Judy Garland

THE VOICE OF MGM

Judy Garland

The Voice of MGM

Scott Brogan

Essex, Connecticut

An imprint of The Globe Pequot Publishing Group, Inc.
64 South Main Street
Essex, CT 06426
www.globepequot.com

Distributed by NATIONAL BOOK NETWORK

Copyright © 2025 by Scott Brogan

All rights reserved. No part of this book may be reproduced in any form or by any electronic or mechanical means, including information storage and retrieval systems, without written permission from the publisher, except by a reviewer who may quote passages in a review.

British Library Cataloguing in Publication Information available

Library of Congress Cataloging-in-Publication Data
Names: Brogan, Scott, 1960– author.
Title: Judy Garland : the voice of MGM / Scott Brogan.
Description: Essex, Connecticut : Lyons Press, 2025. | Includes bibliographical references and index. Summary: "This volume will be the definitive book about Garland's legendary career at MGM, pulling back the curtain to reveal the truths about that career while also presenting previously unknown details and facts that are sure to delight her fans as well as fans of classic film"— Provided by publisher.
Identifiers: LCCN 2024034747 (print) | LCCN 2024034748 (ebook) | ISBN 9781493086542 (cloth) | ISBN 9781493086559 (epub)
Subjects: LCSH: Garland, Judy. | Women singers—United States—Biography. | Singers—United States—Biography. | Motion picture actors and actresses—United States—Biography. | Motion pictures—United States—History—20th century. | Metro-Goldwyn-Mayer. | LCGFT: Biographies. | Filmographies. | Discographies.
Classification: LCC ML420.G253 B76 2025 (print) | LCC ML420.G253 (ebook) | DDC 782.42164092 [B]—dc23/eng/20241122
LC record available at https://lccn.loc.gov/2024034747
LC ebook record available at https://lccn.loc.gov/2024034748

Printed in India.

This book is dedicated to my late best friend, Andy England. His Judy Garland collection mixed with his Grateful Dead collection prompted us to joke, "Judy goes with everything!"

And to my husband, Doug, who has put up with me through thick and thin and whom I love so very much. And it was he who came up with the title. Thank you!

CONTENTS

Introduction		1
Chapter 1	The Road to MGM	5
Chapter 2	MGM's Newest Contract Player	37
Chapter 3	MGM Magic: *The Wizard of Oz* and *Babes in Arms*	73
Chapter 4	MGM's Singing Sweetheart	101
Chapter 5	MGM's Singing Sweetheart Grows Up	135
Chapter 6	More MGM Magic: *Meet Me in St. Louis*	171
Chapter 7	MGM's Greatest Asset: Garland's Golden Era	191
Chapter 8	MGM Treadmill: *The Pirate* and *Easter Parade*	211
Chapter 9	Vintage MGM: *In the Good Old Summertime*	233
Chapter 10	Nightmare at MGM: *Annie Get Your Gun*	243
Chapter 11	Goodbye MGM: *Summer Stock* and *Royal Wedding*	259
Chapter 12	Post-MGM Highlights	279
Appendix A	Judy Garland's MGM Filmography	303
Appendix B	MGM Prerecordings and Records	325
Appendix C	Decca Records	345
Acknowledgments		365
Notes		367
Bibliography		385
Index		387
About the Author		405

Judy Garland, "The Voice of MGM," 1943 promotional photo. From the author's collection.

INTRODUCTION

Judy Garland was the voice of Metro-Goldwyn-Mayer (MGM) both during her time at the studio and after, a distinction that lasts to this day. She was the studio's top leading lady in its musical films during the golden age of the MGM musical, and she's now recognized as the greatest female musical star in the history of film. Any documentary or news story about MGM's golden age will feature at least one clip of Garland singing. Usually, it's "Over the Rainbow" from *The Wizard of Oz* (1939). If "Singin' in the Rain" was the studio's unofficial theme song, then "Over the Rainbow" was its unofficial ballad. Garland's film performance of "Over the Rainbow" alone would have given her eternal fame. But there are more legendary performances, such as her often imitated (but never equaled) "Get Happy" while sexily wearing a tuxedo jacket and a fedora, or the boundlessly joyful "The Trolley Song," or soulful ballads such as "But Not for Me." The number of perfect performances given by Garland while at MGM is astounding.

Garland's life and career at MGM have come to represent both the good and the bad of classic Hollywood more than any other star. She's a top example of a victim of the studio system (reportedly, she hated being called a "victim"). The one-dimensional image of an always suffering and always tragic Garland is a cloud that hangs over her public persona, to the extent that too many people with access to a computer and a search engine crank out error-laden hack articles. This is a great insult to everything Garland achieved at MGM and after. The truth is more nuanced, more joyful, and more exciting. She was an inherently positive, joyful, and funny human being. This is part of what makes her film appearances so timeless. MGM was the best possible place for her talent to grow and thrive, and thrive she did. Garland was at the right place at the right time. From the age of two and a half to when she auditioned at MGM at thirteen years old, she had already lived a full life on the vaudeville stage, honing her craft. In hindsight, it seems inevitable that the little girl with the great big voice and pitch-perfect vaudeville instincts would become the ultimate vaudevillian. Garland had the talent early on, but she also had a natural instinct for retaining and learning from every experience. Audiences responded to her unique talents by applauding and cheering, even while watching the relatively passive medium of film. While she was at MGM, her personal appearance tours simultaneously charmed and electrified audiences even during her first one at thirteen. Local papers are filled with accolades.

Garland's three-era career (vaudeville, movies, the concert stage) is unique for a movie legend of her stature. In her short forty-seven years, she managed to conquer every entertainment medium of the twentieth century. Garland's story has it all. And through it all, her exceptional, once-in-a-lifetime talent never fails to dazzle and mesmerize us. No one since has come close to achieving the same blend of exalted status in the movie musical genre.

Like most kids of my generation, I was introduced to Judy Garland through *The Wizard of Oz* via the annual network TV broadcasts in the United States. We lived mostly overseas, but for several years, we were stateside, and I was at the right age for *Oz* and Garland to work their magic on me. Until the home media revolution in the early 1980s, the only way to see *Oz* was during its once-a-year broadcast. The event was anticipated for weeks prior by all the kids (and more than a few parents) in the neighborhood and at school. No "making of" books had yet been published, and the Internet was decades away, so all we had was what was made accessible, which wasn't much. There was the MGM Records soundtrack album, which truncated the music and dialog onto one 12″ LP and didn't even include "The Merry Old Land of Oz" (the shame!). So one year, I taped my little cassette recorder's microphone to the speaker of the TV in the guest room and recorded the whole broadcast. Within weeks I had the whole film memorized. To this day, I can still lip-synch the entire movie (such a gift!). Later, I found out I wasn't the only one who taped the broadcast on their little cassette recorder, nor was I the only one who memorized the entire film as a result. Garland fans are creative at an early age!

The Wizard of Oz was my "gateway drug" to Garland fandom. I loved her voice, and I wanted to find out more about her. Then several things happened within the span of just a few years. First up was her death in 1969. I was eight, and Mom called us in from playing outside to see something on TV. It was Garland's funeral. The famous scene of her casket, covered in bright yellow roses, being carried out of Frank Campbell's Funeral Home in New York City had a huge impact on me. Mom told us it was Judy Garland, the girl who played Dorothy. I said, "But she's a little girl." That's when I found out that *Oz* had been made many years before. The only other time Mom brought us in to witness something on TV was the moon landing. That's how important it was to her. Mom was obviously a Garland fan too, having grown up with her movies. The apple didn't fall far from that tree. Shortly thereafter, the biographies began to appear, and *That's*

Entertainment! was released. I devoured the film's two-record soundtrack long before finally seeing the film. I had begun randomly buying Garland records (mostly Decca and Capitol compilations) while MGM Records was rereleasing their soundtrack albums. Now we were back overseas, and these albums were all I could get my hands on. Imagine my surprise when I finally saw the films and found out just how edited down many of the musical performances were on those records. I ordered, via mail, every Garland and MGM soundtrack available in the catalogs. It really did take the advertised six to eight weeks for delivery from the United States via military mail. And that was normal. But it made them that much more special once they arrived. They were like movie musical treasures rationed a record at a time. Meanwhile, Mom was reading *Judy* by Gerold Frank, and I picked up a paperback copy of *Young Judy* by David Dahl and Barry Kehoe. I was fascinated by her life, especially those MGM years. The more I read, the more I wanted to know.

By the time of the Internet age, I had read every Garland biography (even the bad ones) and every book about movie musicals and MGM that I could find. It seemed that every few years, new details and facts were revealed. And now, thanks to the availability of newspaper, trade, periodical, and fan magazine archives, my ongoing research continues to uncover new nuggets of information about many aspects of Garland's years at MGM. For example, Garland's MGM personal appearance tours, and especially the USO tours, were mentioned in the biographies, but details about when and where she went and what she did at each city or army camp were nonexistent. In reading the local newspaper accounts of each stop on these tours, one thing is very clear: the public adored Garland. Thousands of people showed up to see her. She really was America's Singing Sweetheart. It's no wonder that when the chips were down for her, Garland's public rallied to her defense, providing unprecedented support at a level never seen before.

This book has been a long time coming and has been a joy to write. It is my hope that after reading it, you will come away with a better understanding of Garland as a performer and as a human being. She wasn't perfect, as some biographers make her out to be. She wasn't all sadness and tragedy, either, as others try to portray her. She was, like all of us, a complicated and flawed person; yet, ultimately, she was a true entertainment genius. How lucky we are that Garland shared her great talent with the world and left so many amazing performances that we can enjoy whenever we wish. She gave us one of the greatest of all gifts a human being can give to another: her legacy of performances.

Scott Brogan, 2024

Introduction

Garland as Dorothy in *The Wizard of Oz*, artwork by Andy England. From the author's collection.

CHAPTER 1

The Road to MGM

To understand Judy Garland's life and career at MGM, one must understand her life and career before MGM. Understanding Garland's formative vaudeville years helps us understand the choices she made, the choices others around her made, and why things happened the way they did. If anyone was "born in a trunk," it would be—at least euphemistically—Judy Garland.

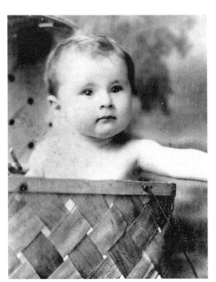

Baby Gumm (Judy Garland) circa 1922. From the author's collection.

Judy Garland was born Frances Ethel Gumm in Grand Rapids, Minnesota, on June 10, 1922. Her parents were former vaudevillians Frank and Ethel Gumm, who had settled in Grand Rapids to raise a family. Frank was born Francis Avent Gumm in Murfreesboro, Tennessee, on March 20, 1886. He grew up to be a handsome young man with a beautiful voice, and, like his youngest daughter, Frances (Garland), he had an alternating romantic, optimistic, and melancholy disposition. Frank had an early interest in show business and later told of how he ran away at ten and joined a minstrel show. Whether the story is true is unknown, but it speaks to his romantic side and his early semi-transient history. At thirteen, Frank already possessed a beautiful voice, which prompted a sponsorship by a family friend, local rich man George Darrow, to both finish his grammar school and begin college at the University of the South in Sewanee, Tennessee, on condition of his services to the school's choir. Frank called his time in Sewanee "six of the happiest, the most beautiful years of my life."[1] In late 1905, with just two of the eight years of school left, he quit and moved back home to help care for his ailing father.

There might not have been a Judy Garland at all if Frank's life had taken a dramatically different turn at this juncture, as it almost did. Frank was popular, singing at Sunday afternoon socials and in church. His frequent duet partner Nene White, who also had a lovely voice, thought Frank had the most beautiful voice she had ever heard.[2] They sang together often until Frank decided to propose, and although White adored him, she turned him down. Had she not done so, you wouldn't be reading this book.

Frank Gumm (right) with an unidentified man in front of an unidentified theatre in Ironwood, Michigan, 1911. Note the poster advertising Frank's act. From the collection of Michael Siewert.

The rejection prompted Frank to leave town, ending up in Tullahoma, Tennessee, living with his younger brother Allie and his sister Mary. He worked as an office manager and bookkeeper, while the local church choir and variety shows provided him with outlets for his performing talents.[3] In 1911, Frank, Allie, and Mary followed brother Robert up north to Ironwood, Michigan. Frank worked as an office clerk for the Oliver Iron Mining Company. His voice got him noticed and a nighttime job as a performer for the owner of several local area theatres, eventually becoming the manager of Ironwood's Temple Theatre, his first time managing a theatre. Frank and Robert formed "The Gumm Bros.," leasing and managing two theatres in Cloquet, Minnesota.

Frank Gumm (*left*) clowning with a friend on the Columbia River, Portland, Oregon, 1912. From the collection of Michael Siewert.

Frank Gumm on the Columbia River, Portland, Oregon, 1912. From the collection of Michael Siewert.

In December 1911, Frank gave his half of the business to Robert and left town again, this time settling in Superior, Wisconsin, where he got lucky and was immediately hired as a singer by the owner of several local theatres. He romanced Kathryn Francis McGraw, the daughter of a local real estate agent. Frank proposed but then kept putting off setting the date until Kathryn finally gave up. In an interesting twist, she married the famous vaudevillian and later film star, comedian Joe E. Brown, a marriage that lasted fifty-eight years.[4] One of Frank's singing engagements was at the local movie theatre, the Bijou Theatre, where he met and eventually became smitten with the theatre's pianist, Ethel Milne.

Ethel was born Ethel Marion Milne in Marquette, Michigan, on November 17, 1893, and, unlike Frank, she hadn't ventured far from her hometown after her family moved to Superior when she was fifteen. The two dated, and it looked as though they were heading for marriage when, in late March 1912, again, Frank abruptly left. He traveled quite a bit in a short time, working for the People's Amusement Company. The bulk of his time away was spent managing and performing in the Crystal Theatre in faraway Portland, Oregon. He became entrenched in the Portland theatre community, performing at other theatres (such as the Sunnyside Theatre) as well as being a founding member of the People's Amusement Company's new Screen Club, serving on its advertising committee. In late 1913, he returned to Superior.[5]

More clowning by Frank Gumm (*far right*) with unidentified friends on the Columbia River, Portland, Oregon, 1912.
From the collection of Michael Siewert.

THE ROAD TO MGM

The reasons for his pattern of abrupt departures weren't due as much to itchy feet as they were to the fact that Frank was homosexual and had affairs with and made advances at local young men. Either he was being run out of town or he left when rumors began to circulate and before he was found out.

Frank's vaudeville partner in Superior, Maude Ayres, noted about Frank's earlier exit from Cloquet, Minnesota, "He was accused of being a pervert, and he had to skip town and get out fast."[6] His reputation eventually followed him back to Superior, becoming known not long after he and Ethel married on January 22, 1914. According to Ayres, who was still his stage partner and a friend to the couple, "Everybody in Superior was talking about it. . . . I was shocked because I had had no idea that there was anything like that going on."[7] It's unknown whether Ethel knew of these rumors yet (she eventually would); if she did, it appears that she kept her feelings to herself. After a brief honeymoon, they left Superior and ended up in Grand Rapids, Minnesota. Frank went into business with Fred Bentz, becoming the manager and in-house singer at the town's movie theatre, the newly opened Grand Theatre. Not long after, the couple tried their luck in vaudeville as a duo act named "Jack and Virginia Lee, Sweet Southern Singers." Sweet they were; successful they were not. After three months on the road, while in Chicago, Ethel was hit with pneumonia and was bedridden for three weeks. They returned to Grand Rapids on February 20, 1915. Frank was able to purchase co-ownership of the Grand with Bentz from the theatre's other owner, James Barlow (in 1918, Frank and Bentz also purchased the Lyceum Theatre in nearby Deer River, Minnesota). Frank dubbed the Grand in Grand Rapids the "New Grand," although the trade magazines during Frank's co-ownership years referred to it as simply the "Grand."

Frank Gumm in front of the Crystal Theatre, Portland, Oregon, 1912. From the collection of Michael Siewert.

The Gumms' first child, Mary Jane, was born on September 24, 1915, and their second, Dorothy Virginia, was born on July 4, 1917. As soon as the girls could walk, they learned the family business, and after some extensive home training, they premiered as a song and dance team at the Grand in 1921. Life was good as the family became a fixture of the town, providing entertainment for local events and church functions. Then, in late 1921, Ethel discovered she was pregnant again. The news was not welcome. Another mouth to feed could put the family under a financial burden. The couple drove to Minneapolis to get advice from their good friend, Marcus

Frank Gumm shows off his flair, similar to that of his youngest daughter (Garland), at the train station in Pendleton, Oregon, 1912. From the collection of Michael Siewert.

Rabwin, who was a medical student at the time. Abortion was illegal, and Rabwin knew it, even though the couple hinted at wanting one. Ethel and Frank had tried to abort the baby on their own using a variety of known home remedies.[8] Rabwin convinced them not only that an abortion was dangerous to Ethel's health and illegal but also that they would not regret having a third child, saying, "After the baby's born, you wouldn't take a million dollars for it."[9]

Rabwin was right. Frances (Judy Garland) and Frank instantly bonded. He gave her the same nickname that he had grown up with: "Baby Gumm."[10] Garland later recalled, "My first two Christmases, I slept in a dressing room while the rest of the family was onstage performing."[11] For the rest of her life, Garland had fond memories of Grand Rapids and the happy times spent at the Grand, especially her father singing popular songs to her. "Danny Boy" was a favorite, which she would later record at MGM and during her concert years.

In the late spring of 1924, Frances had her public singing debut at an annual "Style Show" put on by the local Itasca Dry Goods Company store. After that event, the family visited relatives in Tennessee. Frank's cousin Anna Lee Mirtz later recalled that Frances "was already a charmer and even sang then."[12] Frances had already been singing informally, wanting, like any youngest sibling, to be a part of what her older sisters were doing. The wife of Frank's Tennessee cousin Ashton Pruett, Alice, later remembered a picnic during which Frances climbed on the top of a log and sang as though she were on stage: "Judy Garland could stand on a tree trunk and sing like a birdie when she was only two years old."[13] By the time of the Christmas season in Grand Rapids, the Gumms were ready for the official stage debut of the youngest member of their family troupe, Baby Frances Gumm.

There have been different versions of Frances's official stage debut at the age of two and a half years old on Christmas Eve at the Grand. For years, the story had Frances watching her two sisters perform, with mom Ethel at the piano, and she either broke free from sitting on her

THE ROAD TO MGM

grandmother's lap or was let go on purpose and bolted onto the stage. She sang the only song she knew, "Jingle Bells," over and over to the loud delight of the audience. Ethel yelled at her to get off the stage, but she kept singing, prompting Frank to go out, pick her up, and carry her off, which elicited more cheers and applause. In truth, her appearance was planned. Earlier in the week, Ethel had made a costume for her (her first), and during Mary Jane and Virginia's performance of "When My Sugar Walks Down the Street" (a song Garland later recorded for 1954's *A Star Is Born*, although it was cut prior to the film's release), the two sisters parted to reveal Frances. Frances proceeded to sing "Jingle Bells," ringing the family's little dinner bell. It's true that she wouldn't stop repeating the song thanks to the encouragement of the very approving applause of the audience. After singing the song for a sixth time, Frank, who was laughing so hard he had tears streaming down his face, walked out onto the stage, threw her over his shoulder, and took her off, still singing.[14] This was the beginning of Judy Garland's love affair with her audience.

Baby Gumm (Judy Garland), 1925. From the collection of Michael Siewert.

The stage debut of Baby Frances Gumm became the first of many legends in Garland's life story. Almost immediately after Garland signed with MGM eleven years later, the studio's publicity department began to spin many fabricated stories about this event and others, which usually were barely rooted in truth. But at the time, no one in the general public would have known. That Friday after her debut, Frances had her first newspaper mention. The *Grand Rapids Independent*, in their notice for the Christmas Day and post–Christmas Day billing for the Grand, noted, "Added attraction for Friday eve-

The Gumm Sisters, 1925.
From the collection of Michael Siewert.

10   CHAPTER 1

Early on, the incorrect story of Garland's early years was being disseminated, as shown in this syndicated newspaper panel published on August 12, 1939. From the author's collection.

ning: the three Gumm girls will entertain in songs and dances featuring Baby Frances, two years old. . . . The little girls will appear between the shows at 9 o'clock."[15] Mary Jane, Virginia, and Frances became "the Gumm Sisters" and performed regularly at the Grand, as well as at various social events around Grand Rapids—sometimes even out of town. An early engagement at the Lyceum Theatre in nearby Deer River resulted in the local paper noting that the sister act was "delightful."[16]

In 1925, a strange illness hit Frances. It got so bad that Frank and Ethel drove eighty miles in a snowstorm to St. Mary's Hospital in Duluth, Minnesota. The doctors couldn't figure out what was wrong and thought she might not recover. But she did, and a week later, they returned to Grand Rapids. This was her second serious illness. Previously, in 1924, Ethel took Frances to the doctor with a serious ear infection. They lanced her ears, and for months after, she endured a treatment that required her to wear socks filled with hot salt hanging over her ears. Although she was very young at the time, the event had an impact on her, and she remembered the details for the rest of her life, such as being held down to have her ears lanced without anesthesia ("You'd scream bloody murder") and then having to wear socks with hot salt "an awful lot of the time." She joked that she looked "like a cocker spaniel."[17]

CALIFORNIA

In the summer of 1926, Frank announced to Grand Rapids that the family would take a working vacation trip to California. They had been given good reports about California by Frank's older brother Robert, who was now living in Brea, California, managing the local Red Lantern movie theatre and the La Habra Theatre in nearby La Habra, and their friend Marcus Rabwin, now a doctor and living in Los Angeles. It was also the center of the movie business, a fact that most likely didn't escape Ethel's notice. They decided to visit Rabwin and Robert Gumm and look around for theatre owner/management opportunities.

The Gumm family sang and danced their way across Minnesota, North Dakota, Montana, Idaho, and Washington State before heading down to San Francisco and finally Los Angeles, California. The trip was a source of happy memories for Garland. She enjoyed telling the story of how Frank and Ethel would cheer for the girls as they performed, and then the girls would, in turn, cheer for Frank and Ethel's performances. Garland said, "The one thing I remember about that trip was [my mother would] come out and sing a song and play the piano and sing 'I've Been Saving for a Rainy Day,'" which was so sad it would make Garland cry: "It just broke my heart, you know."[18] They were usually billed as "Jack and Virginia Lee and Kiddies." No matter how small-time a venue might have been, the family had fun. Garland later joked about how they played "rotten" vaudeville—"We were in *lousy* vaudeville"[19]—and then proceeded to tell funny stories about other performers on the bill from this trip and their later stage experiences on the West Coast.

Baby Gumm (Judy Garland) circa 1929. From the collection of Michael Siewert.

In Los Angeles, they looked up Rabwin and stayed for a month at the Hotel Iris (later renamed St. Moritz) in Hollywood while Frank looked around for theatre owner/management opportunities. The sisters had their Los Angeles stage debut on July 10, 1926, at the Erlanger Mason Theatre. As "the Gumm Sisters," they performed during an afternoon kiddies' matinee of the film *Topsy and Eva* starring the Duncan Sisters, which was the act that had allegedly inspired them. The Duncan Sisters (who were there in person) were so impressed with the Gumms, especially Frances, that they insisted the family keep in touch with them.[20]

Judy Garland's first time inside the MGM Studios was not in 1934 or 1935, as most have assumed, but rather during this trip in the summer of 1926. Frank had tried to find the sisters' favorite movie star, Fred Thompson. The family visited (the outside of) the various studios before finally seeing Thompson driving into MGM. Frank used his charm on Thompson and said, "My kids have been dying to meet you!" They were given a tour of the studio and saw a few films being made.[21]

During their visit, the Gumms decided that Los Angeles was the place to relocate to permanently. The family traveled back to Grand Rapids, this time without the frequent stops to perform. They wanted to get home quickly so they could take care of business (Frank and Bentz sold the Grand) and move as soon as possible. The change wasn't due solely to Ethel's ambitions and insistence on a film career for the girls, as later assumed, nor was it due to any problem with the business of the Grand. Rather, the move was prompted by a resurgence of the rumors about Frank's homosexual activities. Ethel had been concerned about Frank's proclivities for years and usually turned a blind eye, but now the word was slowly beginning to spread again.[22] For a brief time after the birth of Frances, the situation seemed to subside, but Frank couldn't deny his feelings for long and resumed his liaisons, this time allegedly putting most of his focus on one young man (whose name is unknown now). The rumors were sufficient for townspeople to claim later that Frank was asked to leave, in spite of how well liked he was.[23]

At this time, especially in small-town America, the topic of homosexuality was taboo, and homosexual activity of any kind, whether sexual or not, was not tolerated. Gay men and women were either run out of town or, worse, killed. There was no such thing as having an "alternative lifestyle," nor was there any knowledge (let alone any understanding) of what we now know as the LGBTQIA community. Gay people led double lives, playing the straight marriage game while either stepping out on the side or suppressing their natural inclinations altogether, resulting in a lot of substance abuse ("self-medicating") and/or suicide. Frank was no different. In another era, he might not have married at all but instead lived as an out and proud gay man. Frank probably would have also been very proud that his supremely talented daughter became one of the greatest gay icons of all time, linked forever with the beginning of the modern American gay rights movement.

The family gave their final performances at the Grand on October 8, 9, and 10, 1926, followed by a string of going-away parties. On October 27, they left Grand Rapids for good. Their first stop was Duluth, Minnesota, where Frank and Ethel left the girls with relatives before traveling via train to Tennessee to visit some of Frank's family. After traveling back to Duluth, the family drove to Kansas City, Missouri, where Ethel and the girls stayed while Frank drove ahead to Los Angeles to find a place to live. It's safe to assume that the sisters performed in vaudeville shows at the local Kansas City theatres, although there are no known listings or reviews in the local newspapers. After a couple of weeks, Frank sent for them, and they traveled via train to Los Angeles. By mid-November, they were living in the Atwater district of Los Angeles. Frank continued looking for theatres while Ethel continued refining the sisters' act.

In March 1927, Frank finally found a theatre to lease and manage eighty miles from downtown Los Angeles in the desert town of Lancaster. The New Lancaster Theatre had been open only since that previous Christmas and was more modern than the Grand back in Grand Rapids, boasting a seating capacity of over 450. Frank renamed it the "Valley Theatre." The family wasn't thrilled about living in this rustic town far away from Los Angeles, especially Ethel. It meant long trips into the city for engagements and professional schooling for the sisters. In an effort to not only announce the new management but also ingratiate the family with the skeptical locals, Frank announced their arrival with a big advertisement in the local paper: "Mr. and Mrs. Frank Gumm and Daughters will present a cycle of songs and dances between shows each evening. . . . Having purchased the theater, I am taking this method of introducing the family to the good people of Lancaster and Antelope Valley. It is my intention to continue presenting the high class picture program as given by Mr. Claman [the former owner]."[24]

In 1926, Ethel began a long association for herself and the sisters with the Ethel Meglin Studio. The Meglin Studio served as a combination training class and talent agency for show business children in the Los Angeles area. Usually billed as the "Meglin Kiddies," the child performers were booked mostly at various movie theatres as part of vaudeville-style stage shows that accompanied the films. On December 10, 1926, the sisters appeared on the Loew's State Theatre stage in Los Angeles for their first time in a Meglin show, billed as "100 of California's Cleverest Children" in the "Twinkle Toe Kiddie Revue" (named after the film currently being shown, *Twinkletoes* starring Colleen Moore). The engagement lasted six nights.

That December engagement would be the last major engagement for the Gumm Sisters for almost two years. For all 1927 and half of 1928, the sisters performed almost exclusively in Lancaster and the surrounding communities. This relatively inactive period of professional activity was due to a combination of reasons. Frank was establishing the theatre, which included family stage performances, mostly on the busy days and nights of the weekend. The sisters had to attend the local schools, naturally participating in school plays. At the same time, the whole family became involved in performing at many local events and activities such as parades, picnics, church functions, and, of course, their father's theatre.

Then, in early 1928, Frances became ill again, suffering from the same mystery infection that had plagued her in 1925. Rabwin got her into the Los Angeles County Hospital, where she stayed for almost a month. Luckily, the mystery illness went away. It's unknown what effect this issue had on Frances's voice, which, even at this early stage of her life, was being noticed. Whatever effect it had was short lived. Her voice, obviously, turned out fine.[25]

In the latter months of 1928, Ethel decided it was time to leave the semi-bucolic life they had established in Lancaster and enter real show business again. During a trip to Santa Monica, she heard about an audition for the local Los Angeles KFI radio station's show *Children's Hour*. The sisters got the job, singing "Avalon Town" and "You're the Cream in My Coffee."[26] Lancaster's local paper, the *Ledger-Gazette*, reported that the numbers "went over very well."[27] They must have since they returned to the program off and on through October of that year.

Ethel renewed their association with Ethel Meglin, resulting in the sisters taking part in the "Famous Meglin Kiddies Recital" on October 28, 1928, at the Breakfast Club in Los Angeles. The surviving program reveals that the show featured seventy-six numbers(!). The Gumm Sisters had a few numbers toward the end of the show: Mary Jane performed "Song" (apparently it was unknown what song she would sing when the program was printed), the sisters performed "Harmony" (again, exactly what is unknown), and "Baby Frances Gumm" performed "Laugh, Clown,

14   CHAPTER 1

Ethel and Frank Gumm circa 1930. From the collection of Michael Siewert.

Laugh" as song number 74, just two songs before the end "Finale" (in which the sisters most likely took part). Frances's placement toward the end of the program is an indication that her talents were already sufficient to get her one of the best spots in the show.

In her recorded 1960 sessions with author and screenwriter Fred Finklehoffe for a proposed autobiography, Garland was candid about her mother's actions around this time, stating that Ethel used her as a pawn in arguments she would have with Garland's father. The arguments mostly centered around Ethel's affair with their friend in Lancaster, Wil Gilmore:

I don't think anything in the world frightens a child more than their mother and father [fighting]. [Mother would] come in the middle of the night and wake me up and dress me and say, "We're leaving Daddy" and I'd say, "I don't wanna leave Daddy," then she'd make me feel terrible because she'd say I didn't love her and make me feel very guilty about loving my father. . . . She would put me in the back seat of the car, wrap me up, and to release her frustrations, she'd just drive hour after hour, 90 miles an hour, hell-bent for election, around mountain curves . . . and I was just terrified, and I don't think I ever went to bed at night without wondering whether I was going to be awakened and taken out in the night. And then she'd take me to Los Angeles, where we'd register at a crummy hotel somewhere . . . and we'd stay there sometimes for about three or four months.[28]

Garland continued to explain that during those times, she would perform around Los Angeles in nightclubs and theatres while Ethel would get jobs as a music or singing teacher. Sometimes Ethel would get bookings for the trio, and the sisters would join them. She remembered the Strand Theatre in Long Beach, remarking, "We always worked there." She talked about working in the Hippodrome Theatre, "where all the actors would say they're working because they're breaking in a new act; that isn't true because it was such a terrible place they always used that as an excuse. . . . The rats backstage were so big we named them. And that's where we worked on the bill with a man who threw up for an act!"[29]

The story about Hadji Ali was one she told often; the specifics would vary, but the main story remained the same. Hadji would come out in a big turban, swallow "twenty-seven hazelnuts and one walnut," and bring them up on command and finish by building a fire, drinking water, and then drinking kerosene. He would then bring up the kerosene to get the fire going and subsequently bring up the water to put it out. She laughed, "And God help the audience if he had any lunch that day! We worked with all kinds of *class acts* like that."[30]

Garland's memories were, like anyone's, conflated in her mind. While the Hadji story is true (his act survives in an early sound film), there isn't anything to support her claim that her mother would angrily or vindictively leave her father, with Garland in tow, for months on end. She was most likely confusing that with the times she and Ethel went into Los Angeles for bookings when her sisters had to stay behind for school. However, there's no reason not to believe her when she said that Ethel used her as a pawn, knowing that Frances was Frank's favorite, and, in an effort to hurt him or to make him acquiesce to her needs, would take her away. Whether the drive into the mountains happened more than once will never be known, although it was most likely a one-time occurrence that traumatized her. Garland was known to exaggerate, and by the time the 1960s rolled around, her exaggerations became the truth in her mind.

December 1928 saw one of Frances's early successes as a solo artist. Ethel seemed determined to get more exposure for her, and so, through their association with Meglin, Frances was one of the one hundred children, "ages ranging from four to fourteen,"[31] who were part of Meglin's new holiday revue show. The show was previewed at the Shrine Auditorium in Los Angeles on December 13, which was part of a massive Christmas benefit that featured more than four hundred stars. This event was probably similar to the benefit at the Shrine as portrayed in Garland's screen comeback in *A Star Is Born* (Warner Bros., 1954), which accurately shows the crowded hustle and bustle of all the acts (stars or otherwise) backstage waiting to go on. Imagine one hundred children and their parents added to that already crowded scene. The whole Gumm family attended the Shrine event in support of Frances, who sang one of 1928's biggest hits, "I Can't Give You Anything But Love, Baby." Garland later recorded studio versions of the song for Capitol Records in 1958 and 1960, and she performed it on TV and in many of her concerts. The Meglin act then moved to its final destination: a week's engagement at Loew's State Theatre that began on December 21. Although Frances wasn't singled out in the newspapers, the act as a whole was given positive reviews, and the *Los Angeles Record* reported, "We have no names with which to lay tribute to. One small miss shook these well-known rafters with her songs a la Sophie Tucker," which is assumed to be a reference to Frances.[32] Originally, Frank did not want Frances to be a part of the show but eventually gave in, with the understanding that Ethel and Frances would return to Lancaster each night. In spite of the grueling schedule and Frank's reservations, the family saw the engagement as a success.

By March 1929, the situation of driving back and forth between Lancaster and Los Angeles had become too much. Ethel and the girls moved into an upstairs apartment at 1814 1/2 South Orchard Street near the Los Angeles theatre district. The Lancaster *Ledger-Gazette* reported, "Mrs. Frank Gumm and daughters leave next week for Los Angeles where they will reside indefinitely so that the girls may pursue special studies. They will spend their weekends in Lancaster, Mrs. Gumm furnishing the music at the theatre [the Valley Theatre, run by Frank]. Mr. Gumm will continue to reside at the family home on Cedar Avenue."[33]

In June, the association with the Meglin Kiddies resulted in the sisters making their big screen debut in the Vitaphone film short *The Big Revue*, shot at Tec-Art Studios in Hollywood. They sang "That's the Good Old Sunny South" live on the set. The film has survived, giving us a chance to see Judy Garland at the ripe old age of seven, singing and dancing with her sisters. Even at this young age, it's obviously Judy Garland. Always the professional, when she flubs a step in the dance and looks up at her sisters, it doesn't deter her, and she catches up so quickly that it's barely noticeable. The "Garland Sound" isn't there yet—in her solo lines, she shouts more than sings, "Yassir!"—but in harmony with her two sisters, she blends in just fine. The shouting is no doubt a result of their stage training. In those days, there were no microphones or speakers on stage. A singer had to be heard throughout the theatre.

The sisters appeared in three more shorts filmed in November and December 1929, a result of their association with Flynn O'Malley's Hollywood Starlets organization. Billed as the "Three Kute Kiddies," they appeared in *A Holiday in Storyland*, singing "When the Butterflies Kiss the Buttercups Goodbye," with Frances getting her first on-screen solo, "Blue Butterfly"; *The Wedding of Jack and Jill*, in which Frances gets another solo, the prophetic "Hang onto a Rainbow"; and *Bubbles*, featuring the sisters singing "The Land of Let's Pretend," with Frances getting a short solo bit toward the end of the song. These shorts were shot in the early two-strip Technicolor process on the Warner Bros. lot, Frances's (Garland's) first time at the studio.

The audio for all of the films has survived thanks to Vitaphone's process of using audio discs to accompany the films as the soundtracks. *Bubbles* is the only one of the three films to survive (in black and white only). For Frances's solo bit in "The Land of Let's Pretend," she's filmed in a nice close-up. We see her reaching out to the audience as she's singing and already displaying some of that future legendary Garland charisma. Her voice is by far better here (and in the audio of "Hang onto a Rainbow"), indicating that she was learning her craft—fast. It had been only five months since their first film, but Garland seemed to have gained several years' worth of expertise.

On March 4, 1930, "Baby Frances Ethel Gumm" participated in the "Eighth Annual *Los Angeles Evening Express* 'Better Babies' Exposition" at the Paramount Studios in Hollywood, placing second. She won a kewpie doll presented by screen legend Mary Pickford. Garland had competed in the same contest the previous year, at which time she was given an honorable mention and a $10 gift certificate to the Broadway department store. She kept the doll, and, twelve years later, it made an appearance in the film that showcased her first adult role at MGM, 1942's *For Me and My Gal*. For the "Oh, You Beautiful Doll" musical sequence, supporting actress Lucille Norman hands the doll to Garland's costar George Murphy. The use of the doll was an in-joke, a nod and a wink to Garland's vaudeville roots in a movie about vaudeville performers.

THE ROAD TO MGM

STOPPING THE SHOW

In the early 1930s, the sisters were making a name for themselves in Los Angeles and along the West Coast. Frances tried out "Gracie Gumm" as a new stage name. It didn't stick. She was also billed as "Baby Marie Gumm," but that didn't stick either. The most common billings for Frances at the time were as "Baby Gumm" or simply "Frances Gumm." The sisters together were usually billed as the "Gumm Sisters," the "Three Gumm Sisters," or the "Hollywood Starlets Trio." For a short while, there didn't seem to be any consistency, with the billing alternating between the "Gumm Sisters" and the "Hollywood Starlets Trio." It would be another several years before "Garland" and "Judy" were combined.

For an extensive time, the sisters were part of the kiddie "Big Brother Ken Show" as well as Maurice Kusell's Theatrical Dance Studio, the latter resulting in the sisters taking part in Kusell's "Stars of Tomorrow" shows. Kusell was enthusiastic about Frances, giving her a solo spot in the show and on the playbill as "Baby Gumm" at the show's engagement the week of July 10, 1931, at the Wilshire Ebell Theatre in Los Angeles. The sisters, as a trio, were featured in three numbers. The engagement was successful enough for the *Los Angeles Times* to label it "a decided hit." The paper also gave a shout-out to the "Gumm Sisters" at the top of its list of "interesting specialty numbers" in the show. Kusell introduced Ethel and the sisters to George Frank of the Frank and Dunlap Talent Agency. They signed Frances to a five-year contract, giving her the name "Frances Gayne." However, soon after signing, the contract's "option clause" was exercised, and Frances was let out of her contract because Frank objected, feeling that she was too young.[34]

These appearances, as well as the smaller ones in various shows in the Los Angeles area, began to get the sisters noticed. Being noticed meant more engagements. The school year kept the sisters from performing as often as they did in the summer months, but that didn't stop Ethel from ensuring they kept busy performing on the weekends, usually in Los Angeles but also at their father's theatre and other events in Lancaster, such as the local Kiwanis Club and school talent shows. They were performing part-time in Los Angeles and part-time in Lancaster while Ethel spent most of her time in Los Angeles, having been hired by Kusell as a "personality and harmony jazz singing teacher."[35] Judging from the dates of the Los Angeles engagements, it appears Ethel tried to confine the sisters' engagements to the weekends. One weekend engagement on January 23, 1932 (a Saturday), was a solo engagement for Frances that turned out to be a milestone for her. She performed at the famous Cocoanut Grove at the Ambassador Hotel in Los Angeles. It was her first time at the Grove, where she would have one of her biggest concert successes decades later: her 1958 engagement that resulted in the very first Judy Garland concert album, *Garland at the Grove*, released by Capitol Records.

On August 25, 1932, the sisters began a very successful weeklong engagement at the Paramount Theatre in Los Angeles. They performed a twenty-minute act five times daily, six on the weekend. The engagement resulted in their first review in the trade paper *Variety*, with Frances

18 CHAPTER 1

The Gumm Sisters in 1931. From the collection of Michael Siewert.

being singled out:

> *Gumm sisters, harmony trio, socked with two numbers. Selling end of the trio is the ten-year-old sister with a pip of a lowdown voice. Kid stopped the show, but wouldn't give more.*[36]

Frances, again billed as "Baby Gumm," made an impact in Kusell's "Juvenile Christmas Revue" at the Million Dollar Theatre in Los Angeles, which ran from December 29, 1932, through January 4, 1933. The *Los Angeles Record* reviewed the show and stated that Frances was "astounding. Her singing all but knocks one for a loop, her dancing is snappy and clever. She handles herself onstage like a veteran pro."[37] This is another indication that Garland's voice was already developing into the sound we know today and that her natural stage presence was already electrifying audiences.

Frances regularly stopped the show during most of these engagements. However, not everyone was impressed. A year after that first *Variety* review, the sisters received their second *Variety* review, this time along with Frank and Ethel. The whole family took an engagement at the Golden Gate Theatre in San Francisco from August 2 to August 8, 1933. Frank opened for the sisters while Ethel played the piano. This time, the review in *Variety* was negative:

> *The Gumm Sisters, with Mama Gum [sic] at the piano, and Papa Gumm in advance, deuced. Three girls of assorted sizes who sing in mediocre voice and style, with majority of the burden falling to the youngest one, a mere tot, who lustily shouted three numbers, decidedly not her type. And much too long.*[38]

However, the *San Francisco Chronicle*'s critic, George C. Warren, raved about the show and noted, "[The sisters] harmonize, and have a strong-voiced small woman who imitates and sings in a big way."[39] The amusing mistake of audiences assuming that Frances was a grown woman had become fairly regular. She already sounded much more mature than her years, and many audience members assumed she was a young woman rather than a child. The act showcased this by having Frances sing the torch song "Bill" from *Show Boat* while sitting on top of a piano, in the manner of the song's originator, Helen Morgan. The song would start with a pin spot on just

Frances's face. At the end of the song, the lights would come up to reveal that this young woman was a child. The usual audience response was first gasps, then applause, and sometimes cheers.

The sisters were back in the Los Angeles area theatres by the middle of the month. Their weeklong engagement at the West Coast Theatre in Long Beach brought additional praise for Frances:

> *Little Frances Gumm of the Gumm Sisters Trio is a "natural." She fools everybody with her matured voice and sings quite as lustily as her two sisters twice her size.*[40]

> *The Three Gumm Sisters present an entertaining harmony act with a real surprise "punch" in the appearance of Frances Gumm of KHJ fame.*[41]

At the end of the month, they had a dual engagement that began at the Warner Brothers Hollywood Theatre in Hollywood from August 24 through August 30, 1933; then they moved over to the Warner Brothers Downtown Theatre in, naturally, downtown Los Angeles, from August 31 through September 6, 1933. *Variety* reviewed the act again, and once more it was negative.

> *In the deuce spot are the Gumm Sisters, three harmony warblers, with Mother Gumm accompanying at the piano. Two of the sisters are grownup, while the third is a precocious juve whose mild attempts at comedy add nothing to the offering.*[42]

Viola Hegyi of the *Hollywood Citizen* is the critic who gave Frances the "leather-lunged" moniker popular with biographers when reviewing the August 24 performance:

> *Little leather-lunged Frances Gumm, child singer, delighted last night's audiences with solos and harmony numbers in which she appeared with her two grown sisters. This oddly mature faced child possesses an extraordinary musical and rhythmic gift.*[43]

In late 1933, the sisters joined another organization of child performers, the Lawlor's School for Professional Children. In her 1979 autobiography *Hollywood's Children: An Inside Account of the Child Star Era*, former child star "Baby Peggy," Diana Serra Cary, wrote extensively about this era of child performers. Cary recalled Garland's first day at "Mom" Lawlor's, which she remembered as taking place in early 1934, although, in reality, it was late 1933:

> *Judy was a quiet, plain little girl whose dresses were a trifle too long and obviously homemade. She looked too old for a child, but she did not yet have the body of a woman. Mom [Lawlor] brought her into our study hall, introduced her, and then asked her if she would sing a number for us. Ethel Gumm settled herself on the bench, and Judy clambered onto the top of the old upright piano. When she crossed her legs, I noticed the limp, worn taffeta bows on her tap shoes. They reminded me of my own tap shoes, whose soles had several times worn through, and what they told me about her made me want to cry. I thought it was needlessly cruel of Mrs. Lawlor to put this obvious amateur through such an ordeal; after all, she knew we were an audience of hardened professionals, and this was a poor little kid from the godforsaken desert town of Lancaster.*

But we had misjudged both Judy and Mom. After Ethel Gumm swept through the introductory bars of the popular "Blue Moon," an incredibly rich voice charged with a mature woman's emotional power was flooding the room: "Blue Moon / You saw me standing alone / Without a dream in my heart / Without a love of my own."

When Judy finished there were tears of pride in Mom's eyes, and every student in the room was applauding wildly and cheering the forlorn little newcomer. Even then Judy was a professional's professional. At our annual Lawlor shows, staged at the Wilshire Ebell Theater, we kept giving Judy encores that sometimes kept her singing until two o'clock in the morning. She seemed unable to say no to an audience.[44]

This was the heyday of child performers. They seemed to be everywhere, but very few were as talented as Frances Gumm. The mania of parents exploiting their children would eventually yield great talents such as Mickey Rooney, Ann Miller, Donald O'Connor, Shirley Temple, Gypsy Rose Lee, and her sister, June Havoc. There were plenty of organizations and shows that were only too happy to hire the children with their parents' enthusiastic blessing. The stereotype of "the stage mother" wasn't for nothing. Ethel became one of the most famous, known at the time for her tenacity and seemingly boundless energy. If it weren't for her supremely talented daughter, she would have faded anonymously into history along with the thousands of now nameless and faceless stage mothers of the era. Ethel's ambition led to the sisters being signed up for several child performer organizations over the next several years. She usually helped pay for these associations by providing her services for anything musical, from piano accompanist to vocal arranger and coach. The associations included I. C. Overdorff's Hollywood School of Dance and Flynn O'Malley's Hollywood Starlets (the inspiration for the sisters' sporadic billing as the "Hollywood Starlets Trio").

From February through March 1934, the sisters went on a tour with the Paramount Circuit up the West Coast to a series of engagements in Washington State, Idaho, and finally San Francisco on their way back to Los Angeles. In Spokane, Washington, the *Spokesman-Review* noted, "The Three Gumm Sisters are harmony singers in a dainty bit of vocal entertainment that features the youngster of the lot in a clever imitation of Helen Morgan. The crowd gave the girls a great hand."[45] The sisters returned to their normal routine for a few months, highlighted by a few engagements with the Gilmore Circus, including one at the Agua Caliente Hotel in Agua, Mexico, that was broadcast on KHJ Radio, and one at the State Theatre in Long Beach, California, which earned Frances another rave review: "Frances Gumm, a charming youngster who is the 'baby' of the troupe, sings 'That's What a Darkie Is,' and 'Dinah' in a singularly grownup little voice."[46]

It wasn't just the critics and audiences who were recognizing Garland's supreme talents; so did her family. Ethel no doubt knew, as did Frank, that great things lay ahead. Always the proud father, Frank sent a letter to the editor of the *Rutherford Courier* in his hometown of Murfreesboro, Tennessee, published on April 27, 1934. He touted the trio's success on their tour up the West Coast and their upcoming engagement in Los Angeles as part of the "Movie Star Frolic" show at the Gilmore Stadium: "The youngest girl, Frances, who is 11 years old, is a big sensation, and a brilliant career is predicted for her as she will shortly be featured with many of the prominent stars of the screen." He also noted that Ethel and the girls would soon go on tour to Chicago and New York. Perhaps he was anticipating Garland's future monetary success for the family with "Should I ever accumulate much of worldly wealth, nothing could afford me more real happiness than to return to dear old Murfreesboro."[47] Frank then sent a letter dated May 20, 1934, to the editor of the *Los Angeles Times* thanking him for a recent review of one of the sisters' engagements and singling out Frances. He also supplied an anecdote for the paper to possibly print:

My Dear Sir:

As a reader and an appreciative one of your excellent column, I am presuming to write you a line in regard to my little girl, Frances Gumm, whom you were kind enough to notice in your column when she appeared with Teddy Joyce at Warner's Hollywood theater; you will recall perhaps that you referred to her as "little hotcha singer and a show stopper." We appreciated this so much and the article is in the little girl's scrapbook.

All three of the girls are appearing on the frolic at the Gilmore Stadium this week-end; working at Leon Errols Beer Garden and going over, if I do brag a bit, very good indeed.

The other day the little one, Frances, 10 years old, made a wisecrack that I think is "hot" and I thought maybe you could use it. If you can I would get a big kick out of it and if you can't there is no harm done in asking anyway I hope. It would run something like this.

The other day little Frances Gumm, the ten-year-old member of the Gumm Sisters trio who appeared last week-end at the Movie Stars Frolic at the Gilmore Stadium, wanted to go downtown in Los Angeles alone. Her mother protested that such a thing would be out of the question. Frances wanted to know WHY and her mother advised her of the danger of being kidnapped. Frances said "Well mother why would anyone want to kidnap ME?" Her mother replied "Well they would kidnap you and HOLD you for RANSOM." Little Frances thought for a moment and replied, "Why mother, what's the matter with 'RANSOM' can't he HOLD his own girls?"

Again thank you for giving the baby the nice little mention you did and assuring you if you can use this gag I would be grateful to you I am with sincere wishes,

Very truly yours,

[Frank A. Gumm]

GUMM TO GARLAND

In mid-June 1934, Ethel and the sisters embarked on a cross-country tour to the Chicago World's Fair. The fair had been going on since 1933, and Ethel convinced Frank that it would benefit the act to take a weeklong engagement at the Old Mexico Cafe on the boardwalk of the fair, as well as two solid weeks of engagements in Colorado along the way, including Denver, Littleton, and Colorado Springs. Frank, who was opposed to the idea of "a woman and three girls driving more than halfway across the country by themselves,"[48] soon relented and gave them some traveler's checks for insurance, and they drove to Chicago. They opened at the Old Mexico Night Club in Chicago on July 15. For part of their time in Chicago, they stayed with some of Frank's relatives from Murfreesboro, including a distant cousin, Mrs. Barbara Goenne, who later recalled that Frances "was a happy girl with a fine sense of humor . . . and she was so natural and unaffected."[49] The shows were successful, so much so that the man in charge of special events for the fair, "Captain Riley," gave Frances the honor of being one of the star performers for the fair's Children's Day on July 19. Frances got to ride in the lead car of the procession along Leif Ericson Drive to one of the auditoriums, where she and others entertained the kids and their parents with a "special program" of songs and dances.[50] It was at the Old Mexico Night Club that they first met then–trumpet player Jack Cathcart. Cathcart eventually married Mary Jane and became a musical arranger for Garland during her legendary concert years in the 1950s, including her television premiere on the *Ford Star Jubilee* in 1955, as well as some of her Capitol recordings.

The engagement at the Old Mexico Night Club began well enough, but the management was slow in making their payments until, finally, the venue closed without paying the performers the remaining money owed to them. According to Garland biographer Gerold Frank, Ethel went to the manager and demanded payment but got nowhere, so she went to the local William Morris Agency, who told her to enter the sisters in the open "tryouts" on Friday nights at the Belmont Theatre. "The agency screened new acts there [and] a Morris man would be there to catch their act."[51] The information about this sequence of events is sketchy. Other sources note that the engagement at the Belmont was not on a Friday but on a Wednesday and that it was a booked appearance rather than an open night for random acts.

Things had also gotten so dire money-wise that Ethel was forced to finally cash some of the traveler's checks Frank had given her—something she had tried to avoid to prove they could make their own way. Then Cathcart called them. A fellow musician told him that a singing act at the Oriental Theatre had been fired. This was the kind of break they needed. The Oriental Theatre was one of Chicago's biggest movie/vaudeville theatres and was the type of local top-tier theatre that Ethel had been unsuccessfully trying to get into. Ethel and the sisters rushed over, arriving barely in time to go on. They got the job.

The weeklong engagement at the Oriental became one of Judy Garland's biggest career milestones. Comedian George Jessell was the headliner, and, after noticing some laughs from the audience when he introduced the "Gumm" sisters, he took it upon himself to rename them

THE ROAD TO MGM

"Garland," allegedly after his friend, New York critic Robert Garland. Another, more far-fetched version of the name change has Jessell exclaiming that Frances was "pretty as a garland of flowers." Twenty years later, Jessell attended the star-studded opening of Garland's comeback film, *A Star Is Born* (Warner Bros., 1954), and told his story about naming Garland. In his pre-premiere article, columnist Leonard Lyons reported about Jessell's renaming the sister act:

> *Earlier that day he'd received a message reminding him to send a telegram to Judith Anderson, who was opening on Broadway. The wire to Miss Anderson still was in his mind: "Dear Judy, may this new play add another garland to your Broadway laurels." Now George was introducing Frances Gumm, and his tongue resisted the clumsy name. He finished his spiel, leading up to the name. "And here she is now," he concluded, then blurted "Judy Garland."*[52]

The first scenario is the more realistic of the three stories. Lyons's story was apocryphal. Frances renamed herself "Judy," but not until 1935. Jessell took great pride in having named one of show business's greatest legends and would often quip, "You couldn't have hidden that great talent if you had called her Tel Aviv Windowsill," which he repeated that night at the premiere of *A Star Is Born* in 1954.

The local William Morris Agency handled the rest of their summer tour, which included the first-ever billing of the "Garland Sisters" at the Uptown Theatre in Chicago on August 21, 1934. Amusingly, that first billing as Garland came on the heels of being billed as the "*Glumm* Sisters" at the Marbro Theatre, also in Chicago. The sisters were booked throughout September and October in Detroit, Michigan; Milwaukee, Wisconsin; and (on their way back home) Kansas City, St. Joseph, and Jefferson City, Missouri.

They were a big hit in St. Joseph, appearing for two nights at the local Dubinsky's Electric Theatre on October 5 and 6. The *St. Joseph News-Press Gazette* promoted the show with an ad that mistakenly lists the "4 Garland Sisters 'Harmony Singers'" and this promo copy:

> *The Garland Sisters offer a singing and dancing act and present the youngest member in a Helen Morgan torch number.*[53]

Of interest is the fact that the film being shown, *Desirable*, featured a story about a "stage mother who interfered with her daughter's happiness because of her own selfish, professional ambitions," much like Ethel's ambitions for Garland. The *St. Joseph News-Press Gazette* raved about the first night's show:

> *The opening number on the program is the four Garland sisters, one of them a mere child but with a voice and expression that reveal both ability and training. She imitates Helen Morgan in "Along Came Bill" ["Bill"] but the number gets a little tiresome when she repeats the chorus. The audience would like to hear more harmonizing. These girls can sing, but use the "hotcha" stuff with restraint, dropping back into good old dominant seventh chords with pleasing effect.*[54]

The *Kansas City Star* noted that Garland sang "Little Man, You've Had a Busy Day" during their engagement there and mixed up Frances's and Virginia's names in a short review titled "A Young 'Show Stopper.'"

> *Virginia Garland, the youngest member of the Garland Sisters, three girls from California, almost stopped the show on its first performance with her impersonation of Helen Morgan sitting on a piano and singing "Bill," and then repeated later before a microphone with "Little Man, You've Had a Busy Day." The girl has personality, as have her sisters, not to neglect them, and the act gets loud and long applause.[55]*

After their engagement in Jefferson City, Missouri, Ethel and the sisters headed directly back to California without stopping to perform. Once back in Los Angeles, the sisters were alternately billed as "Gumm" and "Garland," with the last known "Gumm" billing being at the Strand Theatre in Long Beach, California, from November 9 through November 11. From that date forward, they were known as the "Garland Sisters." Just prior to that last Gumm billing, the sisters received an often-quoted *Variety* review of their engagement at Grauman's Chinese Theatre in Hollywood, listed as "Gumm Sisters (3)."

> *Hardly a new act, this trio of youngsters has been kicking around the coast for two years, but has just found itself. As a trio, it means nothing, but with the youngest, Frances, 13-year-old, featured, it hops into class entertainment, for, if such a thing is possible, the girl is a combination of Helen Morgan and Fuzzy Knight. Possessing a voice that, without a p.a. system, is audible throughout a house as large as the Chinese, she handles ballads like a veteran, and gets every note and word over with a personality that hits audiences. For comedy, she effects a pan like Knight and delivers her stuff in the same manner as the comic. Nothing slow about her on hot stuff and to top it, she hoofs. Other two sisters merely form a background.*

> *Kid, with or without her sisters, is ready for the east. Caught on several previous shows, including the 5,000 seat Shrine Auditorium here, she has never failed to stop the show, her current engagement being no exception.[56]*

Frances had obviously eclipsed her two sisters in talent and stage presence. This development didn't bother Mary Jane and Virginia. They were getting older (Mary Jane was almost twenty) and were not as interested in show business as their little sister was. For the past several years, Frances had been the main attraction of the act and the main focus of Ethel's ambitions. If any of the sisters had what it took to succeed in show business, it was Frances.

The sisters enjoyed a very successful engagement at the Wilshire Ebell in Los Angeles, opening on December 8, 1934, in the "Irving Strouse Vaudeville Frolics," during which Frances created a lot of buzz in the local entertainment community. This engagement resulted in the false claim by the Wilshire Ebell that Garland was discovered there. The facts are much different, as noted later in this chapter.

The sisters received more great reviews. The *Los Angeles Times* noted:

THE ROAD TO MGM

The Garland Sisters scored a hit, with the youngest member of the trio practically stopping the show with her singing.[57]

W. E. Oliver of the *Los Angeles Herald-Express* was especially smitten with Frances's performance. The headline of his article read, "12 Year Old Girl Is Sensation at Frolics." Foreshadowing Garland's future concert years and her effect on audiences, he said:

If the godfathers of the new vaudeville can discover one personality a month of the caliber of a little, 12-year-old girl who appeared this last weekend in the Frolics at the Wilshire-Ebell theater, their anew born ward will soon be up and flourishing as it was in the days before the talking picture dealt it a lethal blow.

This young maid is Frances Garland, of the three Garland sisters. Besides appearing with her two sisters, little Frances sat on a piano and with her mother accompanying, sang in a way that produced in the audience sensations that haven't been equaled for years.

Not your smart adult-aping prodigy is this girl, but a youngster who had the divine instinct to be herself on the stage, along with a talent for singing, a trick of rocking the spectators with rhythms, and a capacity for putting emotions into her performance that suggest what [stage legend Sarah] Bernhardt must have been at her age. It isn't the cloying, heavy sentiment that her elders so often strive for, but simple, sincere feeling that reaches the heart.

The three girls together are an act that anyone would want to see. Frances alone is a sensation, and last Saturday's audience realized it by the way they encored. Much of her individual style of singing was culled by the little girl from her parents' old act, although she must have the divine spark to be able to sing as she did.

Take a tip and see this little Frances Gumm if you want to experience a thrill. She would make any show.[58]

Carl Combs of the *Hollywood Citizen News* reviewed the show as well:

Frances Garland, a livewire little miss, who appeared with her two older sisters in a couple of harmony numbers and who appeared alone in a smoothly executed "Helen Morgan" piano-sitting sob song about "Bill," vied for the big hand with Fuzzy Knight.[59]

These are examples of just how well known the Garland Sisters had become, as well as Frances's effect on audiences. She wasn't as unknown in the entertainment circles on the West Coast as some have assumed. On December 15, 1934, the *Oakland Tribune* reported on the upcoming Christmas show at San Francisco's Curran Theatre and listed Garland among the performers as "Francis [*sic*] Garland, a recent discovery." On December 23, 1934, the *Los Angeles Times* noted that the Frolics show was moving up to San Francisco and that "the three Garland sisters will sing new songs, and Francis [*sic*] Garland, the youngest, will again do several solos."

The Frolics show opened at the Curran Theatre in San Francisco on December 25, 1934, and ran through the end of the year. The sisters were initially listed in the Curran's newspaper advertisements as the "Garland Trio," but by the last several days that billing was changed to "Frances Garland." In his December 27, 1934, review of the vaudeville acts currently playing around the Bay Area that late December 1934, the *Oakland Tribune*'s Wood Soanes noted:

> *Of the group [of acts,] the Garlands [Garland Trio] have the best novelty. They consist of three girls with mother at the piano and they sing. But the virtue of their performance lies in the talent of the youngest, Little Francis [sic]. I loathe child actors particularly in vaudeville, but this youngster sings a song called, I think, "Night and Day" in a fashion that would do justice to Helen Morgan. Little Francis [sic] will undoubtedly go places—but not with mama and sisters Virginia and Mary Jane.*[60]

Eighteen years later, on May 25, 1952, Soanes (still a critic for the *Oakland Tribune*) remembered his 1934 review when writing in anticipation of Garland's upcoming concert at Curran. By 1952, Garland had already achieved legendary status thanks to her recently launched "concert years." Soanes included his original 1934 review in his 1952 article. He definitely called it in 1934!

In early 1935, the film career of Judy Garland almost began on a completely different trajectory. On January 10, the Garland Sisters signed a one-picture deal with Universal Pictures to appear in *The Great Ziegfeld*. *Variety* noted that "Francis [sic] Garland landed a part in Universal's 'Great Ziegfeld.'" A few days later, the sisters performed at Universal cofounder Carl Laemmle's sixty-eighth birthday party at Universal Studios. It's very likely that they performed at other Universal functions. There are no records of any other activity at the studio that involved the sisters, although there is a surviving eight-by-ten promotional photo of Frances (taken during the 1934 Chicago trip) that she signed to Edward Miller and Universal Studios Inn. As late as May, while the sisters were up in San Francisco with the Wolf and Marco Revue, the *San Francisco Chronicle* raved about Frances being the star of the show and mentioned her role in *The Great Ziegfeld*, but by the time of that review, the project had been sold to MGM without the Garland Sisters attached. The resulting MGM version is a huge, extravagant musical that won the studio Oscars for Best Picture, Best Actress (Louise Rainer), and Best Dance Direction ("A Pretty Girl Is Like a Melody") for 1936, out of seven total nominations. There is no spot in the film that features a young sister act.

The sisters continued their stage engagements, including one at the Paramount Theatre in Los Angeles, which resulted in the only known photo of the trio performing on stage. The engagement generated another *Variety* review that singled out Frances:

> *Garland Sisters, three femmes, one of whom, Frances, is still a child and about 80% of the combination, are excellent harmonists, but it remained for the youngster to tie things up in a knot. Girl looks like a bet for pictures and should make rapid headway. However, she should be coached more proficiently in her foreign tongue songs, particularly the German, as her pronunciation is none too accurate. Otherwise, the kid is tops and deserved everything she drew today.*[61]

Yet another Garland milestone occurred on March 29, 1935, when the sisters recorded test records for Decca Records. With Ethel at the piano, the trio sang "Moonglow," and Garland soloed on "Bill" and a medley of "On the Good Ship Lollipop" / "The Object of My Affection" / "Dinah." Only the latter two have survived. The recordings are the very first studio recordings of Judy Garland singing. They're also the first recordings of her voice since the 1929/1930 film shorts. Comparing those with these studio recordings shows how much her voice had developed. Although she's only twelve years old in these 1935 tests, the Garland voice is there. "Bill" is a revelation. Garland displays that vulnerability for which she would later be famous. She also gets a chance to engage in a dramatic recitative break similar to her later 1937 breakout song "(Dear Mr. Gable) You Made Me Love You." In the medley, she displays her incredible expertise and versatility after the deceptively simple opening of "On the Good Ship Lollipop." She turns up the jazz with "The Object of My Affection," and by the time she ends with "Dinah," she's in full vaudeville mode, selling it all the way to the back row with her "hot" vocal stylings. In one short medley, she transitions from cutesy child to jazzy singer to experienced vaudevillian, transitions that singers twice her age would have trouble with. Much has been assumed and written about Ethel's motivations for (and alleged horrible treatment of) Garland in her quest to make her a star, but these recordings prove that, at least vocally, she had her on the right track. When Garland came under the tutelage of Roger Edens at MGM, she didn't need much polishing, and lucky for her and us, he knew exactly what to do. Decca rejected the tests. The recordings were thought lost until the early 2000s when a woman from Los Angeles did some research on two records that had been in her family, mostly forgotten, since the early 1960s. They were finally released to the public in 2010. The complete story is in the Decca Records appendix.

In April 1935, Frank lost the lease on the Valley Theatre in Lancaster and joined Ethel and the sisters in their rented home at 842 North Mariposa Avenue, near the 20th Century Fox studios in Los Angeles. The reason for the move was that rumors were spreading in Lancaster that Frank had been engaging in inappropriate sexual behavior with several local young men. As much as the community in Lancaster liked the Gumms, this was something they couldn't tolerate. It was "suggested" that Frank leave town.[62] He soon managed to find a new theatre to lease, this time in Lomita, California.

In early May 1935, as part of the Franchon and Marco Hollywood Review, the sisters returned to San Francisco for another successful weeklong engagement at the Orpheum Theatre. Ada Hanifin of the *San Francisco Examiner* wrote a review of opening night (May 3), in which she amusingly referred to Garland as "Julia" and not "Judy."

> *Among his featured performers, little Julia [sic] Garland is the star, and incidentally, a "find." She is only 12. But this little bundle of vitality and vivacity has much individually. She dances, talks to the audience with the aplomb of one who was practically born on the stage, has the fullness of voice that comes with much older years, and sings songs in English, Yiddish, Polish, Spanish, and French.*

When she was in the Southland, the movie moguls wasted no time putting her under contract. She has been given a role in "The Great Ziegfeld." Her two sisters, the three are known as the Garland Sisters, make good harmony, but for the most part they are just background for Julia.[63]

It's interesting that *The Great Ziegfeld* was still being mentioned, probably as part of the biographical info that Ethel would have given to the theatre and newspapers. After their return, the sisters continued performing in the Los Angeles area, including a return to the Paramount Theatre in May, resulting in their sixth *Variety* review:

Class act on bill is the Three Garland Sisters, which, for the Paramount booking, seem to have concentrated heavily on Francis [sic], the youthful member of the family. Girls do only a couple of harmony numbers, leaving rest of performance to kid sister, who is talented beyond doubt, and who scores heavily with her rendition of "Eli, Eli," plus a couple of songs in foreign tongue.[64]

The reviewer's note that the act focused mostly on "Francis" is a reflection of Garland's progression into the obvious star of the act and the fact that Virginia and Mary Jane were ready to leave the act and start their own lives, which they soon did.

The last major engagement for the sisters was from June 15 through 26, 1935, at the Cal-Neva Lodge at Lake Tahoe, in the Sierra Mountains in northern California on the Nevada border. It was during this engagement that Garland decided to change her name from Frances to Judy, based on the recent Hoagy Carmichael song of the same name. On the way back to Los Angeles, Ethel and the sisters had to return to the Cal-Neva to retrieve (depending on what story you read) a hatbox full of hats and/or some musical arrangements. Garland ran into the lodge, where she was intercepted by the manager, "Bones" Remer, who snagged her and said, "C'mon, kid, there's some people here you just got to sing for."[65] The people that Remer wanted her to sing for were none other than Harry Cohn, head of Columbia Pictures; Lew Brown, songwriter and executive at Columbia; songwriter Harry Akst; and agent Al Rosen. Garland sang, "Zing! Went the Strings of My Heart" and allegedly a few other songs before Akst asked her whether she knew any other songs; she replied that she knew "Dinah," for which Akst (the composer of the song) accompanied her on piano.[66] The men were enthusiastic, and Brown tried to convince Cohn to sign Garland to a studio contract. For unknown reasons, Cohn declined, probably because of Garland's age. However, by August 8, "Judy" Garland was in the Los Angeles Superior Court with her parents for the final approval/signing of a contract designating Al Rosen as her agent. The *Los Angeles Times* reported on the event on August 9, 1935, and included a photo of Garland taken at the courthouse. Unfortunately, as the article states, the petition was denied:

The petition of Al Rosen for judicial approval of a contract for him to act as manager of 12-year-old Judy Garland in obtaining stage and motion-picture work for her was denied yesterday by Superior Judge McComb.

The court ruled it was without jurisdiction to approve a contract involving a minor whereby she would have a manager who was to receive a commission for obtaining work for her in the future.

The child actress was accompanied to court by her parents, Ethel and Frank Garland.[67]

It's interesting to note that the *Times* went to the expense of sending a photographer to take pictures of Garland in court to get her contract approved. Rosen probably arranged it with the paper, or the photographer might have been there for other reasons and stumbled onto the contract approval hearing. The *Times* felt it was newsworthy enough to publish the photo with the news blurb. This is another indication of the Garlands' local fame, as seen in the paper's coverage of the Garland Sisters act breaking up just six days later.

The final professional engagement for the Garland Sisters was their appearance in the Technicolor short film *La Fiesta de Santa Barbara*. The sisters filmed the short on location in Santa Barbara, California, on August 12, 1935. The short was independently produced by Lewis Lewyn and released by MGM on December 7, 1935. This is the first time Garland was filmed in the then-new three-strip Technicolor process. She did not appear in another color film until *The Wizard of Oz* in 1939. The sisters sing one song, "La Cucaracha" (about marijuana!), and it's the only known recording and footage of the sisters after their earlier 1929 shorts. Garland's voice stands out in their harmonies.

Just three days later, the *Los Angeles Times* published an article about the breakup of the Garland Sisters act, as Suzanne (the nickname the oldest sister, Mary Jane, had taken) left by plane to Reno, where she wed musician Lee Kahn. She had met Kahn during their engagement in Lake Tahoe. The accompanying photo shows Garland and Jimmie (the nickname that Virginia was now using) posed on Suzanne's right and left as she's boarding the plane to Reno.

On August 8, 1935, Judy Garland's new agent, Al Rosen, attempted to get a contract approved designating him as her agent. Despite failing to get approval, Rosen still worked on Garland's behalf. From the author's collection.

CUPID ROBS RADIO TEAM

Suzanne Garland Flies to Reno to Become Bride of Musician

The radio-stage-screen trio of Suzanne, 22; Jimmy, 18; Judy, 12 [Judy was already thirteen at this point but apparently mom Ethel shaved a year off her age just as MGM would soon do]; familiarly

The end of an era. On August 14, 1935, Garland's oldest sister, Suzanne (Mary Jane), broke up the Garland Sisters act to fly to Reno, Nevada, to get married. From the author's collection.

billed as the Garland Sisters, yesterday became a duet.

Romance, in the person of Lee Kahn, musician, broke up the successful trio when Suzanne boarded a United Air Lines plane at Union Air Terminal for Reno.

Kahn, a member of the Jimmy Davis orchestra playing at Cal-Neva Lodge, Lake Tahoe, drove to the Nevada city to meet Suzanne's plane. The two were to be married there last night.

With the conclusion of the Tahoe season, Kahn goes to San Francisco for an engagement and the couple will make the Bay City their home, Suzanne said.

During a tearful parting with her two sisters at the airport, Suzanne revealed that Jimmy Garland is now engaged to Frankie Darro, of screen note.[68]

On the same date, the *San Francisco Examiner* published a similar notice with the headline "At Reno She'll Make It a Duet!" and a photo of Suzanne. Part of their text read, "She may sing again, but not unless her husband wants her to, 'because he's the leader of the orchestra now,' she said."

It was the end of the Gumm/Garland Sisters as an act and the end of an era. The time was right for the youngest Garland sister, Judy Garland, to become strictly a solo act. For all intents and purposes, Garland had been a solo act for some time, with reviewers commenting that the older sisters provided mostly backup (even in the trio numbers) to their obviously more talented younger sister. Now it was official.

THE AUDITION

After the act broke up, things moved quickly for Garland. Rosen was able to get her an audition at MGM on September 13, 1935. Over the decades, legends, assumptions, and faulty memories have clouded the sequence of events that led to this audition, the details of the audition itself, and the subsequent sequence of events.

Although Los Angeles County didn't approve that contract with Rosen that previous August, that didn't stop his determination to get Garland into the movies. He reportedly procured auditions for her at all the major studios, including MGM, Columbia, Fox, RKO, Warner Bros., and Paramount (where she allegedly sang for Cecil B. DeMille). The general consensus was that she was too young and her voice was too mature. They might have been charmed by Garland, but they all passed. However, although Garland had previously auditioned for MGM at least once, she was given another chance when Rosen was able to procure another audition for her. It all happened very quickly on that fateful day in mid-September 1935.

When the call came to the Gumm home from Rosen for Garland to head to MGM right away for the audition on September 13, Ethel was out running errands, so Frank took her without having her change out of her play clothes or put on any makeup. Frank played the piano before musical arranger Roger Edens stepped in at the urging of the studio's resident songwriter (and soon-to-be producer), Arthur Freed, who said, "That guy is the worst piano player I ever heard. . . . Roger, go over and do a song with the little girl."[69] Garland sang "Zing! Went the Strings of My Heart." Freed and Edens were shocked at how amazing Garland was, to the point that Freed ran out and headed over to MGM studio boss Louis B. Mayer's office: "Ignoring receptionists, he burst in as Mayer was dictating to his secretary. It took some doing to induce Mayer to walk from the Administration Building to Stage 1, two city blocks away. By the time Freed and Mayer arrived, a crowd had gathered (in a studio, news travels fast). Judy sang again and again. And then again for Mayer. When she finally sang 'Eli, Eli,' Mayer had tears in his eyes."[70] In 1961, Edens said about the audition, "I knew instantly, in eight bars of music. The talent was that inbred. I fell flat on my face. She was just so high and chubby, wearing a navy blue middy blouse and baby-doll sandals, with lots of hair and no lipstick. I really flipped. I called Ida Koverman, L. B. Mayer's secretary, and she called Mr. Mayer, and he called the lawyers, and she was signed to a contract that day. It was like discovering gold at Sutter Creek."[71] Some of this account, especially the Sutter Creek remark, has been quoted often in stories about Garland's audition. By 1961, even Roger Edens's memory was clouded, although he was probably sincere in his feeling that discovering Garland was like discovering gold.

That is one story. Another, as told by biographer Gerold Frank, is that Rosen secured an audition for Garland with Mayer's secretary, Ida Koverman. She sang a couple of songs for Koverman, who then rang Edens, who "politely replaced Frank at the piano." Koverman convinced Mayer to hear her, so they took Garland to Mayer's huge office (her first time in that famous—or infamous—all-white office), where she sang three songs. Mayer sat "impassively" be-

32   CHAPTER 1

fore Frank became angry that they were being so cold about everything and took Garland home. The next morning, Rosen again called, this time because Koverman wanted them to come back and have Garland sing again for Mayer, the implication being that this second trip to the studio was due to Edens's enthusiasm for her. Edens again provided accompaniment, with the addition of producer Jack Cummings and Freed in attendance. This also allegedly happened on MGM Soundstage 1. Garland sang "several Jazz numbers" before singing "Eili, Eili." The group convinced Mayer to sign her without a screen test.[72]

Another version begins again with Rosen calling the Gumm home and Frank taking Garland to MGM. This time, she sang for MGM talent chief Jack Robbins, who complained, "I'm looking for a woman singer. Why are you bringing me a child?"[73] Garland sang "Zing! Went the Strings of My Heart" for Robbins, who then called Koverman and Edens in to listen. Edens took over for Frank at the piano. Koverman called Mayer, hanging up the phone and exclaiming, "He's coming!"[74] Mayer appeared, and Garland sang "Zing!" again. He listened without emotion and then left. This is when Frank became angry and took Garland home.

In his interview with Albert Johnson, published in the spring 1958 issue of *Sight and Sound* magazine, Edens said:

> *The biggest thing to happen to the MGM musical was the discovery of Judy Garland. . . . She was terrific, right from the beginning. I remember, she was brought in and auditioned; she sang "Zing, Went the Strings of My Heart" and I almost fell off the piano bench. When she finished, I went straight into Mr. Mayer's office and said he just had to sign her.*[75]

In Gerald Clarke's biography of Garland, he tells the story differently. He notes that by September 1935, Garland had already been rejected by MGM at least twice. Koverman sent Edens to the offices of an MGM-owned publishing house to hear her sing, with Ethel providing the piano accompaniment. When Edens took over, he asked Garland what she planned to sing. She replied, "Zing! Went the Strings of My Heart," and then she asked him whether he could change keys. He said, "Yes, can YOU?" Edens immediately recognized Garland's talent and said, "Mrs. Koverman, Mr. Mayer must hear this girl." This incident resulted in the audition at the studio on September 13.[76]

Fifty-plus years later, MGM director George Sidney claimed to have "discovered" Garland in 1934. In December 1934, writer (and future producer/director) Joseph L. Mankiewicz took Sidney and Mayer's secretary, Ida Koverman, to the Wilshire Ebell Theatre to see Garland perform. Sidney said:

> *They used to have amateur acts that would go on. And one of these acts was three girls called the Gumm Sisters and their mother played the piano. The poor mother walked out with the bad feet and she played the piano and these three little girls sang, and Mr. Louis B. Mayer's executive secretary, Mrs. Koverman, said "that girl's good, bring her out to the studio." Me, I at that time, was the test director at MGM and I made all the screen tests of all the new people so I went backstage to this little girl and I said, "You*

THE ROAD TO MGM

33

come to MGM tomorrow morning, Monday, and at 1 o'clock, we're gonna make a screen test of you."
And she came out there and on Stage 16—I can remember it—and we rolled out the mat and the mother
came with the bad feet and she walked, and the other two sisters, and we said, "No, you two sisters sit
over there, we just wanna do this with this little girl here." And she [Garland] said, "What do I do,"
and I said, "Remember you sang a little number with a baseball bat and you just sing it right here to me
in front of the camera," and she did it, and they saw it the next day and they signed her.[77]

Christopher Finch, in his 1975 biography on Garland, reported that the screen test directed by Sidney, with the baseball routine and Ethel playing the piano, happened "a few days" after the audition on September 13, 1935, and not in December 1934. In this version, Edens was going to accompany Garland on piano, but the routine was complicated and included props, so Ethel played. Garland didn't hear anything for a couple of weeks when they were contacted to see the test. Frank went with them. The enthusiasm in the screening room told them it was considered highly satisfactory.[78] Finch doesn't give any source material in his book, although the way it reads, one would think Finch spoke with Sidney directly. Sidney's various recollections have not been verified by any studio documentation, and the footage of this alleged test no longer exists. There are no surviving records from MGM of any Garland screen test happening, nor is there anything in the trade publications (which were already well aware of Garland) of Garland signing with MGM in 1934. Sidney told his story fifty years later. Considering the other inconsistencies and mix-ups in his stories told at the same time, it's clear that his recollections are not reliable. Another false narrative is that Garland was tested at MGM in early 1935. This could be confusion over the brief association at the time with Universal and *The Great Ziegfeld*. It's been claimed that at this alleged early 1935 audition (and the real audition in September 1935), Mayer himself took Garland around the entire studio and made her sing for everyone. It's preposterous to think that Mayer would have had the time to take Garland all over MGM, showing her off, no matter how talented she was, expensively halting the many films currently in production—and then not even sign her to a contract.

MGM kept incredibly detailed records, which makes it inconceivable that all of the print documentation and, to a lesser degree, the film footage regarding at least two separate alleged Garland auditions or screen tests would have become lost. Due to Sidney's stories, the Wilshire Ebell Theatre now incorrectly claims that Garland was "discovered" there and that the engagement (on December 8, 1934) led to her MGM contract. If that claim were true, it would have resulted in a completely different sequence of events in Garland's life and career than what actually happened in the months between December 1934 and September 1935. But it makes for more dynamic article copy and good promotion for the Wilshire Ebell in spite of it being a lie.

The MGM publicity department contributed to the false legends almost immediately after Garland signed with the studio. As early as November 1, 1935, not even two months after her audition, columnist Wood Soanes noted the absurdity of a recent MGM press release stating that Garland "wandered into the Metro-Goldwyn-Mayer studios one day last week and said she wanted to sing." The press release went on to tell the story that she was given an audition and was being hailed as "the baby Nora Bayes" and was "said to be one of two or three players ever signed without the formality of a screen test." Soanes noted how difficult it was to get into any of the studios and that the idea of a young girl just "wandering in" was ridiculous.[79] MGM also stuck to the studio line of giving Garland's age as twelve rather than thirteen, an attempt to make her seem even more precocious. The studio continued to shave a year off her age for the next several years.

On November 20, 1935, *Variety* carried the story (dated November 19) that Sam Katz of MGM was looking for a property to star "Metro's 12-year-old torch singer" Judy Garland (she was thirteen). The story incorrectly claimed that Garland went to MGM when *The Great Ziegfeld* did and that no one at MGM noticed her until she sang at a "night spot." The unnamed author reported that Universal changed Garland's last name from "Gumm" to "Garland." The article is pure fiction, aside from the fact that Garland was indeed contracted to Universal for the film. It's noted here because it's another indication that even though Garland had been at MGM for only a little over a month, the studio was already getting her name in the trade publications and creating false narratives of how she ended up at MGM.

The complete truth about exactly who was or wasn't at that legendary Garland MGM audition on September 13, 1935, will most likely never be known for sure. It can be assumed, with about 95 percent confidence, that Rosen called the Gumms, Frank took Garland "as is" to MGM, and Rosen, Koverman, Freed, and Edens listened to her sing "Zing! Went the Strings of My Heart" prior to calling Mayer to do the same. Mayer sat stone-faced as Garland sang "Eili, Eili" and left without saying much (if anything at all). He then ordered that a standard seven-year contract be drawn up.

According to the local newspapers, Garland was part of another Kusell show in Pasadena, California, at the Pasadena Community Playhouse, titled "Rhythm Madness," which opened on September 24, 1935. Garland's participation in the show was short lived. These stage engagements at movie theatres were usually a week long, but Garland's first day at MGM was just a few days later, on October 1, 1935. The result is that "Rhythm Madness" holds the distinction of being Garland's last professional engagement before beginning her MGM career.

All the years of singing and dancing across half the United States had paid off. Judy Garland won the ultimate show business prize: a contract with the biggest, most glamorous, and arguably the best of all the Hollywood studios, Metro-Goldwyn-Mayer. She was on her way. But first, she still had to prove herself.

Garland poses in the same manner that she sang "Bill" on stage in dozens of shows (Chicago, 1934). From the author's collection.

C H A P T E R *2*

MGM's NEWEST CONTRACT PLAYER

On September 16, 1935, just three days after Garland's audition for the studio, MGM executive F. L. Hendrickson sent a detailed memo to the contract department that began, "Please prepare contract for the services of JUDY GARLAND as an actress." Hendrickson laid out the details:

Original term of this agreement is for a period of 6 months, commencing October 1, 1935, at a salary of $100.00 a week, 20 week guarantee. We have the following options:

6 months $200.00 per week, 20 week guarantee

1 year 300.00 per week, 40 week guarantee

1 year 400.00 per week, 40 week guarantee

1 year 500.00 per week, 40 week guarantee

1 year 600.00 per week, 40 week guarantee

1 year 750.00 per week, 40 week guarantee

1 year 1000.00 per week, 40 week guarantee

Miss Garland is a minor. The details of her birth, however, her parents name and address, will have to be given to you later. We will also verify whether or not the above name is her real or professional name.

A provision should be included in the notice clause that all notices which may be addressed to the artist shall be sent to her care of her agents, Al Rosen Agency, 6404 Hollywood Blvd.

Hendrickson added a postscript to the memo that gave more details, including Garland's birthname and birthplace, the names of her parents, and their home address. He incorrectly noted that she was born on January 10, 1923. The contract was approved in the Los Angeles Superior Court on September 27, 1935, with Garland's parents accompanying her to sign on her behalf. An MGM photographer was on hand to take a photo of Garland at the courthouse, which was the first MGM photograph taken of Judy Garland. The contract began on October 1, 1935—Garland's first day of work at the studio.

MGM initially took its time with Garland's film career. The studio was big enough that it could afford to sign talent to a standard studio contract without any clear plan for them. If they worked out, great; if not, they could easily be released when one of the contract renewal options came up, which was usually at six-month intervals. With Garland, the studio had a unique set of challenges. She had a million-dollar adult singing voice in the body of a typically awkward and plain (in MGM terms) thirteen-year-old girl. The studio's quandary in not knowing how best to present Garland is reflected in the first portrait session she endured on November 6, 1935. She is dressed in an ill-fitting, frilly outfit with nondescript hair. Her expressions show a girl who is clearly uncomfortable but still smiling. The people at MGM's portrait gallery apparently didn't take the sitting seriously or weren't used to making awkward young girls look glamorous. As she would sing a few years later, Garland was an "in-between." She wasn't a budding glamour girl, nor was she a child. Decades later, she joked on Jack Paar's TV show that MGM didn't know what to do with her because "you either had to be a *Munchkin* or [motioning having large breasts] . . . there was no in between."[1]

MGM's resident songwriter and soon-to-be producer Arthur Freed and his musical right-hand man, Roger Edens, knew exactly what to do with Garland. They were her earliest and biggest champions at the studio, along with studio boss Louis B. Mayer's powerful secretary, Ida Koverman. The three of them instantly recognized Garland's

Judy Garland's first portrait sitting at MGM, November 6, 1935. From the author's collection.

unique potential. Both Freed and Edens hitched their wagons to Garland's star. They would have succeeded regardless, but in Garland, they found their perfect muse.

At this time, Arthur Freed and fellow songwriter Nacio Herb Brown were MGM's resident songwriting team. Like Garland, Freed found his way to MGM through vaudeville. Born Arthur Grossman in Charleston, South Carolina, on September 9, 1894, he started off as a "song plugger" for a Chicago music publisher. He met the mother of the Marx Brothers, Minnie Marx, and toured the vaudeville circuit with their act. He first collaborated with Brown in 1921 while also collaborating with other songwriters, including Gus Arnheim and Abe Lyman, with whom he collaborated on 1923's "I Cried for You," which was his first hit song. He ended up in the Los Angeles nightclub circuit, and, in the late 1920s, he was hired by Irving Thalberg at MGM as a lyricist and assigned to write songs with Brown. The duo put out a string of hits, beginning with the studio's first all-talking, all-singing, all-dancing extravaganza, the Oscar-winning *The Broadway Melody* (1929). Their hits include "Singin' in the Rain," "The Broadway Melody," "Broadway Rhythm," "All I Do Is Dream of You," "Good Morning," "Temptation," and many more. Freed was ambitious and wanted to do bigger things by becoming a producer. He got his wish, first as an uncredited associate producer on *The Wizard of Oz* and then with his first producing credit, *Babes in Arms*, both released in 1939 and both starring Garland.

Roger Edens was born Rollins Edens in Hillsboro, Texas, on November 9, 1905, and came to MGM via his association with another singing legend, Ethel Merman. Edens made his way from Texas to Broadway as the accompanist to the ballroom dancers Tony and Renee De Marco. In 1930, he was one of the musicians in the now-famous pit orchestra for the new Gershwin musical *Girl Crazy* starring Ethel Merman and Ginger Rogers (Edens provided the music adaptation for the 1943 film version starring Garland and Mickey Rooney). The pit orchestra included future big band legends Tommy Dorsey, Gene Krupa, Glenn Miller, and Harry James. Edens became Merman's accompanist and vocal arranger, and in a couple of years he went with her to Hollywood. Freed saw and heard Edens accompany singer Patricia Ellis at Warner Bros. and immediately arranged for Edens to move to MGM.[2] His first job at the studio was as the musical supervisor on the Jean Harlow musical *Reckless* (1933). He became the musical supervisor for most of the studio's musicals, chiefly tap dance sensation Eleanor Powell's films, appearing on screen as her accompanist in 1935's *Broadway Melody of 1936*.

Edens provided the musical foundation of what became the Freed Unit. The Freed Unit quickly became the studio's (and then the movie industry's) premiere musical makers. Edens gave invaluable input for most of the studio's musical films and always seemed to know what was right, musically speaking, writing songs and sometimes serving as an associate producer. The special material and songs that he wrote specifically for Garland throughout her career are legendary; the most famous of these is the "Born in a Trunk" sequence in *A Star Is Born* (Warner Bros., 1954) and her "Judy at the Palace" medley, which she regularly performed in concert and on television. Edens was an early proponent of advancing the "integrated musical," in which the songs are integrated into the dialog and advance the story in one way or another. It became a hallmark of the greatest MGM musicals.

Initially, Garland's daily schedule at MGM consisted of song rehearsals with Edens and going to school at MGM's Little Red Schoolhouse (which wasn't red), along with other young contract players, including Freddie Bartholomew, Mickey Rooney, and Jackie Cooper. Fifteen-year-old Rooney had a series of Mickey McGuire shorts on his resume as well as impressive supporting performances in various films, including a scene-stealing performance as Puck in the Warner Bros. adaptation of *A Midsummer Night's Dream* in 1935. Rooney and Garland had already known each other, their friendship going back to their time at Lawlor's School for Professional Children and probably even before that, backstage during their vaudeville years. The two bonded and became best friends for life. In his article about Garland for the July 1943 issue of *Photoplay* fan magazine, columnist Sidney Skolsky wrote a fictionalized version of how they met:

> *It was while she was going to school at Lawlor's, in Hollywood, that a freckled-faced boy was ushered into the classroom and given the seat next to her. The boy began tapping his foot and whistling softly. Then he took a comb from his pocket and proceeded to get his hair so tangled that he couldn't remove the comb. She reached over and unknotted the mess. Giving her a big grin, he stuck out his hand and said, "Thanks, my name is Mickey."*
>
> *This was her first meeting with Mickey Rooney. She fell in love with him.*
>
> *A few weeks later Mickey told her he was leaving school. He had just signed a contract at Metro-Goldwyn-Mayer and had to attend the studio school. She felt miserable that he was leaving. "I'll call you tomorrow," he said. He never did. She didn't see him again until she was signed by the same studio.[3]*

The first work assignment MGM gave Garland was singing at the Los Angeles Coliseum during halftime of the University of Southern California Football Game on either October 5 or October 12 (the details are sketchy). She sang "Fight on for Good Old USC."[4] In mid-October, Garland was penciled in for a role in the upcoming MGM production of *This Time It's Love*, starring Robert Montgomery. According to a letter that Garland's father, Frank, sent to a friend in Lancaster, she was to appear opposite Buddy Ebsen in the film.[5] *This Time It's Love* eventually became *Born to Dance*, starring Eleanor Powell, with James Stewart replacing Montgomery, and was released in 1936. Garland's part was written out of the screenplay before she would have begun any work on the film. On March 10, 1936, songwriter Cole Porter noted in his diary that to his "great joy," *Born to Dance* would include "Buddy Ebsen and Judy Garland."[6] Even though Garland was still relatively unknown to the greater American public, Porter knew who she was and had no issue that she would be singing his songs. He later wrote the score for 1948's *The Pirate* starring Garland and Gene Kelly.

On October 26, 1935, MGM "officially" introduced Garland to a nationwide audience

40   CHAPTER 2

on the NBC Radio variety show *Shell Chateau Hour* hosted by MGM star Wallace Beery. The show was typical of its time, serving to promote MGM films and stars. Beery introduced Garland as being twelve years old (she was thirteen), and she enthusiastically exclaimed, "I want to be a singer, Mr. Beery. And I'd like to act, too!" She sang the latest Freed/Brown hit, "Broadway Rhythm," and received a loud reception from the studio audience.

After a few appearances at various industry and MGM-related events, including entertainer Frank Fay's show at the Cafe Trocadero on November 10 (where she was photographed with stars Spencer Tracy and Una Merkel), Garland's next big assignment was her return to the *Shell Chateau Hour*, again with Beery as the host, broadcast live on November 16. Beery led the audience to believe that Garland had just signed with MGM due to her first appearance on the show and had been immediately cast in producer Sam Katz's new film *Yours and Mine*. None of that was true; it was more fiction the studio publicity department concocted. This appearance is notable because, at the time of the broadcast, Garland's father was in the hospital suffering from a sudden case of spinal meningitis. A radio was placed at his bedside so he could listen to his daughter. Garland sang a stirring rendition of "Zing! Went the Strings of My Heart" and then an equally stirring reprise after a quick chat with Beery. The audio for this performance (and the previous *Shell* appearance) has survived. These are the earliest surviving recordings of Garland's voice after the Decca test records she recorded in March 1935 and before the early film and radio performances in 1936. When comparing the Decca tests and this radio performance, one can hear the influence of Edens on Garland's delivery. Her vocals are a bit more polished. Edens, like Ethel before him, had Garland on the right track.

In an early sign of the kind of control MGM would exert over Garland's personal life, rather than allowing her to go to the hospital to be with her father after the Beery show, MGM sent her to sing at the MGM Club Dance at the La Monica Ballroom in nearby Santa Monica.

Frank Gumm died the following day, November 17, 1935. Garland was devastated. She later said that it was "the most terrible thing that ever happened to me in my life."[7] Ever since, Garland fans and Garland herself have pondered how different her career and certainly her personal life might have been if Frank had lived. Could Frank have shielded her from future overwork and her reliance on prescription medication? Would he have been able to stand up to the studio grind in a way that her mom, Ethel, couldn't (or wouldn't)? In that misogynistic world, MGM might have given Frank more respect than they gave Ethel because he was a man. It's one of the biggest of the many what-ifs of the Garland legend.

As if the death of her father weren't enough, November 17 was also Ethel's birthday. Frank, unbeknownst to the rest of his family, had planned a surprise party for Ethel that evening. They had been sitting around the living room, stunned over Frank's death, when, out of the blue, people began to arrive with "Surprise! Happy Birthday!" on their lips. No one knew how to stop it because no one knew that Frank had planned the surprise or whom he had invited. Virginia later said, "All these people they [Frank and Ethel] knew came to the door with presents. Some of them were from Grand Rapids. That's the saddest thing I can remember. My mother was lying on the couch and all these people came to the door and said, 'Happy Birthday!'"[8] Compounding the tragedy of it all for Garland was that due to her professional obligations the night before Frank's death, she never had the chance to say goodbye to him.

Ten days later, on November 27, 1935, Garland recorded two more test records for Decca: "All's Well" and "No Other One." These were the first studio recordings Garland made after beginning her MGM career, but, unfortunately, they have not survived. They must have made an impression because, at that same time, Decca president Jack Kapp was visiting Los Angeles from New York and signing new talent for the label. A week after the recording session, *Variety* reported that Kapp had signed several artists before returning to New York, including Garland, "the 12-year-old Metro contractee-songstress."[9] The details of that first contract are unknown, as no documents have survived. It was most likely a per-record contract, which wasn't unusual. Garland didn't record for the label again until seven months later, on June 12, 1936, when she recorded "Swing, Mr. Charlie" and "Stompin' at the Savoy" while in New York. The songs became the first Garland single ever released. No other records exist regarding any contract for this 1936 New York session, which was most likely either another per-record contract or perhaps the fulfillment of that 1935 contract/agreement that *Variety* reported on. Nothing else happened between Garland and Decca for over a year, and then, in August 1937, a contract was written for an initial six months. By that point, her star was obviously on the rise, and Decca was happy to sign her for longer terms. That was the beginning of Garland's ten-year association with the label.

For the rest of 1935, Garland continued her daily activities at MGM as well as her personal appearances, including more singing at various studio and industry events, which kept her relatively busy. Even at this early stage in her movie career, she was a popular addition at Hollywood parties, as she would always be. In her March 1936 column, Louella Parsons reported on the "Studio Party" MGM put on at the Ambassador Hotel on February 29, mentioning, "Usually these parties are frankly a bore, but the entertainment in this one was so good everyone lingered on and on [with] Judy Garland called back again and again."[10]

Over the ensuing decades, the assumption has been that MGM forgot about Garland or that since they didn't know what to do with her, she basically twiddled her thumbs, waiting for a

KAPP BACK WITH FILM SIGS FOR DECCA DISCS

Jack Kapp, prez of Decca, is back from a month's stay in Hollywood lining up recording talent and setting more dates. Among the new Decca artists are Frances Langford, Ginger Rogers, Dick Powell, Judy Garland, latter the 12-year-old Metro contractee-songstress.

Miss Langford and Powell were last on Brunswick, shifting to Decca.

Crosby also recorded eight numbers under Decca's personal supervision, chiefly pops, which is a departure for the crooner since he's been in pictures, preferring to can only the numbers he introduced in his Paramount filmusicals. Being between pix for so long, however, he's done 'Treasure Island,' 'Boots and Saddle,' 'Red Sails in the Sunset,' 'Silent Night and 'Adeste Fideles' for the Xmas trade, and others.

Variety notice about Garland's first contract with Decca Records, December 4, 1935. From the author's collection.

chance. But it's obvious from her activities in these early months that someone at MGM was getting Garland exposure and increasing mentions in the newspapers. Although MGM still hadn't figured out how to present Judy Garland to the public on film, at least they were getting her out there.

One notable industry event was the "Show of Shows" put on by the Will Rogers Memorial Fund at the Shrine Auditorium in Los Angeles on December 1, 1935. On November 25, the *Los Angeles Times* listed Garland among those added that week to the notice of the lineup of eighty-six stars scheduled to participate. No records exist regarding what Garland sang or whether she sang at all. She posed for photos backstage with film stars Joe E. Brown and May Robson and child stars Edith Fellows, Mickey Rooney, and Freddie Bartholomew. The photos show a very gangly and awkward-looking Garland wearing another ill-fitting outfit, this time a child's jumper dress with an oversized bow in her hair. The outfit contrasted with the more glamorous fur coat, dress, and hat that Fellows, who was one year younger than Garland, was wearing. Fellows was being presented as "glamorous" (for a "tween") while Garland was the non-glamorous kid. The contrast is just like "Dainty June" and "Rose Louise" portrayed years later in *Gypsy*. The image of Garland as the ugly duckling surrounded by glamorous girls started early.

On December 18, *Variety* published a short blurb (dated December 17) that MGM was preparing an adaptation of Edgar Allan Woolf's *La Belle Dolly* as Garland's first film, costarring the seventy-four-year-old opera diva Madame (Ernestine) Schumann-Heink. Heink was a legendary opera star who was forced out of retirement when she lost everything in the Crash of 1929, working as a vocal coach and, of course, singer. Harold W. Cohen picked up the story for his column "The Drama Desk" on December 24, 1935, but mentioned only Mme. Schumann-Heink and Woolf's names, not Garland's. It's unknown

Garland (*far right*) is seen with Edith Fellows, Mickey Rooney, May Robson, and Freddie Bartholomew at the Will Rogers Memorial Fund "Show of Shows" at the Shrine Auditorium in Los Angeles, California, December 1, 1935. From the author's collection.

MGM'S NEWEST CONTRACT PLAYER

whether the intent was to have Garland sing in a more operatic style or her typical jazzy style. This role sounds more like the kind that would later be played by Deanna Durbin (who wasn't at MGM just yet). The property had been at MGM for at least a few years. In 1933, *Variety* noted that the film would star the young Jackie Cooper with the older non-singing actress Marie Dressler.

The following day, December 19, 1935, Garland sang at the Elks Movie Star Benefit at the Rosemary Theatre in Ocean Park, Venice, California. The benefit featured big-name stars, like MGM's Clark Gable and Jean Harlow, and was billed as the "annual all-star stage, screen, radio show, and Hi-Jinks." It was probably Garland's biggest singing assignment since signing with MGM and singing on the *Shell Chateau* radio shows. A few days before, on December 16, the *Evening Vanguard* newspaper out of Venice Beach noted, "Judy Garland, 12-year-old [again, she was really thirteen] sensation known on the vaudeville stage as the 'Baby Nora Bayes' has also offered her services." The article went on to list some of the scheduled acts, including "the Garland Sisters, Orpheum headliners now making an MGM picture." The Garland Sisters act was not a part of the show, but this kind of mistake isn't unusual regarding Garland's association with MGM at this time. We know that the sisters had broken up the act that previous August and that Judy had been signed solo by MGM that previous September. The pre-event press text that MGM sent to the paper was probably a mix-up of info from Garland's studio file, like it was in 1935, or it could have been a poorly executed copy job on the part of the paper, using info from previous articles. In the article published in the same paper the day after the benefit, there's no mention of "the Garland Sisters," which makes sense, as that article would be more accurate, assuming the writer was actually at the event and able to document the stars and acts correctly. Included in that list are the "Mullane Sisters." Could they have been mistakenly listed as "Garland" in the previous article? Garland was again singled out as "Judy Garland, vaudeville's 'Baby Norah [*sic*] Bayes.'" There is no mention in either article of Garland having recently signed with MGM or being a part of MGM in any way (even though most of the talent in the show came from MGM), aside from that single mention about the Garland Sisters making an MGM film.

A couple of days later, on December 21, Garland took part in the first annual show for the "Forgotten Child of Hollywood" charity event at the Marcel Theatre on Hollywood Boulevard in Los Angeles. The show took place early, at 11:00 a.m. The event is notable because it shows that Garland was already being included with other, more well-known child and juvenile stars at important events. The roster reads like a who's who of young Hollywood: Mickey Rooney, Rose Marie, Dickie Moore, Jane Withers, Baby LeRoy, Virginia Weidler, Jackie Cooper, Cora Sue Collins, and even members of the *Our Gang* shorts and Captain Jack, the movie stunt dog. The event raised money and took gifts, food, and clothing donations for "the forgotten, homeless, and penniless children whose addresses may not be known by old St. Nicholas." It's not noted what Garland sang.[11]

Rooney and Withers joined Garland at the Shrine Auditorium on December 30. The

44   CHAPTER 2

three were not part of any show but were photographed together backstage. The photo was syndicated on January 1, 1936, with the headline "On Their Way in Movies," noting that the trio was "the three foremost up-and-coming juvenile stars in Hollywood."[12]

After the new year, Garland, her mother Ethel, and her sister Jimmie moved into a home in Hollywood at 180 South McCadden Place that featured Garland's first swimming pool, a reflection of the family's new prosperity. At MGM, Garland's workload continued to be light, but her personal appearances continued at a regular pace. On April 3, she was one of several juvenile "child film players"[13] who were a part of the Junior Troupers' benefit show and fashion parade at the Hollywood Masonic Temple, along with Rooney, Deanna Durbin (billed as Edna Mae [sic] Durbin), Cora Sue Collins, Scotty Beckett, and Dickie Moore. The papers also reported that Garland was a guest at eight-year-old "screen cowboy" Dickie Jones's party at the Hollywood Brown Derby on May 15, along with another laundry list of Hollywood child performers, including Jane Withers, Frankie Darro, Virginia Weidler, and Edith Fellows.[14]

FINALLY ON FILM

Garland finally got to appear in an MGM film—sort of—in the spring of 1936 when she and another teen singer newly under contract, the classically trained Deanna Durbin, filmed a one-reel test film. The test was not shown to the public but instead was shown solely at the MGM exhibitor's convention in Chicago, Illinois, between May 11 and 16 of that year. Nothing more is known about the test because it's a lost film.

That test with Durbin had a positive impact on MGM's opinion of Garland because not long after, in early June, the studio sent her to New York for the first time. Mayer's secretary (and Garland champion), Ida Koverman, wrote a letter of introduction dated June 1, 1936, for Garland to take with her and present to local New York MGM representative Florence Browning. Koverman's letter is revealing in that it gives us a glimpse into how Garland was perceived at this time and how she was still relatively unknown outside of Hollywood, necessitating the letter of introduction. Koverman wrote:

Dear Florence:

This will be presented to you by little Judy Garland, who is under contract to us.

She is twelve years old and an extremely clever little artist. Her mother, who will be with her, plays her accompaniments, and I hope you will be able to arrange to hear her sing a few numbers. She is really a marvellous [sic] child.

Her agent is taking her East to try to book her in some of the theatres, and I think it would be very wise to have someone connected with our office see the child before she gets into opposition house[s]. [This is a reference to ensuring that Garland would appear only at theatres owned by MGM's parent company, Loew's Inc.]

She sings very well, is an excellent dancer, and does the Eleanor Powell routines, and is a little genius.

In addition to this she is a dear little thing, I am devoted to her. I know you will like her too.

Garland wrote back to Koverman, telling her that she had met with Browning and other MGM executives and that she "hoped my singing pleases them." She spent her time in New York appearing on a few local radio shows, including Rudy Vallee's popular series and the *Broadway Melody Hour*. In his syndicated column, Sidney Skolsky noted of Garland's appearance at the Trocadero nightclub, "Judy Garland, a truly great singer of popular songs—New York will acclaim her after she debuts on the Rudy Vallee program—sang 'Broadway Rhythm,' and the Times Square crowd gathered at the troc [*sic*] took it big."[15]

On June 12, 1936, Garland was at the Decca Records New York studio recording the two songs that made up that first-ever Garland single release: "Swing, Mr. Charlie" and "Stompin' at

Deanna Durbin and Garland with director Felix Feist during the filming of *Every Sunday* (1936). From the collection of Hisato Masuyama.

the Savoy." Bob Crosby and His Orchestra backed Garland, and, amusingly, Crosby's manager, Gil Rodin, asked that the band not be listed on the record label because he "didn't want to use our name on the same record label with this unknown girl."[16] Seven years later, Crosby and his orchestra backed Garland on two songs in a scene in *Presenting Lily Mars* (1943). By that time, they definitely had no problem with "this unknown girl."

After Garland returned from New York, she went to work on her first official film assignment for MGM, the "Tabloid Musical" short *Every Sunday* costarring Durbin, who had returned to MGM specifically for this project. On June 30, 1936, Garland and Durbin prerecorded their songs for the short. The surviving *Daily Music Report* documents that Garland and Durbin recorded at least seven takes of their duet "Opera vs. Jazz," two of which were "printed" (kept for use by the sound engineers to mix into the film), and Garland recorded at least six takes of her solo "Americana," with four of those being printed. Filming began soon after and was finished in a few short weeks.

Durbin left MGM for the last time and found instant stardom at Universal Studios in *Three Smart Girls*. That film's producer, Joe Pasternak, later stated that he wanted Garland for the role. The subsequent legend, as repeated over the decades but without any documentation, is that he (or Universal) was denied by MGM, so the script was changed to accommodate Durbin's talents. There are no records of Universal making a request for Garland's services to MGM, nor are there any records of the script for the film being rewritten due to a Garland/Durbin swap. Pasternak was a Garland fan and might have "wanted" Garland for the role, but he was in no position to make that kind of request of Universal, and, frankly, the then-minor studio didn't have the budget to pay for the loaning of an MGM contract player for a low-budget film, which is what *Three Smart Girls* was.

MGM releasing Durbin and keeping Garland has resulted in more legends and assumptions. The version put forth by Hollywood columnist Hedda Hopper in her book *The Whole Truth and Nothing But*, published in 1963, states that Mayer planned to let Garland go, but, "by a fluke," the studio let Durbin's contract lapse. Mayer was in Europe and "went berserk" about the alleged mix-up when he returned, saying, "I'll take this fat one, Garland, and make her a bigger star than Durbin."[17] Neither Garland nor Durbin appear "fat" in the film. There are a couple of scenes in which Garland looks heavier than in the rest of the film, a foreshadowing of her propensity to lose and gain weight quickly during production and have it show on screen, but for the bulk of the film, she's slender.

The basis of these stories is the popular image of Garland as the unattractive one that glamorous MGM was stuck with after the prettier Durbin was mistakenly let go. This perspective made the story of Garland's success at the studio more dramatic. Durbin was a teenage version of the studio's resident soprano (and number-one singing star) Jeanette MacDonald, which no doubt worked in her favor. Traditional singers like Durbin and MacDonald were seen as more legitimate and classier than the current "swing" singers, such as scrappy vaudevillians like Garland. However, when watching *Every Sunday*, Garland is the one who comes across best. Durbin sings beautifully, but she's stiffer and less dynamic than Garland, who is more natural, and when Garland sings, she steals the film. Although Mayer was known to have loved the "classy" opera singers, he also loved singers of all styles, male or female. He adored and respected Garland's talents, as he would prove years later. Durbin had a lovely voice; Garland had a one-in-a-million voice. The "drop the fat one" story is apocryphal.

Trade advertisement for *Every Sunday* from the *Motion Picture Herald*, December 19, 1936. From the author's collection.

Another version states that the studio decided there wasn't room for two teen singers on the lot, and one had to go. Garland's voice was the tiebreaker. This story is at least partly true. While Garland's voice was not any kind of a tiebreaker, MGM let Durbin go because, according to the studio's casting director, Bill Grady, the studio didn't have any films with parts for a fourteen-year-old opera singer. Durbin came back to MGM to make the short, solely to fulfill that contractual obligation. The studio had a clause in her contract that they could call on her services up to sixty days after the termination date of her contract, which wasn't unusual. That obligation was *Every Sunday*, which neatly fell into that time frame. As with so many of the Garland legends, the tiebreaker stories are more dramatic. In this case, they're moot because Durbin was no longer under contract except for that clause. It appears the true explanation of the story is the simplest one: there just wasn't room for Durbin at MGM.

At the same time the studio let Durbin go, they also released other young performers for whom they had trouble finding suitable parts, including Joan Leslie, Dennis Morgan, and Peggy Ryan.[18] Leslie and Morgan went on to stardom at Warner Bros. Ryan, just twelve at the time and similar to Garland as a singing tween but nowhere near Garland's league, ended up at Universal in a series of teen musicals with Donald O'Connor and Gloria Jean, which were pale imitations of the hugely successful MGM teen musicals starring Mickey Rooney and Judy Garland.

It could very well be true that Mayer was angry about losing Durbin, but that would have been after her success at Universal. At the time of her release by MGM, Durbin was not a sure thing for movie stardom any more than Garland was, regardless of her voice. However, MGM obviously realized that great things lay ahead for Garland. Why else would they go to the expense of sending her to New York if they didn't have any plans for her? It was just a matter of time. *Every Sunday*, released on November 28, 1936, was more popular with exhibitors than most shorts due to the talents of both girls and was in circulation or at least available to theatre owners for over a solid ten years. When Garland appeared in person at the Stanley Theatre in Pittsburgh, Pennsylvania, in 1938, the rival Alvin Theatre obtained a print of *Every Sunday* and gave it top billing in newspaper ads.[19] It's interesting to note that local theatre ads initially gave Durbin top billing (or solo billing) due to her early success. Then Garland received top billing when the short was shown in the mid-1940s, as her success began to eclipse Durbin's. Although the short was Garland's first film assignment with MGM, it wasn't her first film to be released to the public since joining the studio (excepting the brief appearance in the 1935 short *La Fiesta de Santa Barbara*, filmed before her September 1935 audition but released two months later). That honor went to *Pigskin Parade*, which was Garland's feature film debut, but it wasn't an MGM production; it was made at 20th Century Fox and released more than a month before *Every Sunday*.

MGM loaned Garland to Fox for *Pigskin Parade* in early August 1936, the only time they loaned her out to another studio. She spent five weeks in August and September reporting to the Fox lot to prerecord her songs and film her scenes. The film's plot features some screwball comedy situations mixed in with lots of music. It's a simple narrative about the mistake of a small-town Texas college football team being invited to play against the Yale team. Stuart Erwin plays a local farm boy with natural throwing gifts, and the Texas team's coach, future Tin Man Jack

48   CHAPTER 2

Pressbook for *Every Sunday* (1936). From the author's collection.

SIX 8 x 10 BLACK AND WHITE STILLS

Order from M-G-M Exchange for

**NEWSPAPERS
WINDOW AND
LOBBY DISPLAY**

Pressbook for *Every Sunday* (1936). From the author's collection.

Pressbook for *Every Sunday* (1936). From the author's collection.

Haley, thinking Erwin can lead the team to victory against Yale, entices him to join the team. It's a typical mid-1930s musical comedy, with lots of songs and young talent, and thoroughly enjoyable.

Pigskin Parade was one of Fox's major productions featuring quite a few well-known personalities, including a pre-stardom Betty Grable, Johnny Downs, Patsy Kelly, Tony Martin, Arline Judge, Dixie Dunbar, Elisha Cook Jr., and even an unknown Alan Ladd as a student. For MGM, loaning Garland to Fox for *Pigskin Parade* cost them nothing to see how she would fare in her first feature film role. She wowed audiences and critics alike, taking full advantage of Fox's generosity in giving her two solos ("The Texas Tornado" and "It's Love I'm After") and the bulk of the production number "The Balboa." Garland prerecorded an additional song for the film, "Hold That Bulldog," which was deleted. Neither the footage nor the prerecording exists today. The only existing recording of Garland singing the song is from her appearance on the *Jack Oakie's College* radio show on January 5, 1937, which is most likely the way it was performed on the lost Fox prerecording. It's a novelty number typical of the era, in which "Judy Barks!"—part of the song features her and the chorus barking "Woof! Woof!—Woof! Woof!" That could be part of the reason it was cut.

Garland doesn't appear in *Pigskin Parade* until forty-two minutes into the film. The film then teases the audience with a running joke in which her character, Sairy Dodd, keeps boasting, "I can sing! Y'all wanna hear me?" only to get shot down each time. About twenty minutes later, she finally gets to sing when she takes the stage during "The Balboa." The impact on unsuspecting filmgoers was electrifying. Since Garland's MGM short *Every Sunday* was released after *Pigskin Parade*, this was the first exposure most film audiences had to Garland and her talents. Her solos are powerhouse performances; it's easy to see why people took notice. During "The Texas Tornado," her costars' expressions of genuine amazement are obvious. When Garland performed "It's Love I'm After," there were shouts of "Bravo!" from the cast and crew. Haley went over to her, hugged her, and said, "You're terrific! *Now* I remember you." He remembered the first time her saw her perform when she appeared at Frank Fay's show at the Trocadero in November 1935.[20] Grable became a lifelong Garland fan after working with her on this film. Garland's remake of *A Star Is Born* (Warner Bros., 1954) was one of Grable's favorite films and one of the last films she had privately screened for her prior to her death.[21] Fox knew what they had, too, and they exploited her talents—in a good way. The *Film Daily* noted, "Fifteen-year-old Judy Garland, given her first screen chance, delivers solidly with 'It's Love I'm After.'"[22] *Picture Play* noted, "[One of the highlights] is the singing of Judy Garland, a deep-chested youngster who is all the more remarkable if her given age of thirteen years is true."[23] Both reviews had Garland's age wrong; she was fourteen when she made the film. Columnist Colleen McPherson singled out Garland as "a crooning girl-wonder" and was impressed by the realistic-looking snowstorm (during which Garland amusingly belted "It's Love I'm After" while being pelted with snow).[24] T. H. C. of the *Kosuth County Advance* commented on Garland's "triumphal debut" and then oddly noted, "There is something vaguely suggestive about Dixie Dunbar in Miss Garland's characteristics, and in

52   CHAPTER 2

spite of her rather large mouth she bids fair to go far."[25]

Although she was getting raves and public recognition for her role, Garland herself wasn't thrilled with her performance or her physical appearance in *Pigskin Parade*. She would later half-joke that she assumed she'd look like a glamorous movie queen when she saw herself on screen, but, instead, she thought that she looked like a "fat little frightening pig with pigtails."[26] She was only fourteen years old but already insecure and hypersensitive about her physical appearance.

In 1937, Garland's workload began to increase significantly. She started off the year with the first of what became weekly appearances on the CBS Radio show *Jack Oakie's College*. Garland's radio show appearances were incredibly important to furthering her career. There was no television at the time. Every home had a radio, and it was almost always on, with listeners tuning in to their local stations to hear their favorite shows, as they later would with television. Having Garland as a regular on a weekly show gave her a familiarity with audiences so that when they saw that a film at their local movie house featured Garland, they knew who she was and would, presumably, buy a ticket. She no doubt garnered many fans due to her radio appearances. As they did with all of their stars' radio appearances, MGM ensured that in her appearances, mention was made of the studio's latest film. Garland continued to be a popular guest on radio shows throughout her career at MGM.

Many recordings from the *Oakie* show have survived, and they document a unique part of Garland's career. She was fourteen years old (her last appearance on the show was just after she turned fifteen), which makes them even more amazing than they already are. Garland had the chance to flex her vocal talents and sing all types of songs, from swing to ballads to comedy numbers. She also got to engage in some skits and scripted banter, which showed off her natural flair for comedy. But it's her songs that are the real gems, including "They Can't Take That Away from Me," "Always," "Smiles," "You Couldn't Be Cuter," "Pennies from Heaven," and the first known nationwide radio performance of the new Rodgers and Hart song "Johnny One Note" from their recent Broadway hit show *Babes in Arms*. The song wasn't included when MGM loosely adapted the show into the first Garland/Rooney musical, *Babes in Arms*, in 1939, although Garland later got the chance to perform it in 1948's *Words and Music*. Comparing the young Garland with the adult Garland on the same song, twelve years apart, is a rare treat. The two versions aren't very different aside from the fact that the earlier version includes some extra music and lyrics ("original interpolation," as noted in the official show transcripts[27]) provided by Edens and meant to show off Garland's vocal versatility. The young Garland naturally sounds younger, but her command of the song is there, as it was again in 1948. She sang it seemingly without effort in both instances. Another notable Garland performance on the *Oakie* show happened on February 23, 1937, when she premiered her first "identifier song": "(Dear Mr. Gable) You Made Me Love You."

An interesting sequence of events led to the creation of "(Dear Mr. Gable) You Made Me Love You." Edens and actress Carmel Myers had previously created some special material for Myers to perform on Rudy Vallee's radio show centered around the Harold Arlen song "Let's

Fall in Love." Myers had the idea to recite a nearly three-minute monologue (which Edens set to music) about a chambermaid at the Biltmore Hotel in Los Angeles and her adoration of Clark Gable. To cheer herself up after an argument with her boyfriend, she takes a bus to the gate of MGM in an attempt to meet her idol. She falls asleep at the gate and dreams of spending part of the day with Gable, only to wake up and find out she missed seeing him for real. A couple of years later, Edens was tasked with coming up with something for Garland to perform for Ben Bernie on the February 2, 1937, edition of his popular NBC Radio show, *Ben Bernie and All the Lads*. Garland wanted to sing the Ethel Merman torch song "Drums in My Heart." Edens had to convince her that the song was too adult for a fourteen-year-old to sing. They both knew that vocally, Garland could handle the song without any problems, but it would be uncomfortably indecent for a young girl to sing such a torrid torch song to the forty-six-year-old Bernie. Edens asked Myers whether she would allow him to adapt their idea into a more tongue-in-cheek young fan's adoration of Bernie. Myers admired Garland and gave Edens her blessing. Edens rewrote the material and coupled it with the 1913 song "You Made Me Love You," popularized by Al Jolson.[28]

Concurrently, Ida Koverman asked Edens to provide some entertainment for Gable's upcoming birthday party, while, at the same time, the newspapers were reporting about a woman being arrested for attempting to extort money from Gable. She claimed that Gable, going by the name "Frank Morris," had fathered her illegitimate child while visiting England in 1922. None of it was true; Gable had never been to England. The press printed the contents of the letter she sent to Gable via MGM, which began "Dear Frank." Edens rewrote the Bernie routine as "Dear Mr. Gable," poking gentle fun at the incident, made more amusing by the fact that Garland was just a year older than the fictional Gable daughter.

On February 1, 1937, Garland premiered the number at Gable's birthday party on the set of his latest film, *Parnell*. Edens brought Garland out, sitting on the top of an upright piano. Although the routine was partly satirical, Garland's soulful performance amazed and charmed everyone in attendance, including Louis B. Mayer. As with most Garland milestones, this one also had different versions of the event told over the years. One version claims that Garland popped out of a big cake. This story could be derived from Gable's teasing Garland in later years, telling her he was always afraid that at birthday parties, if a big cake were wheeled out, she would pop out and sing the song. Other versions claim that MGM decided to put Garland and the song into *Broadway Melody of 1938* because of this party. In reality, the earliest mention of Garland attached to the film was in a short news blurb published on October 30, 1935, when it was titled *Broadway Melody of 1937* (to be released in 1936). The routine, with the recitative dialog rewritten by Edens into a more audience-friendly little girl's fan letter to Gable, was added for Garland to perform in *Broadway Melody of 1938* after the success at the Gable birthday party—that is certain. Garland's performance at Gable's party was so impressive that she was taken that same evening to the Trocadero to give her first public performance of the song. However, when she appeared on the

54   CHAPTER 2

Performing "Everybody Sing" in *Broadway Melody of 1938* (1937) with Delos Jewkes, Sophie Tucker, and Barnett Parker. From the author's collection.

Bernie show the following evening, she sang "Oh, Say, Can You Swing?" but, strangely, not "Dear Mr. Gable."

Garland began work on *Broadway Melody of 1938* on March 5, 1937, prerecording her other big number in the film, "Everybody Sing," with Sophie Tucker, Barnett Parker, J. D. Jewkes, and the MGM Studio Chorus. It was her first recording session for an MGM feature film. She later prerecorded "Dear Mr. Gable" on May 7, 1937. Tucker was an early supporter of Garland and labeled her the "Next Red Hot Mama" (Tucker had been billed as the "Red Hot Mama" for years in vaudeville for her similar song-belting style). There are quite a few promotional photos of Tucker and Garland. Tucker hosted Garland and fellow MGM child star Freddie Bartholomew at her home with an MGM photographer present to snap photos of the kids enjoying Tucker's pool, all to promote her motherly approval of the young stars and as a kind of passing the baton to Garland as a "belter." Almost two decades later, in 1954, Tucker attended the premiere of Garland's screen comeback, *A Star Is Born*, and its post-premiere party.

It was around this time that MGM's Special Services Department assigned an assistant to Garland, Mary Schroeder. When Garland arrived at MGM each morning, Schroeder would give her the rundown of whatever work she had for the day, which included anything from interviews to acting lessons to photo sessions, presumably keeping Garland on track with the ever-increasing obligations on her time.[29]

By June 1937, Garland's weekly appearances on the *Oakie* radio show ended. She wasn't a regular on another major radio series until the end of the year. However, she still made random appearances on a variety of radio shows and was featured in a limited series of fifteen-minute shows titled *Frank Morgan Varieties*. The Morgan shows, sponsored by the Dodge car company and hosted by MGM star (and future "Wizard of Oz") Frank Morgan, premiered on May 30, 1937, with promotional notices touting Garland, "the 15-year-old prodigy who sang her way to sensational success," as one of the show's rotating guests. A sign of MGM's new focus on promoting Garland is reflected in the number of times she was noted as one of Morgan's main guests in newspaper listings for the shows that aired on June 6, 14, 21, and 28; July 5, 12, 19, and 26; and August 2 and 9. She's not listed in the final three episodes of the series on August 16, 23, and 30. No recordings of any of the shows are known to exist, so it's unknown what Garland sang or even whether the shows were live at all. It's possible that due to their short running time, they featured MGM prerecorded content, such as the studio's "air trailers" (titled "Leo Is on the Air"), which were on disc and therefore easy to broadcast as fifteen-minute filler, or, in Garland's case, possibly some prerecordings from *Broadway Melody of 1938*.

At this time, Garland was already battling with MGM regarding her weight issues. She gained weight easily, and, on her tiny frame (as an adult she was 4 feet, 11 inches), just a few extra pounds made a big difference on screen. It's unclear when MGM's doctors first prescribed pills to Garland to control her weight, but it was most likely not long after she signed that first contract in 1935. Prior to the MGM contract, during the vaudeville years, Ethel had given Garland and her sisters pills for energy, allegedly stating to dancer Ann Miller's mother, "I've got to keep these girls going!" When they couldn't sleep, Ethel gave them sleeping pills.[30] It's possible the pills Ethel gave her daughters were caffeine pills, which were easily obtained at the time. She might have switched to Benzedrine when it was first marketed in 1933. Benzedrine was seen as a new "miracle drug." Most people either didn't realize how addictive these pills could be or chose to ignore it. Such drugs were prescribed by doctors, which added a layer of legitimacy and a false sense of safety in using them. It seems shocking in the twenty-first century that anyone would so freely give barbiturates (or even caffeine pills) to a child or teenager, but show business in the mid-1930s was a different world. Child stars were more popular than ever, thanks to Shirley Temple's giant movie success. Parents across the nation would and did do just about anything to make their children stars. Magic pills that could keep those kids going were welcomed; plus they had the added bonus of killing one's appetite, which kept the fat off.

To help keep Garland's weight down, the MGM commissary allegedly was given the instruction to serve her chicken broth (or chicken soup or chicken noodle soup) no matter what she ordered. Garland told the story of how, during her first six months at the studio, she was given only chicken soup "but not a noodle in it because I had *baby* fat."[31] That legend, retold in most Garland biographies, originated with Garland herself when columnists interviewed her in the late 1930s and early 1940s. For example, in his column published in early February 1942, John Truesdell gave a synopsis of Garland's life story up to that point. He noted, "Once she got too heavy and the studio waitresses were ordered to serve her clear soup regardless of what she ordered for lunch."[32] Two years later, in 1944, columnist Inga Arvad told the same story, but this time Garland was given chicken soup rather than clear soup, and she quoted Garland, "'Look, she is fat,' a producer said in apparent disgust, and for years whatever I ordered for lunch at the commissary was never served to me. They brought me a bowl of chicken soup and nothing else."[33] In 1957, Garland said, "For months the waitresses at the MGM commissary had orders to bring me consommé, no matter what I ordered or how hungry I thought I was. I'd be hungry after working

56   CHAPTER 2

all morning, and consommé wasn't my idea of a filling lunch."[34] Whether it was true is unknown. It was probably an isolated incident that Garland, known as a creative raconteur, embellished for effect. Garland's claim that she was brought soup "for years" sounds like exaggeration rather than fact. Whatever happened, and whether it was an isolated event or a series of events, it had a big enough impact on Garland for her to stick with variations of the story for the rest of her life.

Garland was under enormous pressure to succeed at MGM. Regardless of her incredible voice and, as yet, largely untapped other talents, she still had to prove herself. She had the singing down pat, but her image was another issue, and she knew it. MGM wasn't the most ideal place for a young girl with body-image insecurities. They didn't seem to be very sensitive to the feelings of their stars and stock players in this regard. In fact, they could be quite brutal at times. MGM was the most glamorous of all the movie studios, and Garland was not glamorous, nor was she a character actor, for whom it didn't matter that they didn't conform to MGM's beauty standards. Garland wasn't a budding young Joan Crawford or Jean Harlow; she wasn't a cutesy child like Temple, either. MGM didn't want its glamorous stars (or, in Garland's case, stars in grooming) to be fat. Garland was more on the chubby side than fat at the time, but at MGM any extra poundage on screen was seen as just plain fat. Although true addiction didn't come until later, Garland developed a habit of using the pills as a hunger suppressant, a source of energy, and an emotional crutch that gave her false confidence that masked her insecurities. Part of the reason that Garland became addicted to her "medication" (as the pills would later be called) more than others who also took them on a similarly regular basis was two-fold: she had a genetic predisposition for addiction, and the chemicals were introduced to her during early puberty. Practically everyone in Hollywood took the pills from time to time, but in Garland's case, as her body grew into womanhood, she grew with a greater physical need for the chemicals than normal. But for now she was young, strong, and eager to please. If the pills gave her some false confidence and helped her to better conform to MGM's idea of female beauty, no one was the wiser. And no one could know that a decade later, it would all come crashing down. In 1937, Garland might have been a casual user of the pills, but images of Garland as "always drugged up" or evil studio staff forcing pills down her throat throughout her career at MGM are false and offensive to Garland and her talents.

Broadway Melody of 1938 was previewed on August 13, 1937, at the Village Theatre in the Westwood area of Los Angeles, near the MGM studios in Culver City. Decca Records president Jack Kapp was once more in Los Angeles from New York and attended the preview. He was again taken with Garland, and the result was that first six-month contract. Garland's first recordings under the new contract were "Everybody Sing" and "All God's Chillun Got Rhythm," recorded on August 30 and released the following month. A few days prior, on August 24, Garland was sent on a quick trip to the Bay Area in northern California for a personal appearance at a matinee of *Broadway Melody of 1938* at the Fox Theatre. On August 26, she was back at the recording studio at MGM, prerecording "Swing, Mr. Mendelssohn" for the upcoming production

MGM'S NEWEST CONTRACT PLAYER   57 of *Everybody Sing* (1938) while also working on her next film, *Thoroughbreds Don't Cry* (1937).

Filming on *Thoroughbreds Don't Cry* went along at a fast pace. It was released just a few months later, in November 1937. The film is a minor "B" comedy that didn't tax the cast's talents, least of all Garland's. Her role wasn't in the original script but was added after her success in *Broadway Melody of 1938* in an attempt to capitalize on her new popularity. Only one of her songs made the final cut: "Got a Pair of New Shoes." Her ballad "Sun Showers" was deleted, but the prerecording survives. It's possible it was deleted because Garland sounds very mature, and her emoting, while perfectly executed, is out of sync with the lightness of the rest of the film. Tucker costars again, but this time she doesn't get any songs, a situation that contributed to her discontent with her career at MGM and her decision to leave the studio. Ronald Sinclair played the role intended for child star Freddie Bartholomew, who couldn't make the film because, as Garland later joked, his voice was changing. *Thoroughbreds Don't Cry* is most notable today as Garland's first on-screen pairing with Mickey Rooney.

While working concurrently on *Thoroughbreds Don't Cry* and *Everybody Sing*, Garland continued to appear regularly on radio shows, including becoming a regular on the NBC Radio show *Good News of 1938*, again sponsored by MGM. She also continued to show up at industry events, such as Eddie Cantor's party at the Ambassador Hotel on October 28, 1937. She recorded "(Dear Mr. Gable) You Made Me Love You" and "You Can't Have Everything" for Decca Records on September 24. The latter song was from the Fox musical of the same name.

Garland's career was now gaining steam. Her recent successes in film, on radio, and on records was more proof to MGM that Judy Garland could become a lucrative star for the studio. It's been written over and over that Deanna Durbin's success at Universal is what lit the fire of MGM's interest in making Garland a star, and that's possibly partly true. But there's no denying that Garland succeeded on her own merit and hard work and not just on a corporate grudge. It was Garland's unique talents and her hard work that led to her success.

MGM was now heavily promoting Garland as a "typical" American teen to the American moviegoing public. The studio's publicity department was very clever and adept at creating mostly fictional scenarios for the newspapers and fan magazines to print, such as a photo of Garland and her mom enjoying hot dogs just like anyone else or a photo of the two admiring a new refrigerator. There were stories of how Garland was studying to become a lawyer or a doctor, and one in which she planned to create a publishing house for "juveniles only, ranging up to 18 years."[35] One alleged interview had Garland exclaiming that her "greatest ambition" was to build a hospital and that she was afraid she would go bald: "It's really serious. But my hair just doesn't grow. I haven't had a haircut in eight years."[36] Another article presented "that Garland Gang" and featured a group of photos of Garland and the other juvenile contract players horsing around at the studio. Of course, "gang" in this context meant clean and wholesome fun: "Juvenile stars of the movies worry just as much about their nickels as any other kids. Judy Garland, the child singer, today submitted conclusive proof on the side of the little professionals. They run in gangs, enjoy their little

58   CHAPTER 2

Two typical American teens, Mickey Rooney and Garland, go roller skating, 1937. From the author's collection.

disagreements and swear by their childish loyalties, exactly as youngsters do in every neighborhood in America." For the record, Garland's "gang," according to the article, consisted of Delia Bogart, Leonard Barrett, Mickey Rooney, Freddie Bartholomew, Jackie Cooper, Ronald Sinclair, Deanna Durbin, and Suzanne Larson (soon to be Susanna Foster).[37] The fact that Durbin is listed in a 1938 article about Garland's gang on the MGM lot is a clear indication that it's all fiction. Durbin was firmly established at rival Universal Studios by this point and wouldn't have been hanging around MGM.

But not all of the stories were fiction. The MGM publicity department was also happy to report about real events that showed Garland attending parties, movie premieres, and outings with the younger set of child and teen stars and contract players that included Rooney, Bartholomew, Cooper, and Betty Jaynes. MGM created puppy-love romances for Garland, linking her mostly with Cooper or Bartholomew; in some stories, Cooper and Rooney competed for her affection in a kind of puppy-love triangle. According to Cooper, he and Garland did have a real, albeit brief, puppy-love romance, although how much of that was nudged by MGM (or the kids' parents; the moms of both kids were friends) is anyone's guess. These stories and many others were published in different papers on varying dates over several months at a time or in monthly fan magazines. This publicity served to keep the budding stars' names in the papers while, as always, promoting their latest films. It was all very innocent and as all-American as apple pie. The reality was much different. These kids were experiencing a world far removed from anything normal, innocent, or all-American.

From this time into the early 1940s, and despite seeing Garland as unglamorous, MGM promoted her as a teen model, having her pose in the latest teen fashions. There are many surviving MGM publicity photos of Garland posing in various teen fashions that were originally sent out to newspapers and magazines. It was all very modest compared to the treatment the glamour girls were getting, with wholesome frocks targeted toward middle-American teen girls. It wasn't long before "Judy Garland" dresses and handbags were being advertised for sale in stores around the country. By November 1939, the "Judy Garland as Dorothy" doll, complete with the gingham dress (but with the standard black shoes rather than ruby slippers), was advertised in time for the holiday season. A year later, a new doll of Garland was promoted for *Little Nellie Kelly* (1940). On November 18, 1940, the movie trade magazine *Film Daily* published the following notice: "Metro [MGM] has made a national tie-up with the Ideal Novelty Manufacturing Co, giving it the right to produce and sell a Judy Garland doll. First promotion under this co-operative arrangement is in conjunction with 'Little Nellie Kelly.'"[38] Naturally, MGM had Garland pose for publicity photos with the doll and its plethora of outfits, with studio-provided text on the back of the photo for a newspaper to print: "I'LL NEVER GROW UP. . . . At least not enough to give up my favorite doll! And Judy Garland poses with her pet doll. The young Metro-Goldwyn-Mayer star is proud of the wardrobe she has acquired for the doll. She claims it's more complete than her own." The doll was heavily promoted in articles and with movie theatre tie-in contests. Even MGM star Hedy Lamarr was photographed posing with the doll. "As beautiful as Judy Garland herself!" she's quoted as exclaiming.[39] As with most of the Garland tie-in products approved by MGM, Garland never saw a penny of profit from the sales of the dolls, but it helped MGM get Garland's name and persona to the ticket-buying public.

Garland's next film was *Everybody Sing* (1938). It was the first film specifically tailored to her talents in which she

Another day at the MGM photo studios, August 6, 1937. From the author's collection.

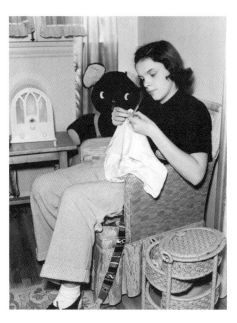

MGM promotional photo of Garland at home. From the collection of Michael Siewert.

60 CHAPTER 2

plays the main character, with crooner Allan Jones and comic legend Fanny Brice providing solid support. The three share top billing in the ads, posters, and lobby cards. Also in the cast is future Glinda, the Witch of the North, Billie Burke, playing Garland's mother, with Reginald Owen, Lynne Carver, and Reginald Gardiner supporting. The MGM star-making machine was in full swing, building up Garland as a rising star. "Judy Garland will become an overnight sensation!" touted the film's trailer, while print and poster ads proclaimed, "It's a little early to predict but here's a prophecy for 1938! Judy Garland—Stardom!" But even with this star buildup, the writers at MGM couldn't resist putting lines in the script referring to Garland's character as an "Ugly Duckling," which was the original title of the film. Thankfully, that title was changed, first to *Swing Fever* and finally to *Everybody Sing*.

Garland proved she could handle the bulk of the dramatics and comedy in the film, and she's given several chances to show off her vocal versatilities. She has a charming comedic duet with Brice ("Why? Because!") in which she's Little Lord Fauntleroy to Brice's famous stage and

Garland poses with her doll and the doll's clothes. The suggested studio text accompanying the photo reads, "I'LL NEVER GROW UP. . . . At least not enough to give up my favorite doll! And Judy Garland poses with her pet doll. The young Metro-Goldwyn-Mayer star is proud of the wardrobe she has acquired for the doll. She claims it's more complete than her own." From the author's collection.

Deseret News (Salt Lake City, UT) ran a free Judy Garland doll giveaway with subscriptions, November 23, 1940.

MGM'S NEWEST CONTRACT PLAYER 61

radio character Baby Snooks. It's the only film record of Brice as Snooks. The number was prerecorded on December 21, 1937, with Garland and Brice performing eleven takes, of which seven were printed, although some of it was recorded live on the set during filming. Twenty-six years later, on her TV series *The Judy Garland Show*, Garland performed with the woman who would go on to play Brice on Broadway and in the film *Funny Girl*, Barbra Streisand. Garland also performed in the series with Jones's son, Jack Jones, bringing the connection to *Everybody Sing* full circle.

MGM advertisement promoting Garland, 1937. From the author's collection.

A highlight of *Everybody Sing* is Garland's powerhouse rendition of "Down on Melody Farm," which practically stops the show. She engages in some amazing vocal stylings and "vocal gymnastics" that are, again, beyond the scope of more seasoned, older singers. She also sang "Swing Low, Sweet Chariot" with some special lyrics by Roger Edens. Her beautiful vocal is unfortunately marred by her appearance in blackface while dressed as a "pickaninny." In the context of the film, she's in costume to hide her identity in order to audition for the show being produced, but to twenty-first-century audiences, it's offensive. At the time the film was made, blackface and minstrel shows were still accepted styles of performing, popping up in films all over the place, usually as a device to get cheap laughs. To label Garland as racist based on this performance and to assume that she had any agency over her film image is wrong. Garland had no serious input at this point in her career as to what she would sing and how she would be costumed. She did what she was told, as she had done her whole life up to this point.

During this time, and for most of the rest of her MGM career, Garland rarely worked on a film without having other obligations that included recording sessions for Decca, personal appearances (film premieres, industry events, etc.), tours, and radio shows. Most of these extra obligations took place in the evenings after long days of filming. In late 1937, while *Everybody Sing* was still in production, Garland began new weekly appearances on *Good News of 1938* show on NBC Radio, which had previously been *New Faces of 1938*. She first appeared on the show when it changed its name on November 4, 1937, anticipating 1938. She was also tapped to perform "Silent Night" for an MGM Christmas trailer by the same name. She recorded and filmed a

Garland and Fanny Brice perform "Why? Because!" in *Everybody Sing* (1938). From the author's collection.

short chorus of the song in three days, from November 6 through November 8, in time for MGM to send it out to theatres for the 1937 Christmas season. The prerecording surfaced a few years later when Garland and Rooney were featured on the annual *Leo Is on the Air* (MGM) holiday show, broadcast live on November 28, 1940, from "Santa Claus Lane" (Hollywood Boulevard) in Los Angeles. Garland and Rooney rode in the parade on one of the floats, and MGM cleverly inserted this 1937 prerecording of "Silent Night" into the broadcast under the guise of being sung live by Garland from "Santa Claus Lane."

NEW YORK STAGE DEBUT

When *Everybody Sing* was completed, MGM sent Garland, her mother Ethel, Roger Edens, and a small entourage that included her tutor (Garland was still under California education and labor laws) via train to Miami, Florida, for the film's world premiere at the Sheridan Theatre on January 24, 1938. This was the beginning of what became Garland's first major film promotional tour. The amount of attention given to Garland and *Everybody Sing* by local MGM executives and theatre owners/managers is reflected in this blurb in *Variety* about the events surrounding the train's short stop in Houston, Texas, while en route to Miami:

> *Because the train on which Judy Garland was heading east stopped for half an hour at Houston, Lionel H. Keene, of Loew's State, got an hour for publicity work, aided by Homer McCallon, his press agent. The extra half hour is explained by the fact that McCallon took a couple of reporters 40 miles up the line to board the train and get interviews before the city was reached.*
>
> *Once in the station, the big event was a 15-minute interview over KPRO, the NBC outlet. It opened with a greeting from Mayor Fonville, the arrival of a guard of honor, composed of 25 girls from the Sam Houston high school, who held the autograph seekers at bay during the broadcast, six children dressed as she was in "Everybody Sing" gave her a box of pralines, after which she was questioned about her trip by announcer Gene Wyatt.*
>
> *The remainder of the time was given over to autographing albums and posing for motion pictures for local showing at the State. It all made a great advance stunt for "Everybody Sing," which*

was the house's underline and all it cost was a lot of hard work.[40]

The train also stopped in Mobile, Alabama, where two sisters boarded and met with Garland at the station restaurant in the train's next stop at Flomaton, Alabama. The sisters' basketball team had just lost a game, but their meeting with Garland perked them up, as reported by the local newspaper: "Judy told them of her school life in California, where she is a student in the eleventh grade, her ice skating and her fondness for eating which she displayed in stops at the Mobile, Flomaton and Pensacola station restaurants."[41] The "fondness for eating" comment is notable because it foreshadows later reports of Garland sneaking food whenever she was away from the constant hovering and watchful eye of MGM and the strict diet they imposed on her in these early years.

Garland and her entourage arrived in Miami on January 24 at 4:30 p.m. local time. Immediately on arrival, she was interviewed for WIOD Radio by Eddie Cohen of the *Miami Daily News*, which was broadcast live from the train station at 4:45 p.m. According to the *Miami Daily News*, Garland was scheduled to end the interview and leave the train station after a train carrying some of MGM's New York executives arrived, and then she would go to her room at the Roney Plaza Hotel to rest and prepare for her personal appearances at the theatre, which premiered the film at 8:00 p.m., with another screening at 10:00 p.m. The premiere was a big success. In his article for the *Miami News*, Cohen noted Garland's ability as an actress:

> *When M-G-M let Deanna Durbin slip through their fingers somebody on the lot must have been sore. We can just hear him bellowing, "Alright, find me another!" Judy Garland is the result. While Durbin is a singer who happens to be an actress, Garland is an actress who happens to be a singer, and in the long run, it is our belief, M-G-M has got something that will even spell greater "box office" than Durbin, because little Judy's appeal is to the masses. She sings our language when she "swings" out and she is thoroughly human at the same time.*[42]

Variety reported that after the premiere, "Judy Garland, her ma and Harry Rapf guests of Mr. and Mrs. Nicholas Schenck at Patio Moresque" in Miami Beach.[43] A decade later, Schenck became a villain during Garland's personal and professional struggles at MGM. While in Miami, Garland also posed for more teen fashion photos on the grounds of her hotel, looking very chic in white slacks and a light jacket. The photos were widely published in papers around the country.

The Garland entourage left Miami and headed to New Orleans, Louisiana, where, on January 28, Garland presented an autographed photo to mayor Robert Maestri and had time to sing for charity at a local hospital. While Team Garland was on its way back to Hollywood, MGM decided that since the recent premiere and personal appearances had been so successful, they would extend the trip and have Garland make her New York stage debut at Loew's State Theatre, followed by an extended tour. Team Garland immediately turned around and headed to New York. This meant a scheduled and publicized stop in El Paso, Texas, on January 30 did not happen. There was a quick stop in Jacksonville, Florida, on February 4, where Garland and her

Garland and her mom, Ethel, arrive in Miami, Florida, for the world premiere of *Everybody Sing*, January 24, 1938. From the author's collection.

Garland poses in some teen fashions while in Miami, Florida, January 1938. From the author's collection.

mom were photographed having breakfast in the back of the Florida Theatre with theatre owner Guy Kenimer and more local MGM executives before they traveled up the East Coast, arriving in New York on February 7. The last-minute change by MGM and their booking of Garland at Loew's State Theatre in Times Square was monumental. As it is today, New York in 1938 was the pinnacle of show business. Garland had already gotten the big Hollywood prize of a contract at the biggest and best studio; now her name would be blazoned over Times Square in larger-than-life lights: "In Person Judy Garland." MGM would not have given her this honor if they hadn't already known (or at least suspected) that in Garland, they had the total package. She was as natural on stage as she was in film, and she already possessed a stage presence that drew people in both musically and emotionally. MGM saw the dollar signs. According to the trade magazines, she increased the house box office wherever she appeared.

Garland opened at Loew's State on February 10, with the Albertina Rasch dancers, the Four Franks, and rising comedy duo Abbott and Costello on the same bill, in the vaudeville format still popular at the time. Her appearance at the State grossed $10,000 more for the theatre than their average weekly gross at the time. On February 16, 1938, *Variety* reported Garland's week at the State Theatre grossed $30,000, which was "very katish":

Youngster is a resounding wallop in her first vaudeville appearance. Comes to the house with a rep in films and after a single date on the Chase and Sanborn radio show. Apparent at the outset that the girl is no mere flash, but has both the personality and the skill to develop into a box-office wow in any line of show business.

Offered three numbers at last show Thursday (10), and then bowed out. Applause was solid and insistent, however, she encored twice, finally begging off with an ingratiating and shrewd thank-you speech. Her 20-minute stint didn't seem that long, and she could have stayed indefinitely.

Kid is ballyed as 14 years old, which seems about right according to her appearance, mannerisms, dress, etc. She's big for her age, however. Voice is pleasant in its quieter tones. At such times it has exact pitch, with expressive warmth and not a little richness. She has a tendency to turn on the steam, however, and then her voice becomes nasal, strident and loses its expressive shadings. She knows how to put over the appealing parts of a song, builds a number well and has definite rhythmic sense, but she must learn the discipline of modulation. Enunciates clearly.[44]

Take a Peak at Summer Chic --In Tropic Preview

Snow Dodging Film Star Displays Lively Play Togs, from Tyrolean Motifs to Gay Fun-Spot Prints

Typical MGM promotion of Garland in the latest teen fashions, February 28, 1938. From the author's collection.

In addition to her show at Loew's State, Garland made many personal appearances in the city, including wowing the crowds at the Casa Manana nightclub on February 13, which prompted a mention in columnist Walter Winchell's world-famous column along with a photo of Garland (in some markets): "The most deafening applause ever heard by these ears greeted Judy Garland at Casa Manana Sunday Night."[45] On February 14, the WEW radio station held a Judy Garland look-alike contest and "audition," with the winner receiving cash and the other contestants receiving guest tickets to see Garland at Loew's. The Famous-Barr Co. department store, "which handles Judy Garland clothes," created elaborate window displays promoting Garland and the show at Loew's.[46] MGM's local promotional team did their job well.

After the success in New York, the *Everybody Sing* tour moved on to engagements in Providence, Rhode Island (February 18 through 24), and Pittsburgh, Pennsylvania (February 25 through March 3), where Garland was given membership in the local "Sekatary Hawkins Club."

The Pittsburgh crowds were so big, the local papers reported, that traffic was stopped for half an hour, and the crowd was four abreast, with "thousands pushed and strained."[47] *Variety*'s review of the Pittsburgh show noted, "Anything trying to follow Miss Garland is immediately behind the eight ball" (the show featured other acts) and "Youngster delivering as few others have around here in several seasons," singling out the song "Bei Mir Bist Du Schoen" as "very slick."[48] On March 2, the crowds were still large enough that, in spite of it being Ash Wednesday, Garland ended up giving six shows that day. The *Pittsburgh Post-Gazette* said of Garland, "For encountering the young lady in person at the Stanley, you realize at last what a distinguished song stylist she really is, a remarkable artist every inch of the way."[49]

It was during this time that the news broke that Garland had been cast as Dorothy in *The Wizard of Oz*. It was also reported that Garland was cast in a screen version of *Topsy and Eva*. That project never happened. MGM's publicity department most likely cooked up the story.

Garland's next stop was Columbus, Ohio (March 4 through 10). The Columbus appearance is notable because it resulted in Garland's first time being featured in *Life* magazine. She was honored as the "Sweetheart of Sigma Chi" by the Alpha Gamma Chapter of the Sigma Chi Fraternity at Ohio State University. The event was photographed and presented in the magazine's March 28, 1938, issue as that month's entry in their "Life Goes to a Party" series. *Variety* noted about the Columbus shows that Garland "does four songs with piano accompaniment only, in front of curtain. . . . Opens with 'Shine on Your Shoes.' Follows with 'You Made Me Love You.' Then novel arrangement of 'Bei Mir Bist Du Schoen,' which puts over well-worn tune like a new one. Encores with 'Melody Farm' and gets off with curtain speech."[50]

During her *Everybody Sing* tour, Garland posed with newspapers from various cities as part of the promotional campaign for the film. This one shows Garland reading the *Boston Globe*, as published in that paper on February 18, 1938. From the author's collection.

The tour was finally beginning to wind down and headed west for a weeklong run at the Chicago Theatre in Chicago, Illinois, from March 11 through 17. Garland and Ethel stayed at the Palmer House, and Ethel wrote to a friend that Garland's fan mail had increased to over one hundred letters a day, necessitating the hiring of a young woman to come in a few times a week to help with the workload. Garland composed a letter on Palmer House stationery to fellow vaudeville performer Perry Frank of the sibling act the Four Franks. Frank was one of Garland's major early crushes. He and his siblings performed on the bill with her in New York, which is where the romance started. Her gushing love letter has survived and includes declarations such as the following:

My darling Perry—I love you. There! . . . When I was in the Phi theater, I went in onto the stage and sat in our old place. It was an awful feeling, sitting there all alone without you dripping (but good) in front of me. If I don't see you before you go to England, I'll die. But please darling, always remember this. When you come back, no matter how many years from now, if you still want me, I'll be yours for the asking. And if we were older, and you asked me to be yours forever, I'd say yes in a minute. That's how much I love you, and always will love you. My only hope is that you love me half as much as I love you. That's a pretty big order. I can't understand why you haven't received more letters from me. I've written every day, sometimes twice a day. What's with the mail?[51]

The romance with Frank continued, at least in the columns, into early 1940. Later, in the summer of 1938, he was in Los Angeles and photographed with Garland on July 8, 1938, at the Cafe Trocadero after the two attended the premiere of MGM's *Marie Antoinette*, even though Garland was officially Freddie Bartholomew's date, and the two are seen in newsreel footage signing the premiere guest book on arrival.

The next stop on the tour was Detroit, Michigan (March 18–24), where Garland was made a Campfire Girl and sneaked out from her scheduled shows to attend a wrestling match at the Detroit Arena Gardens. It was reported that half the crowd recognized her, while the other half thought she was the wife of English wrestler Bob Gregory, "Princess Valerie," who stayed out of the arena: "It was the first time [Garland] had ever been two celebrities in one night."[52] The sneaking-out incident could have been an early teenager attempt at rebellion by Garland against the enormous pressure and tight schedule she was enduring. The tour ended in Detroit on March 24, and everyone traveled back to Chicago, where Garland appeared at the Oriental Theatre (the site of the Gumm-to-Garland name change in 1934) for two nights (March 26 and 27), and then, according to *Variety*, she was quickly flown back to Los Angeles to take part in an MGM air show event. "Air show" in *Variety* meant a radio show, not an air show featuring airplanes. The trip to LA was a quick one because, by March 29, she was back in Chicago. *Variety* noted of Garland's two nights at the Oriental in Chicago, "Kid singer added considerable gross over weekend and on that start house should get $20,000 or better."[53]

The reason Garland was flown back to Chicago was to make a previously planned trip to her birthplace of Grand Rapids, Minnesota. It was Garland's first and last time returning to the town after her family had relocated to California in 1926. The entourage took the train to Minneapolis, Minnesota, arriving late on the night of March 30, where Garland met with fans at her hotel before traveling to Grand Rapids on March 31, where they spent two days visiting the old Gumm home and the high school Garland would have attended. She was given a luncheon at the Pokegama Hotel and performed at the Rialto Theatre, which was next door to the closed Grand

Theatre, where Garland had her stage debut. They returned to Chicago on April 2 to catch the Super Chief train back to Los Angeles. The train took thirty-eight hours and forty-five minutes, which included fourteen stops, to return. On April 3, the train stopped in Albuquerque, New Mexico, where Garland had time to be interviewed by the local paper and photographed waving from a train window. The subsequent article published the following day quoted Garland's happiness to be off the train for a bit: "It's too grand to be cooped up in there." The paper interestingly noted Garland's beauty: "Red hair and freckles do not detract from Judy's beauty, and her off-screen personality is as pleasing as it is on the camera." Garland met with fans and asked a reporter to mail a letter for her (she bought the stamp) addressed to "a gentleman in Washington, D.C., Romance in the offing?"[54] It was probably a letter to Perry Frank.

BACK TO MGM AND ON TO CARVEL

Garland returned to MGM triumphant, thanks to the success of the *Everybody Sing* tour. She immediately went back to her weekly (more or less) appearances on the *Good News of 1938* radio show while also beginning production on her next film, *Love Finds Andy Hardy*. It was the fourth installment in a new series of increasingly popular films centered around the Hardy family of the fictional all-American small town of Carvel, Idaho. The series began with 1937's *A Family Affair*, which was based on the Broadway show *Skidding* by Aurania Rouverol. *A Family Affair* was a kind of sequel to MGM's 1936 film adaptation of Eugene O'Neill's Broadway hit *Ah! Wilderness*, which was also about an all-American small-town family. It featured most of the same cast as *Ah! Wilderness*, but when it was decided to turn *A Family Affair* into a series, Lewis Stone replaced Lionel Barrymore as Judge Hardy, Fay Holden replaced Spring Byington as Mrs. Hardy, and Ann Rutherford replaced Margaret Marquis as Andy Hardy's girlfriend, Polly Benedict. Mickey Rooney was Andy Hardy from the beginning and the breakout star of the series, which put the focus on Andy's trials and tribulations with his on-again, off-again girlfriend, Polly; his wooing of or being wooed by a variety of girls; and his "man-to-man" talks with his father, the wise Judge Hardy. Andy always learned a valuable life lesson or two in each film. MGM boss Louis B. Mayer loved the series not just because the films were cheap to make and brought in tons of profits but also because they epitomized his idealized version of what he thought small-town America should be.

Love Finds Andy Hardy is the best and quintessential Hardy film. Garland appears as Betsy Booth, the visiting (from New York City) singing granddaughter of one of the Hardy family's neighbors. It was the first of three appearances Garland made in the series as Betsy Booth. It was also Garland's first time filming on MGM's new permanent "New England Street" on Lot 2 (the first film shot on the street was *Ah! Wilderness* in 1935), which provided the street where the Hardy and Booth families lived. It became one of the most famous spots on the backlot and was informally known as "Andy Hardy Street." In *That's Entertainment!* (1974), Rooney comments about basically growing up on the street and indicates that Polly Benedict's home was across the street from the Hardy home when, in fact, it was located on the nearby "Small Town Square" on the same backlot. Between the Hardy films and their "Let's Put on a Show!" musicals, Garland and Rooney spent countless long days and nights filming on the fabled street.

Another young starlet, Lana Turner, made her MGM debut in *Love Finds Andy Hardy* (not counting an uncredited bit as an extra in 1937's *Topper*), and although she was just one year older than Garland, she might as well have been ten years older. There was no mistaking Turner for anything other than an MGM "Glamazon" in the making. Garland's Betsy Booth character was an adolescent, a kid, someone Andy Hardy saw as a pal but not a love interest, whereas Turner's Cynthia was an obvious object of sexual desire. Garland was fifteen when *Love Finds Andy Hardy* went into production, and, like any girl her age, she longed to be seen and portrayed as a glamorous and sexy woman. She and Turner became friends, but Garland also envied Turner's beauty and how she was treated at the studio and socially. Garland seemed to be surrounded by an endless parade of glamorous women, including Joan Crawford, Greta Garbo, and Norma Shearer. It probably didn't help much that in *Love Finds Andy Hardy*, her big solo is the song "In-Between," in which she laments that she's not a child but not yet an adult. Similar to "Dear Mr. Gable," Garland gets a recitative break in the song with lines like "I'm allowed to go to picture shows, that is if nurse is feeling able. But we only go to Mickey Mouse; I'm not allowed Clark Gable." For the time being, MGM was more than happy to keep portraying Garland as an adolescent. It would be several years before she was allowed to grow up on screen.

Garland was almost written out of *Love Finds Andy Hardy*. Early in production, on May 24, 1938, she was involved in a car accident that resulted in a sprained back, three broken ribs, and a punctured lung. Luckily, none of the injuries were life-threatening, and she recovered quickly enough to be back at MGM working on the film by June 11.

The success of the addition of Garland and Turner to the Andy Hardy series began a tradition at MGM of trying out various new contract players by putting them in the series to see how they fared, gauge audience response, and give them a bit more experience before graduating to larger roles. Included in the growing list were Donna Reed, Kathryn Grayson, Ray McDonald, and Esther Williams. Garland was the only star to make return appearances in the series, still as Betsy Booth, and in both return appearances, she's helping Andy navigate the world of her hometown, New York City.

Originally, it was planned for Garland to go directly into work on *The Wizard of Oz* after *Love Finds Andy Hardy*. On April 29, 1938, she posed for Max Factor hair and makeup tests for *Oz*, her first work on the film, and the earliest surviving photos of Garland as Dorothy. However, preproduction was taking longer than planned, so the start date was pushed out. In the interim, MGM rushed a quickie "B" movie into production, *Listen, Darling*, to get more on-screen exposure of Garland to movie audiences. Garland costarred with Freddie Bartholomew, Mary Astor, Walter Pidgeon, Scotty Beckett, and Alan Hale Sr. in a story centered around two teens, Pinkie Wingate (Garland) and Buzz Mitchell (Bartholomew), and their attempt to find a suitable husband for Pinkie's widowed mom (Astor) by kidnapping her in the family trailer and going on a husband-hunting

70   CHAPTER 2

road trip. Although it's a short seventy minutes long, the film features three songs. "On the Bumpy Road to Love" is a group number sung, not surprisingly, while they're driving. The other two are Garland solos: "Zing! Went the Strings of My Heart" (her MGM audition song) and "Ten Pins in the Sky." The two were shortened before the film's release. For "Zing!" Garland recorded two versions, one as a ballad and one with a partial jazz midsection, similar to her 1935 radio performance. The surviving prerecording of the ballad version is three minutes and thirteen seconds; in the film, it's cut to two minutes and thirty-three seconds. It's unknown why the song was trimmed. Perhaps it was thought that a full ballad coming so early in the film would slow it down too much. "Ten Pins" is one of Garland's most beautiful MGM ballads and also one of the least recognized. Her vocals are subdued and tender, similar to her vocal on "Over the Rainbow," prerecorded that same year, just a few months later.

Garland's work on *Listen, Darling* was in its last weeks when she began costume tests and prerecording sessions for *The Wizard of Oz*. Over the next year, most of her time was spent either working on *Oz* or with *Oz*-related duties, as well as completing another film, *Babes in Arms* (1939). It took MGM less than four years to make Judy Garland a star.

British sheet music for "It Never Rains, But What It Pours" from *Love Finds Andy Hardy* (1938). From the author's collection.

MGM'S NEWEST CONTRACT PLAYER

MGM studio portrait used to promote *Listen, Darling* (1938). The suggested studio text accompanying the photo reads, "Brown, Grosgrain Bows, and a back veil, are youthfully charming on this high-crowned, roll-brim brown felt hat chosen for fall by Judy Garland, appearing in Metro-Goldwyn-Mayer's 'Listen, Darling.'" From the author's collection.

CHAPTER *3*

MGM MAGIC

THE WIZARD OF OZ AND BABES IN ARMS

The making of *The Wizard of Oz* has been the subject of many books that range in quality from poor to excellent. It would be futile to try to encapsulate the now legendary production of the film here in one chapter. Instead, the following is an overview of the production followed by the quick production of *Babes in Arms*, Garland and Rooney's tour of the East Coast leading up to the New York premiere of *The Wizard of Oz*, and the rest of Garland's activities in that golden year of 1939.

In late February 1938, the news broke that MGM was producing a film version of L. Frank Baum's *The Wizard of Oz* with Mervyn LeRoy as producer and Garland as Dorothy. Producer/director Mervyn LeRoy had been lured away from Warner Bros. by MGM boss Louis B. Mayer to replace the recently deceased "Boy Wonder" chief of production Irving Thalberg. LeRoy immediately said he wanted to make a film of Baum's classic children's book. At the same time, MGM studio songwriter Arthur Freed was aspiring to become a producer. Allegedly (there is some debate), Freed also wanted to adapt the Baum book for the screen as a musical. Mayer told Freed to apprentice as an associate producer for LeRoy, telling him the project was too big and expensive for a first-time producer. This decision turned out to be a blessing for the production. Freed, along with Roger Edens, took charge of the musical aspect of the production. One thing was clear from the beginning: everyone wanted Judy Garland as Dorothy.

MGM's version of *The Wizard of Oz* might not have happened at all were it not for the blockbuster success of Walt Disney's *Snow White and the Seven Dwarfs* in late 1937. That masterpiece of animation showed Hollywood that musical fantasies, when executed correctly, could be successful both critically and financially. We have Disney to thank for putting the wheels in motion that resulted in MGM's production of *The Wizard of Oz*. Most studios were looking for fantasy properties, and Baum's classic was at the top of everyone's list. Independent producer Sam Goldwyn owned the film rights to the book. MGM purchased the rights from Goldwyn on February 18, 1938, a few weeks after Freed's early character outline, which shows how confident Freed was even though the studio didn't yet own the rights.

As early as April 29, 1938, Garland had her first work on the film, posing for some Max Factor hair and makeup tests. From this point until the first day of filming, six months later, on October 13, 1938, a myriad of activities occurred. Several screenwriters were engaged to develop a viable adaptation, which resulted in some amusing and fortunately unused ideas. For example, there were ideas for characters such as a prince and a princess of Oz, both of whom sang opera (Garland would sing jazz). Miss Gulch had a nasty nephew at one point and was "Mrs." Gulch. Casting the roles wasn't easy, either. W. C. Fields wanted to play the wizard but asked for too much money. Oscar winner Gale Sondergaard was tasked with playing a glamorous wicked witch (similar to the evil queen in *Snow White*) and posed for several costume tests. After enduring "ugly" makeup, hair, and costume tests, she left the project. Margaret Hamilton was brought in at the eleventh hour to play the redesigned, hag-looking Wicked Witch of the West. They toyed with the idea of having a real lion play the Cowardly Lion. Enough little people had to be found to play the Munchkins. Costumes had to be designed, produced, and fitted for everyone from Dorothy down to each Munchkin, each extra who played the citizens of the Emerald City, the Flying Monkeys, and the Witch's Winkie Guards. Creating an entire fantasy world from scratch took a lot of time and a lot of trial and error. This difficulty was compounded by the relatively new Technicolor process and its cumbersome cameras, which were in limited supply and available only as rentals to the studios. But if any studio was poised to undertake the task of creating a live-action musical fantasy film in Technicolor, it was MGM. The studio rightfully boasted of having the best of the best under contract in all areas of production, not just in front of the camera. For *The Wizard of Oz*, everyone provided career-defining work. The phrase "the stars were aligned" is more than appropriate here.

Then there was the music. Freed and Edens decided that Harold Arlen and E. Y. "Yip" Harburg were the right songwriting duo to handle composing the score. This choice turned out to be fortuitous. Arlen and Harburg were instrumental in creating not just the songs but also the Munchkinland musical sequence in which almost everything is rhymed and set to music, and Harburg helped with parts of the script. The brilliance of that decision cannot be overstated. Munchkinland is our first glimpse of Oz, and if the sequence didn't work, it would ruin the rest of the film. Herbert Stothart composed the underscore, leaning heavily on the Arlen melodies. His score is so perfect that it won the Oscar for Best Original Score over Max Steiner's seminal score for *Gone with the Wind*.

Once the screenplay was completed, more or less (thankfully sans the extra characters and

Garland posed for portraits for *The Wizard of Oz* (1939), February 25, 1939. From the author's collection.

plot points), and once the songs were written and (most of) the cast was in place (having endured many costume, hair, and makeup tests), it was time for the first prerecording session on September 30, 1938. According to the surviving *Daily Music Report*, Garland, Ray Bolger (the Scarecrow), Buddy Ebsen (the Tin Man), and Bert Lahr (the Cowardly Lion) prerecorded "If I Only Had a Brain," "If I Only Had a Heart," "If I Only Had the Nerve," and "Wonderful Wizard of Oz" ("We're Off to See the Wizard") (the duo, trio, and quartet versions). Garland prerecorded "Over the Rainbow" on October 7, 1938. Six takes were printed (that is, kept for audio mixing), takes 1, 2, 4, 6, 7, and 8. The version heard in the film was edited together by taking the first verse of Take 5 and joining it to the bulk of Take 6.

Filming was originally scheduled to begin on September 15, 1938, under the direction of Richard Thorpe, but it was delayed to October 13, 1938. After twelve days, the production was halted. No one liked what was being seen in the rushes. Worst of all, the original Tin Man, Buddy Ebsen, had been unknowingly poisoned by the "silver" makeup and had to be taken off the film to recuperate from his near-death experience. Thorpe was fired, not because of Ebsen but because his direction was wrong for a musical fantasy. None of the Thorpe footage has survived, so it's impossible to know how wrong he was. It must have been *very* wrong for the studio to stop and scrap everything and start anew.

Director George Cukor came to the production for a week without the intention of directing the entire film. His contributions turned out to be genius and more than helped the resulting success of the film. Cukor changed the look of all of the main characters, most famously changing Dorothy from honey blonde to brunette and using makeup for Garland that was more natural. The acting advice he gave her was also to act naturally. She was an innocent farm girl from Kansas. The assumption is that Thorpe had her acting affectedly. At the time, Garland was quoted as saying, "I learned more in the two days [Cukor] was on 'The Wizard of Oz' than I ever learned at any one time before. It isn't that the other directors aren't wonderful, but they don't know how to handle people my age. It takes a very special kind of understanding to cope with in-betweeners."[1] Cukor also pulled Margaret Hamilton's hair back into a bun to make the Witch look more severe, as well as giving her a protruding chin and nose. Even the Yellow Brick Road was changed from oval bricks to standard rectangular bricks and given a curb.

Production began again on the updated Cornfield set on November 4, 1938, with veteran MGM director Victor Fleming at the helm. For a while, filming went smoothly without any major issues, with scenes shot in the following order:

- Cornfield (November 4 to the week of November 7)
- Tin Man's Forest (week of November 7 to November 19)
- Lion's Forest (November 21 to November 26)
- Poppy Field (week of November 28)
- Witch's Castle (including the melting of the Witch) (December 1 to approximately December 14)
- Munchkinland (December 17 to December 30)

A notable event occurred on November 25, 1938, during filming on the Lion's Forest set: MGM officially promoted Garland from "featured player" to "star." She was presented with her very own dressing room trailer, and the cast and crew were assembled for the event. It was just a little over three years since her 1935 audition.

On December 28, 1938, the good fortune of the relatively smooth previous weeks of filming ended. Things went wrong in the scene in which Margaret Hamilton's Wicked Witch of the West exits Munchkinland in a blast of flames and smoke. Everything was fine until after lunch when the scene was filmed again. The trap door on the floor of the stage that contained an elevator rigging to lower Hamilton didn't work properly, and she was severely burned. The green makeup had copper in it, resulting in her being so badly burned that she was immediately rushed to the hospital and out of the film until mid-February. She suffered first-degree burns on her face and second-degree burns on her hands. Thankfully, she recovered and understandably refused to do any more special effects shots. The shot you see in the film is the single good shot they were able to get that day before lunch and the accident.

After the new year, production resumed with the cast on the Haunted Forest set and proceeded as follows.

- Haunted Forest (January 3)
- "I'd Turn Back If I Were You" scene (January 6)
- "The Jitterbug" (January 9, 11, and 13)
- The scene on the Yellow Brick Road after waking up from the poppies (January 12)
- Emerald City Sequence (January 14 through mid-February)
- "The Merry Old Land of Oz" (January 17, 19, and 20)
- Wizard's Balloon Sequence (including the tearful goodbyes) (last week of January)
- "If I Were King of the Forest" plus Wizard's hallway and Throne Room (late January through mid-February)
- Wizard's Throne Room (February 3)
- Toto's Escape from the Witch's Castle (February 7)
- Wizard's Presentations (February 12)—this was director Victor Fleming's last work on the film before leaving to rescue the troubled production of *Gone with the Wind*. They were also the last Oz sequences to be filmed. King Vidor came in to take over beginning with the Kansas sequences, which were the last sequences filmed.
- Kansas Sequences (February 19 through mid-March)
- "Over the Rainbow" (February 23, possibly also 24)
- Miss Gulch scenes, Professor Marvel scenes, Cornfield retakes (late February into mid-March)
- Retakes/pickup shots with Glinda (Billie Burke) (May 1 and/or 2)
- More retakes (according to the assistant director's report for *Babes in Arms*, Garland was "on Wizard of Oz retakes" on June 30). This was Garland's last work on *Oz*.

Once principal filming was completed, *The Wizard of Oz* went into the postproduction phase, including recording the Oscar-winning background score, creating the groundbreaking special effects, and the final editing. In mid-July 1939, the first previews of the film were held unannounced at theatres outside of the greater Los Angeles area. The elaborate production number "The Jitterbug" was removed after the first preview, and "Over the Rainbow" was removed for at least one preview. There was a debate by studio executives about the song's merits and whether it slowed down the film, plus concern that the sheet music (still a very lucrative market at the time) wouldn't sell. Mayer held a meeting during which Freed exclaimed, "The song stays—or I go! It's as simple as that."[2] The song stayed in the film, and Freed stayed at MGM.

The rest, as they say, is history. Unlike reports given decades later, *The Wizard of Oz* was a big hit. It was also recognized as an instant classic. The reviews were almost unanimous in their praise. However, *The Wizard of Oz* did not immediately turn a profit due to the high cost of the long production and the extensive publicity campaign. It was MGM's most expensive production and most expensive and biggest ad campaign to date. Added to that was the fact that a majority of the ticket sales were at children's prices. To further compound things, most of the European market closed a month after the premiere when World War II began. Because the film didn't turn a profit until the 1949 rerelease, later authors dubbed it unsuccessful, and to this day, that misconception is wrongly reported as fact. Some of that flop scenario is tied to the film becoming an annual tradition on American television in the late 1950s. That makes for more dynamic copy for articles and books that incorrectly claim the film was a flop until it was rescued by TV.

The Wizard of Oz was nominated for five Academy Awards (* winner):

- Best Picture (winner: *Gone with the Wind*)
- *Music (Song)—"Over the Rainbow," Harold Arlen and E. Y. Harburg
- *Music (Original Score)—Herbert Stothart
- Best Art Direction (winner: *Gone with the Wind*)
- Best Special Effects (winner: *The Rains Came*)—this one is especially puzzling considering what they achieved on *The Wizard of Oz*, including the realistic tornado

Garland received a special Juvenile Oscar for her performances on film in 1939 (both *The Wizard of Oz* and *Babes in Arms*). Newsreel footage shows Mickey Rooney presenting the award to Garland at the February 29, 1940, ceremony at the Cocoanut Grove in the Ambassador Hotel.

Director Victor Fleming won the Best Director Oscar for *Gone with the Wind*. If he hadn't been nominated for that film, he might have been nominated for *The Wizard of Oz*. The year 1939 was incredible for the movies, considered by most the best year for classic films, topped off by the mega-hit *Gone with the*

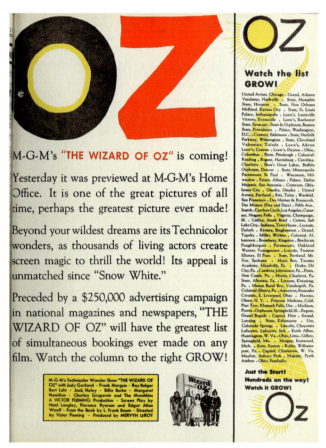

MGM trade ad as published in the *Film Daily* trade magazine on August 2, 1939. From the author's collection.

78 CHAPTER 3

Wind. There were more than enough great films to go around. However, it's a bit puzzling that *Oz* wasn't nominated in some of the other categories, such as Sound Recording, Film Editing, or Color Cinematography.

Due to its legendary status, there have been many misconceptions and urban legends surrounding *The Wizard of Oz*. They're perpetuated today in poorly researched clickbait articles on the Internet, equally poor magazine articles, and even some "legitimate" books. The following explains some of the most persistent and incorrect urban legends.

SHIRLEY TEMPLE AS DOROTHY

A common misconception about this casting is that MGM and/or the producers initially wanted Shirley Temple from 20th Century Fox to play Dorothy. That misconception is understandable. Temple was the number one box office star, and she was the right age, judging from the illustrations in the original books (Baum's book doesn't give Dorothy's age). The legend of Temple missing out on the role and Garland getting it as a second choice was accepted as fact for so long that in 1974's *That's Entertainment!*, the dialog Garland's daughter Liza Minnelli provided as part of the narration about her mother also told this story. It's not true. Everyone wanted Garland. The film's producer, Mervyn LeRoy, later reported that studio head Louis B. Mayer had no problem with Garland playing the role.[3] The role was written for Garland, as were the songs. Freed's early casting outline from January 1938 lists Dorothy as "an orphan in Kansas who sings jazz." That definitely wasn't Temple. Roger Edens went to Fox to meet Temple to test her out, musically speaking. He came back and reported that while she was charming, she wasn't up to the intended vocal demands of the role. It's also safe to assume that Fox had no intention of lending their biggest box office star to MGM for an extended production schedule. On February 28, 1938, columnist Louella Parsons reported, "Judy Garland to Play Dorothy in Metro's 'Wizard of Oz' Film."[4]

THE HANGING MUNCHKIN

When the home media market began in the early 1980s, the prints of the film made available on videotape and early LaserDiscs were faded and slightly fuzzy, similar to what had been broadcast on TV over the previous decades. Viewers mistakenly thought that some of the movement in the background of the scenes in the Tin Man's Forest were people rather than what they really were: exotic birds. This error morphed into the legend that a Munchkin actor hanged himself while a scene was being shot, and it was mistakenly left in the film. Another version claims this incident happened on the Munchkinland set, while yet another version claims it happened right behind the Wicked Witch while she's on top of the roof of the Tin Man's cottage threatening Dorothy and her companions. The legend has persisted over the past several decades.

The Wizard of Oz was filmed on closed sets because it was more costly and tricky to shoot than most films. Everything was accounted for, and it makes no logical sense that a random little person would find their way onto the set during a day of filming to hang themselves.

THE ACTUAL WORLD PREMIERE

The world premiere of *The Wizard of Oz* quietly happened in New Bedford, Massachusetts, on August 9, 1939. The film was previously thought to have premiered in Green Bay on August 10, 1939, but according to the August 23, 1939, issue of the trade magazine *The Exhibitor*, the world premiere was actually, and unintentionally, at the State Theatre in New Bedford, Massachusetts.

The reason for the discrepancies is that the Hollywood premiere was originally scheduled for August 10 but was moved to August 15 at almost the last minute. The film was already scheduled to open on several dates in several spots around the country. The dates of those engagements were not changed. Newspaper records show that the film was scheduled to premiere in several cities and towns in the Midwest on August 11. However, the owners of the State Theatre in New Bedford, the Zietz Brothers, jumped the gun and showed the film "before a capacity house" on August 9.[5] This was probably because Garland and Rooney were in the area as part of their personal appearances tour leading up to the New York premiere, which the Zietz Brothers took advantage of.

The pre-Hollywood premiere showings of the film were as follows:

- August 9: New Bedford, Massachusetts
- August 10: Green Bay, Wisconsin
- August 11: Cape Cod, Massachusetts; Kenosha, Neenah, and Appleton, Wisconsin
- August 12: Oconomowoc, Wisconsin

Oconomowoc has claimed to be the location of the film's world premiere on August 12, and it was reported as such for several decades. Now we know it quietly premiered on August 9 in New Bedford, Massachusetts. In fact, since the film had been playing for several days ahead of the official world premiere in Hollywood, there was time for the *Green Bay Gazette* to publish an early review of the film on August 12, 1939, giving it "the highest of the many praises one may heap upon the splendid technicolor [*sic*] picture, 'The Wizard of Oz,' playing currently at the Orpheum theater, is this: it doesn't let us down."[6]

- August 13: Portsmouth, New Hampshire; Racine, Rhinelander, and Sheboygan, Wisconsin

MUNCHKIN SHENANIGANS

There are legends galore about what the little people who played the Munchkins were up to both off the set and on. In fact, much of the plot of the thankfully forgotten 1981 movie *Under the Rainbow* was based on these legends. The legends include stories about lecherous behavior, attempted murder, drunkenness, prostitution, running amok at the studios, and even harassing Garland (and various other people on the MGM lot). Garland herself didn't help when she joked on TV in the 1960s that the Munchkins "were *drunks!*"[7] As previously noted, Garland was known as a raconteur. She liked to tell exaggerated stories for comic effect. She joked that the studio picked up the

80   CHAPTER 3

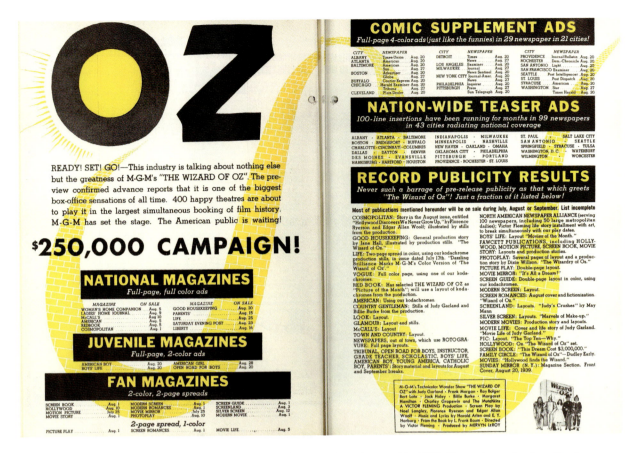

MGM trade ad published in the *Film Daily* trade magazine, August 11, 1939. From the author's collection.

little people at night in butterfly nets and that one little man asked her out. She said that when she politely replied that her mother wouldn't like it, he allegedly said, "Aw, come on, bring your ma, too!"[8] At the time that she told these stories, everyone knew she was embellishing.

These stories have been blown out of proportion. It didn't help that before and during the decades after the production, little people were the butt of insensitive and offensive jokes and harassment due to their size. There were most likely isolated incidents, as there would be with any large group assembled like this and staying at the same hotel for an extended time. "Work hard, play hard." But the image of little people running around Los Angeles like something out of a Looney Tunes cartoon or a scene in *Who Framed Roger Rabbit?* isn't a fair one. The little people worked just as hard as everyone else on the production, getting to the studio in the early morning hours to endure hours of being made up and costumed for long six-day workweeks. There wasn't much time for the kind of mischief that's been attributed to them.

One aspect of the film that's not an urban legend was Garland's charm and the respect she earned from the cast and crew. In a 1977 interview, Margaret Hamilton (best known as the Wicked Witch) said, "Once we started to work with her, we realized there was something special about her. . . . No one impressed me quite as much as Judy did those first days. She had those marvelous, expressive eyes, and there was a whole feeling of wonder in that little face. Her enthusiasm was contagious." She talked about the film's enduring popularity, citing as an example the famous deletion of "The Jitterbug" number prior to the film's release: "I remember when they cut a scene because it included a jitterbug dance that they feared might date the movie. I asked them how long they expected it to play," she recalls. "When they said, 'about 10 years,' I said, 'you're crazy!'"[9]

Immediately after her work on *The Wizard of Oz* was completed, MGM sent Garland on a short promotional trip to New York, with Ethel and Edens among the entourage, back to the Loew's State Theatre in Times Square, where she had triumphed the year before. They arrived on March 31, and Garland appeared on local radio, notably on the CBS Radio show *Tune-Up Time* on April 6, in which she sang "F. D. R. Jones," "Sweet Sixteen," and "It Had to Be You." Another guest on that radio show was Kay Thompson, who became Garland's closest female friend in just a few years when she joined the famous Freed Unit at MGM in the mid-1940s. Her influence on Garland's life, especially her later singing style, was monumental. She was so close to Garland that she was chosen to be godmother to Garland's first child, Liza Minnelli, who later cared for Thompson in her final years.

True to form for MGM, Garland didn't appear just at Loew's State; they had her make as many appearances as possible. On April 8, Garland amusingly attended a convention of twins at the Loew's Ziegfeld Theatre, where she reviewed a "parade of doubles."[10] Garland took part in the New York Easter Parade on April 9, riding in a carriage with future Broadway legend Mary Martin. Nine years later, the famous annual event became linked to Garland thanks to her smash hit, the 1948 MGM musical *Easter Parade*, costarring Fred Astaire. Prior to her opening night at Loew's, Garland made a whirlwind of appearances at the Loew's theatres in the New York area over two nights.

- April 10: Yonkers at 7:45 p.m., Orpheum at 8:45 p.m., Triboro at 9:25 p.m., Valencia at 10 p.m.[11]
- April 11: Jersey City at 8:30 p.m., 175th Street at 9:30 p.m., Paradise at 10 p.m.[12]

Due to the appearance times given and taking into account the time to travel, Garland's appearances at the theatres weren't stage shows; rather, she was meeting and greeting her fans. The local papers reported that when Garland appeared at "a Jersey theatre," she was "forced to appear in the lobby at the demand of her fans."[13]

On April 13, Garland opened at Loew's State in Times Square, again with her name in lights bigger than the theatre's marquee. This time, she was accompanied by Joe Venuti, "The Swing King," and His Orchestra and a vaudeville show featuring Don Darcy, Barrett Deems, Chick Robertson, the Gaudsmith Brothers (who did the poodle act that they also performed in the Garland/Gene Kelly musical *The Pirate* in 1948), and Stafford & Louise ("Outstanding American Dance Stylists"), plus "international comedians" and "a program of sophisticated jazz." The

82   CHAPTER 3

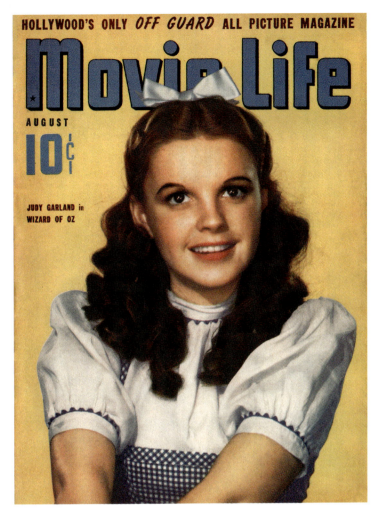

Garland as Dorothy makes a lovely cover for the August 1939 issue of the fan magazine *Movie Life*. From the author's collection.

featured film was the MGM version of Mark Twain's *The Adventures of Huckleberry Finn*, starring "America's Favorite Boy!" Mickey Rooney.[14] Incidentally, that was the film that director Norman Taurog left *The Wizard of Oz* to direct. Taurog was the original director of *Oz* (before Richard Thorpe) but left the project before any shooting began, knowing he wasn't the right director for it.

Garland's Loew's engagement lasted for a week, ending on April 19, and was another big success. Walter Winchell noted in his column that Garland took "the box office record at Loew's State away from [boxer] Jack Dempsey."[15] Another notable New York appearance for Garland was at the Press Photographers' tenth annual ball, held on April 14 in the grand ballroom of the Astor Hotel in New York City. The Astor later played a pivotal part in the plot of Garland's dramatic debut in *The Clock* (1945).

It was during this New York trip that Garland had one of her early crushes on an older man when she met composer, pianist, and wit Oscar Levant. As was her way, Garland obsessively showered him with phone calls, letters, and copies of her poems. At this point in her life, Garland had a pattern of roller coaster crushes, almost always with older men. Levant was attracted to her but kept the relationship platonic, probably because he harbored love for starlet June Gale. Garland's intensity of affection prompted Gale to stop resisting Levant's marriage proposals and marry him. Levant also had an addiction to prescription medicine and later quipped that if he had married Garland, "she would have given birth to a sleeping pill."[16] In the late 1940s, Levant had a brief career at MGM and would have been one of Garland's costars in *The Barkleys of Broadway* had she been able to complete the film.

On the way home from New York, Garland and her entourage stopped for an engagement in Cleveland, Ohio. On April 21, she sang the national anthem at the opening game of the Cleveland Indians baseball team. She was photographed at the game with the team's owner, Alva Bradley, manager Oscar Vitt, and Cleveland mayor Harold Burton. The local paper featured a photo of Garland at the game wearing a traditional Native American headdress, which must

"Where or When"—Garland and Mickey Rooney in *Babes in Arms* (1939). From the author's collection.

have been placed there for the photo op, as other photos show her in normal clothing for the game.

Garland returned to MGM on April 30 and went directly into rehearsals for her next film, *Babes in Arms*, costarring Mickey Rooney. This was their third film together and the first of what became a subgenre of the movie musical, the "Let's Put on a Show!" teen musical. Arthur Freed, the uncredited associate producer on *The Wizard of Oz*, chose the 1937 Rodgers and Hart musical *Babes in Arms* for his first film as a full-fledged producer. The stage version had a similar plotline to the film—about teenagers in a small town who put on a show to avoid being sent to a work farm when their show business parents go out on the road. The main difference is that in the stage version, the parents are never seen. Freed wanted to change that and make the plot more sentimental. "I want to . . . have the vaudevillians show that time has passed them by and that they couldn't catch up. . . . That's why in the last scene when [Rooney] gets his big chance at success, I want him to send right away for his father."[17]

Freed and Edens decided that most of the songs from the stage version were too "adult" for teens Garland and Rooney, so they removed "My Funny Valentine," "The Lady Is a Tramp," "Johnny One Note," and "I Wish I Were in Love Again." The latter three were later featured in the 1948 MGM musical biopic about Rodgers and Hart, *Words and Music*, and performed by Lena Horne, Garland, and Garland and Rooney, respectively. One of the new songs added to *Babes in Arms* was written by Freed and his usual collaborator Nacio Herb Brown, "Good Morning," sung as a duet by Garland and Rooney in the opening of the film. Their unique chemistry is magical and immediately lets the audience know that the film they're about to see is special. It was later performed to great effect by Gene Kelly, Debbie Reynolds, and Donald O'Connor in 1952's *Singin' in the Rain*. An older Freed song was dusted off and added, "I Cried for You," written in 1923; it became another one of Garland's best film vocals and on-screen ballads. She performs the song similarly to "(Dear Mr. Gable) You Made Me Love You"; however, this time, she sings to a photo of Rooney rather than Clark Gable. The dialog break in the song includes lines like "I know I'm no glamour girl like Baby . . . like her! And maybe someday you'll realize that glamour isn't the only thing in this world. You can't eat glamour for breakfast . . . I might be pretty good-looking myself when I grow out of this ugly duckling phase . . . time is a great healer." The lines are melodramatic corn, but Garland had a natural ability to make even the corniest of dialog completely normal, believable, and impactful, as she would prove time and again.

Babes in Arms was also the first MGM film directed by Busby Berkeley. Freed hired Berkeley for a one-picture deal (for the time being) from Warner Bros., where he had phenomenal success reinventing the early movie musical with his kaleidoscopic and extravagant musical numbers, beginning with 1933's *42nd Street*. Berkeley was a taskmaster and tough on performers. It didn't help that he suffered from alcoholism, which fueled his erratic and abusive behavior. He became especially tough on Garland. He felt that her eyes were her best feature and would scream at her, "Eyes! Eyes! I want to see your eyes!" while working her, Rooney, and everyone else to exhaustion during long days of shooting.[18] This treatment caused Garland to harbor an intense hatred of him that famously blew up a few years later. But in 1939, all of that was in the future. On *Babes in Arms*, there are no known incidents of Berkeley's future mistreatment. The daily production notes show that on most days, the cast was expected to be on the set at 9:00 or 10:00 a.m., after spending a couple of hours in hair, makeup, and costume, and ended in the 4:00 to 6:00 p.m. range. Perhaps Berkeley was on his best behavior, trying to prove himself to MGM. This was his first time being required to work in a more intimate setting, with clearly defined character development in addition to songs and dances that were mostly driven by the script and not the usual stage-bound production numbers that could be interchangeable, as had been the case with most of his work at Warner Bros. He would need to conform to the new style of musicals developing in the Freed Unit if he were to succeed.

MGM publicity photo of Garland in her home in Bel Air, Los Angeles, 1940. The studio publicity text on the back reads, "IT'S PLAY TIME FOR JUDY GARLAND. . . . And during every moment free from her role in Metro-Goldwyn-Mayer's 'Strike Up the Band,' in which she again costars with Mickey Rooney, the young starlet spends time in her garden of her home, enjoying the relaxation in the sunshine." From the author's collection.

The "Freed Unit" was the name given to Freed's staff of supremely talented people in front of and behind the camera. In 1939, the Unit wasn't a unit yet. Freed was gathering talent, mostly from Broadway, sometimes other venues or studios, which formed what became the greatest pool of musical talent in film history. Along with great acting, singing, and dancing talent, he hired great behind-the-scenes talent. Over the years, Freed brought to his unit, among others, stars Gene Kelly, Lena Horne, June Allyson, Frank Sinatra, Gloria DeHaven, Vera-Ellen, and Lucille Bremer. Behind the scenes, there were Kay Thompson, Hugh Martin, Ralph Blane, Charles Walters, Jack Martin Smith, Lemuel Ayers, Irene Sharaff, Conrad Salinger, Johnny Green, and many more.

Garland celebrated her seventeenth birthday on the set of *Babes in Arms*; later in the evening, she and some friends (including her new crush, the decidedly more mature bandleader Artie Shaw) partied at Garland's home in the Bel Air area of West Los Angeles. Garland and Ethel had the home built and moved into it in early 1938. It was a sign of Garland's success and her confidence (most likely driven by Ethel) that she would continue to succeed at MGM. Located at 1231 Stone Canyon Road and designed by architect Wallace Neff, the 5,513-square-foot home was built on just under three acres of land. Mabel, the mother of Jackie Cooper, Garland's friend, designed the interior. Garland lived in it with Ethel until her marriage to David Rose in 1941 and sold it on March 21, 1943. MGM used this setting to its advantage, taking photos of Garland on the grounds, tending the garden, and posing in various rooms, including a music room where she played records.

Although MGM promoted Garland doing "homey" things at her new home, like tending a garden or listening to records, the reality is that she rarely had time for any of these activities. It was all part of the studio's intense promotional campaign, which ramped up in the months ahead of the premieres of *The Wizard of Oz* and *Babes in Arms*. According to MGM, Garland, despite her talent, fame, and money, was just another teenager with many crushes and ambitions. Depending on which newspaper or magazine article was being read, Garland wanted to be everything from a doctor to a lawyer to a veterinarian. Articles provided to columnists by MGM and/or allegedly written by an author instead of MGM's publicity department quote Garland saying things like claiming that the best way to learn to sing outside of having a teacher was through records: "For all ambitious beginners phonograph records are invaluable. They offer the world's greatest singing stars in all fields of music as teachers."[19] Another amusing article, published in late 1939 and attributed to author Mayme Ober Peak, titled "Judy Garland Builds Home of Her Dreams," purported to be a personal tour of the new home with Garland. "I want to show you MY room," Garland allegedly said. "My goodness, did I have to fight to get it like I wanted it! They thought I ought to have a French room or a room with a four-poster bed and a canopy. But I don't like pinks and blues and ruffled things. I'm not the ruffle type. I like everything tailored."[20]

Another Garland-related address featured in newspapers and fan magazines at this time was 5421 Wilshire Blvd., in Los Angeles. This was the site of "Judy Garland Flowers." MGM sent out several publicity photos and stories about the shop allegedly owned and run by Garland. Photos showed her serving customers, including her sisters and director George Sidney. Most of the photos were taken in December 1938, and at least one was part of the official promotional set of photos for *The Wizard of Oz*; the promotional text on the back of that photo reads, "'WIZARD OF OZ' . . . was not the only activity that kept Judy Garland busy, for the young Metro-Goldwyn-Mayer star is the owner of her own flower shop, 'Judy Garland Flowers Inc.'" The studio promoted the shop as something Garland would help run during her time off. The truth is that aside from these photo sessions, Garland didn't spend much time at the shop because she was too busy at the studio and with her many other obligations.

Over her birthday weekend, Garland and some of her peers at MGM were invited to Mayer's beach house to celebrate. Garland was filmed having fun with "the gang," including Rooney, Ann Rutherford, and Jackie Cooper. She's seen cutting a huge birthday cake, with Mayer hovering like a proud father. Because MGM had been shaving a year from Garland's birth date

Label of the Decca Records 78-rpm-release of "Over the Rainbow" from the 1940 album of songs from the film. From the author's collection.

in publicity for so long, the voiceover on the newsreel and the text in various newspaper articles and fan magazines incorrectly reported that it was Judy's "Sweet Sixteen" birthday. Cooper later said that the whole day was scripted. The teens were told what to do and where to do it, all for the cameras. They never had any real time to themselves.

On June 29, 1939, the NBC Radio show *Maxwell House Coffee Time—Good News* devoted its entire show to *The Wizard of Oz*. The episode pretends to go behind the scenes of the making of the film. It featured the premiere public performance and first radio performance of "Over the Rainbow" by Garland. It's also the only known recording in which Garland publicly flubbed the lyrics to the song. Garland's costars Ray Bolger and Bert Lahr, the *Good News* musical director Meredith Willson, and the film's songwriters E. Y. Harburg and Harold Arlen joined Garland on the show. Arlen accompanied Garland on piano for her "Over the Rainbow" debut. As if this wasn't enough of an obligation, Garland was busy at MGM filming parts of the title number for *Babes in Arms* before the show and after. The partial nighttime shoot began at 1:00 p.m. and ended at 10:00 p.m. The assistant director's notes state, "Judy Garland worked on Good News program between 4:00 p.m. and 6:30 p.m."[21] In other words, Garland was sweet Patsy Barton in *Babes in Arms* for half the day, then she scurried over to the NBC Radio studios and played a fictionalized version of herself learning "Over the Rainbow," and then it was back to MGM and Patsy Barton. While she was at NBC Radio, director Busby Berkeley used her stand-in for the shot in the film that ends the "Babes in Arms" number. It's laughingly obvious that it's not Garland. It's most likely that audience members of the time noticed the switch since they would have seen it blown up on a huge movie screen and probably got a kick out of it. Spotting gaffes in films goes back to cinema's early years when lip readers would get a laugh "reading" what silent film actors were really saying to each other.

Garland began a new one-year contract with Decca Records on July 15, 1939. Ethel signed the contract as "Judy Garland by Ethel M. Garland" because Garland was still a minor. Ethel had been using the last name Garland since she and Frank had begun using it in 1935, although neither she nor Garland had legally changed their names. The new contract called for twelve songs to be recorded within the year, for which Garland would be paid a royalty advance of $250 per completed song. She recorded seventeen songs. Her royalty rate was as follows: if

They're Tired, but Also Happy—

Oscar A. Doob suggests the reader be not misled by the woeful expressions of Joe Vogel, center, and Harry Shaw, extreme right. He says they really are very happy, but tired in this picture which was made after Mickey Rooney and Judy Garland jammed 'em into Loew houses in New Haven, Hartford and Bridgeport. During it all, Vogel, as in Washington, and Shaw served as ushers, bodyguards, pacifiers and utility men at large. At the left is Les Peterson, studio representative. He is making the tour with the two youngsters.

The August 1939 Judy Garland–Mickey Rooney promotional tour was chronicled by the *Box Office* trade magazine. From the author's collection.

Garland had a song on both sides of a single, she would receive two cents for each single (78 rpm) sold in the United States and Canada and 10 percent of the wholesale price in other countries; if Garland had only one song on one side of a single, she would get one cent per disc sold in the United States and Canada. She was also paid 50 percent of whatever Decca was paid for public performances or broadcasting. As far as what Judy would record, the contract states, "The Artist agrees to record such selections as Decca may choose within the Artist's repertoire."

On July 28 and 29, Garland recorded eight songs under the new Decca contract, including her first studio recording of "Over the Rainbow." It was released in September 1939 on Decca single number 2672 with "The Jitterbug" on the B-side and peaked at the number 5 spot on the Billboard charts.

Two of the four songs recorded on July 29—"Zing! Went the Strings of My Heart" (another Garland studio first) and "Fascinating Rhythm"—remained unreleased in the United States until they were included on the 1943 compilation album *Judy Garland Second Souvenir Album*. "I'm Just Wild about Harry" was released only on Decca's Brunswick label in England and Australia in the spring of 1940. It was not released in the United States until 1984, when it was included on the MCA Records LP *Judy Garland—From the Decca Vaults*. The fourth song, "Swanee," was rejected, and no copy has survived. Garland rerecorded it on October 16, 1939.

Some examples of MGM's advertisement artwork are shown in the September 6, 1939, edition of *The Exhibitor* trade magazine. From the author's collection.

GARLAND AND ROONEY GO ON TOUR

Garland completed her work on *Babes in Arms* on August 2, 1939. Four days later, on August 6, 1939, she and Rooney left Los Angeles by train for Washington, DC, where they kicked off a quick tour of a few cities in the Northeastern United States, culminating in the New York premiere of *The Wizard of Oz* on August 17 at the Capitol Theatre. The duo's entourage included MGM publicity executive Les Patterson, "orchestra leader" Georgie Stoll, music arranger Roger Edens, and Garland and Rooney's mothers.

Loew Notes: *Lester Isaacs, chief projectionist, has been in New Orleans trying out the new double track sound device for "Wizard of Oz" . . .*

The tour went as follows:

August 9, 1939: Garland and Rooney met with teens who won contests to meet the duo at a reception at the Willard Hotel, Washington, DC. According to one article, Garland and Rooney had only ten minutes to eat before meeting with the guests.

August 10, 1939: The entourage arrived in Bridgeport, Connecticut. They drove to New Haven, Connecticut, where the duo was given a reception in their honor at the Hotel Taft. On the following morning (August 11), they were driven to Hartford, Connecticut. Also on this day, the *Film Daily* trade magazine published an early review of *The Wizard of Oz* with the headline "Handsomely Mounted Fairy Story in Technicolor Should Click Solidly at the Box Office," referring to the film as "a corking achievement all the way through."

Judy, Mickey, the Capitol and "Oz"—
Master Mickey Rooney and the young Miss Garland at one of the many parties, all with an eye to the press, arranged in connection with their appearance at the Capitol and the run of "The Wizard of Oz." To the right is an off-angle, roof shot of the line that created a policing headache on the opening day.

The *Box Office* trade magazine noted the New York premiere of *The Wizard of Oz* as well as a new "double track" soundtrack for the film, August 26, 1939. From the author's collection.

August 11, 1939: The duo performed at the Loew's Poli Theatre in Hartford, Connecticut. They gave four shows this day between showings of *Lady of the Tropics* starring Hedy Lamarr and Robert Taylor. They had arrived that morning from their appearance and overnight stay at the Taft Hotel in New Haven just an hour before their first scheduled show at 10:30 a.m.

August 12, 1939: The entourage returned to Bridgeport, Connecticut, where the duo performed and then spent Sunday, August 13, at the Long Island home of Mr. and Mrs. Nicholas Schenck before heading to New York.

August 14, 1939: The entourage, accompanied by Loew's New York executive Joseph

MGM MAGIC

R. Vogel, arrived at New York's Grand Central Station at 12:10 p.m. to a crowd of more than ten thousand fans. They were taken to their hotel, the Waldorf Astoria, for press interviews.

August 15, 1939: The official world premiere of *The Wizard of Oz* took place at Grauman's Chinese Theatre in Hollywood.

August 16, 1939: The duo presided over a luncheon event at the Waldorf Astoria Hotel in New York. They met teen representatives from the area (chosen from a recent local MGM promotional contest) and members of the Mickey Rooney and Judy Garland fan clubs. George Jessell and Jack Haley emceed.

August 17, 1939: The New York Premiere of *The Wizard of Oz* took place at the Capitol Theatre. Garland and Rooney gave twenty-six-minute (approximately) stage shows between screenings. They performed five shows a day during the week between seven showings of the film, and seven shows per day on the weekends between nine showings of the film! They performed from mid-morning until midnight. Garland's songs in the show included "The Lamp Is Low," "Comes Love," "Good Morning" (with Mickey), "God's Country" (with Mickey), and "Oceans Apart." This engagement grossed $100,000 in its first week, with the duo performing to approximately thirty-eight thousand people daily, give or take. *Variety* said of their show, "It's grade-A showmanship by both kids: they're young, fresh, and on the upbeat in the public's affection and imagination—a tousle-haired imp, and a cute, clean-cut girl with a smash singing voice and style."[22]

August 23, 1939: The duo took a time-out from their shows at the Capitol Theatre to pose for a photo session for the *Daily News* color magazine cover.

August 24, 1939: The duo took another break from their shows at the Capitol Theatre and made a quick visit to the World's Fair. Newsreel footage and photos show them

"THE WIZARD OF OZ." Conducted by Captain Volney Phifer, under the direction of exploitation manager William R. Ferguson, this original "The Wizard of Oz" carriage, and trailer-van, is touring the north and eastern portions of the country in behalf of the Metro production. Here are seen (upper left) the carriage before New York City's Capitol; (upper left) Mickey Rooney and "Dorothy" (Judy Garland) utilizing her carriage; (center) the bannered van; (bottom) the carriage.

The Munchkinland carriage used in *The Wizard of Oz* went on tour, as chronicled in the September 6, 1939, edition of the *Exhibitor* trade magazine. From the author's collection.

MGM promotional picture, 1939. From the author's collection.

chatting with New York's Mayor LaGuardia.

August 30, 1939: The last day of appearances for Garland and Rooney at the Capitol Theatre. Rooney had to go back to MGM in California. Later that night, the duo appeared at Madison Square Garden for the Harvest Moon Ball dance competition. Some footage of the duo sitting in the audience after performing (but no actual performance video) has been released on various *Oz* home media releases.

August 31, 1939: Ray Bolger and Bert Lahr joined Garland in the show at the Capitol Theatre. For this new show, Garland added "F. D. R. Jones" and "Blue Evening" to the lineup. The engagement ended a week later, on September 6, when Garland returned to MGM.

An amusing incident occurred at the beginning of the tour in Washington, DC. The duo's appearance violated the District of Columbia's child labor laws, which stated that girls under the age of eighteen could not work on stage between 7:00 p.m. and 7:00 a.m. The transgression was noted in the papers with headlines such as "Judy Garland Causes a Row" and "Judy's Show Brings Charges."

The lines went around the block when Garland and Rooney opened at the Capitol in conjunction with the New York premiere of *The Wizard of Oz* on August 17. As was the case at every stop on their tour, the duo triumphed. The *Hartford Courant* noted that fifteen thousand people showed up to see Garland and Rooney at the local Loew's Poli Theatre. MGM representatives and theatre owners around the country had been busy with promotional events that included newspaper coloring contests, look-alike contests, and ticket giveaways. In Atlanta, Georgia, there was an *Oz* character dress-alike contest, with prizes of $20 each going to the best Dorothy, Scarecrow, and Tin Woodman; $8 to the second best of the three; $5 to the third best. A local clothing store in Appleton, Wisconsin, gave away free tickets to the film with each purchase of a "Judy Garland" dress. At most of the stops on the duo's tour, local contests were awarding a lunch or meet and greet for local teens with Garland and Rooney. In the New York area, one local high school boy and girl were chosen to represent each Loew's theatre. The lucky teen couples got to take part in the reception luncheon for Garland and Rooney at the Empire Room in the Waldorf Astoria Hotel in New York on August 16.

Up to this point, the teen market had been largely untapped by the movie studios. However, with the recent successes of Deanna Durbin at Universal, Rooney in the Andy Hardy films, and Bonita Granville in the Nancy Drew films, it was clear that child stars didn't need to be little children like Shirley Temple to be very lucrative for the film studios. Garland and Rooney proved to be the era's most popular movie teen duo.

When Garland returned to California in early September 1939, MGM gave her a bonus of $10,600 for her efforts on the tour. For all of her *Oz*-related work, the promotion, and the tour, Garland received a total of just $30,749.98.[23] She (and the rest of the cast) never received any royalties for the film, but, as Ray Bolger noted in an interview in the 1970s, they received a "kind of immortality" with *The Wizard of Oz*. To date, one doesn't need to know a thing about Judy Garland to know who she was due to her now iconic (in the true sense of the word) image as Dorothy and her timeless rendition of "Over the Rainbow" as performed in the film. All one has to do is say, "She was Dorothy in *The Wizard of Oz*," and there is instant recognition. Almost a century after *The Wizard of Oz* was first released, its imagery, music, and dialog remain a part of the American (and the greater English-speaking world's) lexicon. It's one of the few films to come out of Hollywood that can truly be called timeless.

Garland puts her hand and footprints in the forecourt of Grauman's Chinese Theatre on October 10, 1939, assisted by Mickey Rooney and a Grauman's staff member. *Photofest*.

Babes in Arms had its world premiere at Grauman's Chinese Theatre in Hollywood on October 10, 1939. The star-studded event was highlighted by Garland placing her hand and footprints in cement in the forecourt. She was the seventy-fourth star to receive this honor. As if anyone needed proof, this was the sign that she was now a true movie star. The film was a hit

MGM promotional portrait, 1939. From the author's collection.

and eclipsed *Oz* at the box office and in initial popularity. It spawned a series of Garland/Rooney "Let's Put on a Show!" musicals, all produced by Freed, that lasted as late as 1943's *Girl Crazy* (the last of the series). Rooney even received an Oscar nomination for Best Actor. Garland was relegated to the honorary award category as the recipient of a "juvenile" miniature Oscar for her work in 1939 in *The Wizard of Oz* and *Babes in Arms*. She was also one of only two women to make the top ten box office list, the other being Bette Davis.

For the rest of 1939 and into early 1940, Garland enjoyed a period of relative inactivity. She had been working almost non-stop for the past eighteen months, and this lull must have been a welcome respite. Her only major activity from September 1939 through early February 1940 was a recording session for Decca Records on October 16 and a return to her weekly appearances on the NBC Radio show *The Pepsodent Show Starring Bob Hope*. December saw a few personal appearances due to the holiday season, including attending the opening of the Arrowhead Springs Hotel in Palm Springs, California, which was broadcast over the radio. She sang "Comes Love." On December 22, Garland and Rooney participated in a Christmas party/show at the Los Angeles Coliseum. According to the *Los Angeles Times*, Garland was introduced by Santa Claus and sang "Silent Night." Also on the bill was the latest iteration of the Meglin Kiddies troupe, as noted in that same *Times* article: "Singing, dancing, comic and acrobatic groups of children from Ethel Meglin studios next held the spotlight on the large outdoor stage." Just a few years prior, Garland would have been one of those nameless children; now she was one of the top stars supported by the group. It's not a big stretch of the imagination to think that Ethel Meglin might have told the children backstage, "See Judy Garland? She was part of our group; now look at her. You, too, can become a big star if you work hard enough."

Garland was also hitting the nightclub circuit and dating older men, which didn't make MGM very happy. Staying out until the early morning was the opposite of MGM's carefully crafted image of her as America's Sweetheart. One news blurb reported, "Judy Garland is going for the gay life in a big way. You can view her these evenings up to 2 or 3 a.m. in local night haunts," noting that MGM "protested" her actions. Garland is quoted as saying, "It's not in my contract when I have to go to bed. And until I have another picture to make, I'll go to bed when I like."[24]

Garland and her sister Sue (Mary Jane) pose with Mrs. Philip Norris while visiting Natalie Norris in the hospital, December 1939. From the author's collection.

One appearance in December 1939 received some press and is an early example of Garland's lifelong passion and charity toward ailing and special needs children. On December 2, 1939, Garland and her sister Sue visited a young girl in the Santa Ana, California, hospital. According to the papers, the girl, Natalie Norris, was recuperating from "a major operation" (the details of the operation were not given). Her condition was critical for several days, and at one point she had a "nightmare of delirium" in which she thought she was Dorothy in *The Wizard of Oz*. Her doctor thought a call from Judy would help her recovery. An in-person visit was arranged, and Garland gifted the girl a set of photos (two signed by Garland as Dorothy), a doll, some books, and a personal performance of "Over the Rainbow." The story was picked up by several columnists, complete with a photo of Garland and her sister outside the hospital, and was

Jackie Cooper escorts Garland out on the town, probably taking her to a rendezvous with Artie Shaw, circa early 1940. From the collection of Michael Siewert.

mentioned as late as early 1940. The *Oz* publicity photos that Garland gave to the girl are the only known surviving *Oz* promotional photos that Garland signed as Dorothy.

ARTIE SHAW

The lull in activity at this time gave Garland time to obsess over her latest romantic crush: musician and bandleader Artie Shaw. They first met in New York in 1938 when Garland was on her personal appearance tour. Later, during the filming of *The Wizard of Oz*, on February 10, 1939, Garland attended Shaw's opening at the Palomar nightclub in Hollywood. In the middle of his performance, Shaw collapsed. He was being treated for a recent strep throat infection with sulfanilamide. It turned out he was allergic to sulfa-based medicines. He was hospitalized, and it was then discovered that he had the blood disease agranulocytosis. Garland insisted on visiting him in the hospital multiple times. He woke up to see her face staring at him: "That absolutely marvelous little face, with freckles, the brown eyes, the reddish hair, looking at me with consummate tenderness."[25] Perhaps it was partly the Florence Nightingale effect, but Garland fell hard for Shaw, believing she was in love despite their age difference (most likely because of it). Shaw, however, did not reciprocate that love. He adored her as a friend, and, like everyone else, he was in awe of her talent. Of Garland, Shaw said, "Judy was marvelous! Bubbly, laughing, full of joy, just starting life. I was enchanted by her, crazy about her. I 'dug' her. That's better than 'loved' or 'cared for' . . . I felt that she was the best friend I had had in a long, long time."[26] Garland took it on herself to help him recuperate while he was convalescing at home. They went on long drives, with Garland pouring her heart out to him. He saw her as "the closest thing to a little sister I ever had."[27] Unfortunately, this was the image she desperately wanted to shed. There were times when he would attempt to give her an innocent "good night" kiss on the cheek and then she would move in and begin to kiss him passionately. He would pull back—"What are you up to, you idiot?"—and an embarrassed Garland would try to laugh it off with "Nothing, nothing!"[28] Garland did not want a friend or a big brother figure; she wanted a lover, but Shaw kept her at arm's length. He was known as a notorious womanizer and was already twice married, which didn't sit well with Ethel, who tried to dissuade Garland from spending time with him.

After filming *Dancing Co-Ed* for MGM, costarring Lana Turner (whom he was definitely sexually attracted to), Shaw left Hollywood and did not return until early 1940, which is when Garland began to see him behind Ethel's back. By this point, she had forbidden Garland to see Shaw, so Garland came up with the ruse of having friend and fellow MGM star Jackie Cooper pick her up under the guise of going out together, only to deliver her to Shaw. Cooper, like most people, couldn't deny Garland's very persuasive charms. She was adept at getting what she wanted. He would kill time before bringing her back home. Cooper had to bow out of the ruse when he began to date someone on his own, so Garland came up with the idea of telling Ethel she was going to see her sister Jimmie and Jimmie's daughter Judalien (named after Garland), but instead she went to see Shaw. Jimmie trusted Shaw not to take advantage of Garland, knowing that Shaw was dating Betty Grable.[29] Despite the "dates," the Garland–Shaw relationship remained platonic. This arrangement probably helped feed Garland's fantasies, as she was, despite her talent and star status, still an impressionable and romantic teenage girl.

In early 1940, Shaw eloped with Turner. Garland was devastated. Shaw running off with glamorous Turner reinforced Garland's insecurities about her looks and sex appeal. When Ethel told Shaw that he broke Garland's heart, he claimed to be surprised.[30] It's hard to believe that someone as suave and savvy as Shaw didn't see at least some of Garland's pining for him in all the time they spent together. It was reckless and callous behavior on his part. Ethel wasn't much help in dealing with her daughter's devastation. She was known as a fairly cold person who, for instance, didn't reciprocate hugs—not just with her daughter but with anyone.[31] Garland didn't have any substantial female role models in her personal life, nor did she have many close female friends. She was basically on her own, trying to navigate the conflicted emotions that any girl her age would be going through. MGM was aware of Garland's obsession with Shaw and wasn't happy that their innocent "kid next door" was more than eager for adult romance with a known and more mature womanizer. In another one of those studio-fed articles of the time, Garland is quoted as saying, "I go out with all the kids in our crowd. I'm not interested in any one boy— boys don't mean very much to me. I get very annoyed when they have me engaged. Why, they actually had me engaged to Artie Shaw; he certainly is a little too old for me!"[32] The obviously made-up quote could have been an attempt at damage control on MGM's part in response to the gossip columns and fan magazines that noted Garland's obsession with Shaw.

The extreme highs and lows of the relationship with Shaw, coupled with Garland's emotional devastation at his rejection of her, are indicative of her need for a father figure. Just a few years earlier, Frank Gumm's death had left a void in Garland's life that impacted her for the rest of her days. It didn't help that on November 17, 1939, the fourth anniversary of Frank's death, Ethel secretly eloped in Yuma, Arizona, with family friend Will Gilmore.

Will and Laura Gilmore had been friends with Frank and Ethel Gumm in Lancaster. The two couples spent a lot of time together. After Laura had a stroke, and with Frank busy in town (and most likely not sexually interested in Ethel anymore), Ethel and Will spent more time together. The rumors around Lancaster were that there was more to the relationship than friendship. Baby Gumm (Garland) knew something was wrong but didn't fully understand the situation until much later. There were bitter arguments between Ethel and Frank that Garland could hear from her bedroom.[33] By 1938, Frank Gumm and Laura Gilmore had died, and Ethel and Will were dating, which didn't sit well with Garland or her two sisters. They did not like Gilmore's colorless personality or his strict ways. The fact that Ethel married Gilmore on the anniversary of Frank's death only made it worse for Garland, who never forgave her mother for that transgression. It didn't matter that the date was also Ethel's birthday. Garland treated Gilmore with contempt. He was living with them at the Stone Canyon house, and she avoided him as much as possible.[34]

Garland didn't need to worry much about running into Will Gilmore very often. In early 1940, she began the busiest period of her MGM years and would soon break free of Ethel and Gilmore with her first marriage. The Ethel Gumm/Will Gilmore marriage lasted less than four years, ending in divorce.

Garland Glamour, 1940. From the author's collection.

CHAPTER 4

MGM's Singing Sweetheart

When 1940 began, Judy Garland was on top of the entertainment world thanks to the recent dual successes of *The Wizard of Oz* and *Babes in Arms*. She also enjoyed a fairly long period of inactivity at MGM, not beginning work on her next film until February 1940, seven months after completing *Babes in Arms* in July 1939. It was the last time until her pregnancy with Liza Minnelli in 1945/1946 that she would enjoy such a long break from the studio grind. But she wasn't completely idle. During this time in late 1939 and early 1940, Garland continued her weekly appearances on NBC Radio's *The Pepsodent Show Starring Bob Hope*, made a few personal appearances, and recorded more singles for Decca Records.

Just after the new year, Garland and Ethel took a short pleasure trip to New York through Chicago. From Chicago, they took a jaunt up to Milwaukee, Wisconsin, to visit relatives and for Garland to see her former crush, teen performer Perry Frank, who was appearing with his siblings (as the "Four Franks") at the Milwaukee Riverside Theatre. Over a month later, columnist Landon Laird of the *Kansas City Times* noted Garland's surprise appearance at the theatre, commenting that "there has been considerable talk of a romance between Judy and Perry Frank. The gossip seems confirmed because when the boy walked on the stage, Judy shouted, 'There's Perry!' and dropped a box of candy that rolled on the floor." Laird quoted Garland, who said about Frank, "Oh, he's wonderful, and I'm so happy to see him! Don't you think he's wonderful if we'd come all this way to see him? All the Franks are!" Garland also shot down the persistent rumors about a romance between her and Mickey Rooney: "I wish people would quit circulating stories about us. We mean nothing to each other. We're just good friends."[1] The New York trip was short; for a change, it was for pleasure rather than centered around personal appearances dictated by the studio. Garland was back in California to resume her weekly appearances on the Bob Hope show on January 16.

By February, Garland was finally working on another film, her second guest appearance in the Andy Hardy series in *Andy Hardy Meets Debutante*. In this edition, Andy is crazy about a New York debutante played by starlet Diana Lewis. Garland's Betsy Booth character is, once again, Andy's gal pal and living in New York, so, naturally, she's friends with the debutante and can arrange a meeting when the entire Hardy family visits the city. The production never left MGM, utilizing the studio's famous back lots and some rear projections to give the appearance (sometimes successfully, sometimes not) of the action actually taking place in New York. In the same basic scenario as 1938's *Love Finds Andy Hardy*, Andy doesn't see Betsy's charms until she wows him with her singing. In *Debutante*, Garland had one of her best on-screen performances, reviving the 1921 song "I'm Nobody's Baby," thanks to Roger Edens's unwavering genius for knowing exactly what song, old or new, was right for her talents. It was a perfect choice. Garland's studio version for Decca Records, recorded on April 10, 1940, was among her most popular for the label, peaking at the number 3 spot on the Billboard chart. Edens dusted off the Arthur Freed/Nacio Herb Brown ballad, 1935's "Alone," written for the Marx Brothers film *A Night at the Opera* (1935). Two more songs were prerecorded but ultimately deleted: "All I Do Is Dream of You" and "Buds Won't Bud." Garland recorded the latter for Decca on April 10, but, for unknown reasons, she didn't record studio versions of "Alone" and "All I Do Is Dream of You."

Garland's achievements continued at the twelfth annual Academy Awards ceremony on February 29, 1940. She was awarded the Juvenile Oscar for her film work in 1939 in both *The Wizard of Oz* and *Babes in Arms*. The newsreel footage shows Rooney awarding her the miniature statuette and asking her to sing "Over the Rainbow." Unfortunately, the newsreel cuts away before she sings. Rooney was nominated in the Best Actor category for his role in *Babes in Arms*. It's always seemed unfair that he would be in the running in that adult category while at the same time Garland, whose performance in *Oz* was more than worthy of a Best Actress nomination, was relegated to the Juvenile Award. Garland wouldn't have stood a chance against the *Gone with the Wind* juggernaut and Best Actress winner Vivien Leigh's performance in that epic, but a nomination would have been a better acknowledgment of just how much Garland's performance in *Oz* contributed to its success and stature as an instant classic. While appreciative, Garland later half-jokingly dubbed her miniature Oscar her "Munchkin Award."[2] Garland almost had a role in *Gone with the Wind*. In a memo dated November 26, 1937, producer David O. Selznick noted that he wanted to set up a screen test for her in the role of Careen (Scarlett O'Hara's younger sister) among tests of other stars in other roles, including *Oz*'s Glinda, Billie Burke, in the role of Aunt Pitty Pat. The tests never happened, and the Careen role went to MGM star (and Andy Hardy's girlfriend) Ann Rutherford. Laura Hope Crews memorably played Aunt Pitty Pat.

While filming *Andy Hardy Meets Debutante*, the news broke about a plot to kidnap Garland.

JUDY ENTERTAINS HER GUARDS

WIREPHOTO (AP)
Movie Actress Judy Garland, 17, passes refreshments to Detectives J. A. Everson (left) and L. F. Ennen, who were posted as guards at her Hollywood, Cal., home after phone call warned that she would be kidnaped.

Garland entertains detectives sent to her home after a failed kidnapping attempt, March 7, 1940. From the author's collection.

On March 7, Robert Wilson of Buffalo, New York, called the Hollywood police and told the night desk sergeant, W. A. McDonald, that "Judy Garland will be kidnapped tonight." Wilson asked McDonald whether he knew Garland. McDonald answered "Yes." Wilson then asked, "Do you know where she lives?" and after McDonald answered "Yes" again, Wilson gave McDonald Garland's correct address, which prompted McDonald to take action. Wilson and his accomplice, Frank Foster, had cased Garland's home for two nights, and Wilson told McDonald that they knew the servants would be off that night. They planned to take Garland at midnight into the mountains and ask for a ransom of $50,000. Police traced the call to a Santa Monica hotel and arrested Wilson. Wilson had planned to meet Foster at Sunset Boulevard and Stone Canyon Road and then walk up to Garland's home at 1231 Stone Canyon Road. At the last minute, he panicked and anonymously called the police, not realizing his call would be traced and a hotel employee would identify him. According to the newspaper reports, a group of reporters, photographers, and sixteen policemen descended on Garland's home, where she and her sister Virginia were entertaining some friends. The officers guarded the home. "I've never been threatened before," Garland calmly told them. "I'm sure everything will be all right—but make yourselves at home."[3] The newspapers featured Wilson's mug shot and a photo showing Garland serving refreshments to the detectives. Garland's mom and stepfather, Ethel and Will Gilmore, were in Santa Cruz when the events happened and returned home immediately after police wired the Santa Cruz authorities.

Fortunately, the kidnap plot never endangered Garland, but it was another indication of her new star status and already rabid fan base (the "Garland Cult," as it became known). The event resulted in the first of three case files the FBI opened regarding Garland during her lifetime. The other two were opened in 1941 (after MGM received an ominous letter about Garland) and in 1968 when Garland filed a claim that two rings had been stolen from her.[4]

STRIKE UP THE BAND

Garland began work on *Strike Up the Band* on April 3, 1940, while continuing her work on *Andy Hardy Meets Debutante*. The overlapping of film assignments became a new normal for her, especially during the early years of the 1940s when her workload was at its heaviest. For three months, Garland did double duty on *Strike Up the Band* and *Andy Hardy Meets Debutante*. Once she was finished with *Debutante*, she worked on *Band* alone for less than two weeks before beginning work on her next film, *Little Nellie Kelly*, which she then worked on while finishing *Band*. While she was working on multiple films simultaneously, Garland also continued appearing on the radio in the evenings and often recorded for Decca Records in the same evening before getting home late. Those early calls to be in the makeup chair at the studio were brutal. April 15, 1940, is a good example (of many examples) of this increased workload. Garland had a day of rehearsals for the "Gay Nineties" routine for *Strike Up the Band*. She was due on the set at 9:00 a.m. and was not dismissed until 6:00 p.m. She then had her weekly appearance on Bob Hope's radio show, followed by a recording session for Decca Records. She and songwriter Johnny Mercer recorded the popular Cole Porter song "Friendship." In an extensive sixteen-page promotional ad spread placed by MGM in multiple trade magazines in early September 1940, the following Garland films are listed among the MGM films in production: *Strike Up the Band, Little Nellie Kelly, Ziegfeld Girl, Babes on Broadway*, and *The Youngest Profession*. The first two were released in 1940; the second two were released in 1941. The latter was taken off Garland's schedule and given to MGM teen star Virginia Weidler. Garland wasn't the only star with multiple films listed, but she and Spencer Tracy were the only two with more than four films on the list. Tracy ended up appearing in just three, and one of those wasn't until 1947. Garland's films were musicals that required longer, more grueling schedules than dramas or comedies due to the addition of music and dance rehearsals, prerecording sessions, and longer days of filming.

Garland and Mickey Rooney in *Strike Up the Band* (1940). The May 1941 *International Photographer Magazine* selected this as the first-place winner in the Best Action Still category. From the author's collection.

An increase in workload meant an increase in Garland's use of the pills to get her through the long days at MGM followed by long evenings of more performing in one way or another that lasted into the night.

Strike Up the Band was the follow-up to *Babes in Arms*, with Garland and Rooney again costarring and putting on a show. This time, the story is not far removed in plot and tone from the Andy Hardy films, just with a bigger budget and elaborate songs and dances. Garland and Rooney play high schoolers who love swing and live in a small town named Riverwood. Jimmy Connors (Rooney) is a drummer in the school band who dreams of being a famous big band leader. Mary Holden (Garland) sings with the band and pines over Jimmy, wanting to be his girlfriend. He sees her only as, no surprise, a gal pal. The film's plot is a bit more involved than *Babes in Arms*, but not by much. This explains the running time being a solid 120 minutes, longer than the average musical at the time. Jimmy and Mary convince the school principal to let them put on a dance to raise money to form a big dance orchestra for the school. The dance in the school gym, the "La Conga" production number courtesy of Busby Berkeley, is a success, allowing them to start that big band. "La Conga" remains one of Berkeley's best numbers. The choreography, the music, and the sheer size of it are astounding, and its palpable energy and excitement endure. It helps that both Garland and Rooney, along with the supporting cast and stock dancers, are giving their best.

Things become complicated when local pretty rich girl Barbara Frances Morgan, played by June Preisser in the same basic teenage femme fatale role she had in *Babes in Arms*, sets her sights on Jimmy. Meanwhile, the younger Willie (Larry Nunn) loves Mary, who sees him only as a friend, given that she's still pining over Jimmy. The teens put on an elaborate stage show that's a re-creation of the old melodramas, titled "Nell of New Rochelle," to raise enough money to travel to Chicago and participate in a nationwide band contest sponsored by real-life bandleader Paul Whiteman. Whiteman plays himself and appears earlier in the film as the guest band at a party at Barbara's fancy home. "Nell of New Rochelle" was meant to give the adults in the movie audience the pleasure of seeing Garland, Rooney, and the rest of "the kids" performing old favorites, deftly poking fun while also paying homage to the then-archaic melodramatic style of performing. Jimmy, Mary, and their band are all set to head to Chicago when they discover that Willie's injury from a fall during the show has become serious, and he urgently needs an operation his family can't pay for. After some serious soul searching, Jimmy learns what's truly important in life and uses the Chicago money to get Willie the operation. When it seems Jimmy will never realize his dream, Barbara's father hears of his sacrifice and comes through with the money. They rush to Chicago and win the contest and the $500 grand prize. Jimmy leads all of the bands in a finale medley, with Mary as the lead vocalist, ending with the appropriately patriotic Gershwin song "Strike Up the Band," complete with the US flag waving and America's favorite teens, Garland and Rooney, superimposed on the flag just before the fade out. You can't get any more patriotic than that.

Producer Arthur Freed had initially wanted the Garland/Rooney re-teaming to be a remake of MGM's early sound musical *Good News* (1930), based on the 1920s Broadway hit about 1920s college life and featuring the songs "The Varsity Drag" (drag in this case was a type of dance and not female impersonation) and the evergreen ballad "The Best Things in Life Are Free." MGM boss Louis B. Mayer suggested a film titled "Strike Up the Band" featuring the Gershwin song of the same name because "it sounds so patriotic."[5] War had come to Europe, and it was becoming increasingly evident that the United States would enter the conflict soon. Mayer, who was very patriotic, believed in the America idealized in the Andy Hardy films. *Strike Up the Band* was everything he could have asked for with its portrayals of wholesome American youth, homespun life lessons, and loud patriotism.

It was during this time that Freed first brought Garland's future husband Vincente Minnelli to MGM from Broadway. Freed was constantly gathering top musical talent for the studio, not just performers but also the talent behind the camera. He told Minnelli he could watch and learn before getting any directorial assignments. Minnelli lent his talents to the "Our Love Affair" number in *Strike Up the Band*. Freed asked him to take a stab at making the number, which takes place in the confines of a home parlor and adjoining dining room, into a larger production number. Minnelli hit on the idea of having the pieces of fruit in a bowl on the dining room table come to life and play the musical instruments, based on a *Life* magazine article he had seen. That did the trick. After they duet the song, Jimmy and Mary walk over to the dining room table, and Jimmy demonstrates how he would set up his big dance band, positioning the fruit as band members. The number segues into a fantasy sequence showing the audience what Jimmy is imagining, with the various pieces of fruit coming to life and playing different instruments thanks to some clever puppet work. It was a brilliant idea that worked perfectly. Minnelli was on his way to becoming MGM's top musical director. At this time, his interaction with Garland was minimal, but he later remembered, "I was attracted to her open manner, as only a man who has been reserved all his life can be."[6]

"Our Love Affair" (written by Freed and Edens) became a standard and was nominated for the Oscar for Best Song. It lost to "When You Wish Upon a Star" from Disney's *Pinocchio*. *Strike Up the Band* was also nominated for Best Scoring (Edens and Georgie Stoll), losing to *Tin Pan Alley*, and Best Sound Recording, which it won, awarded to MGM's sound director Douglas Shearer. Another accolade the film received was in May 1941. The *International Photographer Magazine* awarded MGM studio photographer Ed Cronenweth first prize in the Best Action Still category of the Hollywood Studios' Still Photography Show for his photo of Rooney flinging Garland around. The photo was used extensively in MGM's promotional materials.

Edens also wrote "Nobody" for Garland, which Berkeley filmed beautifully in a rare, subdued manner, focusing on Garland and her velvety vocals. It's another of Garland's best. She also got to show off her swingy side with "Drummer Boy" (another new Edens and Freed song) and her flair for satire in the "Nell of New Rochelle" sequence. On a budget of $838,661.40 (a big amount for the time), *Strike Up the Band* grossed $3,494,000.[7] Although some reviewers found the film a tad on the long side, most agreed it was great entertainment and a worthy successor to *Babes in Arms*. The basic format for the "Let's Put on a Show!" teen musicals was now set.

> Judy Garland, however, steals scenes from Rooney by her newly-acquired art of underacting. When the two are together, it seems Mickey works too hard while Judy is completely relaxed. This draws attention to her and every pout provokes a laugh. She is at her best in the title song number, flirting, cavorting—giving in the notes swing manner.
> —Ed Parker, "From the Back Row," *Winnipeg Tribune,* Winnipeg, Manitoba, Canada, November 7, 1940

LITTLE NELLIE KELLY

Little Nellie Kelly was a George M. Cohan Broadway musical from 1922, which was seen as old-fashioned even at that time. Although Freed's version altered the plot and eliminated most of the songs, the film was no less old-fashioned and corny, even by 1940 movie musical standards. Only Cohan's "Nellie Kelly I Love You" and "You Remind Me of My Mother" were retained from the original production; the latter was a solo for Garland's costar Douglas McPhail that went unused. The film was significant in Garland's career for a few reasons: it was a step forward in MGM's grooming her for adult stardom; it was centered around her talents without frequent costar Mickey Rooney (she gets top single billing and, in many cases, above-the-title single billing); and it was the only film in which she has a death scene. The mother, Nellie Kelly (Garland) dies giving birth to Little Nellie Kelly (Garland again). Edens later said, "This film gave Judy her first opportunity to portray an adult, acting both the wife and daughter of George Murphy. But the studio executives didn't at all like the

Through tieup effected by Ward Farrar on "Strike Up the Band" at Loew's, Indianapolis, with local music store, guest admissions were offered to all children under 16 for a special morning showing of the picture. In addition, cooperating merchant devoted entire window, as shown above, to display of various musical instruments. Background featured cutouts of Whitman, Rooney and Garland.

An example of the elaborate window displays some theatres would create to promote their films is this one for *Strike Up the Band* (1940) from the November 9, 1940, *Motion Picture Herald* trade magazine. From the author's collection.

MGM'S SINGING SWEETHEART

idea of Garland's growing up. Mr. Mayer, a very sweet old guy, was in the centre of the debate about making Judy both the mother and the daughter. 'We simply can't let that baby have a child,' he'd say."[8] If there were any doubts at MGM about whether Garland had the acting versatility to pull off an adult (however brief) role, her death scene most assuredly erased them. George Murphy, who was in the scene with Garland, later stated that he'd never seen such incredible acting:

I assure one and all this was one of the greatest dramatic scenes that I have ever witnessed. It took me longer to get over it than it took Judy. And you might be interested that when it was finished, the complete set was empty, with the exception of Norman Taurog, the director, Judy, and myself. The grips, electricians, carpenters and all these so-called hard-bitten workers were so affected that they had to get off the set so that their sobs would not disturb or disrupt the sound track.[9]

Despite the very thin story and a cartoonish characterization of Little Nellie Kelly's grandfather by Charles Winninger, the film was enormously popular and made a considerable profit. The *Detroit Free Press* called it "the finest Irish picture ever made." That was part of an article about how the local old Corktown Club of Detroit named Garland "Miss Corktown of 1941" (the article was published December 1940) "in honor of her performance in the title role of 'Little Nellie Kelly.'"[10] The Utah Theatre in Salt Lake City, Utah, went to the extreme and blazoned "Judy Garland" in ten-foot bubble lights in their lobby over the row of snack vending machines. The critics were mixed about the film overall but nearly unanimous in their praise of Garland's talents and performance.

Judy plays her dual role in grand style, emphasizing her maturity and status as a top-flight actress with loads of wholesome charm and assurance. She sings several familiar Irish songs and a swing version of "Singin' in the Rain."
—Eddie Cohen, *Miami News*, Miami, Florida, December 13, 1940

Judy Garland . . . proves that she is a top notch actress. She has loads of personality and wholesome charm. She goes through the picture without showing any signs of acting, which is an ability that many a veteran tries to achieve without reaching that goal.
—P. F., *Honolulu Star Bulletin*, Honolulu, Hawaii, December 23, 1940

Made to order for small situations and everyone who saw it praised it highly. We played it in the worst blizzard here in ten years so didn't get any of our rural crowd. Just made rental on film but glad we played it. We're going to bring it back when roads open.
—Walter R. Pyle, manager of the Dreamland Theatre, Rockglen, Saskatchewan, Canada, *Motion Picture Herald*, December 6, 1941

Little Nellie Kelly gave Garland a couple of great songs that stayed in her ever-growing repertoire: "A Pretty Girl Milking Her Cow" (an eighteenth-century Irish folk song updated by Edens) and "It's a Great Day for the Irish" (a new song written by Edens), which is now an unofficial anthem for St. Patrick's Day celebrations. On her TV series in 1963, just before singing it, Garland joked about "A Pretty Girl" being "a rather obscure Irish folk song that fit the picture quite well, and we did it, and they released the picture, and the song became an obscure Irish folk song! But I like to sing it."[11] She definitely liked it. Garland sang it in concert and recorded studio versions in 1940 for Decca Records and in 1955 for Capitol Records. She also recorded studio versions of "It's a Great Day for the Irish" in 1940, again for Decca (and then, twenty years later, in 1960, for Capitol). One musical highlight she performed only in the film was her rousing rendition of "Singin' in the Rain," which is equaled only by Gene Kelly's iconic performance twelve years later. As with "I'm Nobody's Baby" in the recently released *Andy Hardy Meets Debutante*, Garland sings the song in a party setting in an MGM idealized version of a clean and wholesome teenage social world. All of the party guests (extras) are well-mannered and well-dressed American youth, and when Garland sings, they're enthralled by her. In both, Garland's magic again bounces off the screen, giving the films a level of entertainment they otherwise wouldn't have had.

One of the film's delights is the "Nellie Montage" sequence, which shows little Nellie Kelly growing up. MGM used actual photos of Garland from her childhood to give the sequence authenticity—a pleasant surprise to unsuspecting Garland fans, especially during late-night television showings decades later.

Also of note, and a staple of future MGM Records soundtrack compilations, is the outtake of Garland's beautiful rendition of "Danny Boy." Her moving performance was possibly a result of the fact that one of her cherished childhood memories was of her late father singing it. Two separate takes have survived and have been released in various audio formats over the years. The song replaced "The Stars Look Down" (unrecorded), which was to be Garland's first song in the film. Then "Danny Boy" was replaced by a quick chorus of "A Pretty Girl Milking Her Cow."

On February 13, 1940, Garland's peer and friend Lana Turner married bandleader Artie Shaw. The event was devastating for Garland, who, as noted in the previous chapter, had been madly in love with Shaw and still harbored intense feelings for him. Garland's devastation was born out of obsession. Obsessing over older men had become a pattern with her and was even noted in the gossip columns of the time. Naturally, she dated some of her peers in the movie industry who were her own age or thereabouts, including Jackie Cooper, Robert Stack, Leonard Sues, Dan Daily Jr., Peter Lynd Hayes, and Billy Halop of the Dead End Kids fame, among others. Garland also dated orchestra leader Jimmy Cathcart, who, according to the papers, stole her away from Robert Stack and gave her his Kappa Sigma "sweetheart" ring from Indiana University. Garland wore the pin when Cathcart escorted her to see the Broadway show *Meet the People* when it was in Los Angeles.[12] Cathcart was the brother of Jack Cathcart, who married Garland's older sister, Mary Jane (a.k.a. Sue or Suzy), in 1941 (divorced 1963). The relationship with Jimmy Cathcart didn't last long, but Garland had a longer "relationship" with brother-in-law Jack. He became her musical conductor and director for most of her concerts in the 1950s, provided the vocal arrangement for her comeback film *A Star Is Born* (1954), and even played a trumpet solo on her 1955 studio recording of "Carolina in the Morning" for Capitol Records (which he also conducted).

Barron Polan was another brief but important romance. Polan was Mervyn LeRoy's assistant and more to Garland than just a romance; he was also a friend, having accompanied her to film premieres and being part of her entourage for her 1942 tour of army camps, serving as one of her managers. She apparently felt great affection for him. He was one of the few recipients of her book of poetry *Thoughts and Poems, by Judy Garland*, which she had privately printed in a limited quantity to give out as Christmas gifts in 1940. She dedicated it to Polan: "To Barron in appreciation for his many kindnesses to me." Garland had taken up composing poetry as an outlet for her romantic fantasies and longings. Her poems are not on par with those of Emily Dickinson, but they do provide a

Garland is escorted to the Los Angeles premiere of Disney's *Pinocchio* by her dear friend Barron Polan, February 9, 1940. From the collection of Michael Siewert.

peek inside Garland's mind and romantic expectations at the time. In many ways, she was still an impressionable, emotionally innocent girl.

MY LOVE IS LOST

My love is lost.
I held it as a handful of sand, clenching my fist
to hold it there.
Yet, bit by bit, it slipped through my straining fingers.

Now, nothing but memories of every smile, every kiss,
and, above all, every word.
For 'twas not into my ear you whispered but into
my heart.

'Twas not my lips you kissed, but my soul.
And when I opened my tired hand and found
my love was gone
I trembled and died.

I struggle to hide my deadness.
To conceal the emptiness in my eyes,
that sparkle with tears always so close
but never come.

My mind quivers and screams, fight, fight to live
But why?
My handful of existence has vanished.
My love is lost.
My love is lost.[13]

Like most teenagers her age, Garland's obsessions burned super white hot but usually didn't last long. Likewise, the Turner/Shaw marriage lasted even shorter than any of Garland's obsessions. It ended in September 1940, which probably gave Garland some private satisfaction. She claimed not to want to marry "for three or four more years," but the truth was that while she was still nursing her broken heart from the Shaw debacle, she continued to go out with other, usually older, men. It didn't take her long to find someone new to whom to direct her romantic obsessions.

DAVID ROSE

Garland rebounded from the Shaw obsession to another notable, albeit brief, romance, this time with songwriter Johnny Mercer. The two even recorded a duet for Decca Records, their version of Cole Porter's "Friendship." In a reversal of how Garland's romances usually went, it was Mercer who was the obsessed one, and although it was a friend who convinced Garland to end it, she apparently didn't have a problem obliging. Mercer remained obsessed and went on to write the lyrics to two standards about his love for Garland: "That Old Black Magic" (music by Harold Arlen) and "I Remember You" (music by Victor Schertzinger). Garland recorded the former for Decca Records in 1943. Mercer went on to co-write the Oscar-winning "On the Atchison, Topeka, and the Santa Fe" with Harry Warren for Garland's 1946 hit musical *The Harvey Girls*. He also cofounded the Capitol Records label, to which Garland was successfully contracted from 1955 to 1966. The label produced some of her greatest recordings, including the masterpiece *Judy at Carnegie Hall* album in 1961.

MGM'S SINGING SWEETHEART

While she was still carrying on her romance with Mercer, Garland was also dating musician David Rose. She had first met Rose a few years before, introduced to him by Jackie Cooper. On the night of the day that the news broke about Shaw marrying Turner, Garland was backstage for her weekly appearance on the Hope show and was hysterical and inconsolable over the news. Singer Margaret Whiting was there and tried to comfort Garland, who exclaimed (while allegedly banging her head against a wall), "He said he wanted to marry me! . . . I'm going to kill myself!" Whiting later said, "Never have I seen anybody so devastated as Judy was that night."[14] Rose was working as the orchestra leader on a show across the hall while Garland was in her dressing room, killing time between rehearsal and show time. She spent that downtime time crying and wailing. Rose knocked on the door. When she answered, he handed her a slice of chocolate cake with whipped cream on the top and said, "My mother made it. I had some left. It's for you." They shared the cake and that night they went out on the first of many dates.[15] Rose was the opposite of Shaw—quiet, unassuming, mature—and, at thirty, he was twelve years Garland's senior. Rose and Garland had two major things in common: each was coming off relationships that had recently hurt them, and they were both musicians who loved learning, sharing, and performing music. Garland was still hurting from Shaw, and Rose had just ended a bad marriage to comedian and movie star Martha Raye. Before anyone had time to think of it as anything more than a brief affair, the Garland/Rose relationship had become serious, and Garland was ready to hear wedding bells being rung for her.

In the beginning, Garland's mom, Ethel, was opposed to her daughter's relationship with Rose. Garland would tell Ethel that she was spending the night with her friend Betty O'Kelly or that she was out with her girlfriends seeing a movie. She was really at Rose's place. His place was on the way between the Garland household and the home of Garland's sister Virginia and her husband, Bobby Sherwood. One night, Ethel drove by and saw Garland's car parked in Rose's driveway after being told she was spending time with friends. Ethel is quoted as calling Rose and saying, "Judy's there at your house, and you better damn sure have her here in fifteen minutes, or I'll have the law on you!"[16] This made Garland furious, and a heated argument ensued between mother and daughter. But that didn't stop Garland from continuing to see Rose. Ethel purposely drove by Rose's home late one night, and, sure enough, Garland's car was again in the driveway. This time, Virginia warned Garland that Ethel had seen her car and encouraged her to call Ethel rather than come home cold to an angry mother waiting to pounce. Garland called, but it didn't help. They had another nasty argument. Ethel would have been really incensed if she found out that Garland and her friend Betty had slept in the rooms of their male companions (Rose and O'Kelly's date, Buddy Pepper) rather than with each other during a weekend trip to a new hotel in Lake Arrowhead, California.[17] If the story is true, it's hard to believe that Ethel wouldn't have put two and two together. If the story isn't true, it's at least a scenario in keeping with the lengths Garland would go to deceive her mother in the name of romance. Ethel could threaten to "tell Mr. Mayer," as she often did, but it was to no avail. Garland was more than ready (at least in her own mind, if not in reality) to marry and leave the nest, and she was determined to get what she wanted.

Garland entered into a new contract with MGM in September 1940, two years ahead of the expiration of her original contract from 1935. The new seven-year contract, signed on August 28, 1940, and filed in the Los Angeles Superior Court on September 26, 1940, immediately raised her weekly pay from $600 to $2,000 (the workweek was Monday through Saturday) for three years, then $2,500 for the next two, and then $3,000 for the last two. Ethel signed a rider, as the "mother of the artist," guaranteeing that Garland would carry out "each and all of her obligations" as set out in the agreement, and she and Garland would take care of compensation for her work outside of the contract. After some heated discussion between Garland, Ethel and her husband, Will Gilmore, and Ethel's lawyer, Harry Rabwin, they settled on a stipend for Ethel of $125 per week paid out of this new contract.[18] The contract stayed in place until 1946, when a new one was drafted giving Garland even more money and (so it seemed) more control over her career and workload. This 1940 contract was another example of MGM's faith in Garland's marketability. She was currently in transition from child star to adult star. That transition ruined the careers of most child stars. Based on the figures of this new contract, it appears MGM was confident that Garland would successfully make that transition, becoming a bigger asset for them. Indeed, Garland turned out to be one of the rare cases of a child star becoming not just an adult star but, eventually, a living legend.

Filming on *Little Nellie Kelly* ended the day after Garland's new contract with MGM was filed in the Los Angeles Superior Court. On October 1, 1940, after finishing looping work on the film, Garland was admitted to the Cedars of Lebanon Hospital for a routine tonsillectomy. The studio was nervous about whether the procedure would affect the now famous (and lucrative) Garland voice. The procedure went fine, and photos of Garland convalescing at home with a nurse were published, along with articles that mentioned the studio's angst.

Garland and Rooney reprised their *Strike Up the Band* roles in the CBS *Lux Radio Theatre* adaptation on October 28, 1940. It was Garland's first of eight appearances on the radio series from 1940 to 1953. The program presented adaptions of films and plays, usually performed live in front of a studio audience and abridged to fit the hour-long time slot (including commercials). Garland re-created some of her MGM film hits on the program. She also got the opportunity to stretch her dramatic talents in ways MGM wouldn't let her, including an adaptation of the Katharine Hepburn role in *Morning Glory*. On December 28, 1942, she played the lead in the radio adaptation of the original 1937 non-musical film version of *A Star Is Born*, which had brought Oscar nominations to its two leads, Janet Gaynor and Fredric March. It was this successful radio performance that planted the seed of Garand's desire to play the lead in a musical film remake. Garland made her wishes known, but MGM was not interested in their singing sweetheart in a dramatically heavy film portraying a struggling young actress who falls in love with and marries an alcoholic film star. It didn't fit their carefully crafted image of Garland as presented in their lighthearted musicals. They had found a formula that worked both critically and financially, and they weren't about to jeopardize it.

ZIEGFELD GIRL

In October 1940, Garland began rehearsals for her next film, the big-budgeted and extravagant *Ziegfeld Girl*, produced by Pandro S. Berman and directed by Robert Z. Leonard, with the musical numbers again directed by Busby Berkeley. Garland was a late replacement in a role originally intended for dance legend Eleanor Powell. As late as mid-September 1940, Powell's name was still attached to the project as one of the three female leads, along with Lana Turner and Hedy Lamarr (both of whom stayed on the project). The change in the character from dancer to singer was due to the fact that Powell's popularity was waning, while Garland's name on the marquee ensured a strong box office. Tony Martin and James Stewart costarred, supported by Jackie Cooper, Edward Everett Horton, Charles Winninger, and Eve Arden. Turner's brief marriage to Artie Shaw had ended that

America's Singing Sweetheart in 1941. From the author's collection.

previous September, and later biographers have pondered whether that had any impact on Garland's friendship with Turner and their ability to work together so soon after the Shaw events. From all appearances, it seems that Garland had moved on. She and Turner were lifelong friends, and if they compared notes about their experiences with Shaw, it's unknown what was discussed.

The story of *Ziegfeld Girl* follows three young women and their experiences in show business. Even in 1941, when the film was released, it wasn't the most original story, having been told with variations in many films and stage shows. This time, it's their experiences in the famous Ziegfeld Follies that provide the setting. One finds stardom (Garland), one finds marriage (Lamarr), and one finds heartache, alcoholism, and, in this case, implied death (Turner). This version is supposed to be about the heyday of the Ziegfeld Follies, circa 1920s, but there is no serious attempt to make it an accurate period piece, with the styles of the clothing, hair, and costumes being very contemporary. None of that mattered to audiences at the time, who responded to the spectacle by making it a hit.

In *Ziegfeld Girl*, Turner and Lamarr get the glamour treatment and the adult storylines, while Garland is relegated to another "kid sister" role. Her character is a peppy young vaudevillian who engages in some puppy love with Jackie Cooper and endures the stress of trying to bring her old-fashioned vaudevillian father into the more modern performing style while also briefly serving as a "Little Miss Fixit" to Turner's character. It's Garland's character's voice that sets her apart and finally gets her noticed, much like how Garland felt about her own life and how she was perceived as a voice rather than how she wanted to be seen, as a desirable and glamorous woman. Even so, Garland is the top-billed female star in the film and on most ads and posters, second only to James Stewart, who was riding the success of his recent film hits and Oscar win (won while *Ziegfeld Girl* was in production). The dichotomy of Garland being given top billing and promoted as the main female star while playing the non-glamorous teen role in a film about the apex of female glamour, with two of MGM's biggest Glamazons as her costars, most likely was not lost on Garland. She was already known in social circles as a highly intelligent person who was acutely aware of everything around her, especially regarding her body image.

Ziegfeld Girl is Lana Turner's film more than anyone else's. She has the meatier role, with the screenplay focused more on her character's dramatic narrative than anyone else's. This is the film that solidified Turner as a star (MGM gave her a hefty raise in salary and a star dressing room trailer as a result). The addition of Garland to the cast was more a case of MGM capitalizing on her popularity than any attempt to further her career. It's a brief detour from her films produced by the Freed Unit, being produced by Pandro S. Berman. Her star power, and that of Stewart and Lamarr, was needed to make the expensive project a profitable film. Lillian Burns, the studio's drama coach who coached most of the major actresses on the lot, including Garland and Lana Turner, talked about Garland's insecurities. One day, she praised Garland's work in *Ziegfeld Girl*: "Judy, I'm so glad the picture's so good." Garland cut her off with "What does it mean to me? So, I have a scene where I cried again." On another occasion, Burns told Garland she had a "priceless gift" and could do anything she wanted. Garland replied, "Except one thing, except that when I sit down at a table opposite a man, all he can see is my head. I haven't any neck." Burns went home in tears.[19]

Obviously, Garland was the only choice to handle the musical numbers along with crooner Tony Martin, and she has several notable songs. "Minnie from Trinidad" is a novelty number made into a huge production number by Berkeley, expertly sung by Garland. As big of a production number as "Minnie" is, the centerpiece production number of the film is built around the new song, "You Stepped Out of a Dream," as sung by Martin, and featuring the MGM Glamazons (the bevy of beauties that graced MGM movies) on full display wearing insanely over-the-top costumes by designer Adrian. The number is a celebration of MGM's idealized version of feminine beauty. Garland doesn't get any vocals and, at the end of the number, is in the background with the other "cute" and non-glamorous group of girls, whereas Martin, Turner, and Lamarr take center stage surrounded by the other Glamazons. "We Must Have Music" is another elaborate production number, this time featuring Garland with Martin. It was filmed but cut before the film's release. Photos of Garland in her drum majorette costume, as she was costumed in the number, were still circulated as part of the extensive promotional material for the film. The only surviving footage that exists is a brief clip of Garland singing the number that opens an MGM short, also titled "We Must Have Music," about the studio's music department. Even with this deletion, the film runs a long 132 minutes. "We Must Have Music," although deleted before the film was released, was mentioned in some local reviews of the film because of the early promotional material that MGM sent out. This happened occasionally when it was decided to edit things out of films at the last minute.

Garland's best number, another one of her best screen performances and vocals, is "I'm Always Chasing Rainbows." The song, already in the public domain, appeared in several musicals of the 1940s, and yet Garland's rendition is magical. The surviving prerecording sessions give us a peek into Garland's genius at work. Each take is a mini masterpiece. Any of the takes would have been just fine in the film, but, true to MGM's insistence on perfection, musical direc-

Surrounded by Glamazons. Garland (*center*) is seated between Lana Turner (*left*) and Hedy Lamarr (*right*) in this publicity still for *Ziegfeld Girl* (1941). From the author's collection.

tor Georgie Stoll, or perhaps it was director Leonard, had a tough choice in picking the winner. It's alleged that during the filming of "I'm Always Chasing Rainbows" Turner said to Garland, "I'd give all my beauty for just half your talent. The look on your face when you sing."

Finally, the film's finale sequence is a medley of songs and melodrama that features clips from the studio's 1936 Best Picture Oscar Winner, *The Great Ziegfeld*, mixed in with new footage of Garland and Martin. The sequence opens with Garland singing the new song "Ziegfeld Girls," which segues to the former film's "You Gotta Pull Strings," followed by a montage of clips from the 1936 film's famous production numbers. As if that's not enough, Martin appears and reprises "You Stepped Out of a Dream." Turner's character, now deathly ill but watching from the audience, removes herself to the lobby, walking down the stairs one last time to Martin's voice in the background, only to slump forward and collapse. On top of that, after her death scene (the prettiest deathbed scene since Greta Garbo in *Camille*), the film cuts to a re-creation of part of *The Great Ziegfeld*'s famous wedding cake set as featured in its centerpiece number, "A Pretty Girl Is Like a Melody." Only now it's Garland in a copy of the original costume worn by Virginia Bruce, complete with a blonde wig, filmed in medium shot and then spliced in to look as though when it cuts to the long pull-back shot of the original number, the audience believes it's still Garland on top of the cake singing "You Never Looked So Beautiful Before" with the MGM Studio Chorus swelling to a final ultimo. The End. They don't make them like that anymore! This montage sequence wasn't the first idea for the finale. The original idea for the finale was to open with music provided by the world-famous MGM Studio Orchestra, then Garland and Martin in the "We Must Have Music" number, followed by a bit performed by the musical group Six Hits and a Miss, and then ending with the reprises of "You Stepped Out of a Dream" (Martin) and "I'm Always Chasing Rainbows" (Garland). However, toward the end of production, it was decided to make the finale more elaborate, so Garland was called back a month before the premiere date to prerecord and film her sections of the new finale.

Ziegfeld Girl was released on April 25, 1941. The critics (then and now) complained about the film's length, the story, the anachronisms, and even Adrian's wonderfully outlandish costumes. But there was no denying the sheer size of it all and the fact that, despite its flaws, it's still enjoyable to watch, thanks to the charisma of the stars and the professionalism of the production, the kind that only MGM could produce. Audiences loved it, and it made a profit of double its cost, grossing over $3 million on a production cost of $1.5 million.

MGM spared no expense on the film's promotional campaign. MGM's director of advertising and publicity, Howard Dietz (who also co-wrote the song "That's Entertainment!" among others), organized a lavish $100,000 "Caravan of Beauty" that toured the county, usually arriving in a city just before the film opened there. This was in addition to the normal publicity blitz that went out for a high-profile film like *Ziegfeld Girl*. The caravan featured costumes from the film as well as oil paintings of the various Ziegfeld Girls by noted American artists, plus displays of the winning artwork from a contest conducted in connection with the film. The exhibit was

MGM'S SINGING SWEETHEART

accompanied by two of the young women who appeared in the film as Ziegfeld Girls, Virginia Cruzon and Myrna Dell. They modeled some of the gowns featured in the film. The promotion line was that the girls were chosen because they represented the "perfect Ziegfeld Girl of 1941."

Another fictional but no less fun story cooked up by MGM was about the baton Garland used in the film. In the deleted "We Must Have Music" production number, Garland is costumed as a drum majorette, twirling a baton. A publicity article circulation claimed that the baton Garland used was her own from when she was four years old, which was "among her souvenirs of 'The Gumm Sisters' era." The article continues that Garland used it in her first feature, *Pigskin Parade*, and "now as the drum majorette in the M-G-M musical's finale number, it once again comes out of hiding," but this time it was painted silver and had "100 sparkling rhinestones

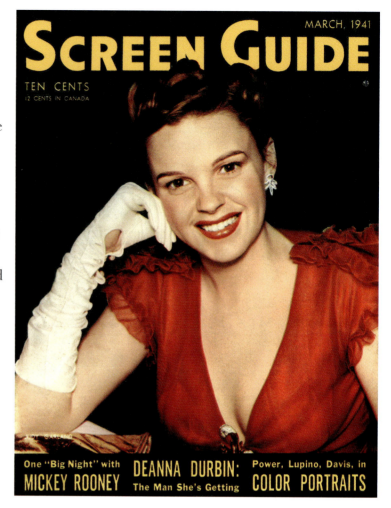

Garland looking radiant on the cover of the *Screen Guide* fan magazine, March 1941. From the author's collection.

studding the head." Garland is quoted chuckling, "I'm sure if it had been as impressive 14 years ago as it is now, we would have received more than 50 cents a piece for our 'Gumm Sisters' act."[20] Garland doesn't wield a baton in *Pigskin Parade*; Tony Martin does, and that baton is obviously too big for a four-year-old girl to use. In *Pigskin Parade*, it looks about as tall as Garland was at the time, pushing 4 feet, 11 inches.

Here is a sampling of the contemporary reviews for *Ziegfeld Girl*:

> It is young Judy Garland, however who provides the greatest entertainment quotient in the play with her true trooper tactics, her magnificent song renditions, and her increasingly fine sense of musical comedy.
> —Ed Parker, *Winnipeg Tribune*, Winnipeg, Manitoba, Canada, May 31, 1941

You'll very much like the way Judy bears down on that old favorite, "I'm Always Chasing Rainbows." That pathetic cry in her voice will do things to you. Another excellent number in which Judy is the principal performer is "Minnie from Trinidad," a delightfully silly novelty.
—Merle Potter, *Star Tribune*, Minneapolis, Minnesota, April 27, 1941

Judy Garland provides a much-needed bounce as the daughter of Pop Gallagher (Winninger). "Minnie from Trinidad" is her hit number, as it probably is also of the Busby Berkeley ensembles.
—Philip K. Scheuer, *Los Angeles Times*, Los Angeles, California, April 16, 1941

[Lana Turner's] performance, combined with the song-plugging talent of Judy Garland, especially "Minnie from Trinidad," are the highlight of the film. In contrast with Hedy Lamarr and Philip Dorn, her violinist husband, Judy and Lana tower above the alien corn. The musical renditions are left strictly to Judy and Tony Martin, who is in fine singing voice, even if his slim acting moments leave something to be desired.
—Frank P. Gill, *Detroit Free Press*, Detroit, Michigan, April 18, 1941

At the end of 1940, Garland's name appeared on the list of the top ten box office stars of 1940. It was her first of three times on the list; the other two were for 1941 and 1945. This first appearance was on the strength of both *The Wizard of Oz* and *Babes in Arms*, which were released in the latter part of 1939, and their success continued into 1940. Garland's other films in 1940, *Strike Up the Band*, *Little Nellie Kelly*, and *Andy Hardy Meets Debutante*, also contributed to her new status. She and Warner Bros. star Bette Davis were the only two women on the list.

Garland followed the glitz and glamour of *Ziegfeld Girl* with her final appearance in the Andy Hardy series in *Life Begins for Andy Hardy* (1941). The film is arguably the worst of Garland's MGM films, although it still turned a profit due to the star power of Garland and Rooney and the popularity of the Hardy series. It was quickly made with poorly executed rear projection shots designed to represent New York. In this entry, Andy returns to New York to begin his life as an adult, with Betsy (Garland again) helping out. Garland doesn't sing at all. It's not considered her dramatic debut, but, technically, it is her first non-singing role, though only because all the songs she recorded were deleted. She recorded "Abide with Me," "The Rosary," and the Cole Porter standard "Easy to Love." It's unknown why the cuts were made or even whether all the songs were filmed. The prerecordings survive and are up to the usual high Garland standard, especially "Easy to Love." In the film, Garland sings only a quick a capella version of "Happy Birthday" as recorded on the set during a scene. The only positive thing one can say about this Hardy film is that it features some great shots of various parts of MGM's famous "New York Streets" section on Lot 2.

At this point, Garland's romance with David Rose had morphed into a marriage engagement. On June 2, 1941, invitations went out, inviting guests to Garland's Stone Canyon home for the official announcement of her engagement to David Rose (his divorce from Martha Raye was finalized on May 15, 1941). The party took place on June 15, 1941, from 1:00 to 5:00 p.m. It was attended by more than six hundred people (luckily, the size of Garland's home and the grounds could handle a large number of guests). Studio photographers were on hand to mark the occasion by snapping photos of Garland in a formal afternoon outfit with her guests, which the publicity department wasted no time getting out to the newspapers and magazines. Although her mother and the studio weren't happy about her engagement (she had just turned nineteen), there was nothing they could do. Ethel didn't want her daughters to marry musicians, but that didn't stop them—and it didn't stop the divorces, either. MGM wasn't as concerned about Rose's vocation as a musician as they were about the fact that, in the public's eye, she was now a young lady engaged to an older man and not as innocent as they would have liked to keep her. Little Judy Garland had grown up, and there was nothing they could do about that, either.

For a month after the engagement announcement, Garland was in the early stages of production on the third of the "Let's Put on a Show!" musicals with Rooney, *Babes on Broadway*. She rehearsed and prerecorded the new song "How about You?" and posed for costume tests; she even had a French lesson for her Sarah Bernhardt impersonation. She was also exhibiting more tardiness getting to the set, causing delays, or not showing up. This pattern soon created a bad reputation of unreliability for her, which would haunt her for the rest of her life. The bad behavior could be because she and director Busby Berkeley didn't mix well, and her newfound independence of being engaged and stepping out on her own was manifested in the passive-aggressive behavior of being habitually late or a no-show. It was a good way of exerting control over situations that she probably felt she had no control over.

Garland exerted more of that control over her life when, without warning, the couple took a quick and unannounced plane trip to Las Vegas, Nevada. Judy Garland and David Rose married on July 28, 1941, at 1:00 a.m. in Las Vegas. Garland sent a telegram an hour later to producer Arthur Freed, which read, "Dear Mr. Freed, I am so very happy. Dave and I were married this AM. Please give me a little time and I will be back and finish the picture with one take on each scene. Love, Judy."[21] Here was Garland exerting some more independence but still bowing to the studio's control over her life, an example of her conflicted emotions. Freed didn't pause production on the film so Garland could have a honeymoon. On the next day, July 29, she was back on the set at 9:00 a.m., ready to film her next scene. She was dismissed at 5:57 p.m. For a few days, she didn't have any time off; finally, she wasn't needed for work that Friday, August 1, and Saturday, August 2. She was back on the set that following Monday, followed by two sick days. It appeared that for the time being, Garland was mostly true to her word to Freed and was not absent for the next several weeks and was out (or delayed the production) only for a few sporadic days toward the end of filming in early November.[22]

120   CHAPTER 4

During the production of *Babes on Broadway*, from July through November 1941, Garland's extracurricular professional work outside the studio was light—for her. She appeared on only four radio shows (that are known) and had just two recording sessions with Decca. In contrast, she had another four radio show appearances in the last two months of the year after the film had been completed. However, Garland and Rose had an active social life. They were seen out and about in restaurants and clubs, socializing around Hollywood, as shown in photos in fan magazines and some random comments by columnists like Hedda Hopper. Hopper liked Garland and fed the gossip in some creative ways; many times, it was complete fiction.

Garland and her new husband, David Rose, return to Los Angeles after getting married in Las Vegas, Nevada, on July 28, 1941. From the author's collection.

BABES ON BROADWAY

Babes on Broadway followed the formula of the previous two "Let's Put on a Show!" musicals. The kids were growing up, so, in this installment, they're now struggling young actors in New York City hoping for that big break. The plot centers around Rooney as Tommy Williams, part of a trio act that gets the chance to audition for the biggest producer in New York, Thornton Reed (James Gleason). Along the way, he meets Penny Morris (Garland), who just happens to have a beautiful voice. With his act going nowhere, Tommy gets the idea that they should produce their own show. Since they don't have any money for a theatre, he has another idea to use a charitable cause to help raise the funds. Tommy finds his cause at the children's tenement house where Penny works. The tenement house doesn't have the money to send the children on a trip to the country, so Tommy arranges to produce a block party featuring all his unemployed performer friends under the guise of helping the kids but also helping Tommy, who has begun to show his opportunistic character. Then a new cause presents itself:

refugee children from England being sent to the tenement house are scheduled to have a short-wave radio hookup to speak to their parents during the scheduled block party. Tommy callously exclaims that they don't need the kids and their trip anymore, thinking that the radio hookup will give him and his friends more exposure (and more money). This decision creates conflict between him and Penny. The radio hookup/block party succeeds and gets Tommy in the papers. Meanwhile, Reed's new show has experienced dismal out-of-town tryouts and needs a replacement act for a spot on the show. Reed's assistant, Jonesy (wonderfully played by Fay Bainter), who has an affection for Williams and his act, can't get a "name" replacement for Reed, so she decides to take a chance on Tommy and his friends. Tommy learns a lesson in selflessness when he realizes it would be better to take the high road and turn down the offer from Jonesy and produce his show as originally planned to raise money for the kids' trip to the country. He and Penny give Jonesy the news, prompting Jonesy to let them use an empty, broken-down theatre owned by Reed, free of charge, to mount their show, on the condition that they fix it up. On opening night, a city inspector stops the show during the performance, citing code violations. Tommy tells the audience they can't continue and will refund their money. As they're cleaning up and getting ready to leave the theatre, it's discovered that no one asked for a refund, and some even donated more. The kids can go to the country, but Tommy is back where he started. Reed suddenly shows up, having been alerted about the code violations in his building, for which he's still responsible. Realizing that although they can't perform for an audience, nothing can stop them from giving a private show for one person (Reed); they perform for Reed, which fades into the film's finale, which is Reed's production of *Babes on Broadway* at the New Amsterdam Theatre.

There are several great musical numbers to enjoy in *Babes on Broadway*. Garland and Rooney's sublime introduction of the Oscar-nominated song "How about You?" written by Burton Lane and Ralph Freed (it lost the Oscar to Irving Berlin's "White Christmas" from *Holiday Inn*) is an intimate song and dance performed in Penny's apartment. By this point, Garland and Rooney's chemistry was such that they could have performed without rehearsal and blindfolded and still been completely in sync with each other. The production number "Hoe Down" is a typically energetic Berkeley production number, with many dancers, props, and elaborate choreography. This time, it's toned down just enough (in the beginning), so it doesn't hinder Garland's superb vocal intro. Supporting actor Ray McDonald gets the chance to show off his dance talents in a lengthy solo break during the number, temporarily taking the focus away from Garland and Rooney, which was unusual for a big production number in a Garland/Rooney musical. In another effective performance, Garland sings the patriotic "Chin Up! Cheerio! Carry On!" to a group of British war refugees, reflecting the current mood of the United States as an ally to England during World War II. Her vocals are riveting despite the manipulative manner in which the number is filmed with the sad, crying refugee children. It is blatant propaganda meant to convince Americans of their duty to help England in these early years of World War II (conceived and filmed two months before America entered the war).

122   CHAPTER 4

Another effective sequence wasn't directed by Berkeley but by newcomer Vincente Minnelli. For the scene in which Tommy and Penny visit that abandoned, run-down theatre, they imagine what past performances the theatre witnessed. The sequence then becomes the fantasy "Ghost Theatre Sequence," in which both stars perform a medley of songs and dramatic readings paying tribute to the great stars of the past, including Garland's impersonation of Sarah Bernhardt in French. This is the second time that Minnelli provided a creative fantasy sequence for a Freed musical, the first being the "Our Love Affair" fruit orchestra sequence in 1940's *Strike Up the Band*. In this "Ghost Theatre Sequence," Minnelli again successfully displays his soon-to-be-famous signature style of nuance and taste.

The film's finale sequence is an extended minstrel show in which Garland, Rooney, and almost everyone else are in blackface. Berkeley went all out with the size of the finale, and it's a stunner with dozens of backup dancers, enormous sets, and a long, flowing curtain. Unfortunately, the blackface mars it. Garland performs a thrilling vocal of "F. D. R. Jones," which she had first performed on the radio in 1939. She also recorded it as a single for Decca Records, paired with her recording of "How about You?" at the same recording session on October 24, 1941, the only two songs from the film that Garland recorded as singles. Vocally, her performance succeeds, and visually, it almost succeeds. It's not just the blackface. Thankfully, she's not doing a blackface caricature or acting cartoony. Instead, she's manic. It's one of a few times on screen when she seems to be "overmedicated," to put it politely. Others might say "speeding out." Like *Everybody Sing* in 1938, this was a time in film history when blackface was seen as perfectly normal and not anything more than an old-fashioned form of entertainment. To the white audiences, anyway. The filmmakers weren't using it to intentionally make fun of anyone, at least not in this instance. The end of the finale presents Garland and Rooney out of blackface and formally dressed. Garland is shown with her hair up, looking more like a glamorous leading lady than she had for the rest of the film. It's an almost shocking difference, in a good way, and is a taste of what's soon to come to movie screens: the glamorous Garland.

Babes on Broadway was a transition film for Garland. Her character's age isn't specified, but it's clear that she's of the college freshman age. She's presented as a lovely young woman who is desirable to Rooney's character; they even have their first romantic kiss. She and Rooney had outgrown the teen-themed musicals, and although he continued as Andy Hardy, she did not return to that series. Columnist Harrison Carroll reported in his column that since Garland and Rooney were married (to other people), MGM would "divorce" them as a screen team, noting that "they're too old for kid stuff."[23] From this point forward, with few exceptions, MGM presented Garland as an attractive young woman and, soon, a glamorous leading lady.

A few future film heavyweights make early screen appearances in *Babes on Broadway*. Future Oscar winner Donna Reed has an uncredited role as Jonesy's secretary, and a tiny four-year-old Margaret O'Brien, in her film debut, effectively steals the audition scene as a melodramatic child actress. Costar Richard Quine (one of the "3 Balls of Fire" trio with Rooney and

McDonald) went on to become a successful film director, including the 1955 musical remake of *My Sister Eileen* (which he cowrote) starring Janet Leigh, Betty Garrett, Tommy Rall, and a young Bob Fosse in a rare on-screen appearance, as well as the 1958 classic *Bell, Book, and Candle* starring James Stewart and Kim Novak.

Babes on Broadway opened on December 30, 1941, in several cities across the United States. On a budget of $955,300.37, it grossed $3,859,000. Another big hit for MGM.

"Babes on Broadway" bounced onto the screen at the Fox-Oakland yesterday and found a welcoming throng waiting with open arms at the portals, which just goes to show that news of good entertainment travels fast. And this is good entertainment—nothing arty, nothing socially significant, nothing especially new for that matter, but all done with fanfare and with talent constantly in evidence—good entertainment for all classes of theatre patron.
—Wood Soanes, *Oakland Tribune*, Oakland, California, January 14, 1942

Here is a picture in the best traditions of show business which has just about everything needed to bring crowds to the theatre and joy to the hearts of patrons of all ages . . . Mickey Rooney and Judy Garland [are] performing as well or better than ever.
—Martin Quigley Jr., *Motion Picture Herald*, December 6, 1941

Judy puts on one of the most professionally polished performances of her career.
—Sarah Lockerbie, *South Bend Tribune*, South Bend, Ohio, January 25, 1942

An interesting urban legend has grown about *Babes on Broadway*. Without any proof, some overzealous fans have claimed that one (sometimes both) of Garland's two sisters are dancers in the "Hoe Down" number. Ever since the home media era began, we can now own and study films at our leisure, and some of the fans seem to have too much leisure time on their hands. When looking at the film and freeze-framing the image, the girl in question looks similar to Garland's sister Jimmie, albeit younger, but that's as far as it goes. She never appears close enough to confirm that she is one of Garland's sisters. The popular website IMDb (Internet Movie Database) lists both of Garland's sisters as dancers in its entry for the film, thanks to these fans going in and adding incorrect information. Because anyone can go in and make additions to the site, it has become so riddled with errors (in most of the entries) that it's basically useless as a reliable research tool. That is the "proof" people use to argue their case because there is no other proof. Unfortunately, the Internet being what it is, this misinformation has been shared all over cyberspace as fact. IMDb also lists Jimmie as a showgirl in *Presenting Lily Mars* and as a Harvey Girl in *The Harvey Girls*, among a list of other incorrect credits. There are photos of Jimmie and Mary Jane visiting Garland on the set of *Presenting Lily Mars* in 1942 and having a "reunion," which was widely publicized, and yet no mention of Jimmie being *in* the film—only that the two sisters were visiting Garland on the set. Both sisters briefly worked at MGM, but not on screen.

Jimmie Gumm was a script girl at MGM for a time in the early to mid-1940s. This position has been well publicized. One article dated May 16, 1943, has the headline "Judy's Sister Jimmie Is in Movies Too—Works as a M-G-M Script Girl" and explains how Jimmie worked her way up from the accounting department to script girl.[24] If she had been in *Babes on Broadway*, it would have been similarly publicized. MGM would have taken full advantage of one of Garland's sisters appearing in one of her films—the publicity department would have had a field day. In the late 1940s, Jimmie was allegedly a member of the MGM Studio Chorus in the recording studio, not on screen. At least that makes sense, as Jimmie did have a decent singing voice. Sue was noted by columnist Virginia Vale as joining the fan mail department "when her army husband was sent away."[25] In July 1945, Jimmie made a publicized attempt at a nightclub singing career in New York City, but she bombed. It could be that after that experience, she was content to be a voice in the MGM chorus. Another fact to consider is that MGM's dancers were professionals. While Jimmie and Mary Jane (Sue) sang as a part of the Gumm/Garland Sisters trio professionally and did a little dancing in the act, they were not trained dancers on the level needed to be an MGM contract dancer. In 1964, Jimmie was interviewed by Lloyd Shearer for the syndicated *Parade* newspaper magazine insert published on October 4, 1964. Nowhere in the interview does Jimmie say anything about being in any of her sister's films when talking about their professional histories. It's nice to fantasize about Garland's sisters backing up their superstar younger sister in her films, but it's just that—fantasy. The claims about Garland's sisters being in any of her films are false. End of story.

GARLAND GOES TO WAR

At the end of 1941, America entered World War II. When Japan attacked Pearl Harbor, Hawaii, on December 7, 1941, Garland and Rose were at the Fort Ord army camp in Monterey, California, for the NBC Radio show *The Chase and Sanborn Hour* with Edgar Bergen and Charlie McCarthy. Despite the bombing, the show went on, although it was constantly interrupted by news bulletins. On that same day, Garland was made an honorary corporal in Company H of the First Medical Regiment. She was the first major star to be given an honorary appointment in the military during World War II. The regiment's *Esprit de Corps* newsletter noted:

> Judy Garland, lovely star of radio and screen, was given an honorary corporalcy in Company H of the 1st Medical Regiment. . . . Miss Garland was dressed in an attractive black and white outfit. Major Martin had Judy line up with a squad of men from Company H, and 1st Sergeant Marshall Nummel pinned corporal's stripes on each sleeve of Miss Garland's sweater. A corporal's warrant was then presented while a pair of identification tags were placed around her neck.
> —*Esprit de Corps*, Fort Ord, California, December 1941

In early January 1942, Garland and Rose settled into their new home in Sherman Oaks, California. It had once belonged to the late MGM legend Jean Harlow. It was also Garland's first home away from her mother. She was finally independent. She and Rose finally had a bit of a honeymoon, traveling to New York City (photos of the couple at Pennsylvania Station were published on January 8) and Miami, Florida, in mid- to late January, ending their trip in Chicago, which is where they left from to begin their USO tour. After their brief honeymoon, Garland and Rose joined the USO Camp Shows Inc. for a five-camp tour of army camps. It was the first of eight separate tours planned by the USO to be in full swing before the end of January 1942.[26] Garland was noted in the papers as being the first of the Hollywood stars to tour army camps for the USO, followed by Al Jolson, Ann Miller, and Constance Moore. The title of the show that Garland and Rose toured with was "Thumbs Up." Garland and Rose usually performed two to four shows a day at the camps, with Garland singing twelve songs in each show.[27]

The Garland/Rose tour of army camps began in Fort Custer near Battle Creek, Michigan, on January 21. Garland and Rose were accompanied by her mom, Ethel; her manager (and former boyfriend), Barron Poland; and "several studio representatives." About the USO tour, Garland said, "We wanted to do this. Only thing I wish is that more soldiers could see our show. They deserve all the entertainment they can get."[28]

- **January 21, 1942: Fort Custer, Battle Creek, Michigan**—According to the local newspaper, they arrived in Battle Creek at 1:01 p.m. on the Mercury (train) from Chicago, Illinois. Garland is seen in the local papers being mobbed by a crowd. They went to their suite at the Post Tavern Hotel to rehearse and rest before going to the fort to meet Brigadier General Cortlandt Parker, commanding officer of the Fifth Division. While at the hotel and outside of Garland's room, policemen had to keep "autograph hunters and admirers" away. Per the *Battle Creek Enquirer*, one girl, ushered out of the hall near Judy's room by a firm-handed policeman, sputtered, "If I didn't like Judy Garland so much, I'd be mad about this!" When it came to liking Judy Garland, almost everybody felt that way.[29]

  Before performing, Garland was made an honorary MP and met with other ranking officers while dining with them and the enlisted men at the mess hall. She was the first honorary woman member of the military police during World War II. There were two shows that evening; the first started at 6:15 p.m., and the second started at 9:00 p.m. Garland performed one number (what song she sang isn't identified) toward the end of the show and joined in the finale. At the fort, Garland was given a personal bodyguard, MP Technical Sergeant William Dyer, who said to her, "I'm glad to do this for you because you are my favorite actress."[30]

Vivacious Judy Garland made her debut as an Army entertainer with a show at Fort Custer, Mich., and in return was made an honorary "M. P." She is shown above surrounded by members of the Military Police and Army stage hands after the show. Miss Garland is making a tour of mid-western Army posts.

Garland, during her first tour of army camps, was surrounded by adoring soldiers during her stop at Fort Custer, Battle Creek, Michigan, on January 21, 1942. From the author's collection.

The following day, January 22, Garland was scheduled to visit the post's hospital, the Veterans Facility, the American Legion Hospital, and the two service clubs, along with the new USO club on West Michigan Avenue in Battle Creek, at 11:00 a.m., where she was to cut a ribbon, opening one of the rooms to army-enlisted men. All that was planned to happen before Garland and Rose left for Chicago (again on the Mercury train) at 3:00 p.m. Those plans were canceled to allow the couple the chance to leave for Chicago on the earlier 10:47 a.m. train. The reason for leaving early wasn't given. Newspaper reports noted that Garland's mom, Ethel, joined them in Chicago.

- **January 23, 1942: Fort Knox, Louisville, Kentucky**—A two-night engagement, two shows a night. Garland was suffering from an abscessed tooth and rested for most of the day on January 24. One of Garland's cousins on her father's side from Louisville, Kentucky, Edwin Rion, and his family visited Garland and Rose on the 24th and attended one of their shows at Fort Knox. After the shows, Garland, Rose, and their entourage left on the 11:35 p.m. train for St. Louis, Missouri.

- **January 26, 1942: Fort Jefferson Barracks, St. Louis, Missouri**—The entourage arrived in St. Louis on January 25 and went to the fourteenth floor of their hotel, the Hotel Coronado, for a greeting party, "where the 19-year-old star's reddish hair and strikingly sensitive face was an immediate center of attention—especially for the army officers and favored enlisted men who were on hand as a greeting party." When asked whether she had any ambition in the theatre, Garland replied, "I don't inquire into that too much. They [MGM] have been awfully good to me so far, and I'll continue to do what they tell me. I know they have a program for me, which probably includes more mature and more serious parts as time goes on."[31] The papers noted that on the afternoon of Sunday, January 25, Garland disrupted a Millikin alumni meeting when she walked through the room where the meeting was being held, "followed by a group of soldier admirers and was on her way to another room where press photographers were to take pictures."[32] Garland and Rose had a camp tour at 2:00 p.m. and then ate dinner at 5:00 p.m. with the troops in one of the mess halls. That evening, the duo, along with the post's own band, gave two shows at the camp's Tent Arena, the first beginning around 7:00 p.m. Judging from the newspaper photos documenting the event, it looks as though they performed at two different venues at the camp.
- **January 27, 1942: Camp Robinson, Arkansas** (outside Little Rock)—Two-night engagement. On the 27th, Garland was photographed on stage at the camp with Rose at the piano, as well as signing autographs with Rose looking on.
- **January 29, 1942: Fort Worth, Texas**—The entourage was on its way to the final stop of the tour, Camp Wolters, just outside of Mineral Wells, Texas. Garland's train briefly stopped Thursday night (January 29) in Fort Worth, Texas, where Garland was photographed with MPs.

The *Fort Worth Star-Telegram* noted that she slipped through their "town" on her way to Mineral Wells, Texas (west of Fort Worth), arriving there without the usual fanfare: "Mineral Wells citizens chafed at the restrictions that kept them from ballyhooing the visit of one of America's most popular movie queens. But Miss Garland, her studio executives and USO officials had specified that there should be no blowing of trumpets when she arrived. She is here to entertain the soldiers and they were all asleep at camp when she arrived to get a brief rest in her hotel suite before a busy day."[33]

In 2009, local Mineral Wells resident Betty Scott remembered the day that her husband, who worked in the maintenance department at the Baker Hotel, got to meet Garland, who was staying in Room 703:

Lawrence wanted to see her, so the guys in the maintenance department said that the air conditioning in Miss Garland's room had a problem and they sent Lawrence up to her room to take care of it. Miss Garland was in her room at the time, as the story goes. She was sitting at her vanity in her dressing gown. She let Lawrence in to work on the air conditioning, and he got to see her in person. This was probably one of his greatest moments because he told everyone back then he got to see her in person and that she was very nice.[34]

- **January 30, 1942: Camp Wolters, Mineral Wells, Texas**—According to the papers, Garland led "2,000 Mineral Wells school children in a parade to the post office where each will buy a defense stamp in the interest of the Palo Pinto county campaign to sell defense bonds." Garland bought the first stamp.[35]
- **January 31, 1942: Camp Wolters, Mineral Wells, Texas**—The last day/night of the USO tour. During the day, Garland made a special appearance at the Station Hospital at 3:00 p.m. and also visited the camp's Service Club, recreation halls, "and other parts of the camp."[36] In the evening, Garland was a guest of honor at a ball that celebrated President Roosevelt's birthday. This was the first event at the camp's new $83K sports arena, which was opened early for this event (the arena was not officially dedicated until February).

The tour was a resounding success and a great achievement for Garland and Rose. At all the stops, the crowds were huge, and the press coverage was vast. Newspaper archives from the areas are filled with photos and articles about the size of the crowds and how much everyone loved Garland. The tour, while raising money and giving support to the troops, also gave Garland the chance to connect with her fans in a more personal way. She came across as the epitome of what American audiences wanted to see: a young lady who possessed a beautiful voice and demeanor—America's Sweetheart. The men in the camps and all throughout the war might have dreamed of sex with a femme fatale or glamour girl (Lana Turner, Rita Hayworth), but Garland was one of the girls they wanted to come home to, introduce to Mom and Dad, and then marry. She was relatable, an aspect of her stage presence that would draw millions to her. Even at this early stage in her career, audiences felt connected to her, as if she was one of them who just happened to be a movie star. Her friendly nature and natural vulnerability warmly embraced her audiences. The "Garland Cult" was growing.

Garland and entourage returned to Los Angeles on February 2, 1942, where she was immediately taken to the hospital for treatment of a case of strep throat. The newspapers ran news blurbs, usually with a photo of Garland, noting that she had collapsed from her illness while in Mineral Springs, Texas. Garland's physician, Dr. Barney Kully, "said that she would be forced to rest for 'a couple of weeks.'"[37] This is one of the times that's thought to be when Garland had her first abortion. While the papers ran the photos of Garland recuperating at home, the columnists mentioned the rumors that she was pregnant. John

Truesdell noted in his "In Hollywood" column that news of Garland and Rose "expecting the stork" was welcomed by the couple and their friends, "with the exception of her studio bosses, who have not yet adjusted to the fact that she is a married woman."[38] No one in the papers dared to mention abortion. Truesdell was right; MGM wouldn't have been happy with Garland being pregnant any more than they were about her being married. Having a child would, the studio executives assumed, ruin Garland's career, so they, along with her mother, convinced her to have the procedure. The abortion is assumed to be one of the reasons for the breakup of Garland's marriage to Rose. This is most likely true, although the marriage wouldn't have lasted in any case. Garland was too young, and Rose wasn't the kind of man who could shield her from her increasing insecurities, increasing battles with MGM, and increasing dependence on pills.

In the beginning, the marriage to Rose was a happy one. Garland went into it with all of her youthful energy and obsessiveness, as would any girl her age who is in love and newly married. Rose was a model train enthusiast, the kind that Walt Disney famously had at his home. Rose immediately installed a railway on the grounds of the home he and Garland bought and called it the "GarRose Railway." Garland gave him a miniature depot for the train as a wedding gift.

Garland enjoyed her new role as wife. She enjoyed entertaining, telling family friend Dr. Marc Rabwin and his wife, Marcella, "See, now I'm married, and I have my own house and servants."[39] She also enjoyed collaborating with Rose musically, which was the main thing they had in common. According to the August 25, 1941, issue of *Broadcasting Magazine*, when Rose turned the theme music to his weekly radio show *California Melodies* into the song "One Love," Garland contributed some of the lyrics, although the published song credited the lyrics to Leo Robin.

Unfortunately, Garland's schedule at MGM kept her from spending much quality with her husband. He was busy as well, and with her various evening commitments and his on the radio, there were many occasions when the only time they had together was at night. Rose was often up late working on his music, and Garland would be either just getting home or already home and, wanting to be a part of what he was doing, would deprive herself of the sleep she needed. It was noticed many times at the studio that she was coming in already fatigued. The pills helped. Allegedly, Rose wasn't concerned about Garland's habit because, at that time, it seemed as though practically everyone was taking pills to sleep and to get up, and no one thought they were damaging.[40] Garland was no different in that respect. The difference with Garland was that she was subjected to a much heavier workload than most. She suffered from insomnia, caused by her early years in vaudeville, when her schedule was the opposite of that at MGM. She also relied on the pills more and more as a crutch, not just physically but also emotionally. In modern parlance, she was "self-medicating."

The November 1942 issue of *Photoplay* magazine featured an extensive article by writer

Sally Reid titled "The Private Life of Judy Garland Rose." The headline for the article reads, "This is about two young people who love chocolate ice cream, and music, and each other—in a way that will best answer those rumors you've heard about them." The article features promotional photos that MGM took of the couple at home doing "homey" things, such as decorating (hanging a painting), reading, and playing music, and also out on the town. The "Gar-Rose Railway" was nicknamed by *Photoplay* as the "Honeymoon Express." The article is typical fan magazine fare of the time, with some truth and some fantasy. By this point, the separation rumors had already begun, and the article addressed it:

> *Rumors of their separation have continued to crop up, like mushrooms after a heavy summer rain—or like whispers after a quarrel. Judy says, "I won't give life or dignity to any such reports by denying them," and goes back to practicing her scales. Her music teacher is exacting. She must know her lessons or get her fingers thoroughly kissed between chords. Her teacher, of course, being her musician husband who is teaching his wife to read by note.[41]*

Another military honor came Garland's way in early February 1942, just after she returned to Hollywood from her USO tour and before she began filming the most patriotic (and one of the best) of her MGM musicals, *For Me and My Gal*. The 506th Paratroopers in Fort Benning, Georgia, named Garland their "Parabelle." The *Atlanta Consitution* printed a lengthy article about the honor:

> *A seasoned paratrooper has been through the fire—and he has stood the grueling test that has made him a man with a respectful attitude toward life. All that considered—what kind of girl does a paratrooper pick when he's trying to find the woman of his dreams?*
>
> *The boys of the 506th Parachute Regiment here at Fort Benning have given the answer. The paratrooper gives the brush-off to the sweater girl—like Lana Turner. There's not a spare nook in this brain for the willowy, slinking, sophisticated type—like Hedy Lamarr. Girls who peer around the corner of an ambush hair-do—like Veronica Lake—seem to get in the paratrooper's hair.*
>
> *The paratrooper likes his girls sweet. He likes a sweet face and a sweet voice and a girl who acts like a girl. That's why MGM's Judy Garland, the sweet and sprightly little singer of the movies—the girl who reminds the paratrooper of some particular little girl who lived down the street from title of the "parabelle" of the [sic] his house back home—won the 506th—without a dissenting vote.*
>
> *Every man in the 506th went for Judy Garland in a big way when the vote was taken on just who would sponsor this regiment as the date nears for a journey to a battlefront somewhere. They told Judy she had been elected unanimously, and Judy answered just as a young man likes to have a girl answer—simply and sweetly:*
>
> *"I'm glad to be your parabelle. Thank you for the honor. And if you ever come to Hollywood, be sure to drop in." She hit the nail on the head when she wired that message. Dropping in, agreed the*

troopers, is the way a paratrooper would call. . . . The men of the 506th made 1,750 jumps in three hours—averaging 10 jumps a minute. The air was filled with men from the 506th floating down from planes. And a lot of them plummeted to earth with pictures of Judy Garland pasted in the dome of their transparent plastic helmets—the paratrooper's streamlined version of a pin-up girl.

As soon as they can they'll be glad to drop in on Atlanta for another visit and in on Judy Garland for their first visit. They thank her for the honor.[42]

Garland was growing up, both in her personal life and on screen. The latter was progressing much slower than she wanted. Like any young woman her age (she was nineteen when she returned from the USO tour), she was more than ready to be an adult and to be treated as such, which meant she wanted to play adult roles. Her next film did just that, and it presented Garland

January 1942: Inside the *Modern Screen* fan magazine was an article about Garland and her mother (pictured here). Garland is wearing one of her outfits from *Babes on Broadway*. From the author's collection.

as a true triple threat, giving her full rein in showing off not just her singing but also her acting and dancing abilities. It was the best role of her career to date. The Garland career seemed to know no limits.

America's Singing Sweetheart was growing up, January 1942.
From the author's collection.

Small movie star trading cards (also sold as "cigarette cards") were popular with fans. This 1941 colorized version of an MGM promotional photo was one of many Garland trading cards.

CHAPTER 5

MGM's SINGING SWEETHEART GROWS UP

FOR ME AND MY GAL

Once recovered from her "strep throat infection," Garland went into production on her next film, *For Me and My Gal*, costarring with newcomer Gene Kelly in his screen debut. Garland first met Kelly a few years earlier when she was visiting New York in the spring of 1939 between her work on *The Wizard of Oz* and *Babes in Arms*. He was appearing in the musical *One for the Money*, and Garland went backstage to meet him. The two hit it off and became instant good friends. They spent some time together, non-romantically, with Kelly taking Garland "pub crawling" before she had to return to Hollywood.[1] Garland was sixteen during that 1939 trip, and if that story is true, she was underage, but she was Judy Garland and the two probably had no problem being admitted into pubs, or the pub crawling could have happened a couple of years later, when Garland returned to New York for a short vacation in late March 1941 accompanied by her mother. At that time, she saw Kelly again; he was now a star, starring in *Pal Joey*. Not long after, producer David O. Selznick signed Kelly to a movie contract, but he didn't do anything with him. Selznick loaned Kelly to MGM for *For Me and My Gal*, after which he sold Kelly's contract to MGM over the objections of some at the studio who didn't think Kelly was movie material. How wrong they were.

For Me and My Gal began production under the title *The Big Time*, which is the title used on all of the surviving *Daily Music Reports* that document the recording sessions from March through

June 1942, and it's the title of the original story the film is partly based on, written by Howard Emmett Rogers.

The film is centered around vaudeville singer/dancer Jo Hayden (Garland), her relationship with opportunistic Harry Palmer (Kelly), and their ups and downs. It opens with Jo and the act she's with, "Jimmy Metcalf & Co.," arriving in the fictional town of Clifton Junction, Iowa. Also arriving is fellow performer and opportunistic heel Harry Palmer, the headliner at the theatre they're all going to perform in. Jimmy Metcalf (George Murphy) is enamored of Jo but hasn't made his feelings known to her. Jo and Palmer do not initially hit it off, and after he buys the sheet music to the new song "For Me and My Gal" away from Jimmy, he attempts to convince Jo to leave the Metcalf act and join him as

MGM advertising artwork for *For Me and My Gal* (1942). From the author's collection.

a duo. After she bids her visiting brother, Danny (Richard Quine), goodbye at the train station, Palmer persuades Jo to join him for coffee, at which time he shows her the "knockout" song he purchased. The two then perform an impromptu song and dance and realize they're perfect for each other. Unbeknownst to them, Jimmy had been watching them from outside the cafe window, and back at the hotel, he persuades Jo to team up with Harry. Their goal is to be picked up by a big-time circuit and perform at the Palace Theatre in New York City, which was the ultimate goal of all vaudeville performers. Harry will say and do anything to play the Palace, including entering a relationship with big-time opera singer Eve Minard (Marta Eggerth). Jo is in love with Harry and goes to Eve's hotel to confront her. Eve tells Jo she has no designs on Harry and that he is an opportunist and Jo should not get involved with him. Jo tells Eve that she loves Harry. Eve devises a scheme to test Harry's loyalty to Jo and their act by pretending to offer him a job in her show, with one caveat: Jo is not included. Will he leave Jo and the act for Eve and her act? Jo is waiting at her hotel for Harry to return. At first, it seems that he will go with Eve, but then he realizes that he loves Jo. They decide to marry, but only after they have played the Palace. Jo's brother Danny shows up to tell her he's dropped out of medical school and joined the army. Jo and Harry are booked into the Palace only to find out that it's the Palace in New Jersey, not *the* Palace in New York. A representative from the real Palace sees their act in New Jersey and offers them a job. But right before their engagement, Harry is notified that he has been drafted. He tries to get out of it because it means giving up on the Palace. He can't get his draft delayed, so he purposely breaks some of his fingers on one hand, ensuring he won't have to go into the military and can play the Palace. Meanwhile, Jo receives a telegram telling her that Danny was killed in action. As she's grieving, Harry bursts in and tells her they'll be able to play the Palace after all. But Jo figures out that he took the coward's way out and, compounded by the recent death of her brother, tells Harry she never wants to see him again. They go their separate ways. Harry realizes what he has lost and tries to get into any branch of the military, but they won't take him. He runs into Sid Simms (Ben Blue), previously of Jimmy's act and a mutual friend with Jo, who also knew what he did and is now contributing to the war effort by performing and selling Liberty Bonds for the YMCA because he, too, is "4F" and cannot serve. Harry decides also to join the YMCA and goes overseas to help entertain the troops. While in Paris, Harry runs into Jo, who is performing at a YMCA concert. She still rebukes him, fighting her true feelings of love for him. Harry continues performing with Sid, and one night they end up close to the front and become involved in getting a medical convoy to safety. The military phone won't work to warn them, and although Harry tells the others he got through, he didn't. To face his lie, he goes out alone toward the front to warn the convoy. He succeeds, saves the convoy, and is wounded in action. The war ends, and Jo is finally performing for the troops at the Palace Theatre, patriotically in her "army" uniform. She sees Jimmy and Harry in the audience and rushes off the stage to reunite with Harry. She brings him on stage, and the two sing "For Me and My Gal" and then kiss. Fade out.

On paper, the plot might seem corny; however, the film is anything but. Only Garland could deliver lines like "I know you'll never make the big time because you're small time in your heart" or "He's right, and I love him. He's wrong, and I love him. It's no good" and make them completely natural and believable. Garland's all-too-often-ignored ability to act naturally and convincingly is displayed in full in *For Me and My Gal*. She gives a brilliant, nuanced performance, probably infused by her recent real-life tour of army camps and the affection and connection she felt with the soldiers she met and performed for.

It helps that, for once, director Busby Berkeley did not indulge in any of his elaborate production numbers. The musical numbers are organic to the plot, mostly taking place on stage but realistically, as they would in vaudeville. There are no stages that seem to go on forever here. *For Me and My Gal* is the best film representation of life in vaudeville during World War I. Part of that success was the contributions to the film by former vaudeville star Elsie Janis, who served as an uncredited technical advisor, most notably helping Garland with her performance style. The fact that Berkeley, Garland, and others came from vaudeville also helped. Berkeley later claimed this film was his favorite.

Originally, the film was to have two female leads, one a dancer (allegedly Eleanor Powell) and one a singer (Garland), but MGM's acting teacher and production assistant, Stella Adler, suggested combining the roles into one, knowing that Garland could handle the required level of singing, acting, and dancing. The change also created a believable love triangle between Garland, Kelly, and Murphy. Before Kelly's casting, Murphy had been cast in the lead as Harry. Murphy later said that the film was the one that disappointed him the most because he was relegated "to the part of the shnook who never gets the girl. Needless to say, I was disappointed. I'd begun to develop a phobia about this state of affairs."[2] Adler and one of the film's screenwriters, Fred Finklehoff, suggested Kelly for the lead. Garland also gave her encouragement. She famously helped him, showing him how to act in front of the camera and teaching him little tricks of the trade. He stayed a loyal and grateful friend, later commenting, "I owe her an eternal debt."[3] He helped Garland with her dancing, which was much more difficult than in her previous films. Although she wasn't a trained dancer, her natural musical instincts made her a quick study, and she could keep up with the likes of Kelly and, later, Fred Astaire, among others. Both men later said with awe that she could pick up steps faster than most trained dancers.

For Me and My Gal features one of the best scores of any of the great MGM musicals, and yet almost all of the songs are not original to the film but are songs from the World War I era. Roger Edens compiled a brilliant lineup of songs that fit the narrative while evoking the right amount of nostalgia and patriotism. The song list is like a Hit Parade of chestnuts from the era, such as "Smiles," "Oh, You Beautiful Doll," "Pack Up Your Troubles in Your Old Kit Bag and Smile, Smile, Smile," and "When Johnny Comes Marching Home," among others. Garland and Kelly performed an abridged but no less charming rendition of "When You Wore a Tulip" (the duo recorded the full version for Decca Records) and a fantastic song and dance to "Ballin' the Jack" that features some of the best dancing of Garland's career. Four new songs were written for the film: "I'm in Love with a Uniform," "Parlez-Moi D'Amour" (both of which were not recorded or filmed), "The Spell of the Waltz" (Eggerth's solo, recorded but unused), and "Three Cheers for the Yanks." Garland prerecorded the latter song, and it was planned to be the finale of the "YMCA Sequence," but it was never filmed. The prerecording survives, and while it's enjoyable, it's a bit too 1940s sounding, which is probably why it went unused. Garland also recorded the 1915 song "Don't Bite the Hand That's Feeding You," which was planned to follow her duet with Kelly, "When You Wore a Tulip," in the "Vaudeville Montage," but it was also deleted.

"After You've Gone" is another vintage song chosen by Edens as perfect for Garland. Written in 1918, the popular song is given the Garland treatment and is another of her great film ballads. She had first performed it on the *Shell Chateau Hour* radio show on August 6, 1936, with some of those special material lyrics added, again, by Edens. In *Gal*, the arrangement is similar but without the special material. Garland performs it beautifully, with the right amount of pathos at just the right moment, and she looks stunning in close-up. The song became as identified with her as "Over the Rainbow" or "The Trolley Song," and it's another one that she kept in her repertoire for the rest of her life, recording it twice for Capitol Records. It was a popular staple

138   CHAPTER 5

of her concerts and a part of the "playing the Palace" mystique that was created when she really did play the Palace in 1951, bringing vaudeville back to the theatre in a record-breaking run that was her first great comeback after leaving MGM. The decision for her comeback to take place at the Palace was based in large part on her effectiveness in *For Me and My Gal*. The decision makes sense. With this film, moviegoers got to see all of the adult Garland's talents on display. It's also our first glimpse of Garland the concert performer. When she sang "How You Gonna Keep 'Em Down on the Farm," her electric stage presence cast its magic spell on the audience of extras on the set (a rare thing indeed). It's a brief preview of the famous Garland stage presence that later captivated audiences in hundreds of concerts during her concert years.

The song and dance by Garland and Kelly to the title song became an instant classic, and after Garland's "After You've Gone," it's arguably the best number in the film. It's set early in the narrative in an empty late-night restaurant with just the owner present. Harry persuades Jo to listen to the song he purchased ("For Me and My Gal"), but he botches his vocals, which makes her laugh. She takes over the piano and begins the song solo, and then he joins her for a second chorus, leading to their dance. The sequence is choreographed in such an easy, natural manner that the audience forgets they're watching two of the greatest musical talents in the movies; rather, they become two vaudeville performers ad-libbing a song and dance. Garland and Kelly exude a warm, affectionate chemistry together. Their chemistry makes the sequence, and the sequence makes the film. We, as the audience, see their obvious love for each other, which makes the events that follow completely natural and believable. We root for them to find their happily ever after.

For Me and My Gal includes a fun anecdotal in-joke that MGM's publicity department circulated regard-

Garland and Gene Kelly perform the title song in *For Me and My Gal* (1942). From the author's collection.

MGM's Singing Sweetheart Grows Up 139

ing the "Doll Shop Sequence" early in the film. The syndicated article published in the spring of 1942 was headlined "Star's Childhood Dolly Makes Screen Debut."

> *Judy Garland's favorite doll of her "little girl" days will appear in a scene in "Me and My Gal."* [sic] *For a sequence in a doll shop, where Judy and George Murphy dance and sing the old favorite, "Oh, You Beautiful Doll," the "props" department was called upon to furnish various types of old-time dolls. Judy came to the rescue with her own cherished childhood dolly. It was one the young star had won in a contest sponsored by Mary Pickford many years ago.* [4]

In 1930, Garland (still Frances Gumm) was one of fifteen finalists out of twenty-seven thousand children who were up for a film contract with Paramount Pictures in the Prettiest Children contest in Los Angeles. All fifteen finalists were each given "a beautiful $150 doll by Mary Pickford."[5] Garland didn't win the contest or the film contract. No other information is known about Garland's association with it aside from the fact that she received a doll for her participation and that a photo of the finalists was published in the *Los Angeles Express*. The doll is the kewpie doll that Lucille Norman hands to George Murphy during the number. Kewpie dolls were popular in the early part of the twentieth century, beginning in 1912. It's the type of doll that would have been given out at a contest in 1930. The contest was also mentioned in two articles published in Garland's father's (Frank Gumm) hometown of Murfreesboro, Tennessee, with the headlines "Child of Former Citizen Stands High in Contest"[6] and "Child Known Here Wins in Contest."[7] Frank liked to promote his talented daughters, so he is probably the information source for the paper; it's highly unlikely that Murfreesboro would have been paying much attention to kiddie contests out west in Los Angeles.

Garland worked on *For Me and My Gal* from February 29 to July 29, 1942, a little over twenty-one weeks. She was out sick for at least sixteen days, which was low for a Garland film at the time, judging from her previous attendance records. The film premiered at the Astor Theatre in New York City on October 21, 1942, and went into general release on November 20, 1942. It's the first film in which Garland is billed solo above the title, and it's her first adult role. Audiences loved the film, making it one of the biggest hits of the year. On a cost of $802,980.68, it grossed $4,371,000.[8]

MGM heavily promoted the film. The studio's vice president of advertising and publicity, Howard Dietz, conceived the idea of having sing-alongs in various cities to raise money for the current war bond drives while simultaneously promoting the film. The first sing-along was in Times Square, New York, on October 21, 1942, coinciding with the film's opening at the nearby Astor Theatre. It was sponsored by the local YMCA (the YMCA is featured in the film). For the premiere, "ten large bells erected on the towering sign atop the Astor rang out the melody of 'For Me and My Gal' through a special public address system. The bells dangled approximately one hundred feet over Broadway. Each bell pealed out a tone for each of the ten syllables comprising the line, 'The bells are ringing for me and my gal.'"[9]

Garland performed in the sing-along in Pershing Square in Los Angeles on November 21, 1942, along with Douglas McPhail (her romance in *Little Nellie Kelly*), resulting in twenty-five thousand people crowding the square. The first half hour of the show was broadcast on the local radio, followed by a " transcribed rebroadcast over another outlet."[10] *The Showmen's Trade Review* detailed an example of one of the many nationwide promotional campaigns, this one in Toledo, Ohio, which featured the following: art breaks and advance promotions in papers within a fifty-mile radius of the city; fifteen radio spot announcement for three days before the film opened at the local Esquire Theatre; the local YMCA sent notices out; an "entire fleet of Buckeye News" trucks featured advertisements on both sides of their trucks; local music store window displays featured sheet music and posters; even visiting bandleader Joe Venuti and his orchestra played the title song and promoted the film during their engagement at the local Commodore Perry Hotel; and finally, five hundred reserved-table cards were used at the Willard and Secor hotels "and other prominent restaurants" that read, "Reserved for 'For Me and My Gal' starring Judy Garland. . . . Now Playing at the Esquire."[11]

Most of the critics loved the film, especially Garland's performance and the showcasing of her dancing abilities. However, Bosley Crowther of the *New York Times* wasn't as impressed:

> Miss Garland is a saucy little singer and dances passably. She handles such age-flavored ballads as "After You've Gone," "Till We Meet Again," and "Smiles" with Music-hall lustiness and sings and dances nicely with Mr. Kelly in the title song. She also teams with George Murphy to do quite well by "Oh, You Beautiful Doll!" But she is not a dramatic actress. She still sniffles and pouts like a fretful child. And Mr. Kelly, who has a dancer's talents, has been pressed a bit too far in his first film role. He has been forced to act brassy like Pal Joey during the early part of the film, and then turn about and play a modest imitation of Sergeant York at the end. The transition is both written and played badly. Mr. Kelly gets embarrassingly balled up.
> The songs are good, the story maudlin—that is the long and short of it. But maybe that was vaudeville. Two beers "For Me and My Gal."
> —Bosley Crowther, *New York Times*, New York, October 22, 1942

> Judy Garland, vocally and dramatically, has never been better than as the young vaudevillian who leaves George Murphy's act to team up with Gene Kelly.
> —Mildred Martin, *Philadelphia Inquirer*, Philadelphia, Pennsylvania, December 4, 1942

> Judy Garland has gone a long way since she was just a little girl singing. She has developed into an emotional actress of scope and power. But there's something about it all that bothered me. She's too thin, too finely drawn. Slow down, Judy!
> —Mae Tinee, *Chicago Tribune*, Chicago, Illinois, December 25, 1942

> Why can't we have more like this instead of so many war pictures that nobody wants?

Believe it was liked as well as any picture we have ever shown. The first picture we have run that gave us better receipts the third night than the second. We want many more like it.
—S. L. George, manager of the Mountain Home Theatre, Mountain Home, Idaho, *Motion Picture Herald*, April 24, 1943

The hit tunes of 25 years ago cast a spell of pleasant peace and contentment. And how that Miss Garland sings them! There isn't a better song-plugger in all of show business or a more captivating ingenue.
—Harold V. Cohen, *Pittsburgh Post-Gazette*, Pittsburgh, Pennsylvania, December 4, 1942

Judy looks thin and frail throughout the picture, but she seems to have developed enormously as an actress and entertainer since her last screen assignment. She projects the old melodies charmingly . . . and she also dances with grace.
Kate Cameron, *Daily News*, New York City, November 1, 1942

Judy Garland, as slim as an undernourished string bean, plays the role of this little vaudevillian with great flair, not only because of her singing of the old songs, which are many, but because of the emotional quality which she gives the playing. It's needless to say that Miss Garland is fresh and active and that she puts over a song better than most of her contemporaries with vastly more experience.
—Boyd Martin, *The Courier-Journal*, Louisville, Kentucky, November 27, 1942

A few of the reviewers noticed Garland's drastic weight loss. Her weight loss is most noticeable in the film during the "Ballin' the Jack" number, in which she's seen wearing shorts that show off her very skinny legs. For once, those around her encouraged her to eat and gain weight, which she did, and by the time she began *Presenting Lily Mars*, she was in a healthier state and quite lovely. It was during *For Me and My Gal* that MGM finally began to give Garland the glamour treatment, as reflected in her promotional portraits taken at MGM's famous photo studio at this time and going forward. These photos were also used in advertisements for beauty products. Her time as a cute example of teen fashion had ended. Now she was glamorous enough to sell Lux Soap and Max Factor makeup. MGM's singing ugly duckling had blossomed into a beautiful swan.

One aspect of *For Me and My Gal* that goes unnoticed is that Garland's character is ahead of her time (especially for the period portrayed, 1916–1918). Jo Hayden is an independent and strong woman who has complete agency over her own life. She has her own career and goals that are not dependent on a man's control or direction. She's working in vaudeville as part of a deal with her brother to put him through medical school and "then pay me back—with interest." He's thinking of quitting due to his perception that she shouldn't be working. "This is a fine time to quit in your last year. . . . Well, I'm not going to let you quit." Although she's helping her brother, she's not dependent on him or his success, as she makes clear in the rest of her response: "You're not working any hardship on me. . . . I love it; I'd be doing it anyway." Her focus isn't on finding

142   CHAPTER 5

a man to marry, either. She falls in love by chance. They both have the same dream, to play the Palace, but when he shows how reprehensible he can be, she tells him to leave and goes back out on her own.

Garland's professional activities outside of MGM during filming were minimal, with just two major radio appearances (*Command Performance No. 18* on June 18 and "The Chase and Sanborn Hour" on June 21) and two recording sessions for Decca Records, including recording two songs from the film duetting with Kelly, "For Me and My Gal" and "When You Wore a Tulip" (Garland didn't record a studio version of "After You've Gone" until 1955). Garland and Kelly's voices blended so perfectly that it's a shame they didn't record more studio duets. The Decca single "For Me and My Gal" was released in January 1943 and peaked at the number 5 spot on the Billboard chart in 1943, placing at number 19 for the entire year.

PRESENTING LILY MARS

Garland didn't have much time to rest on her accomplishments in *For Me and My Gal*. A month and a half before finishing her work on that film, she began work on *Presenting Lily Mars*. Although most of her recent films were produced by Freed, *Presenting Lily Mars* was produced by Joe Pasternak. Pasternak had recently moved to MGM from a successful producing career at Universal. He had made Deanna Durbin a star after she left MGM in 1936. MGM hoped he could do the same for their new young soprano, Kathryn Grayson, which he did. He would soon head a second musical unit at MGM, the "Pasternak Unit." It was second only to Arthur Freed's musical unit (the Freed Unit). The main difference between the two was that Freed's musicals usually had bigger budgets and were pushing the boundaries of the genre, with an emphasis on dance, while Pasternak's were lighter in tone, no less entertaining, with an emphasis on more simple storylines and an old-world charm. Pasternak preferred the operetta type of musicals and left the experimentation to Freed. Freed also had first dibs on the top musical stars at MGM, which were Garland, Kelly, Astaire, and Frank Sinatra, as well as the top people behind the camera. A friendly rivalry developed between the two units, which provided a lot of employment for MGM's musical staff. Both units shared one important quality, and that was the singular look and professionalism of the MGM Musical. The studio became known for its musicals, making most of the top musicals of the era and also making more than the other studios. When moviegoers went to see an MGM musical, they knew they were seeing the best. Each unit had a few misfires, but even those misfires were at least interesting in their own ways.

Within a short time frame (1941/1942), Garland first worked with the three MGM heavyweights who would come to her rescue, so to speak, in her last two years with the studio: Gene Kelly, Joe Pasternak, and Charles Walters. All three men adored her and helped her through the physically and emotionally rough period of those last years at the studio.

In *Presenting Lily Mars*, Garland is presented as a small-town young woman, just out of

This promotional spread published in the trade magazines in 1943 included Jacques Kaprilik's advertisement artwork for *Presenting Lily Mars* (1943) featuring Garland and costar Van Heflin. From the author's collection.

high school at around nineteen years old, whose goal is to go to New York and become an actress. Local boy John Thornway (Van Heflin) has become a big New York producer, and when he comes back for a visit, Garland's Lily Mars does everything she can to get him to see her act out scenes from Shakespeare and later an old-fashioned melodrama. After conspiring to make Thornway a captive audience of one, she hysterically proceeds to overact Lady Macbeth's sleepwalking scene, which doesn't endear her to him at all. She crashes his formal party, and he throws her out, but not before she gets the chance to sing (the swingy "Tom, the Piper's Son") and charm him, although he doesn't yet know it. She goes to New York and tries to get into his current production. His frostiness for her begins to melt, and he begins to fall for her, which doesn't make his current leading lady, Isobel Rekay (Marta Eggerth in the same basic role she had in *For Me and My Gal*), very happy. Misunderstandings ensue, and a jealous Isobel, temperamental diva that she is, leaves the production. Thornway decides to take a chance on Lily, giving her a crash course in acting. In a deviation from the usual overnight success story, Thornway realizes Lily isn't ready to handle a starring role. He convinces Isobel to return, and Lily is returned to the tiny walk-on role she previously had. Will she show up to play her tiny role, showing she's a true professional and she forgives Thornway? The film ends with a jump forward in time, revealing a theatre marquee displaying Lily's name in lights in a Thornway production, segueing into the film's finale production number, proof that Lily is at last a Broadway star.

The role of Lily Mars has a kind of duality regarding Garland's progression into adult roles. It's a bit of a step back from *For Me and My Gal*, but, even so, she's filmed and presented as a beautiful young woman and not Betsy Booth. At the beginning of the film, Lily Mars is closer in spirit to Garland's Penny Morris character in *Babes on Broadway*. Lily exhibits the peppy, bouncy personality of Garland's previous "Let's Put on a Show!" roles. After Lily gets to New York, she's the maturing, wide-eyed young Broadway hopeful, and then, at the end of the film, she's a Broadway leading lady. After her recent distressingly thin appearance in some of *For Me and My Gal*, Garland had put back on a few pounds, and it makes a difference. She looks lovely and healthy, sporting a contemporary early 1940s wardrobe and hairdo that enhances her natural beauty. "Gal pal" Betsy Booth was finally gone. In the film's finale, Garland is given the full MGM glamour treatment for the first time. She's shown with her hair up and wearing a beautiful black sleeveless gown. She dances with a new MGM contractee, dancer/choreographer (and soon-to-be director) Charles Walters, proving her dancing ability once again, with Walters as her partner to "Broadway Rhythm" and Tommy Dorsey and His Orchestra providing the musical backup on the soundtrack and the screen. The adult Judy Garland had arrived.

The musical numbers in *Presenting Lily Mars* are not as abundant as they had been in *For Me and My Gal*. Even so, Garland is still at her vocal best. In the aforementioned "Tom, the Piper's Son," she shows off her ability to swing effortlessly. The number is basically a "throwaway" song that isn't anything important aside from showing the audience for the first time that Lily can sing. It's made great by Garland's strong vocals and equally strong charm. She's obviously having fun. With Bob Crosby and His Orchestra as backup (the same Bob Crosby whose manager in 1936 didn't want his band listed on the Decca Records label "with this unknown singer"), Garland sings the ballad version of "When I Look at You" in a sweet, dreamy manner and then immediately follows with a satirical version that shows off her natural brilliance as a comedienne. She takes what could have been a forgotten slapstick routine and spins it into gold. Perhaps the most effective number is Garland's duet with actress Connie Gilchrist (dubbed by Mary Kent) as the stage manager Frankie. It's late at night, and newly arrived Lily has no place to go, so she plans to sleep the night in Thornway's theatre. The two bond over their love of show business, and Frankie begins to sing what had been her signature song when she was on the stage, the chestnut "Ev'ry Little Movement Has a Meaning of Its Own," during which Garland joins her. It's sparkling with warm charm. The surviving audio from the prerecording session on July 28, 1942, reveals that it was Take 7 that was used, with Kent telling Garland afterward, "It's been a great pleasure," in an admiring tone.

The film's finale, presenting Lily Mars as a successful musical leading lady, proved troublesome. Garland wrapped up work on the film in early November 1942, immediately going into rehearsals for her next film, *Girl Crazy* (1943), produced by the Freed Unit. Her last work on *Lily Mars* was taken up mostly by the original finale, "Paging Mr. Greenback." The number is a blatantly patriotic song telling people not to be a miser like "that old tightwad Mr. Greenback" and give to the war effort. The footage no longer exists, but the prerecording does. Surviving behind-the-scenes photos reveal a number crowded with dozens of extras in "everyday" dress in front of a backdrop of the US Capitol building that looks suspiciously like the one used in *Babes in Arms* (1939). In his autobiography, Pasternak claimed that friends of Garland's "arranged to see a rough-cut [and then] ran to Judy with wails of pain and distress, all aimed in my direction."[12] The implication was that those around Garland exerting influence (and there were many) felt that she should have been presented in a more glamorous manner. By "friends," Pasternak probably meant Freed Unit biggie Roger Edens and others. Edens created a new finale, almost ten minutes long, centered around his own composition, "Where There's Music," which included a medley of old songs that segued into the finale's big finale, "Broadway Rhythm." Rehearsals, prerecording sessions, and filming on the new finale lasted from February 20 to March 16, 1943.

Presenting Lily Mars was released on April 2, 1943, and was another success. Garland was more than proving herself to be the new musical leading lady at MGM. Critics and audiences liked the film, and while it isn't as well known today as Garland's blockbusters, it turned a tidy profit of over $2.2 million on a budget of $1,045,000. As late as January 1944, *Variety* listed it and *Girl Crazy* in their list of recent "Top Grossers of the [Holiday] Season." A sampling of the kind of reviews the film received:

> A top-flight production which figures to draw in every possible customer and send them home abrim with satisfaction. . . . Judy Garland is at her best, adding to her singing and youthful buoyance a poignancy that invests the role with sincerity.
> —uncredited review, *Showmen's Trade Review*, May 1, 1943

> Metro-Goldwyn-Mayer, which dotes on young Judy Garland, is again having her show off her best points in "Presenting Lily Mars," now at the Capitol. After having agreed so long on Miss Garland's blithe talents there is no point in disagreeing now. Miss Garland is fresh and pretty, she has a perky friendliness that is completely disarming, and she sings and dances according to the mood—sometimes raucous jive, sometimes sweet little ballads that turn out to be quite enchanting. No doubt about it, Miss Garland is a gifted young lady.
> —T. S., *New York Times*, April 30, 1943

GIRL CRAZY

Production of *Girl Crazy* began on November 30, 1942, which was immediately after the principal production of *Presenting Lily Mars* had wrapped. A month into production, Garland had

146

CHAPTER 5

a slight detour to the Pasternak Unit to film a guest appearance in the Gene Kelly/Kathryn Grayson musical *Thousands Cheer*. It was Garland's first time guesting as herself in a feature film and her first time in Technicolor since *The Wizard of Oz* in 1939. She sings "The Joint Is Really Jumpin' Down at Carnegie Hall" with classical pianist Jose Iturbi accompanying her on piano. She's sporting some serious red hair (MGM loved redheads), and the number, while peppy and of its time, doesn't really tax or show off her talents other than her voice, of course, and her ability to make a purse out of a sow's ear, musically speaking. *Thousands Cheer* was released on September 13, 1943. Garland's song proved to be prophetic. She really did have the joint jumpin' at Carnegie Hall when she gave her historic, still legendary concert there on April 23, 1961, forever immortalized on the Capitol Records recording that has never been out of print. If you want to know what Garland was like in concert, *Judy at Carnegie Hall* is the recording that captures that essence as best as any audio recording could.

Girl Crazy was the last of the Garland/Rooney "Let's Put on a Show!" musicals, their last time costarring together, and their last time on screen together until 1948's *Words and Music*. Garland guest starred as herself in one scene. The generally easy, happy time Garland had during *Presenting Lily Mars* evaporated on *Girl Crazy*. The director was again the taskmaster Busby Berkeley. There were several sporadic days in March, April, and May 1942 when Garland was out sick from the production of *For Me and My Gal*, usually three or four in a week's time, but there were no known serious fireworks between her and Berkeley. *Girl Crazy* was another story. It's unknown for sure, but it's possible that the abuse Berkeley heaped on Garland (and everyone else) in the early weeks of filming was due to his alcoholism. Berkeley went crazy rehearsing, staging, and shooting the "I Got Rhythm" number in late 1942 and early 1943. For nine grueling days, he filmed the number, working everyone to the edge of their last nerves. He was especially tough on Garland. "Your eyes! Your eyes! I want to see your eyes!" he would shout at her.[13] He was known to be hard on performers, but in this case, he went too far. He put her through take after take. What weight Garland had gained in the past year, she had lost and was again gaunt and unhealthy at just ninety-four pounds. Berkeley's callousness

Garland is given the full MGM glamour treatment in this photo taken during the last weeks of principal filming on *Presenting Lily Mars*, November 3, 1943. From the author's collection.

MGM'S SINGING SWEETHEART GROWS UP   147

didn't help. In the finished number, as seen in the film, she looks manic. She had sporadically used her prescription medicines for weight loss, sleep, and energy for the past several years, at least, and they continued to be a crutch to help her through the studio workload, starting one film before the last one was finished. Her schedule over the past year or two had been, with few exceptions, constantly working and performing in one way or another. Now it all came crashing down. At Berkeley's hands, she had a complete collapse. The event is one of the most well-known events in Garland's MGM career, usually used as an example of the studio's callous treatment of her. It was dramatized in the 2001 miniseries *Life with Judy Garland: Me and My Shadows* based in part on her daughter Lorna Luft's book. This was the first time that she had a collapse of this magnitude in front of cast and crew. It wouldn't be the last. On January 29, 1943, Garland's personal physician and Gumm family friend, Marcus Rabwin, confined her to bed and ordered her not to dance for "six to eight weeks."[14] Garland's mother, Ethel, told MGM that she could be back in three. Garland was back on the set on February 8, just ten days after the collapse. She was out sick on February 13, 17, and 18. The scenes being shot did not involve dancing. Then, on February 20, she found herself in music rehearsals for the revised finale to *Presenting Lily Mars*. The *Girl Crazy* production worked around her.

Due to Berkeley's behavior, "I Got Rhythm" alone made the film over budget by either $60,000 or $97,000, depending on which book you read. Edens had had enough:

> *The biggest fight I had with Berkeley's techniques, though, was on Girl Crazy. I'd written an arrangement of "I Got Rhythm" for Judy, and we disagreed basically about his presentation. I wanted it rhythmic and simply staged; but Berkeley got his big ensembles and trick cameras into it again, plus a lot of girls in Western outfits, with fringed skirts, and people cracking whips and firing guns all over my arrangement and Judy's voice. Well, we shouted at each other and I said there wasn't enough room on the lot for both of us. But he got his way, even though I persuaded him to cut some of the pistol shots. And I must say that this scene, with all those things I disliked, looked wonderful now on TV.[15]*

Berkeley got his way—briefly. He was soon fired, and Norman Taurog was brought in to direct the rest of the film, with Charles Walters handling the musical numbers.

Charles "Chuck" Walters had been a successful Broadway dancer/choreographer before going to Hollywood in 1942, landing at the RKO Studios. He wasn't happy with his experience and had planned to return to Broadway when Gene Kelly asked him to come over to MGM and help him with his big solo dance number (with chorines) that he was preparing for his follow-up to *For Me and My Gal*, the MGM adaptation of the Cole Porter Broadway hit *Du Barry Was a Lady*. Lucille Ball was his costar. Walters and Kelly had worked together in New York and were good friends. Walters came up with the idea of having Kelly sing the Porter hit "Do I Love You?" to Ball's character in her dressing room and then continue the song via dance out of the dressing room, through the backstage hallway, and into the nightclub audience, ending up on the nightclub stage. When he explained it to the film's producer, Arthur Freed, Freed said, "You think like a director, Chuck."[16] He ended up becoming one of MGM's top musical directors and directed two Garland films, *Easter Parade* (1948) and *Summer Stock* (1950).

After Berkeley's departure (his "I Got Rhythm" became the film's finale), Taurog and Walters guided the production with ease. In early May 1943, the production went to Palm Springs for location shooting. The time was spent on the "Dusty Road" set (as the production notes named the location in the desert they chose to use), filming Garland and Rooney performing "Could You Use Me?" The duet is classic Gershwin and is one of the best of the Garland/Rooney film duets, up there with "How about You?" and "Our Love Affair"; although it's a comic duet, it's no less well performed. The duo re-created their performance almost identically for Decca Records on November 4, 1943, part of the label's album of studio-recorded songs from the film.

The Gershwin score was arranged, scored, and performed to perfection. The film is based on the original 1930 Gershwin Broadway hit featuring Ethel Merman's star-making debut and also making a star of the play's supporting actress Ginger Rogers. The famous opening night pit orchestra included future jazz legends Benny Goodman, Gene Krupa, Glenn Miller, and Jimmy Dorsey. The show featured new songs that became standards, including "Embraceable You," "Bidin' My Time," "Sam and Delilah," "Could You Use Me?," and "I Got Rhythm." RKO turned it into a quickly forgotten movie vehicle for their comedy team, Wheeler and Woolsey. The Garland/Rooney film is the definitive version. The plot is a simple one: New York playboy Danny Churchill (Rooney) is sent to an all-male school out west in Arizona in an attempt to toughen him up and to keep him from his frivolous girl-chasing. He meets and falls for the only girl around, Ginger Gray (Garland), who works for the school's post office. She doesn't reciprocate his feelings at first. There are some typical fish-out-of-water comedy bits with Rooney, as well as some romantic obstacles. Then they find out that the governor plans to close the school due to low enrollment. Danny hits on the idea of having a Queen of the Rodeo contest to attract attention for the school. To get people interested in the contest, he woos the governor's pretty daughter. This situation creates the usual romantic mishaps, but all works out in the end, and, surprise, the new enrollments are from girls. They decide to make the school co-ed. The film ends with Berkeley's "I Got Rhythm" number.

Walters's staging of the musical numbers brings the legendary Gershwin score to life. Garland's vocals are heavenly, giving Walters a lot to work with. As Clive Hirschorn notes in his book *The Hollywood Musical* about Garland's vocals, "It must be said, Gershwin never had it so good."[17] "Embraceable You" centers around her character's birthday. The male students present her with a piano, and she plays and sings the song, which becomes a charming dance number with the boys. Walters himself, in a cameo, takes over and dances with Garland. It's amusing to see the much more mature Walters show up out of nowhere among the very-young-looking college boys. He stands out, looking more like one of the school's teachers than one of its students. The "Bidin' My Time" number gives Garland a chance to show some comedy while performing

MGM'S SINGING SWEETHEART GROWS UP   *149* with some of the boys in a humorous and purposely lazy style. At one point, she mugs directly into the camera, letting the audience in on her enjoyment. By far, the best Garland number is the ballad "But Not for Me." She not only sings it perfectly but also acts it. All the heartache and disappointment we've all felt at one point or another is brought to life in her subdued and yet still gut-wrenching emotional rendition. It's true; Gershwin never had it so good.

Girl Crazy was another big hit. Even with Berkeley going over budget, the film cost just under $750,000 and turned a profit of more than $3 million. The reviews were again stellar.

> And with Judy, who sings and acts like an earthbound angel, to temper [Mickey's] brashness—well, they can do almost anything they wish, and we'll like it even in spite of ourselves. . . . [Mickey] does a hep-cat hoedown with Miss Garland in the finale that must have caused a minor earthquake. Amid these frantic shenanigans Miss Garland's songs, such as "Biding My Time," should sooth [*sic*] even the most savage breast; of all the child prodigies of Hollywood, Miss Garland has outgrown her adolescence most gracefully and she still sings a song with an appealing sincerity which is downright irresistible.
> —T. S., *New York Times*, December 3, 1943

> "This One's Got Rhythm." Here's a musical for showmen to tell the juniors about and get out of their way. . . . It has Judy Garland matching Rooney in their gag sequences, ditto their romantic interludes, and singing songs the way they were born to be sung.
> —William R. Weaver, *Motion Picture Herald*, August 7, 1943

> Judy sings as charmingly as ever and her voice enriches the memorable Gershwin score.
> —uncredited, *Showmen's Trade Review*, August 7, 1943

Notably, the manager of the Paramount Theatre in Seattle, Washington, Dean Gross, created an extensive advertising campaign for *Girl Crazy* that was on par with anything MGM could create. It included special screenings for "Honor Pass" students at the local schools, advertised via four thousand printed heralds and six thousand "Boy and Girl Date Cards" that were distributed at schools and a local football game; elaborate window displays at eleven Stetson store outlets; a Girl Crazy Sundae; stickers on the windows and mirrors of twenty-two chain drug stores; a sneak peek in the local *Seattle Guide* pocket publication; having the sales force of the Harper, Meggee, Inc. record distributor push the sales of Garland, Tommy Dorsey, and Gershwin records; and, of course, lots of newspaper advertisements.

During the time Garland was filming *Girl Crazy* as well as the new finale for *Presenting Lily Mars*, she and Walters were seen out together in the Hollywood social scene. The news broke in early January that she had separated from her husband, David Rose, with the official separation announcement on February 2, 1943. The marriage had been over for a while, and the couple had already been separated for some time. In the 1970s, Walters was interviewed by the BBC. He said he had thought about marrying Garland but was still new to Hollywood and MGM, and

150   CHAPTER 5

MGM advertisement for the last of the Garland/Rooney "Let's Put on a Show!" musicals, *Girl Crazy* (1943). From the author's collection.

he feared he would be "Mr. Judy Garland" rather than his own person.[18] Walters was gay and as open about it as one could be in the studio system in Hollywood. He was a safe date for Garland, who had her own fair share of romances with straight men and probably welcomed having a friend to go out with without expectations, allowing her to be herself. His comments decades later imply that he toyed with the idea of entering a "lavender marriage," which is what most gay men did in that era in Hollywood. Lavender marriages were arranged between a gay man or woman (anyone in the public eye, whether star, director, or otherwise) and a spouse of the opposite sex to avoid gossip and scandal. In modern parlance, the spouse would be the "beard." Many people engaged in such marriages to keep their careers. In hindsight, it seems callous of Walters that he could think so little of Garland's feelings to use her as a "beard" in such a flippant manner, basically to get ahead. It's more than a little presumptuous of him to think she would be naive enough to agree, presumptuous enough that he was still talking about it decades later. Regardless, Walters and Garland remained friends both professionally and personally for the rest of their lives.

When it came to romance, Garland was the opposite of how she was as a performer. She had a natural genius for performing, but in affairs of the heart, she was usually lost. By this point (1943), she had matured and didn't obsess as much over men as she previously had, but that's a low bar. A normal obsession to Garland would be super-obsession to the average person. In the article "The Real Me" written by Garland for *McCall's* magazine, the August 1957 issue, Garland said of her life with David Rose:

> *Even before I met David, I had found the only way I could keep my weight down was to take pills. Diets are fine if you can stay with them—which I couldn't. It was some time before I learned that the*

pills I was taking can be very dangerous. On top of this, I had trouble sleeping. So I also took pills to put me to sleep. A close friend of mine once said I went to sleep with pills and woke up with them too, and he was pretty nearly right. The sleeping pills I was taking were creating a tremendous strain on my nervous system. I wanted to be slim and lovely. I wanted to be calm and placid. And I wanted to sleep nights. There's a pill for every ailment, and I found them all. I was in this mixed-up state when David and I were divorced. [19]

At the time of her official separation from David Rose in the spring of 1943, Garland embarked on two of her biggest love affairs, one that was an intense but brief affair and one that had a profound effect on her life.

TYRONE POWER

The intense affair Garland had was with 20th Century Fox star Tyrone Power, which began in late 1942. The two were still married (Garland to Rose and Power to French actress Annabella), but that didn't stop them from spending as much time together as possible. They fell madly in love. Garland was living in an apartment on Sunset Boulevard where she entertained Power. Not yet twenty-one, she still retained some of her teenage romantic notions, saving corks from the bottles of champagne they shared together and saving the champagne glasses he used. [20] She hoped he would leave his wife to marry her. He gave her a copy of the romance novel *Forever* and told her they should star together in a film adaptation. She confided in her acting coach at MGM, Lillian Burns, who promptly warned her that Power's intentions were not serious. He handed out that book and spiel to other girls. But Garland was undeterred and with good reason. Power was, in fact, also in love with her. During their romance, he was sent to the Marine Officer Candidate School at the Marine Corps Base Quantico in Virginia, near Washington, DC. Garland sent him many passionate love letters, including one that was fifteen pages long. [21]

In an apparent effort to force his hand, Garland told Power that she was pregnant, so he broached the subject of divorce with Annabella, who gave him a flat "no." Whether Garland was actually pregnant is unknown. Some biographers claim she was and that MGM paid for an abortion, which, if true, would make it her second. Others claim she used the threat of pregnancy to get Power to do what she wanted. This latter scenario is most likely the truth. At this time, Garland was known for saying and doing anything to get what she wanted. She was very persuasive, especially when it came to romance. People who grow up insecure in their appearance because of being teased or bullied oftentimes will use sexual conquest as a means of getting self-validation that they are, indeed, desirable. They don't see it as using someone or possibly hurting them. Judging from what Garland's contemporaries have said about her actions during this time and what's already been written, it appears this was at least part of what drove her to act the way she did. Her future makeup artist and good friend, Dottie Ponedel, later explained:

She didn't care. You know, she wanted fun. She wanted to have a good time. And anybody she saw
that she wanted, whether it was your husband or whether it was your sweetheart, if she wanted him,
she'd get him. Cuz it happened right here in this house. She tried to get a sweetheart of mine, but it
didn't work, and she was so mad—I'll never forget it—she said, "He's chicken!"[22]

Annabella flew to DC to talk to Power in person, which he mistook for her having a change of heart and would agree to the divorce. He told Garland to fly to New York, where he would meet her, and they could finally be together. But Annabella was not budging. Garland was defeated. At least, that's according to biographer Gerald Clarke. There are no records that prove that Garland flew to New York "at the end of May," as Clarke claimed. Principal filming on *Girl Crazy* ended on May 19, 1943, so it's possible that Garland could have flown to New York. Clarke also claimed Garland returned to Hollywood from that trip just a few days before her birthday on June 10. The timeline doesn't add up. By the time she had her birthday, she had already been involved with Joe Mankiewicz for some time, long enough for him and his friends to assemble a comical birthday record for her. The two romances did overlap, but the timeline was different. The real final blow in the Garland/Power romance came from Garland's close friend and neighbor, Betty Asher. She told Garland that Power was sharing the contents of Garland's letters with his fellow Marines. Garland was devastated, and that was the end of the affair. Power remained married to Annabella until 1948.

Betty Asher was more than just Garland's friend and neighbor. She was also her publicity aide, assigned to Garland in 1939 when the Shaw "romance" began. What Garland didn't know until much later was that Asher was a studio spy. She had been assigned to Garland by MGM not just as an aide but also to report back on Garland's activities. Asher, as the daughter of a producer for Carl Laemmle, had been a part of the Hollywood world her entire life. She was also the lover of MGM vice president Eddie Mannix. Mannix and MGM's head of publicity, Howard Strickling, were the studio's "fixers"; they fixed all manner of problems and crises that happened to the studio's stars, keeping their sometimes criminal behavior out of the headlines (usually) and out of jail by any means. They also controlled the love lives of their stars, especially when they were carousing with people the studio disapproved of. Garland was not immune. She allegedly had an affair with MGM star Spencer Tracy in 1937 that the studio had to step in and "fix."[23]

Asher became Garland's good friend and confidant while acting as a personal assistant and performing those publicity duties. The Power "letter reading" incident didn't actually happen. Asher concocted it to end the affair on orders from Mannix. It was no accident that Garland took an apartment in the same building as Asher. Garland, no doubt, didn't think anything nefarious was going on, but for Asher, it was an easy way to keep close tabs on one of MGM's biggest moneymakers. It's been written that Asher also encouraged Garland to drink in an attempt to get more information out of her if she were drunk.[24] Asher remained a part of Garland's life for several years, accompanying her on the extensive USO tour in September 1943 and even serving as Garland's maid of honor in her marriage to Vincente Minnelli in 1945. It wasn't too long after that when Garland finally found out, or figured out, Asher's true intentions, which was another devastating blow. "She gave a report to the studio office every week on the people I saw, what I ate, what time I came in at night, and what time I got up in the morning. I can remember crying for days after I found out what she was doing to me."[25]

JOE MANKIEWICZ

Joe Mankiewicz first saw Garland perform at the Wilshire Ebell Theatre in 1934 when he was a new writer at MGM. Like everyone who saw her at that time, he was enchanted. When they became lovers nine years later, he was a well-respected writer and producer. Like almost everyone in Hollywood, male or female (especially female), Garland was dazzled by and infatuated with Mankiewicz's charm and intelligence. Her social circle had already been expanding to the enlightened and creative worlds of people who were arriving at MGM, mostly to the Freed Unit, from the more sophisticated Broadway scene. With her natural gifts for wit and her intelligence (she would memorize dialog and lyrics in seconds and could impersonate anyone), Garland fit right in. She was a popular party guest and thrived in that witty and creative social atmosphere. Mankiewicz introduced her to a broader social scene with even wittier and more intelligent people. For her birthday on June 10, 1943, he and Dore Schary (the same Dore Schary who would be instrumental in Garland's release from MGM in 1950) spearheaded the writing and performing of a satirical sketch titled "The Life of Judy Garland" that featured Mankiewicz and Schary along with Danny Kaye, Keenan Wynn, and Van Johnson. The group performed it for Garland in her Westwood home. Mankiewicz and Schary did their homework, noting the name of Garland's parents' early vaudeville act "Jack and Virginia Lee" (making a joke out of confusing Virginia Lee and Ethel Gumm) and impersonating Baby Gumm's stage debut singing "Jingle Bells" and ringing her bell. The performance was recorded (probably by Garland's in-home equipment), and the record has survived, revealing the sketch as an amusing and purposely silly retelling of Garland's rise to fame. Apparently, word got out about the sketch because, a month later, a syndicated article circulated to the newspapers reported on the event.

Frivolity aside, the affair had become serious, although Mankiewicz was in no position to marry. As much as they felt for each other, the relationship couldn't last. Mankiewicz's wife had recently suffered a breakdown and was a patient at the Menninger Clinic in Topeka, Kansas, so divorce was out of the question. And while Garland was as in love with him as she had been with Artie Shaw (possibly more), he didn't feel the same way about her. He adored her, saying, "I wasn't in love that way. I was in love—and I know this is a terrible analogy—the way you love an animal, a pet."[26] He firmly believed in psychoanalysis, and in Garland, he saw a woman who, however talented, sharp, and intelligent, was in desperate need of therapy. She had serious issues and was incredibly insecure, still immature emotionally, and didn't seem to have any control over her life. Garland was known as a funny storyteller, and she would embellish her stories for better effect. Mankiewicz thought that she didn't just embellish stories but that she lied too much about everything. He saw that most of her deep insecurities were tied to her complex relationship with her mother, including, for example, Garland knowing that she wasn't wanted and even that she was the wrong sex (she was named Frances because Frank and Ethel wanted a Frank Jr.). Then there were her stories about Ethel's cruel treatment of her during those years in Lancaster when Ethel used her as a pawn in her arguments with Frank. Mankiewicz convinced Garland to seek out therapy. Garland agreed to have some sessions with Dr. Karl Menninger, who was visiting from the Menninger Clinic. Dr. Menninger had treated Mankiewicz's wife, so, naturally, Mankiewicz thought he could help Garland. However, Dr. Menninger saw patients exclusively in Topeka. He recommended Dr. Ernst Simmel, who had studied with Sigmund Freud himself. Garland began to see Dr. Simmel regularly, at least five mornings a week. Her sister Virginia, who was now employed at MGM as a script girl, usually drove her to the appointments and waited in the car to then drive to the studio.[27] Initially, Garland would embellish or make up stories to entertain Dr. Simmel rather than open up to him. She thought she was fooling him, but, of course, she wasn't.

Mankiewicz's influence on Garland extended beyond her mental health. He felt that MGM was wasting her, putting her in frivolous roles that barely tapped her deep well of talents. He encouraged her to assert herself at the studio and in her personal life. His influence was such that both Ethel and MGM were alarmed to the point that it became one of the few times MGM actually worked *with* Ethel rather than either ignoring her or banning her from the lot. The romance was bad enough, but the trips to the psychiatrist were too much. As with all of her affairs, the more Ethel tried to stop Garland, the more she pushed Garland further into the relationship. The studio confronted Mankiewicz. He was on the train back to Hollywood after visiting his wife at the Menninger Clinic in Kansas, and Mayer and Strickling were on the same train. They found out he was on board, and Mayer arranged to meet with him, at which time he berated Mankiewicz for having an affair with Garland, who was much younger than him, and exerting influence over her. Mankiewicz replied, "It's none of your business." Mayer hit the roof. "I'm head of the studio!" he bellowed. Mankiewicz responded, "Not at all; you're not talking like the head of the studio; you're talking like a very jealous old man!" The two shouted at each other, and Mankiewicz stormed out of the train car.[28]

The event on the train would have gotten just about anyone else at the studio immediately fired. But Mayer's allegiance was to MGM first, and he knew Mankiewicz was one of Hollywood's top writers/producers/directors. It all came to a head sometime in the late spring or early summer of 1943. Mankiewicz was called into Mayer's office. Eddie Mannix was there, as was Garland's mom. Mankiewicz was ordered to end the affair. There was a lot of shouting by Mayer, Mankiewicz, and Ethel. According to Mankiewicz in a 1978 television interview:

> It was just a screaming fight. The mother got hysterical, Mayer got hysterical. "The idea that MGM movie stars are crazy?" he said. "They're lunatics? How can [you] do this? All this girl needs is a

MGM'S SINGING SWEETHEART GROWS UP

155

mother's love, and there's the mother; how can you deny this?" And tears are rolling down his face. He must have hated his mother. And the mother is saying, "I know exactly what to do with her; you just lock her in a closet. What the girl needs is discipline." And I kept saying, "Look, the girl needs help, and Dr. Karl Menninger said if you'll give me a year, it can straighten out, but the longer you go, the more difficult it's going to be, and there'll come a time when it's no. It's not going to happen."[29]

Garland's sister Virginia lived down the street from the house Garland was living in at the time. Due to her proximity to Garland's home, Virginia was often called on to be a go-between in the battle between Garland and their mother. In the early 1970s, she was interviewed by Garland biographer Gerold Frank. She told the story that one day, Garland told her she was pregnant with Mankiewicz's baby. This conversation apparently happened after the blowup between Mankiewicz and the studio and after he told Garland (according to what she told Virginia) that she should start seeing other men. "I think it might be better if we're not together so much," he said. Garland tried dating other men, and then she told Virginia she was pregnant with Mankiewicz's baby. Virginia convinced Garland to let him know, and Mankiewicz arranged a train trip to New York to visit a doctor "who will take care of me." The reasoning for going to New York was that Garland was afraid that word would get out if she went to a local doctor. Garland and Virginia told Ethel they were going to New York for Garland to audition "for a big radio program." Ethel took the bait. The sisters went to New York, and Mankiewicz had Garland go to a doctor friend. She was tested, and it turned out she wasn't pregnant after all. Mankiewicz bid them a stiff but courteous goodbye. Virginia got the impression that Mankiewicz could not forgive Garland for the false alarm, indicating that he thought it was a ruse on Garland's part. He gave her the silent treatment when she tried to call him multiple times. Whatever anger she might have had subsided because he and Garland would later renew their romance briefly while she was dating Vincente Minnelli.

The exact dates of Garland and Virginia's quick trip to New York are unknown. She was quite busy after finishing *Girl Crazy* on June 9, 1943, going to Philadelphia, Pennsylvania, a few weeks later for her concert debut, which was followed by some time in New York (appearing on *The Pause That Refreshes on the Air* radio show broadcast from New York), which could be the trip Virginia was talking about, although that was not a spur-of-the-moment trip, but rather a short stay in New York before Garland went on a short tour of army camps in New York, New Jersey, Indiana, and Pennsylvania, immediately followed by a second USO tour in the fall and then, finally, the early weeks of production on *Meet Me in St. Louis*. There is nothing in that film's production notes about Garland being in New York for what would have been more than a week (taking into account the train time plus a day or two's stay). However, there's no reason to doubt the events happened. Garland later told her daughter Liza Minnelli a very romanticized version of her trip to New York to see Mankiewicz, complete with movie romance imagery such as the two going on a carriage ride in Central Park.

Garland's first time in concert at the Robin Hood Dell in Philadelphia on July 1, 1943. From the author's collection.

CONCERT DEBUT

On July 1, 1943, Garland made her concert debut at the Robin Hood Dell in Philadelphia. Garland was backed by an orchestra conducted by Andre Kostelanetz, with her piano accompaniment provided by Earl Brent. After signing with MGM, she appeared on stage in various movie theatres and other venues during promotional tours for some of her films, at industry events, and at army camps, but this was her first in-concert event as an adult. The *Philadelphia Inquirer* reported that the concert would consist of Kostelanetz opening with a "Damnation of Faust Suite" by Berlioz followed by Strauss's "Emperor Waltz."[30] Then Garland would come on and sing a program put together by Roger Edens and arranged by MGM's top musical arranger, Conrad Salinger:

- Gershwin Medley ("Someone to Watch Over Me," "Do, Do, Do," "Embraceable You," "The Man I Love," and "Strike Up the Band").
- Kostelanetz performed a "Symphonic Synthesis" of "Porgy and Bess" arranged by Robert Russell Bennett from the Gershwin score.
- Garland returned with a medley of movie hits ("For Me and My Gal," "You Made Me Love You," "It's a Great Day for the Irish," "Our Love Affair," "I'm Nobody's Baby," and the complete "Over the Rainbow").
- Garland then encored with "The Joint Is Really Jumping Down at Carnegie Hall," followed by a finale encore, "But Not for Me."

The concert was a triumph for Garland and Kostelanetz. The newspaper reports in the following days were full of praise. Samuel L. Singer of the *Philadelphia Inquirer* reported:

"She's just as sweet as she is in the movies!" That was the unanimous verdict of the all-time record crowd last night at Robin Hood Dell; regarding Judy Garland, pert and pretty miss from Hollywood who sang for the first time with a symphony orchestra.

It was estimated that 15,000 squeezed their way inside the Dell, with as many more unable to gain admission.

Miss Garland was radiant in a transparent pale blue organdy dress with silver spangles, a small bouquet of white flowers at her waist, her reddish golden hair shining in the stage spotlights. She was cheered by her admirers outside the Dell fence when her car drove in the private entrance; she was cheered again at every appearance on the stage, and hearty applause always drowned out the final notes of each selection.

Miss Garland's accompanist, Earl Brent, did the boogie-woogie last night. Judy really cut loose here, and apparently enjoyed it as much as the audience, for she said, "I think it would be sorta fun if we did the last number over again." In the encore she substituted the words, "Robin Hood Dell" once for Carnegie Hall. Another encore was Gershwin's "But Not For Me."

Andre Kostelanetz conducted, and contributed some worthy orchestral selections, even though the audience lived only for Judy.[31]

The article also noted that Garland was initially nervous but found her footing with "Strike Up the Band," during which "Miss Garland really injected all that personality which made her a leading screen songstress."

On the same day, the paper published a second uncredited article that gave data about how "Judy Garland Sets New Dell Record." The article noted that the Dell's manager, David Hocker, had to turn away fifteen thousand "devotees of swing" and that "at least an equal number, according to Park Guard Lieutenant John Beutler, sat on the grass and in vacant parking lots on adjoining hillsides." The lines began to form three and a half hours before concert time: "By trolley and on foot they came, the ant-like lines increasing every minute." The crowd inside was so big that those standing were pushed to the front of the edge of the orchestra pit, blocking visibility for those in the seats. Hocker went on stage to "appeal for cooperation," pointing out the safety violations, but it didn't work. "Apparently no one dared to violate the OPA's ban on pleasure driving, or if they did they made sure their offense was well concealed," said the paper, which noted that no OPA agents were on hand to "check possible violators." OPA was the new federal Office of Price Administration created by an Executive Order given by President Roosevelt in August 1941. Its purpose was to put a ceiling on the prices of most goods and to institute rationing of goods (which began in May 1942). The paper's comment about a ban on "pleasure driving" was a topical joke about how it seemed like everything was rationed for the war effort, even the act of having fun. Another paper said Hocker tried to clear the aisles twice "but gave up when hundreds pushed to the orchestra pit." Garland had been "nearly mobbed by autograph seekers during the afternoon rehearsals." Prior to the performance, Garland arrived by sneaking unnoticed through the press gate.[32]

All of that information is important because it's the first documented instance of the unique cult-like effect Garland had on audiences as a live performer, even this early in her career. She had already dazzled audiences as a young girl and as a teen in her vaudeville years just before signing with MGM, but this is a clear example of what would come later after she left MGM and began her "Concert Years" in 1951, which solidified her status as an entertainment legend. Garland mesmerizing her audience just by walking out on the stage was written about at length in contemporary articles and reviews. Her stage presence was spoken of with awe, and experiencing it was akin to a religious experience. For many of her most ardent fans, it was. Hence, the term the "Garland Cult" was commonly used long before her death.

Two days after the concert, Garland was in New York and appeared on *The Pause That Refreshes on the Air* radio show accompanied by Kostelanetz. She sang "That Old Black Magic" (which she recorded for Decca Records on July 26, 1942), "This Is the Army Mr. Jones," and "Over the Rainbow." The concert wasn't recorded, but the recording of this show survives. "Over the Rainbow" from this radio show is the only extant recording of Garland with Kostelanetz performing one of the concert songs using the same arrangement, giving us an idea of how the concert might have sounded.

As triumphant as the Robin Hood Dell concert was, MGM did not allow Garland the chance to repeat the in-concert success for the rest of her tenure at MGM. Although she almost did. In August 1945, when Garland and her husband, Vincente Minnelli, were in New York during their honeymoon, they met with executives at Radio City Music Hall and signed a contract for her to appear there in concert. There are photos of Garland, Minnelli, MGM producer Arthur Freed, and Radio City Music Hall executive Gus Eyssell having a meeting and of Garland signing the contract. Unfortunately, the concert never happened. No information is known about what became of the contract, but it's safe to assume MGM most likely paid off Radio City.

RETURN TO THE TROOPS

Garland didn't waste time standing on her laurels. The day after the concert, she arrived in New York City, where she was, according to the *Motion Picture Daily*, paid $5,000 each for three radio shows before going on another USO tour of army camps, this time sponsored by the USO Camp Shows, Inc., and the Post Special Service Office.[33] The ten-camp tour was in the tristate area of New York, New Jersey, and Pennsylvania. Garland was accompanied by her manager, Melvin Heyman, and her mother, Ethel. *Variety* reported that when Garland arrived in New York, she checked in with MGM vice president Howard Dietz, who assigned Si Seadler to accompany her with the following instructions: "1, You are to act as official dancing partner; 2, you are to limit your attentions to the duration of the orchestra; 3, when the music stops you are to put her back into circulation; 4, I shall require a complete report on all eventualities." *Variety* joked, "Dietz is still waiting for the report."[34]

First Sergeant John P. Blazetic presents Garland with a bouquet of flowers after her performance at the Carlisle Barracks, Pennsylvania, part of her extensive tour of army camps, July 19, 1943. *Photofest*.

- **July 8, 1943: Fort Dix and Camp Kilmer, New Jersey**—Garland performed at Fort Dix during the day and then gave two shows in the evening at Camp Kilmer. Earl Brent accompanied her on the piano. About the Camp Kilmer show, the *Courier News* noted that "Miss Garland will intersperse her songs with soldier banter and will invite members of the audience to participate in the program."[35]
- **July 9, 1943: Camp Shanks, Orangetown, New York**—Garland performed one show at the camp's "Victory Hall" at 8:00 p.m. Her appearance competed with her own film, *Presenting Lily Mars*, which was playing that same night in two theatres at the camp.
- **July 10, 1943: Fort Hancock, New Jersey**—Garland became the "New Sweetheart of Sandy Hook" when she performed an hour-long show in the camp's Theatre #2 "before a packed audience" and was photographed with the camp's general, General Philip S. Gage.[36]
- **July 16, 1943: New York**—Garland had just returned to New York for a break before heading out for the last half of the tour when she went to the News One and Three Color Studio, where she posed for color photos, one of which made the cover of the weekly *Sunday Magazine*. Columnist Julia McCarthy was at the photo shoot to interview Garland and her mom, Ethel, who said of the tour, "Camp shows, every night, and a bad cold. . . . Done seven of them for the USO around New York and it'll be a dozen by the time we get home."[37]

CHAPTER 5

- **July 19, 1943: Carlisle Barracks and New Cumberland, Pennsylvania—** Garland arrived as scheduled in Harrisburg, Pennsylvania, at 2:00 p.m., but instead of heading directly to the Carlisle Barracks to sing for bedridden soldiers and have supper in one of the enlisted men's mess halls, she rested. On her way to Carlisle, she stopped at the Army Service Forces Depot (now known as the New Cumberland Army Depot) in New Cumberland, Pennsylvania, which is just outside of Harrisburg. That stop, and the late start, made her ninety minutes late for a scheduled mid-afternoon appearance at the campus of the Carlisle Medical Field Service School (at Dickinson College), where six hundred Air Corps men, "and as many townspeople, had waited patiently since 5 o'clock." She had been scheduled to sing as well as visit with patients in the station hospital and have supper in one of the enlisted men's mess halls. She only had time to make a quick statement before being taken to the Carlisle Barracks.[38] According to the April–August 1943 edition of the school's *Flight Log* magazine, "she said she was sorry that she couldn't stay long enough to sing anything. With a 'God bless you all; I know you'll all get your silver wings someday,' she swept out. You could have run several full-sized locomotives with the steam we blew off after that faux pas."

  The Carlisle Camp Barracks performance was on a special stage built for the show at the camp's Stark Field at 8:00 p.m. and began with a thirty-minute "varied program" by the Medical Field Service School Concert Band.[39] Garland opened the second half of the show by stating, "I didn't come here to tell you how to win the war, and I know you'll win it. I'm here to pay an installment on the debt I owe to the men in uniform." She sang "It's a Great Day for the Irish," "As Time Goes By," and "For Me and My Gal." At this point, Garland opened the show to requests, noting that she had "an awfully bad cold" and that her voice must "sound a little rotten." At one point, she joked about her voice sounding as raspy as Eddie "Rochester" Anderson's. A baby in the audience shouted during one number, prompting Garland to quip, "I don't blame you!" On request, Garland sang "You'll Never Know," "You Made Me Love You," and "Don't Get Around Much Anymore," and then the audience kept shouting "Over the Rainbow," to which she replied, "Oh, I don't know that one." Just before the final number, she asked the audience to "let me sing one I like." She closed with "Exactly Like You" and said, "I hope my coming here has given you as much pleasure as it has me. I hope that it won't be long until we meet again. Until then, God bless you and goodbye."[40]

- **July 20, 1943: Indiantown Gap Military Reservation, Harrisburg, Pennsylvania—**Garland was driven to the reservation, where she "sang several numbers at the Red Cross building" before appearing at Muir Field. As if that wasn't enough, two hours later, she repeated the performance for the men of the Transportation Corps Unit Training Center in their outdoor amphitheatre. She was driven back to Harrisburg en route to

Pittsburgh, Pennsylvania.[41] All that in one day! To relax, Garland went unnoticed to the movies in Harrisburg, seeing Cary Grant's latest film, *Mr. Lucky*.[42]

- **July 21 and 22: Camp Shenango Personnel Replacement Depot, Pennsylvania** (the town is now called Transfer)—Garland arrived in Philadelphia on January 21 and was met by Camp Shenango's special services officer, Captain "Maxcie" O. Brock. Garland visited the camp's headquarters to "pay her respects to the post commander, Col. Zim E. Lawhon."[43] Her performance at the camp's service club was "tumultuous and enthusiastic." Her second performance was the same partial request show she had been giving. She then performed at "a recreation hall show where she sang another request program."[44] A couple of months later, the camp changed its name to Camp Reynolds.
- **July 24, 1943: Fort Wayne, Indiana**—"Judy Garland Chews Bologna with Boys" read the title of an uncredited article about Garland's appearance in Fort Wayne. "For an hour Miss Garland sang songs she had helped make popular" at Baer Field and then asked, "When do we eat?" at which point she ate bologna, "the meat course the chef placed on the table," with the enlisted men.[45]

In the middle of Garland's USO tour, during the week of July 21, the Young and Rubicam advertising agency approached MGM about Garland hosting her own thirty-minute weekly radio show on NBC on Thursday nights from 8:30 to 9:00 p.m., sponsored by General Foods. MGM declined because, as *Variety* reported in its July 28, 1943, issue, "[MGM] seems to be worried that Miss Garland's health won't permit her to take on a weekly radio program in addition to her picture commitments. Metro has stepped up her working schedule so that she can have a sustained layoff." It's unknown where *Variety* got their information, but it's doubtful MGM was planning on giving Garland a sustained layoff; she was too lucrative. She had been so busy over the past couple of years that, in hindsight, it's almost frightening to think what stepping up her work schedule would have meant. It's noteworthy that at this time, Garland's health was already being discussed in newspapers in the context of her ability to fulfill her contractual obligations. It was a topic that would dominate the entertainment headlines in the late 1940s.

When she returned to Hollywood from the USO tour, Garland didn't go directly into another film production, and she didn't have much time off, either. She made one major radio appearance on *Command Performance No. 81* with Bing Crosby. Then she was asked by the Hollywood Victory Committee to participate in their upcoming extensive US Bond fundraising tour titled the Third War Loan Campaign, commonly known as the Hollywood Bond Cavalcade. This time, Garland was one of approximately twelve stars who took part in the tour, stopping in fifteen cities to "Back the Attack," as it was advertised. Some stars would randomly come in for a few shows and then leave, but Garland was one of the core group of stars who completed the entire tour. The stars, staff, and crew had a short week of putting the show together beginning

162　　　　　　　　　　　　　　　　　　　　CHAPTER 5

Garland is besieged by fans on arriving in Boston, Massachusetts, with the "Back the Attack" USO War Bond Tour, September 10, 1943 (photo published on September 11, 1943). From the author's collection.

the weekend of August 28, 1943, before leaving the following Friday, September 4, via train to Washington, DC. The stars who made up the core group were Garland, Fred Astaire, Lucille Ball, James Cagney, Greer Garson, Betty Hutton, Harpo Marx (with companion Muriel Goodspeed), Dick Powell, and Mickey Rooney—plus Kay Kyser and his band (with Harry Babbitt, Georgia Carroll, Julie Conway, Ish Kabibble, and Diane Pendleton) and the Four Starlet Bondbardeers (Rosemary LaPlanche, Doris Merrick, Dolores Moran, and Marjorie Stewart). Joining them later were Kathryn Grayson, Olivia de Havilland, and Martha Scott. Alfred Newman, the musical director at 20th Century Fox, was the musical director for the tour. Writers who contributed to the show's script were enlisted through the "Hollywood Writers' Mobilization," including H. Allen Smith, Eddie Moran, Jerry Gollard, Wilkie Mahoney, Arthur Phillips, Carl Hurzinger, and J. M. Josefsberg.

Columnist John Truesdell wrote, "Judy Garland, who's worn herself to a frazzle movie making, dating Van Johnson, and canteen entertaining, gave up her Mexico City vacation against doctor's orders—to go on that victory bond cavalcade which will tour the country any train time now."[46] Garland was accompanied on the tour by her sister Virginia and her "best friend" Betty Asher.

The tour kicked off in Washington, DC, and went through fifteen American cities before ending in San Francisco three weeks later. Millions of Americans flocked to these events, buying war bonds as their tickets, with seat prices ranging from $18.75 to $1 million. After crossing

10,091 miles, the campaign raised a total of $1,095,614,000 and pushed America's War Loan over the $2 billion mark.

The Hollywood Victory Committee was an organization founded on December 10, 1941, just days after the Japanese bombed Pearl Harbor, Hawaii, which plunged the United States into World War II. Its mission was to provide a means for stage, screen, television, and radio performers who were not in military service to contribute to the war effort through bond drives and improve the troops' morale. It was associated with the Screen Actors Guild. The Committee organized events between January 1942 and August 1945. Its first chairman was Clark Gable.

- **September 4, 1943: Los Angeles, California**—The Hollywood Bond Cavalcade had a big send-off as the stars left Los Angeles by train for Washington.
- **September 8, 1943: Washington, DC**—The Cavalcade arrived in Washington and kicked off the tour with a parade to the Washington Monument for the opening ceremony/festivities, plus a nationwide radio hookup from the White House featuring a speech by President Roosevelt that began at 9:00 p.m. EWT (now called Eastern Standard Time), 6:00 p.m. PWT (Pacific). Newsreel footage survives of the stars in their jeeps going past the White House and around the Washington Monument. After the day's events, the stars boarded their train at midnight and headed to their first stop, Philadelphia, Pennsylvania.
- **September 9, 1943: Philadelphia, Pennsylvania**—Philadelphia went all out, becoming one of the biggest events of the entire tour. There was a bond auction sale on the corner of Broad and Chestnut streets followed by a parade (in which all of the stars participated), with more than one hundred thousand people lined up along the route. Warplanes flew overhead. There were several other events during the day, including rallies at the Navy Yard at Sun Shipyard in Chester, Pennsylvania, where Betty Hutton appeared before eight thousand workers and raised money by selling kisses. Garland participated in the bond rally at the Philadelphia Navy Yard. Fidelity Mutual Life Insurance employees subscribed $1 million at a luncheon attended by Greer Garson, while another luncheon sponsored by the Mid-City Club and attended by Fred Astaire raised another million. The appearance of other stars raised smaller sums at similar events that day.[47]

  The main show was at the Philadelphia Convention Hall beginning at 8:00 p.m., where more than fourteen thousand people attended and purchased a total of $12,250,000 in bonds.[48] James Cagney, the master of ceremonies, was introduced to the crowd by the state chairman of the bond drive, E. A. Roberts. Greer Garson announced the box office receipts for the performance. Garland's part of the shows usually consisted of her singing "The Man I Love," "Embraceable You," and "Blow, Gabriel, Blow" as well as clowning and duetting with Mickey Rooney. Kathryn Grayson joined the tour at this stop. More newsreel footage was filmed, including impressive footage of downtown Philadelphia during the parade. Virginia Safford's column noted what the stars were doing on the train,

164 CHAPTER 5

including "SIGHT OF the week: Judy Garland darning a hole in her precious nylons."[49]

They raised a total of $58,717,122, which went toward the city's quota of $490,048,700.[50] The largest single purchase in the city was $25 million, made by the Penn Mutual Life Insurance Co. The city bought $10 million worth. Pennsylvanians as a whole purchased $180 million on the first day of the Third War Loan Drive, which included the figures raised on this day by the Cavalcade.[51]

- **September 10, 1943: Boston, Massachusetts**—The events in Boston rivaled the popularity and success of the events in Philadelphia. The city developed a seven-point program:

  1. The broadcast from the White House on September 8 was played on the eve of the twenty-four-hour rally at Boston Common's bond stand, the "Victory Platform," in which the army participated.
  2. A million-dollar luncheon where each of the one thousand guests was required to purchase a $1,000 bond to attend. This was followed by an evening parade that ended at the Boston Garden.
  3. Multiple publicity projects were assigned to each of the local newspapers and radio stations, including a contest for the "Bond Queen of Massachusetts" that was open to all housewives. The housewife who sold the most bonds won the title.
  4. A super bomber was displayed in the center of Boston throughout the month. Other bombers and blimps dropped leaflets about the drive during September.
  5. A flying squadron of minute men was organized to cover every public gathering with a short pep talk.
  6. A "Town Meeting" was held in the middle of the month.
  7. A trolley car with twenty-four sheets on each side drove throughout the city for the entire month.[52]

Prior to the arrival of the Cavalcade in Boston on September 8, an "all-night affair" was highlighted by auctions of personal items from the stars.[53] The first parade began at 4:00 p.m., taking the stars through downtown Boston in jeeps. The navy provided each jeep with an escort of two enlisted men wounded in action. As with every parade during the tour, local military units also participated, and in Boston, they showed off "every type of equipment from the jeep and peep to amphibian assault land-and-sea outfits, accompanied by anti-aircraft guns and other heavy arms. Even a barrage balloon will be shown."[54] After dinner at their hotel, the Hotel Statler (where the entire tenth floor was reserved for the Cavalcade), another parade was planned to take them to Boston Garden, but that was canceled for late rehearsals, leaving fifty thousand fans disappointed. The US Army, US Navy, Marine Corps, WACs, WAVES, American Red Cross, Massachusetts Women's Defense Corps, Lexington Minute Men, Coast Guard, and Massachusetts State Guard all took part.[55]

MGM's Singing Sweetheart Grows Up

165

The *Boston Globe* newspaper reported on the events, noting that the Military Police was used to guard the hotel to "keep away curiosity seekers." Six hundred local police officers protected the four major events of the day. Different military units were assigned to accompany the stars in their jeeps. The American Red Cross accompanied Garland. Two hundred fifty thousand people "crowd-packed" the parade route, which the paper noted "consisted mainly of women and teen-age children" who at times attempted to break through the police lines to get close to their favorite stars. The paper published a frightening photo of Garland's jeep being mobbed by fans. Garland's jeep was the last in the procession, putting her "in constant danger of being overwhelmed by her fans. . . . It was only by the vigorous use of mounted police that the star's admirers were prevented from disrupting the end of the procession." The event raised over $200 million in war bond sales.[56]

The all stars of the "Back the Attack" USO War Bonds tour: (*rear left to right*) James Cagney, Lucille Ball, Fred Astaire, Greer Garson, Paul Henreid, Garland, Betty Hutton, Harpo Marx, Marjorie Stewart; (*front left to right*) Sergeant Barney Ross, Kay Kyser, Mickey Rooney, Rosemary La Planche, in Boston, Massachusetts, September 10, 1943. From the author's collection.

- **September 11, 1943: New York City**—The Cavalcade arrived by train at Pennsylvania Station at 10:30 a.m. to a crowd of fifteen hundred. They were then driven to a press conference at their hotel, the St. Moritz. The *Daily News* noted that Garland "had train sickness en route but looked as inviting as a rib roast when she reached the station."[57] Seat prices for the show at Madison Square Garden ranged from $18.75 to $1 million (in war bonds). One box (of seats) alone brought in $40 million.[58] "An eighth of a billion dollars was subscribed in advance as the price of admission" to the event at the Garden, with more bonds sold beforehand and each buyer receiving a ticket.[59] Nineteen thousand people attended the show, and the total tally for the event was originally promoted as $155 million, but on September 15, the New York War Activities Committee of the Motion Picture Industry reported the total was $152,966,625.

- **September 12, 1943: Pittsburgh, Pennsylvania**—The parade (through the "Golden Triangle" of the city) comprised six military divisions, headed by units from all military detachment stations in the Pittsburgh area and the Air Corps band of the University of Pittsburgh, as well as units from the Salvation Army, Civilian Defense Units, and local high school bands. The two-hour parade began at 2:00 p.m. at Fifth Avenue and Dinwiddle Street, then went down Fifth Avenue to Liberty Avenue, and then over to Sixth Street, across the Sixth Street Bridge to Stockton Avenue, past a reviewing stand on Ridge Avenue to Brighton Road. There was a dinner in the Urban Room of the William Penn Hotel at 6:30 p.m. that netted $10 million. The three-hour main show was at Forbes Field at 9:00 p.m.; the stars' appearance was preceded by "a variety of entertainment." The gates opened at 6:30 p.m.[60] The *Pittsburgh Post-Gazette* noted that admittance to the show was by the purchase of a war bond, with seats ranging from $18.75 to $1 million. The show raised $70 million, bringing the total for this stop to $80 million.[61]

- **September 13, 1943: Cleveland, Ohio**—The stars spoke to an assembly of Defense Workers. That night, at the Civic Auditorium, Kay Kyser auctioned off an American flag for $10 million, plus two pounds of butter and three-pound steaks for $100 each! $83 million was raised at the show. Earlier in the day, there was a luncheon that netted $60 million, bringing the total for the day to $143,702,000.[62]

- **September 14, 1943: Detroit, Michigan**—The Cavalcade arrived in Detroit at 1:00 p.m. They were taken to their hotel, the Hotel Statler, where their rooms were provided for free (106 total). Two hundred Military Police had to lock arms to clear a passage for the stars to get into the hotel lobby due to there being about two thousand people there to see them.[63] The $1,000-per-seat show was at the Olympia Stadium in Detroit, where fifteen thousand "E Bond Gallants" were in attendance thanks to their raising that much in bond sales. Local columnist Anthony Weitzel noted the room numbers for the stars at the hotel. Garland was in Room 974. He also noted that the stars were advised that room service was almost impossible, so they ate in the public dining rooms.

- **September 15, 1943: Cincinnati, Ohio**—En route to Cincinnati, the Cavalcade spent an hour early in the morning in Springfield, Ohio, where the local paper noted that the stars slept peacefully while the locals began their workday. The Cavalcade arrived in Cincinnati at 10:30 a.m., where they were then bused through the city on chartered Cincinnati Street Railway buses. An hour later, they had a reception and held a press conference at their hotel, the Netherland Plaza Hotel. Garland missed that due to having a cold but still made the show that night. They held a bond rally at Nippert Stadium, University of Cincinnati, at 3:00 p.m. (Garland most likely missed this event, too). The big show was held at the Albee Theatre at 7:00 p.m. The *Cincinnati Enquirer* reported what the stars did while on the trains between the scheduled stops, noting again that "Judy Garland darns holes in her nylons."[64]
- **September 16, 1943: Chicago, Illinois**—After their arrival, the stars took part in a parade at 12:30 p.m. down State Street. The main show was at Soldier Field at 8:00 p.m., where 115,000 people showed up. Entry to the show required a purchase of an "extra" bond ranging in price from $25 to $1 million, netting $115 million. The total for the Chicago event was $150 million.[65]
- **September 17, 1943: Minneapolis, Minnesota**—Five days before the Cavalcade's arrival, the 2,750 available seats for the show at the Minneapolis Auditorium were sold out, even at bond prices of $50 to $100, for a total of $10 million before the Cavalcade arrived. The Cavalcade arrived at the Minneapolis Great Northern Station at 10:30 a.m. and stayed at the Nicollet and Radisson hotels. The stars were presented with "Warsages" (corsages made from war savings stamps) and visited two war plants in the afternoon. The *Minneapolis Star* reported that when the bus carrying the stars arrived at their hotel, Garland, Rooney, Cagney, and Garson noticed the mass of people across the street couldn't see them because of the bus, so they waited for the bus to leave and then went to the center of the street to say hello to their fans. A local little person, Harvey B. Williams, who was one of the Munchkins in *The Wizard of Oz* and known locally as "the world's smallest mailman," got a chance to reconnect with Garland. The show at the auditorium began at 8:30 p.m.[66]
- **September 18, 1943: St. Louis, Missouri**—An estimated four thousand fans were at the St. Louis Union Station to greet the Cavalcade. The Cavalcade then rode in army jeeps and Red Cross cars in a parade from Union Station through the downtown area at 3:45 p.m., led by the Jefferson Barracks band and including contingents of WAVES, WACs, SPARS, women Marine Reserves, members of the CAP, and the Coast Guard. Most of the stars lodged at the Hotel Jefferson, where police had to chase three hundred autograph hounds out of the lobby. They also had to drag a high school girl out from beneath Fred Astaire's bed. In another incident, surging fans shattered a plate glass window, which tore Garland's dress to shreds. The main show at Kiel Auditorium began at 8:15 p.m.[67]

- **September 20, 1943: New Orleans, Louisiana**—September 19 was an open day in New Orleans, Louisiana, before their official performances on September 20 at the Tad Gormley Stadium. *Variety* reported the crowd at fifty thousand; the *States* newspaper stated it was between sixty-five thousand and seventy-five thousand; while *The Item* newspaper claimed one hundred thousand showed up, despite the actual venue seating only thirty-five hundred.

  The tour officially passed the billion-dollar mark in bond sales in New Orleans, bringing the cumulative total to $1,010,500,000.[68]
- **September 21, 1943: Dallas and Fort Worth, Texas**—Because the tour was such a success, it was decided to add another short stop, a 3:00 p.m. matinee at the Will Rogers Memorial Coliseum in nearby Fort Worth, Texas. The Cavalcade traveled by motorcade from Dallas to Forth Worth to give the matinee performance before returning to Dallas for the originally scheduled evening show. Many in the cast had been sick due to food poisoning from a seafood dinner in New Orleans, but most recovered in time for the show. "Scarcely 30 minutes before Judy Garland reached the stage she was in a faint and under a doctor's care in her dressing room. No one would have guessed it, the way she sang 'Blow, Gabriel Blow,' and two Gershwin tunes, 'Embraceable You,' and 'The Man I Love.' Judy remained on stage to coax some boogie-woogie out of the talented pianist, Jose Iturbi, and when she came backstage she was in a state of collapse."[69]
- **September 22, 1943: San Antonio, Texas**—This stop in San Antonio brought the tour total to $1,074,000,000.[70]
- **September 25, 1943: San Francisco, California**—San Francisco was the official end of the tour, being the last stop for fundraising and giving shows prior to the Cavalcade's return to Los Angeles. The money raised in SF was $21,614,600.[71]

The Cavalcade's appearances in Washington for the official opening and the welcome home to Los Angeles are not listed since no show was given, meaning no bond admissions were charged.

After returning to Hollywood, Garland had some downtime during October. On November 2, 1943, she returned to the Decca Records studios to record "But Not for Me" and "I Got Rhythm" for the label's "original cast album" of songs from the soon-to-be-released *Girl Crazy*. She recorded three more songs from the film on November 4, 1943 ("Embraceable You," "Could You Use Me?," and "Bidin' My Time"). The album was the first of three deluxe cast albums of Garland films that Decca produced over the next few years. The other two were *Meet Me in St. Louis* and *The Harvey Girls*. These albums were not soundtrack albums. That market didn't open up until 1947. The Decca albums featured studio re-creations of select songs from the films featuring Garland and some of her costars. The label had just recorded, but not yet released, a cast album of songs from the recent Broadway hit *Oklahoma!* (the first ever Broadway cast album), so it's probable that Jack Kapp (who was so keen on signing Garland to the label in 1935) realized what could be done on record with show tunes and, knowing the appeal of a Gershwin score, decided to do the same with *Girl Crazy*. Garland and Rooney recorded six songs from the film for Decca. The *Girl Crazy* cast album, with three 78 rpm records featuring a song on each side, was released on April 6, 1944.

On November 3, 1943, Garland returned to MGM for her first major work on the production of *Meet Me in St. Louis*. She prerecorded the songs "Boys and Girls Like You and Me" and "Over the Bannister." Little did she know that not only would the film become a masterpiece of the film musical genre, but it would also profoundly change her life forever.

MGM's singing sweetheart has grown up. From the April 1943 edition of *Photoplay* magazine. From the author's collection.

CHAPTER *6*

MORE MGM MAGIC
MEET ME IN ST. LOUIS

Garland's first official work on *Meet Me in St. Louis* was on November 3, 1943, when she prerecorded "Boys and Girls Like You and Me" and "Over the Bannister." By this point, much had happened behind the scenes to get the film into production with Garland as the star. First and foremost, Garland didn't want to be in it. She, along with those around her (like her on-again, off-again lover of the time, Joe Mankiewicz), felt that taking the role of a love-sick girl in high school in a seemingly bland story about a family in 1903/1904 St. Louis, Missouri, was a step backward for her career. She was finally being seen as an adult in film and with the public. She did not want to turn back. Garland and her supporters had a valid case. On paper, *Meet Me in St. Louis* seemed plotless. The family goes about their business living their lives, and the only real conflict comes late in the film when the father announces that he's moving the family to New York.

There was a consensus among many at the studio that the film would be a big nothing and might be the first flop of Garland's career. It didn't help that it was to be directed by a still unproven Vincente Minnelli. His biggest claim to fame at this time was his helming of the all-black musical *Cabin in the Sky* (1943). That film was nothing to sneeze at, full of great talent (you can't go wrong with Lena Horne, Ethel Waters, Eddie "Rochester" Anderson, and Louis Armstrong, among others), but in the Hollywood of 1943, it was considered a very niche film, not one to be taken as seriously as the "A" musicals. *Meet Me in St. Louis*, the naysayers assumed, would probably be the same.

The story of what became the film *Meet Me in St. Louis* goes back to June 14, 1941. That's the date the *New Yorker* magazine published the first of eight of Sally Benson's stories titled "5135 Kensington." Benson derived her stories from her own childhood, growing up at that address in St. Louis in an era long gone. She wrote four more chapters and published the stories in book format, titled *The Kensington Stories*, which details a year in the life of her family in 1903/1904 St. Louis, Missouri. MGM purchased the film rights (plus the radio and, interestingly, the television rights) for $25,000.

Without a viable script, Freed enlisted one of MGM's best storytellers, Lily Messenger, to tell the story to studio boss Louis B. Mayer. Messenger was one of the few people who could tell a story (or read a script or treatment) in such a way as to make Mayer a fan, regardless of whether it was good or bad. And so she did with the Benson stories. But even with Mayer's support, producer Arthur Freed faced an uphill battle with many at the studio who complained about a lack of glamour and a boring plot. At a conference with studio executives, Freed exclaimed,

MGM studio portrait, 1944. From the author's collection.

"There is no conflict? These people are fighting for their happiness! Where is the villain? Well, the villain is New York!! What more do you want?!" Mayer chimed in with "I think the story is very exciting; there's a lot of action! And what about those girls who have to leave their home and their sweethearts? I tell you, it broke my heart!"[1] At this point, Freed was the golden boy of the producers on the lot. His films were so successful that he had the clout to do almost anything he wanted. He and Minnelli stood firm. They could see the magic in author Sally Benson's original stories. The executives let them have their way.

Several people had a go at the screenplay beginning in 1942. Messenger provided an initial storyline treatment on January 6, 1942, followed by Benson herself with Doris Gilbert, delivering early screenplays in March and May 1942 and additional material later.[2] Screenwriter Bill Ludwig took a stab at it, as did the husband-and-wife team of Sarah Mason and Victory Heerman. That duo had some clout after winning the Oscar for the screenplay of 1933's *Little Women*, another slice-of-life family story. Freed called in Fred Finklehoffe and Irving Brecher. The two had written several films together, and Finklehoffe had written four Garland musicals already. Similar to the script process for Garland's other MGM masterpiece, *The Wizard of Oz*, the final screenplay for *Meet Me in St. Louis* removed extra scenes and subplots, keeping the narrative streamlined. In both cases, less was definitely more. Finklehoffe and Brecher simplified the *St. Louis* story by focusing on the family nucleus. Brecher, in interviews with author Mark Griffin for his biography on Minnelli titled *A Hundred or More Hidden Things: The Life and Films of Vincente Minnelli*, stated that while he and Finklehoffe received cowriting credit, it was Brecher who wrote the screenplay. Finklehoffe provided an outline and then moved on to other projects. Brecher also claimed that he suggested to Freed that Minnelli direct the film.

There were several plot ideas in the various scripts and treatments that Finklehoffe and Brecher removed. These included scenes at Princeton University (which the Smiths' only boy, Lon Jr., attended), Rose having a romance with Colonel Darly (originally Colonel Andrews; the character is briefly seen in the final film), a scene in Mr. Smith's office, a trip to visit grandparents in Minnesota, Rose getting involved with a middle-aged man, and a blackmail plot involving Esther. There were also slight adjustments to names and other minor things, such as Rose and Esther both having auburn hair rather than the initially planned brunette and blonde, Tootie working with the water sprinkler man rather than the ice wagon man, the cakewalk originally danced by the second youngest daughter, Agnes (whom Benson based on herself), rather than Esther and Tootie, Agnes took on the Braukoffs (originally Waughop) instead of Tootie in the Halloween sequence, and Agnes even got the final line in the book, "Right here where we live. Right here in St. Louis," spoken by Esther at the end of the film. Other changes were to names. The boy next door was originally Bluett, not Truett. The Bluett name remained the official studio name of the Truett home built on the "St. Louis Street" on MGM's Lot 3. Rose's boyfriend, Warren Sheffield, was originally Warren Sheppard. The family's maid, Katie, was based on a real-life person who gave MGM's New York office a signed release allowing them to use her name.

When Finklehoffe and Brecher delivered their screenplay in July 1943, the film's casting had been ongoing for several months. In her April 23, 1943, column, Louella Parsons made a big deal out of the fact that Van Johnson would play opposite Garland in the film. Parsons had some of her info wrong, though. She noted that Margaret O'Brien would play "Sally, the youngest of the Smiths, while Judy is Rose and Van is Judy's heart interest." In the actual screenplay, O'Brien is, of course, Tootie, and Garland is Esther, with Lucille Bremer as Rose. Johnson was considered for the role of John Truett, but, ultimately, the pivotal boy next door role went to another handsome young newcomer, Tom Drake.

According to Minnelli's 1974 autobiography, *I Remember It Well*, Garland, in her attempt to get out of the film, went to him and said, "It's not very good, is it?" to which he replied, "I think it's fine, I see a lot of great things in it. In fact, it's magical." Between Minnelli, Mayer, Freed, and Brecher (who read her the entire script) trying to convince her that it was the right film for her, Garland relented. Ultimately, Garland probably realized she could complain and resist to a point, but she had to acquiesce because the studio always had the final say. If she refused to do it, she could be suspended without pay. In 1942, when these discussions most likely first took place, she wasn't a big enough star, nor was she strong enough emotionally, to go on a strike or leave for an extended vacation like Bette Davis (at Warner Bros.) or Greta Garbo (at MGM) had previously, and famously, done.

Another minor drama of sorts played out when Freed and Minnelli decided that dressing up MGM's "New England Street" (a.k.a. "Andy Hardy Street") on Lot 2 wouldn't work as Kensington Avenue. They wanted an entirely new street built with era-appropriate Victorian homes. They were able to get their way again. Freed brought in Lemuel Ayers, the Broadway designer who had designed sets for the original production of *Oklahoma!*, to work with art director Jack Martin Smith on the designs for *St. Louis*. The "St. Louis Street" was constructed on MGM's Lot 3 for $151,575.[3] The street, with its seven beautiful facades of Victorian homes, turned out to be one of the most used and lucrative locations of any on MGM's backlots, showing up in dozens of films, such as a quick appearance in Hitchcock's *North by Northwest* (1959), and later in TV shows, including *The Twilight Zone*, which filmed on the street many times. Other studios also paid to film on the street, such as 20th Century Fox using it for the Gilbreth family home in *Cheaper by the Dozen* (1950). It also appeared in two more Garland films, *Till the Clouds Roll By* (1946) and *In the Good Old Summertime* (1949), although Garland herself was not in any of the scenes shot on the street for those films. Filming *Meet Me in St. Louis* was the only time she spent on the street that was partly created because of her.

As important as the film's design was to its success, the music was even more critical. *Meet Me in St. Louis* wasn't a typical movie musical of the time. There are no chorines or big production numbers on Broadway stages and no backstage show business plot. The songs are organic to the narrative. They flow out of the plot in a natural manner. *Meet Me in St. Louis* wasn't the first film musical to feature an integrated score, but it was the most successful at the time and helped prove that modern film musicals could be sophisticated *and* popular. In addition to featuring the classic title song, the film contained a masterful blend of vintage and new songs. Freed and his frequent songwriting partner Nacio Herb Brown contributed the new song "You and I," which is so perfectly evocative of a typical song of the 1903 era that most audiences don't know the difference. Hugh Martin and Ralph Blane provided the rest of the new songs.

In choosing the songwriting team of Martin and Blane, Freed made another fortuitous decision. The duo had come to MGM, as did most of the Freed Unit at this time, from Broadway. They wrote the songs for *Best Foot Forward*, which MGM purchased and filmed in 1943, bringing them along with the package (also part of that package were newcomers June Allyson and Nancy Walker). The duo provided three new songs that became masterpieces in their own right: "The Boy Next Door," "Have Yourself a Merry Little Christmas," and "The Trolley Song." But writing them didn't come easily.

"The Trolley Song" proved to be the most difficult to create, if not actually to compose. The script didn't give them much to go on. It simply stated, "A trolley is there. Some youngsters on it, but a good number are still outside, chatting gaily. Quentin (shouts) Let her go, motorman!

The trolley starts and the crowd starts to sing."[4] Martin and Blane wrote songs they felt would be perfect for singing on a trolley. They thought writing a song about a trolley would be, as Blane put it, "too corny" and "on the nose." One of their songs for the sequence was a rousing number titled "Know Where You're Going and You'll Get There."[5] Each time they took a song to Freed, he gave them the same reply; he would say that he loved the song and would use it in his ongoing production of *Ziegfeld Follies*, but he wanted a song *about* a trolley. Exasperated, Blane went to the Beverly Hills Public Library and found a book with a photo of a trolley that was captioned "Clang, Clang, Clang, Went the Trolley." "Well," Blane said, "I dashed back—told Hugh the title, and we wrote it in about ten minutes."[6]

The story about the writing of "Have Yourself a Merry Little Christmas" is retold every holiday season in various articles in magazines, papers, and online. Hugh Martin, who later claimed that he alone wrote the music and lyrics for the film's new songs, giving Blane the music credit out of courtesy and never revealing the truth until after Blane had passed, also told the story many times. Composing the song wasn't as difficult as "The Trolley Song." The problem was with the original lyrics. The lyrics were very sad, opening with "Have yourself a merry little Christmas, it may be your last, next year we will all be living in the past." The rest of the original lyrics are equally depressing. Garland loved the tune but was rightfully concerned that if she sang those sad lyrics to Margaret O'Brien in a similarly sad manner, on top of the already sad scene, "the audience is going to say, 'Oh, my God,' and they're going to be leaving the theater."[7] Martin has been quoted saying that Garland said, "If I sing that song to little Margaret O'Brien, the audience will hate me. They'll think I'm a monster."[8] Martin was full of youthful stubbornness at the time and resisted changing the lyrics. It took the boy next door himself, Tom Drake, to take Martin aside and convince him to make the changes. Martin changed the lyrics, and the song became a classic. To date, it's the most covered non-secular Christmas song after Irving Berlin's "White Christmas." In the 1950s, Frank Sinatra asked Martin for updated lyrics that were more generic, such as changing "next year all our troubles will be out of sight" to "from now on our troubles will be out of sight" and "until then, we'll have to muddle through somehow" to "hang a shining star upon the highest bough." It's the updated lyrics that are the most covered.

The third original song by Martin and Blane, "The Boy Next Door," was straightforward enough for them to write and became another all-time Garland classic. It's the first song sung in the film by Garland as Esther, and, like "Over the Rainbow," it's an "I want" song that establishes her character's motivation early in the film. Most original movie musicals are lucky if just one song becomes a classic. Martin and Blane provided three. They also contributed their adaptation of the traditional "Skip to My Lou." The rest of the songs were the traditional "Under the Bamboo Tree" and "Over the Bannister." The former is a charming duet and dance by Garland and O'Brien that's one of the film's highlights. Their fun is infectious. Esther tenderly sings the latter to John.

One more song was planned, recorded, and filmed. Richard Rodgers and Oscar Ham-

MORE MGM MAGIC

175

SCENE No.	COMPOSITION	COMPOSER	TIME	DISC NUMBER	REMARKS	LIBRARY NUMBER	CLASS	USED IN PRODUCTION
2015	Clang, Clang, Clang Went The Trolley	Martin – t 1 / Blane t 2	4:01 / 4:00		Studio orchestra – prerecording. Judy Garland vocalist with chorus			

DAILY MUSIC REPORT
PROD: MEET ME IN ST. LOUIS
FROM: OFFICE OF NAT W. FINSTON — The following recordings were made today:
PROD: 1317 DATE: 12-2-43

Garland recorded "The Trolley Song" on December 2, 1943.
The first two takes were "printed" (saved for use in the film).
From the author's collection.

merstein II had written "Boys and Girls Like You and Me" for *Oklahoma!*, but it went unused. MGM purchased the song, and Freed and Edens intended to use it in *Meet Me in St. Louis*. After "The Trolley Song," the film originally segued to Esther and John walking around the unfinished fairgrounds. The description of the scenes, as given by MGM's music department to Rodgers and Hammerstein's publisher, noted that John goes looking for Esther, who is wandering around the fairgrounds alone. He finds her, and they have a romantic scene walking and talking, with John carrying Esther over a mud puddle. While he's holding her, she sings the song to him.

Hammerstein wrote to Freed, questioning the "feat of strength" of John being able to carry Esther presumably during the entire song. Freed wrote back, letting him know that Minnelli had filmed the song "simply and eloquently" with the camera on Garland's face throughout. Another person who had a problem with the song was Blane. He and Martin were still new, relatively unknown songwriters, and Blane was worried—angry, in fact—that their songs would be overlooked due to the prestige of a Rodgers and Hammerstein song being included.[9] Ultimately, it all worked out in Martin and Blane's favor. The entire sequence was deleted. A few years later, the song was prerecorded by Frank Sinatra and filmed for the 1949 MGM musical *Take Me Out to the Ballgame*, but that version was also deleted. The *St. Louis* outtake footage does not exist; however, the prerecording does. When Freed wrote to Hammerstein again, he mentioned that the sequence was cut for length. It's a lovely song, but, being a love ballad, it and the entire fairground sequence slowed down the flow of the film too much, in addition to adding unnecessary length.

When filming began on December 7, 1943, Garland had already prerecorded all her songs for the film except "Under the Bamboo Tree," which was prerecorded on December 17. When prerecording "The Trolley Song" on December 2, 1943, Garland had only one rehearsal before recording the first take, which was perfect. It's the take used in the film. A second take was recorded "for insurance." It's a testament to her talent that she imbued each song with the right amount of nuanced emotions while still not happy with or having a handle on portraying her character.

Decades after the film was released, an urban legend around "The Trolley Song" prerecording session had fans arguing online over a line dubbed into the film. As Garland sings, an unseen extra is heard, "Hi ya, Johnny!" Some fans claimed it was a mistake inadvertently left in the film, that someone walked into the recording studio while Garland was recording the song and yelled, "Hi ya, Judy!" This is specious to the reality of the prerecording and filming process. Recording sessions were tightly controlled, making it nearly impossible for someone to randomly wander in and be loud enough to be picked up by one of the microphones. When the number was filmed, Garland and the extras would lip-sync to a playback disc on silent film. The pristine prerecording would be added to the film in postproduction, as would the dubbing of noises, including "Hi ya, Johnny!" Finally, since "John Truett" was running to catch the trolley, it makes sense that someone would exclaim, "Hi ya, Johnny!" once he got on.

Filming "The Boy Next Door" in *Meet Me in St. Louis* (1944), December 23, 1943. From the author's collection.

The first scenes shot for the film were shot on the "Exterior Trolley Depot" (the permanent train depot set on MGM's Lot 2), "Exterior Trolley Car," and "Interior Trolley" sets (the latter on a soundstage). This was the performance of "The Trolley Song" with the chorus extras, which is the closest any number in the film comes to being a "production number." The setup is simple: Esther and John have a date to meet with their friends for an excursion via trolley to see the construction site of the World's Fair. John doesn't show up, and Esther reluctantly gets on the trolley without him. As it sets out, everyone is singing happily. Esther is oblivious to everyone's glee, mopily moving up to the top level of the trolley, where she finally sits and stares into space. Suddenly, there's a big commotion, and Esther leans out to see what the fuss is about. John is running after the trolley; he will make it after all! Now overcome with intense joy and happiness,

MORE MGM MAGIC 177

Esther bursts into song: "With my high starched collar and my high topped shoes." Garland's performance is perfection. She displays the right amount of initial despondency that seamlessly morphs into an unbridled expression of joy in "five of the most magical minutes ever proffered in a musical."[10] Minnelli masterfully uses rear projection to give the impression that the trolley is moving down the street, keeping a tight focus on the passengers and Esther, ensuring the rear projection doesn't take away from the action or the song. The sequence is in constant motion, whether it's the trolley, the rear projection, or the movements of the extras. Thanks to home media and our ability to watch and inspect every detail in our favorite films at will, fans of MGM's famous backlots can spot backlot locations in the rear projection footage, including "New England Street" and Andy Hardy's front porch.

It wasn't until December 14 that Garland began to film the non-musical scenes. That's when the issues started. The "Interior Smith Kitchen" (without Garland) was up first, followed by scenes shot on the "Interior Esther and Rose's Room." At first, Garland mocked the script in her delivery, still thinking the character was juvenile. She didn't have a handle on how to por-

A deleted scene from *Meet Me in St. Louis*; *(left to right)* Joan Carroll, Lucille Bremer, Garland, Henry H. Daniels Jr., and Margaret O'Brien. From the author's collection.

tray the character yet. Minnelli was a perfectionist, and, this being his big chance to prove himself—in the persnickety three-strip Technicolor process no less—he had a lot riding on the film. For Garland (at first, anyway), it was simply another assignment. She was unaccustomed to the way Minnelli was directing the film. His style was very different from what she was used to. He loved to rehearse his actors—a lot. For Garland, who was known as one of the quickest studies in Hollywood, with an almost photographic memory, the rehearsals were torturous. In one instance, Minnelli called on everyone at the end of the day for another rehearsal. Garland tried to sneak out of the studio, only to be stopped at the gate by the guard on orders from Minnelli and sent back. She was livid. She went to Freed with her concerns, telling him she doubted her acting ability. Freed relayed the message to Minnelli. Mary Astor, who played the mother, Mrs. Smith, remembered Garland coming to her with similar complaints about Minnelli's direction. Astor said, "Judy, I've been watching that man, and he really knows what he's doing. Just go along with it because it means something."[11]

Just one day after the first day of filming the scene with Bremer, Garland called in sick. She returned the next day (December 17) to prerecord "Under the Bamboo Tree," which took seventy-five minutes to complete, making it a short day. The following day, Garland called one of the film's two assistant directors, Al Jennings (Wallace Worsley Jr. was the other), at 8:00 a.m., saying that she didn't feel well but would come to work if a car picked her up. The car was arranged, and when she got to the studio, she called the soundstage, and David Friedman (the film's unit manager) and Jennings went to her dressing room. They called Dr. Jones (a studio doctor), who checked out Garland and said she should go home. Garland said she wouldn't go without talking to Freed first, which she did, and then left for the day at 10:30 a.m. This scenario is an example of the pattern of behavior that Garland increasingly exhibited throughout the rest of her time at MGM. She would call someone, usually the assistant director, at all hours of the night and early morning to say that she was ill and couldn't come in or didn't think she'd be at her best the next day and couldn't come in or that she hadn't slept (for a variety of reasons) and would be late. Garland being late often meant she wouldn't show up at all. The production logs for the film show that she was out sick for at least sixteen days during the production. That might not sound like much for a shoot that lasted from December 1943 through the end of April 1944, but because she was the star, she was in most of the scenes. Her absences had a big impact. Garland wasn't being a diva—she had long suffered from insomnia due to her late-night vaudeville body clock being at odds with the studio's early morning schedules; plus she had issues with her pills, which she was increasingly reliant on. She would also go out and often didn't get home until after midnight. On top of that, and probably because of the pills, she suffered from severe migraine headaches. She was still riddled with insecurities, and if she felt she wasn't going to be 100 percent perfect, she could talk herself into being unable to perform, so she would find excuses not to perform and, thus, not to show up. At one point in the production, Mary Astor, who had played her mom once before in 1938's *Listen, Darling*, said to Garland, "Judy, what the hell's happened to

Garland resting during the filming of *Meet Me in St. Louis*, February 8, 1944. From the author's collection.

you? You were a trouper—once.... You have kept the entire company out there waiting for two hours.... You know we're stuck—there's nothing we can do without you." Garland giggled, "Yeah, that's what everybody's been telling me." Astor became angry, "Well, then, either get the hell out on the set, or I'm going home." Garland grabbed Astor's hand, saying, "I don't sleep, Mom [her nickname for Astor]." Out of frustration, Astor said, "Well, go to bed early then—like we all have to." Astor later said she wouldn't have been so short with her if she had known the extent of Garland's issues.[12]

As filming progressed, Garland began to warm to Minnelli, his direction, and her role. Just before Christmas 1943, Minnelli filmed Garland's performance of one of Martin and Blane's new songs for the film *The Boy Next Door*, which became a standard and another staple of Garland's repertoire. Most of the song is framed by a window as Esther wistfully gazes at the home of the boy next door and sings about her crush. Garland's appearance and performance are exquisite. If she had any doubts about the role or her appearance prior, those doubts were dashed when she viewed the rushes. The person she saw on the screen wasn't an awkward teenager or Andy Hardy's gal pal Betsy Booth. Minnelli brought out what most people were beginning to notice: Judy Garland had matured into a beautiful woman. Garland's performance of "The Boy Next Door" is even more remarkable considering that the day before had been very long, with filming on the "Exterior and Interior Foyer" (which may have included some of "The Boy Next Door") set from 10:22 a.m. to 6:00 p.m., followed by a recording session for Decca Records that night. Garland recorded "No Love, No Nothin'" and "A Journey to a Star," which were introduced by Alice Faye in the 20th Century Fox musical *The Gang's All Here* (1943).

A significant factor in Garland's luminous appearance in *Meet Me in St. Louis* is the fact that it's the first time Dorothy "Dottie" Ponedel created her makeup. Dottie was the first to give Garland her eventually well-known arched eyebrows and a fuller lower lip. When she first met Garland, introduced by MGM's head hairdresser, Sydney Guillaroff, Garland was holding the rubber disc nose inserts and tooth caps she wore on screen. Dottie told her, "I don't see anything wrong with your nose, and your teeth look perfect to me. Let's put these things in the drawer and forget about them."[13] Dottie did such a great job that Garland insisted she do her makeup on all her films going forward. Part of Garland's new contract with MGM in 1947 stipulated that Dottie would remain her makeup artist for as long as she was "employed by the studio."[14] Dottie was like a mother and a confidant to Garland, helping her through many rough times at the studio. Unlike Betty Asher, Dottie was not a studio spy and had no ulterior motives for being Garland's friend, having genuine love and affection for her. Aside from Kay Thompson, Dottie remained Garland's closest female friend until Garland's death.

At the end of 1943, the film's production notes recorded that Garland was off the film from December 27 through December 31 due to being in the hospital on the 26th and 27th. No records exist that explain which hospital Garland was at and why. It could have been exhaustion, although her schedule outside the studio at this time was light, especially compared to the previous several years, with only a few radio shows and one Decca Records session. After the New Year, Garland was late or absent from the set more often than not. On January 4, 1944, she was out sick. On January 8, 1944, she was late, per the assistant director's notes:

Judy Garland phoned at 8:25 that she was not well and could not be on the set ready to shoot until 11:30 instead of 10:00 (her call). Camera was set up and ready for 10:00 for same dance shot of which we made on take last night and which does not satisfy director. Mr. Freed (by phone at 9:50) requested Mr. Minnelli forget the dance shot and relight for closeup of song, which also includes Miss Garland. Eliminating the dance shot would party compensate for the loss in shooting time due to Miss Garland's lateness. 12:30–12:50—Conference-Mr. Freed, Mr. Minnelli, and Miss Garland. Owing to Miss Garland's illness and failure to arrive on set until 12:30, company was unable to work before lunch.[15]

The company was sent home at 5:40 p.m. What Garland, Minnelli, and Freed spoke about during their conference is unknown. Judging from the fact that she had just been hospitalized, in addition to her recent unreliability, it's possible that she was seriously fatigued, had recurring migraines, and was on the verge of a breakdown. The next day there were no problems, but then, for the following three days, Garland was either very late or out sick. January 13, 1944, was an especially trying day for the production. Garland missed a call to be in wardrobe at 9:00 a.m. She called the assistant director, saying her eyes were bothering her and she didn't want to drive. The studio sent a car. Once in her dressing room, it was discovered that her tooth bridge (worn to make her teeth "Technicolor white") was missing. Another car was dispatched to her dentist to get a spare set. All of this happened before 10:40 a.m., when Garland was finally on set in

CLOTHES, as of 1903, make glamorous Judy Garland into a demure Junior Miss. Stocking stripes fight blouse stripes, do nothing for a girl.

The "demure Junior Miss." A newspaper blurb published on October 29, 1944, shows Garland between takes during the filming of *Meet Me in St. Louis* (1944). From the author's collection.

hair and makeup but still in street clothes. For the next hour, she and Tom Drake rehearsed the scene where Esther and John turn out the lights. Once she was in her costume, eleven takes were made of the scene from 12:16 to 1:30 p.m. After lunch, more rehearsals were interrupted for ten minutes so Garland could rest due to migraines. Another thirty minutes were spent adjusting her costume before more filming could resume. Despite all that, Minnelli managed to complete seven more takes by 7:10 p.m., at which point the production ended for the day.

That day's events are an excellent example of the impact that Garland's issues had on any of her films. Garland's issues weren't the only reasons for delays in filming. It seemed as though everyone was sick or had some other medical issue. Joan Carroll (Agnes) suffered an emergency appendectomy. Mary Astor was away from the film for more days than Garland (twenty-eight) due to a sinus condition that became recurring pneumonia. Tom Drake had throat issues, and Leon Ames (Mr. Smith) had to have ear and sinus issues taken care of. Even Marjorie Main had a standing weekly doctor's appointment (for what is anyone's guess). The most serious of the absences after Garland was the film's other main star, little Margaret O'Brien. O'Brien first had dental problems that necessitated wearing braces for ten days, making her unavailable for shooting. One day after Freed was made aware of the situation, O'Brien's plate came loose, and she was rushed to the dentist. On Sunday, January 30, 1944, O'Brien's aunt, Melissa, contacted Jennings to let him know that O'Brien wouldn't report to the studio the next day as planned. She said that O'Brien suffered from hay fever, the flu, and nervous spells. Their doctor advised a two-week rest period. The next day, they were on their way to Arizona. They then went to Kansas. O'Brien's mother mailed a letter to Freed, apologizing to him while letting him know that not only did O'Brien have hay fever and bad nerves "due to overwork," but she had also been working almost non-stop going from film to film for the past year (seven feature films in which she served either as the star or in small roles, and one short), adding, "Even in the days she didn't work we still had to make a trip to the studio for publicity interviews, lessons, wardrobe fittings etc., and I was beginning to be greatly criticized for allowing my child to work so hard. We couldn't even take a weekend off because we were always on call." O'Brien returned to the set on February 15.[16]

Despite all of the angst, nothing is noticeable on screen. The finished film is beautifully crafted, with each scene seamlessly leading to the next. Each family member has a little crisis that plays out less like a drama and more like a leisurely, pleasant tandem bike ride through the park that hits an occasional small bump—not enough to knock you over, but enough to keep things interesting. Esther wants to date and ideally marry the boy next door (John Truett); Rose wants Warren Sheffield to propose; Lon Jr. (the oldest and only son) wants to take visitor Lucille Ballard to the Christmas ball but ends up having to take his sister Rose, who assumed she would go with Sheffield, who instead is taking Ballard (that's the most complicated plotline in the whole film), while Esther is stuck going to the ball with Grandpa because John Truett's basketball practice went too long and he missed getting his suit from the tailor (Esther proclaims, "I hate basketball!"); Tootie and Agnes have to navigate Halloween; and Lon Sr. drops the bomb, saying they will all move to New York before the opening of the upcoming St. Louis World's Fair. Only Grandpa, Mrs. Smith, and cook Katie seem to have no real crises until the news breaks about the move to New York.

Behind the scenes, some real-life drama ensued when Freed told Minnelli that the Halloween sequence would have to be cut. While "Boys and Girls Like You and Me" and the fairgrounds sequence were deleted without any objections, Minnelli blew his top when made aware that the Halloween sequence was set to suffer the same fate. The film's co-screenwriter Irving Brecher later said that on the day of the sneak preview, Minnelli was crying about it: "Actually crying. His eye makeup was running."[17] Brecher went to Freed and tried to persuade him to keep the sequence in the film for the preview to see how the audience would react to it. Freed told Brecher, "Mind your own fucking business. I'm the producer, not you. Get the hell out of here."[18] But Freed had a change of heart, and the sequence remained in the film for the preview and subsequently stayed in the final cut of the film. It's one of the film's most famous sequences and is a tour de force for O'Brien.

The more Garland saw herself on the screen through Minnelli's eyes, the more she saw how beautiful she looked, and the more she began to love him. It's possible that she thought he was also in love with her because of how he was filming her. Garland never looked so glowingly beautiful. A close second would be how she looked in most of the previous year's *Presenting Lily Mars*, especially in that film's finale sequence. That was in black and white. In *Meet Me in St. Louis*, Garland's beauty is fully displayed in beautiful three-strip Technicolor. Compare how she was filmed in Technicolor in 1943 for *Thousands Cheer* to how she was filmed in 1943/1944 in *Meet Me in St. Louis*; the difference is striking. In the former, she's still pretty but more cutesy, whereas

MORE MGM MAGIC

183

Tom Drake ("The Boy Next Door") and Garland in *Meet Me in St. Louis* (1944). From the author's collection.

in the latter, she's just plain gorgeous. The difference was in the directors. Minnelli did not direct the former. He had fallen for Garland, and his adoration of her shows in every shot of her in *Meet Me in St. Louis*. Like most people in Hollywood, Minnelli was not immune to Garland's powerful charm. As a fellow artist, he also fell for her talent. "The surface wasn't scratched with Judy at all," he said. "She had great potentials [*sic*]. She could have done anything she wanted to. As great as Duse, or Bernhardt, or Garbo. You could tell her twenty things, and you'd never know if you were getting through to her or not because people were messing with her, and making her up, and so forth. And by God, everything would be in place. [She] wouldn't forget a thing."[19]

Was it love or mutual admiration that brought the two together? No one knows for sure, but it lasted longer than anyone in Hollywood thought it would. Hollywood and most of MGM (maybe all) assumed Minnelli was gay. Minnelli's sexuality has been debated since he first appeared on the scene at MGM, wearing eyeshadow and exhibiting very feminine mannerisms. Some thought he was merely "artistic," while others thought he was more in touch with his feminine side than most straight men, but not gay. As progressive as Hollywood might have been in the 1940s compared to the rest of the United States, homosexuality was still a taboo subject—at least publicly. It was easier for the behind-the-scenes talent to be more outwardly gay than the on-screen talent because they weren't in the public spotlight nearly as much. The Freed Unit was jokingly called the "Fairy Unit" because so many talented people who created most of MGM's greatest musicals were gay. For actual stars, it was completely taboo. One of MGM's biggest silent stars, William Haines, was poised to keep enjoying his stardom after passing the sound test in the late 1920s, but after he refused to enter into a "lavender marriage" (as they called marriages of convenience in Hollywood at the time), and follwing some shenanigans in his personal life,

MGM let him go. Luckily for Haines, he had a burgeoning decorating career to fall back on and became a world-renowned interior designer (William Haines Designs is still in business). He and his partner at the time of his split with MGM, Jimmy Shields, stayed together until Haines died in the 1970s. Minnelli was married four times in his lifetime, fathering two daughters (including his daughter with Garland, Liza Minnelli). His private paintings of the female form (including one resembling Garland) reveal a fascination with the female bosom. All are beautiful and very sensual, with a focus on the women's breasts.

Minnelli was nineteen years older than Garland and had a colorful past prior to their initial meeting in 1940. Like Garland, he was born into a show business family on February 28, 1903, in Chicago, Illinois. His father was the musical director of the Minnelli Brothers' Tent Theatre. But unlike Garland, Minnelli found his creative outlet behind the scenes. He began his career as a window dresser for the Marshall Fields department store in Chicago. While at Marshall Fields, he entered into a love affair with future performance artist Lester Gaba. The romance continued after they moved to New York separately but around the same time. They even took a cruise together to Bermuda. Minnelli found success as a set designer and stage director for the then-new Radio City Music Hall, and he was also the color consultant for the original design of the Rainbow Room nightclub. He designed costumes and sets for (and eventually directed) successful Broadway musicals and revues. One of his biggest successes, the Broadway musical *Hooray for What!*, was later tied to Garland in two distinct ways: (1) the show's songwriters,

1945 promotional tie-in for *Meet Me in St. Louis* (1944). From the author's collection.

MORE MGM MAGIC

185

Harold Arlen and E. Y. "Yip" Harburg, were hired by Arthur Freed for *The Wizard of Oz* based on their score for this show, and (2) the show initially starred Kay Thompson, who found her way to MGM as a vocal arranger in the mid-1940s and became not only Garland's best female friend but also a significant influence on her singing and performing style.

While in New York, as in Chicago, Minnelli traveled in the theatrical gay circles at the time. Designer Jack Hurd told Minnelli biographer Mark Griffin that during this time in New York, Minnelli picked him up and took him back to his place to have sex. Hurd said he wasn't attracted to Minnelli because of his feminine ways and pronounced face makeup, so he turned him down. Years later, when Hurd was working at MGM, he bumped into Minnelli and reminded him of their brief time together. Minnelli was distressed enough by the "reunion" that he went to L. B. Mayer and tried to have him fired.[20]

Minnelli's journey to New York's gay theatre community and then to Hollywood was similar to that of film legend Cary Grant. When Grant left New York for Hollywood, he turned his back on his previous gay lifestyle, cutting ties with friends, including William Haines. Haines never forgave Grant for his actions.[21] Both Minnelli and Grant were highly ambitious and knew they had to play the straight game, which meant staying in the closet. Both men married several times and fathered children, which has led many to assume they were bisexual. Maybe. It wasn't uncommon then, and even in the twenty-first century, it's still not unusual for gay men to marry women and have families for a variety of reasons, such as career, family pressures or obligations, the church, or their local societal demand.

The jury will probably always be out (so to speak) about whether Minnelli was genuinely gay, bisexual, or gender fluid. The subject is essential to Garland's story because she was already conflicted about the rumors surrounding her late father. It would turn out that during their marriage, Minnelli, like Garland's father, would have "lapses" and act on his homosexual desires. In the beginning, Garland must have heard the rumors about Minnelli—the studio gossip mill at MGM was both strong and swift—but her growing love for him likely clouded her thinking. Garland typically gravitated toward the strong, masculine type. But with Minnelli, not only did he seem to love her through the camera and in real life, but he was also very sophisticated, which Garland found irresistible. Like Joe Mankiewicz, Minnelli introduced her to a social network of creative, talented people with whom she felt at ease. Many in that crowd had an enormous impact on her performance style and her confidence as a performer.

Ten days after completing her work on *Meet Me in St. Louis*, Garland was at the Decca Records studios on April 20, 1944, for the first of two sessions, recording studio versions of songs from the film for the second Decca cast album of songs from a Garland film (the first was *Girl Crazy* five months prior). She recorded "Boys and Girls Like You and Me," "The Boy Next Door," and "Have Yourself a Merry Little Christmas." The next day, she recorded "The Trolley Song," "Skip to My Lou" (with a Decca chorus), and "Meet Me in St. Louis, Louis." All were included on the Decca cast album. "Boys and Girls Like You and Me" was noted on the album's cover as "Not included in picture" (meaning "film"). The album was released on November 2, 1944, a few weeks before the film's premiere and peaked at the number 2 spot on Billboard's new "album" chart. The songs were also released as singles.

Meet Me in St. Louis premiered in, naturally, St. Louis, Missouri, on November 22, 1944, followed by its New York premiere on November 28, 1944. According to the *St. Louis Star and Times*, "Every one of the theatre's 3,100 seats was occupied and almost 300 persons were standing. . . . More than 2,000 were turned away . . . for the first showing."[22] Freed's story about nothing turned out to be something, and that something was big. It was a blockbuster hit. Audiences flocked to the film, making it MGM's highest-grossing film in its history up to that date, grossing more than $7 million on a $1.7 million final cost. (*Gone with the Wind* (1939) was the highest grosser at the time, but although it was owned by MGM, it wasn't made by or at MGM; it had been produced by the Selznick Studios at RKO.) The critics were just as much in love with *Meet Me in St. Louis* as the public, as these raves reveal:

Let those who would savor their enjoyment of innocent family merriment with the fragrance of dried-rose petals and who would revel in girlish rhapsodies make a bee-line right down to the Astor. For there's honey to be had inside.

And it isn't just the clang-clang-clanging of "The Trolley Song" that will ring in your energized ears, despite the rather frightening impression you may have got from the radio. Nor is it, indeed, the musical phases of the film that are most likely to allure. Except for maybe half a dozen numbers which Judy Garland melodically sings—and which had been planted like favors in a bride's cake—this is mostly a straight family lark, covering a year of rare activity in a house heavily peopled with girls.

Miss Garland is full of gay exuberance as the second sister of the lot and sings, as we said, with a rich voice that grows riper and more expressive in each new film. Her chortling of "The Trolley Song" puts fresh zip into that inescapable tune, and her romantic singing of a sweet one, "The Boy Next Door," is good for mooning folks.

—Bosley Crowther, *New York Times*, November 29, 1944

If you are looking for a picture that represents sheer, unadulterated enjoyment, let me steer you to a theatre showing "Meet Me in St. Louis." You are guaranteed a thoroughly good time. . . . Judy, of course, gives out in song whenever the spirit moves her, which is often enough to please her loyal following, but not too often to interfere seriously with the thread of the story.

—Kate Cameron, *New York Daily News*, December 10, 1944

All set within the year 1903 . . . the result is real, sock ["socko"] entertainment in every way—with the infrequent song interpolations serving as grand garnish. . . . Contrary to what may be expected, it is far from being a musical in any sense of the word. It is

1945 Canadian sheet music. From the author's collection.

homeopathic to the extreme. And the songs do not disturb the story enough to matter. . . . Judy Garland does one of her finest performances.
—Jerry Cahill, *Sacramento Union*, December 24, 1944

"Meet Me in St. Louis" . . . is the kind of picture for which reviewers have trouble finding enough laudatory adjectives. That's a fact. This Technicolor musical has just about everything you could ask for in the way of entertainment. It's wonderfully acted and sung, beautifully filmed, and was brilliantly produced and directed. . . . Judy sings better than ever.
—uncredited review, *Shamokin News Dispatch*, February 1, 1945

This bright jewel, sparkling and brilliant in a rich Technicolor setting, is probably the most attractive bit of filmic entertainment in town. . . . Miss Garland is a sheer delight.
—uncredited review, *Hollywood Citizen News*, January 1, 1945

All that Technicolor and minute attention to the trappings of authenticity can do in behalf of a period play are done superbly for this otherwise plain and unpretentious tale about a family that lived in St. Louis before and during that city's World's Fair in 1904.
—uncredited review, *Motion Picture Herald*, November 4, 1944

Meet Me in St. Louis remains a masterpiece of the film musical genre and one of the greatest film musicals of all time, on par with *Singin' in the Rain* (1952) and *The Sound of Music* (1965). Garland is so luminous she practically glows. She's the teenage daughter, but she's also the leading lady, perfectly portraying a young woman in love for the first time. For war-weary audiences and servicemembers entrenched in World War II, seeing a glowing Garland in a film about a simpler, easier time, however rose-colored the lens might be, made them love and adore her all the more.

1944 MGM studio publicity still. From the author's collection.

Garland was fortunate to be the star of three true movie masterpieces in her film career: *The Wizard of Oz* (1939), *Meet Me in St. Louis* (1944), and *A Star Is Born* (Warner Bros., 1954). After the premiere of *Meet Me in St. Louis* in late 1944, Garland wasn't just a movie star. She was a movie superstar. The fact that she was one of the few actresses MGM could rely on to bring in the crowds with only her name above a film's title clearly indicates her exalted status. From here on out, it looked as though Judy Garland would reign supreme as MGM's premiere musical leading lady. She had become MGM's greatest asset.

The cover of the October 1944 *Movie Stars* fan magazine features Garland in another pose from the same photo session as seen on the previous page. From the author's collection.

CHAPTER 7

MGM'S GREATEST ASSET
GARLAND'S GOLDEN ERA

The phenomenal personal and professional success of *Meet Me in St. Louis* began a golden era for Judy Garland both at MGM and in her personal life. This golden era featured a succession of her best film performances, which led to Garland's status as MGM's "greatest asset."[1] First up was her guest appearance in Arthur Freed's pet project, *Ziegfeld Follies of 1946* (originally titled *Ziegfeld Follies of 1944*). The all-star musical comedy revue was planned as a celebration of MGM's twentieth anniversary in 1944 and a showcase for what the studio was capable of achieving. Set up in the plotless revue format of the stage extravaganzas produced by the late great showman Florenz Ziegfeld, the film presents what Ziegfeld might have created if he had access to the MGM talent pool and immense studio resources.

Throughout the planning stage of *Follies* (which dragged on for a couple of years), Garland's name was penciled in for several skit/song/production-number ideas. Some of the segment ideas that included Garland in song and/or comedy skits were a "Fireside Chat" (with Lucille Ball and Ann Sothern), "As Long as I Have My Art" (with Mickey Rooney), "Reading of a Play" (with Frank Morgan), and, depending on which biography one reads, duetting with Fred Astaire on "The Babbit and the Bromide" or joining Astaire and Rooney in a spoof of the Ira Gershwin/Kurt Weill Broadway musical *Lady in the Dark*.

One idea that made it past the idea phase was a song skit featuring Garland and Rooney reunited and in Technicolor for the first time in "I Love More in Technicolor Than I Did in Black and White." The script for the skit and the song (by Hugh Martin and Ralph Blane) has survived. A printed copy was included in the 1994 LaserDisc boxed set edition of the film. The skit has Garland playing herself, opening with her on stage. The camera then follows her off stage, where she turns down dates with MGM leading men James Craig, Van Johnson, and John Hodiak to keep a date with "an old friend." The old friend turns out to be Rooney. He shows her clips from their previous films and laments that he's only kissed her in black and white. The skit segues into the song, titled "I Love You More in Technicolor Than I Do in Back and White" (the tense changed from past to present). The skit never got past the script stage, which is probably a good thing since, as charming as it sounds, it would probably come across as dated today, especially the short bit with "Mamie," Judy's backstage "colored maid" (as noted in the script), who has lines that even on paper come off as the negative racist stereotype of the era.

A 1944 promotional photo of Garland for *Ziegfeld Follies* (released in 1946 as *Ziegfeld Follies of 1946*). From the author's collection.

Meanwhile, Roger Edens and new MGM vocal arranger Kay Thompson had come up with a sophisticated musical comedy skit that spoofed the image of MGM's drama queen Greer Garson, titled "A Great Lady Has an Interview" (a.k.a. "Madame Crematante"). The "Great Lady" is being interviewed by the press (a group of chorus boys), talking and singing about her biggest dramatic role yet, playing the part of "Madame Crematante," who "toiled . . . suffered" to invent the safety pin. The tone of the piece was high camp. Edens, Thompson, and Charles Walters (who staged the number) auditioned the skit for Garson at Freed's home, accompanied by *Follies* director Vincente Minnelli, who watched the performance along with Garson's mother and her husband, Richard Ney. Edens, Thompson, and Walters had hoped that Garson would be receptive to spoofing her own image. After the trio vigorously performed the number, there was an uncomfortable silence. Garson's mother spoke up first: "Well, I don't think so." Ney said, "No, it's not for you, dear."

The trio left their "audition" completely dejected. When they were getting into their car, Edens excitedly proclaimed, "Goddamn it! It's great for Judy! Do you think she can do it? She can imitate you, Kay—she's a good mimic—I think it'll work!"[2]

Garland began rehearsals of "A Great Lady Has an Interview" with the chorus boys on July 6, 1944, under the direction of Walters. Filming began on MGM's Stage 21 on July 19, 1944. To Walters's dismay, after he staged and rehearsed the number, Minnelli was brought in to shoot it. Walters later reported, "Every bit of action in that number was mine. I almost cried."[3] Freed's insistence on having Minnelli direct the number makes sense. Walters had yet to prove himself as a director. Minnelli was the main director of *Follies*, and he also seemed to be the only person who could guide Garland through a production with minimal issues, and he made her look beautiful. Walters recovered from his disappointment and became one of MGM's greatest directors.

Ziegfeld Follies of 1944 went through a bumpy and lengthy production due to its revue format and the uneven quality of the different segments. A nearly three-hour edit of the film had a disastrous preview at the Westwood Village Theatre in Los Angeles on November 1, 1944, after which everyone wanted to cut something, prompting Edens to quip, "If this keeps on, we can always release it as a short."[4] Songs and skits were added, deleted, or reshot. It was retitled simply *Ziegfeld Follies* and had its roadshow premiere on August 13, 1945, in Boston, Massachusetts. Garland and Minnelli were on their honeymoon trip in New York and traveled to Boston to attend the premiere with East Coast MGM executives Joesph Vogel, Howard Dietz, and William F. Rogers. After a few roadshow engagements, the film was taken out of circulation, and more changes were made. Garland's sequence stayed in the film throughout the entire process. New ads and posters added the "of 1946" to the title, while other ads and lobby cards did not, which has created confusion about the title ever since. Examples of the confusion with the film's title can be seen in the trade magazines published in early 1946. The two-page advertisement for the film in the January 5, 1946, edition of *Motion Picture Herald* lists thirty-two cities across the United States where it was scheduled to open simultaneously on January 15 titled *Ziegfeld Follies*. By the same magazine's February 23, 1946, edition, the film was advertised as *Ziegfeld Follies of 1946*. Although it received mixed reviews, the officially titled *Ziegfeld Follies of 1946* still turned a nice profit, grossing over $5,344,000 on a $3,240,816.86 investment.

"A Great Lady Has an Interview" was one of the film's highlights, and it was singled out for praise by critics and audiences. Garland fans especially loved this new, sophisticated Judy Garland, presented as an ultra-glamorous and slightly campy movie star. Even at this early stage, the "Garland Cult" was growing. Garland biographer Christopher Finch put it best: "Hardcore Garland aficionados swooned over Madame Crematon [*sic*]. This was the Judy they had hoped for, the Judy of their most cherished dreams—a camp madonna."[5] It was a new image for Garland

MGM'S GREATEST ASSET   193 and light-years away from her "girl next door" persona, carefully crafted by MGM. She looks beautiful (if a bit thin), shows a real flair for high comedy, and is obviously having a good time. She also raps. A brief section of the skit was styled in an early form of what would eventually be called "rap," thanks to the brilliance of Kay Thompson. Thompson soon became Garland's best female friend, confidant, and musical mentor. It was Thompson who helped Garland grow artistically and vocally in the late 1940s and helped shape Garland's later performing style in concert. Her positive influence can never be underestimated.

With "A Great Lady Has an Interview" in the can in mid-1944, Garland went into production on her next film, *The Clock*, on July 31, 1944. *The Clock* (1945) stands out in Garland's career and personal life. It was her first solely dramatic role, and it was during the film's production that the love between her and Minnelli blossomed into eventual marriage. That latter chain of events might not have happened if the film had been completed as initially planned.

The original director of *The Clock* was Fred Zinnemann. Zinnemann had recently graduated from directing shorts to directing features, and his directing style didn't gel with Garland. It didn't help that she wanted Minnelli to direct from the beginning, and she seemed to be stalling the production long enough to get Zinnemann replaced with Minnelli. The film was important to Garland; it was her chance to prove that she was more than a musical comedy performer. She rightly knew that Minnelli was the only director who could bring out her best, both in acting and in appearance. He was the only one she trusted. After a few short weeks, Zinnemann was taken off the project, and Minnelli was brought in. Zinnemann wasn't happy about the experience. In a handwritten letter he sent to Minnelli, he put part of the blame on Garland, saying he thought

This massive Pennsylvania Station set built at MGM for *The Clock* (1945). From the author's collection.

Publicity still of Garland and Robert Walker for *The Clock* (1945). From the author's collection.

she "behaved pretty badly," and he put part of the blame on producer Arthur Freed, for whom he said he had "great contempt for [his] conduct both as a producer and as a man."[6] He assured Minnelli he had no hard feelings toward him and wished him well. Zinnemann added three more Oscars to his previous Oscar win for Best Short Subject in 1938, including the classic *From Here to Eternity* (1953).

Minnelli made some changes to Garland's appearance and reshot the bulk of the Zinnemann scenes. He also wisely decided that the third character in the film, after the two lovers played by Garland and Robert Walker, was New York City itself. Minnelli went to great lengths to make the film appear as if it were shot on location and not on MGM's backlot and soundstages. He cleverly mixed location footage of the city with the studio sets and backlots. Some are obvious rear projection shots, but they work. What really works is the constant presence of the city and the fact that it seems to try everything to keep the lovers apart. The city is always looming, hovering over them. Minnelli's attention to detail was such that at a cost of $66,450 (at a 1944 dollar value), the studio built a re-creation of the interior of Pennsylvania Station on Stage 27, complete with working escalators. This attention to detail became a hallmark of Minnelli's directing style.

The story of *The Clock* is a simple one. The very green small-town soldier Joe (Robert Walker) is on his forty-eight-hour leave in New York City. He feels overwhelmed by the city as soon as he arrives in Pennsylvania Station. He bumps into Alice (Garland) in a charming "meet cute" scene that immediately sets up the city and its hustle and bustle as a force against the couple. Alice recognizes the sincerity of his innocence and agrees to spend the afternoon with him, showing him some of the city. The two slowly fall in love. That love is tested by the city separating them and throwing obstacles in their path, but in the end, everything works out. Along the way, they come across a few colorful New York characters. They help an injured milkman make his early morning deliveries, providing us with a nice tour of MGM's "New York Streets" on Lot 2. The couple then have breakfast with the milkman and his wife, who provide the lovers with an example of long-term love and devotion. James and Lucille Gleason beautifully play the couple. Keenan Wynn has a comic bit as a drunken diner patron who gives Gleason his injury. Angela Lansbury's mother, Moyna MacGill, has an uncredited bit as an eccentric woman at a late-night diner trying to ignore Wynn's drunken rants. Alice and Joe manage to get married in spite of more obstacles, and the film ends with Joe saying his farewell to Alice on his way back to camp. The last shot is an overhead pullback showing Alice walking away from the train. She puts her chin up with a slight smile of confidence and determination on her face. She knows everything will be all right. The more the camera pulls back, the more Alice is swallowed up by the city. She's just one of a million wartime love stories. The ultimate fate of the couple is left to the imagination of the audience. Does Joe return from the war? Does their love survive in the long term?

The Clock was a success when it was released on May 25, 1945, making a nice profit for the studio. Garland more than proved herself capable of subtle, nuanced acting, which, when compared to the major dramatic actresses of the era, comes off today as less histrionic and more realistic than many of their more famous roles. Critics enjoyed Garland's performance, and she received good reviews, but her musical genius got in the way. When audiences went to a Judy Garland film, they expected to hear her sing. Some patrons and theatre managers complained about the lack of singing while still enjoying the film.

> Miss Garland, who does not sing this time, and Walker, who is once again in uniform, play their roles with an appealing combination of innocence, bewilderment and confidence in the powers of love.
> —E. A. C., *Motion Picture Herald*, March 24, 1945

> The stars play the thing beautifully all of the way, with innumerable touches making for humor and sentiment. This is [a] perfect teaming.
> —G. L. D., *Democrat and Chronicle,"* Rochester, New York, June 28, 1945

> "The Clock" presents to screen fans a Judy Garland who does no singing. We can report positively that they will like this Judy Garland, the actress, very much. . . . Judy Garland can be—and here is—any American girl of her age. Judy scores solidly as an actress. Under Vincent [*sic*] Minnelli's direction she registers with a trouping performance that would have set her at any time on the screen if no one had ever heard her sing.
> —uncredited, *Lincoln Heights Bulletin News*, Lincoln Heights, Los Angeles, May 10, 1945

Garland didn't make another dramatic film until 1961's *Judgment at Nuremberg*. *The Clock* was released toward the end of World War II, after a steady stream of similar wartime romances,

Garland and her husband Vincente Minnelli relaxing at home in 1945. From the author's collection.

the effect being that it didn't make a mark as it might have if released a few years earlier. Today, the film is seen as a charming classic and one of the better and more realistic (in spite of the rear-projected New York) love stories put out by Hollywood during the war.

In December 1944, *Life* magazine featured Garland on the cover. It was another important sign of her superstar status. Garland's personal life was on a high as well. She and Minnelli were in love, and on November 24, 1944, just a few days after the premiere of *Meet Me in St. Louis*, they boarded a train for New York. They announced their engagement after their arrival. By this point, the couple had been living together, something that did not sit well with Garland's mother, Ethel. Ethel had endured a lot of Garland's seemingly bipolar or manic-depressive mood swings and the situations those brought, but living together outside of marriage was still a taboo and something even Hollywood knew to try to keep quiet, especially when it involved MGM's most popular "girl next door." Minnelli was able to calm Ethel down a bit, claiming that he would keep his intentions honorable until they were able to get married once Garland's divorce from David Rose became final.

The couple enjoyed visiting some of the New York spots portrayed in *The Clock*. Garland was enjoying the bliss of their romance and their professional and personal collaborations. Minnelli introduced her to his New York friends, who, like him, were quite creative and flamboyant. Back in Hollywood, as he had done in New York, Minnelli introduced her to his social set. Garland and Minnelli became a part of the Hollywood elite, going to dinners and parties that included such guests as Laurence Olivier and Vivien Leigh, Gene Kelly, and director George Cukor, among others. In spite of her limited education, Garland more than held her own with her sharp wit and wickedly funny sense of humor. Once again, everyone seemed to love her.

Garland and Minnelli were very active in the broader Hollywood social scene both before and after their marriage. They were featured in most fan magazines of the time, seen in photos and columns that chronicled their socializing at various restaurants and nightclubs. MGM was only too happy to help feed the magazines and newspaper columnists stories about their new golden couple. Garland's heavy workload outside of MGM in the evenings died down quite a bit beginning in late 1943, giving her more time for socializing. She had some radio appearances and recording obligations with Decca Records, but, overall, she wasn't as swamped with work as she had been. This lightening of her load was most likely due to her inability to keep up with that brutal schedule and her studio obligations, which took priority. One of her most famous appearances was on February 15, 1945, when, after a day at MGM, she went over to the Shrine Auditorium and recorded the radio show *Dick Tracy in B-Flat, or For Goodness' Sake, Isn't He Ever Going to Marry Tess Trueheart?* for the Armed Forces Radio Service *Command Performance* series, which was sent overseas

One of many newspaper and magazine blurbs showing Garland and her husband Vincente Minnelli socializing, this one from December 1945. From the author's collection.

to be played over the Allied Expeditionary Force radio stations. The show, while never officially premiered on US radio, was nonetheless popular on records and on nostalgia radio shows in later decades, and with good reason. It features an all-star lineup of most of the top musical talent in film and radio at the time, including Bing Crosby, Frank Sinatra, Bob Hope, Jimmy Durante, Dinah Shore, and the Andrews Sisters, among others. Garland played the role of Snowflake. She sang a short parody of "Over the Rainbow," which was the only time in her career that she spoofed the song in public.

THE HARVEY GIRLS

Once the couple returned to California, Garland went to work on her next film, the big-budget original film musical *The Harvey Girls*. Minnelli went into directing another big-budget original film musical, *Yolanda and the Thief*, starring Fred Astaire and Garland's *Meet Me in St. Louis* costar Lucille Bremer. Both films were produced by the Freed Unit. Garland wanted to work with Minnelli on *Yolanda*, thinking it was a better role. Freed convinced her that the *Harvey* role was the better one for her talents, and he was right. Although Garland might have felt that playing a waitress in a western on the backlot was below the more lofty-appearing role of Yolanda, *The Harvey Girls* presented Garland in the kind of earthy good-girl role that audiences expected. *Yolanda*, unfortunately, sank like a stone at the box office. It was a bit too arty for the general public at the time and Bremer's appeal as a leading lady was limited, at best. Today, it's a cult classic for musical fans due to Minnelli's use of color and surrealism and Astaire and Bremer's dances. When it had its disastrous preview in Pomona, California, Garland was in attendance with Minnelli. On the way out, she turned to Arthur Freed and quipped, "Never Mind, Arthur, Pomona isn't Lucille's town."[7] Garland's sarcastic comment was a reference to Bremer's limited ability to connect with audiences.

The big set piece of *The Harvey Girls* is the production number "On the Atchison, Topeka, and the Santa Fe," written by Johnny Mercer and Harry Warren. The sequence is a mini masterpiece of imagery and music and is still exciting to watch today. Filmed on MGM's Lot 3 on "Billy the Kid Street," the studio installed train tracks to run through part of the street to accommodate the train in spite of the fact that the nearby "Western Street" already had tracks. The reason for

Bing Crosby, Frank Sinatra, and Garland during the recording of the radio show *Dick Tracy in B-Flat* at the Shrine Auditorium in Los Angeles for the Armed Forces Radio Service *Command Performance* series, February 15, 1945. From the author's collection.

MGM'S GREATEST ASSET

this is simple: "Billy the Kid Street" had a more rustic frontier town look (in keeping with the plot) compared to the more modern look of "Western Street." "Billy the Kid Street" was elaborately dressed up to be the fictional town of Sandrock, New Mexico. The "Atchison" number brilliantly introduces the Harvey girls as they are, in turn, introduced to the town, featuring that now-famous pullback overhead shot

A 1945 postcard showing the arrival of the train in *The Harvey Girls* (1946). From the author's collection.

showing the train's arrival. After the Harvey girls and costar Ray Bolger's Chris sing their introductions, we get Garland's show-stopping entrance, which is one continuous shot following Garland as she moves and sings among the chorus and cast. The film's director, George Sidney, later told the story about how the cast and crew had been rehearsing the number with Robert Alton (who staged it) for days when it came time to shoot it. Garland arrived on the set at 1:00 p.m. She went through the number with her "dance-in" (the dance version of a star's stand-in) and said, "I'm ready," and did it perfectly in the first take. "We shot it, and she did it like she had been rehearsing it for six months. It was sheer genius!" exclaimed Sidney.[8] The end of the number features another famous shot showing the cast, chorus, and townspeople vigorously singing and dancing alongside the exiting train as it steams and zips past them, ending on a close-up of Garland for that final note. At the film's preview in Inglewood, California, on July 12, 1945, the audience cheered at the end of the number, as well as breaking into applause throughout the rest of the movie.[9]

The story of Garland's ability to learn and perform the complicated "Atchison" routine is one of many examples of her almost inhuman natural talents. She was revered by her peers and almost everyone who worked with her for instinctively knowing what was right, whether singing, acting, or dancing. She was known for being able to memorize dialog in a first reading or learn a new song after hearing it once or twice. She could listen to a song and sing it back to you. She also learned choreography in the same quick manner. It's no wonder everyone wanted to work with her. Contract dancer Dorothy Tuttle, who was one of the on-screen chorus and dancers in most of the Freed musicals at this time, said, "She was, without a doubt, the greatest natural talent I ever worked with. She would pick up a script and read it for the first time like she'd studied it for two weeks. She was just incredible."[10]

Another big production number in the film that showcased Garland is one that wasn't seen by the public until the early 1990s, the now famous "March of the Doagies." The number originally took place in the narrative late in the film, after the Harvey girls had their big party. It's every bit as big and elaborate as "Atchison," having been filmed over several nights on the back lot and on a soundstage. It ends on a soundstage desert set with Garland on the top of a large rock in front of a huge bonfire, prompting fans to label it "Judy of Arc" or "Judy on Fire."[11]

After that Inglewood preview, it was decided that the film was too long, and "Doagies" was cut, along with its reprise, as was an earlier duet between Garland and costar John Hodiak, "My Intuition." The latter wasn't missed, but the removal of "Doagies" left a small plot hole. There is no explanation or reason given for the entire Harvey House staff and partygoers to suddenly be away from the Harvey House when a fire is set, burning it down. Viewers who caught this would have thought, "Where is everybody?" and, when they all show up out of nowhere, "Where are they all coming from?" This small anomaly didn't hamper the enjoyment of the film or its success at the box office. It became one of *Variety*'s top all-time moneymakers for several decades. It's still one of the most popular of all the famous MGM musicals.

Over at Decca Records, it was decided to produce a cast album of new studio re-creations of songs from *The Harvey Girls*. For the album, Decca went all out with a full orchestra and chorus under the direction of the film's musical director, Lennie Hayton, and vocal arranger Kay Thompson. Kenny Baker and Virginia O'Brien re-created their songs from the film as well. Singer Betty Russell stood in for Cyd Charisse's character. They began the recording sessions while the film was still in production, with the first session on May 14, 1945, followed by another session the next evening.

Decca's elaborate version of the "Atchison, Topeka, and the Santa Fe" number is almost identical to that heard in the film. It takes up both sides of one disc, with the chorus introduction on one side and Garland's entrance, solo, and the finale on the other. These were the standard 10″ 78 rpm records, which were usually housed in albums of four discs, two songs each, eight songs total, and the space (time) on

British sheet music for *The Harvey Girls* (1946). From the author's collection.

each side was limited. They were called albums because they looked similar to standard photo albums. Before the album was released, MGM cut "March of the Doagies" from the film. Decca decided to cut the song from the album as well, ending up with an uneven number of songs, meaning one disc would have an empty side. The remedy was to cut the chorus intro to "Atchison." When it was released on November 1, 1945, the album had only three discs (six songs). To keep the continuity, Decca brought Garland back into the studio on September 10, 1945, to rerecord her solo with a new lyric. They changed the opening line, "What a lovely trip," to "What a lovely day." The "trip" lyric didn't make sense out of context from the now-deleted elaborate intro section. Several years later, this change created confusion when Decca rereleased the songs on various compilations and some-

Picture Show fan magazine with Garland and costar John Hodiak in a publicity still for *The Harvey Girls* (1946), published on May 4, 1946. From the author's collection.

times mistakenly chose the unused "trip" version. Garland fans were understandably perplexed.

While Garland was relatively reliable during the production of *The Clock*, on *The Harvey Girls*, the stress of having another big-budget Technicolor musical on her shoulders became an increasingly heavy burden. She began to exhibit more of her erratic behavior. In spite of how happy she was in her personal life, her insecurities still got the best of her. For example, in mid-January 1945, she was late to the set for a series of mostly consecutive days. She would be required on the set at 10:00 or 11:00 a.m., but that meant that she had to be in makeup around 8:00 a.m. That early morning call was too much for her. She continued her habit of calls to the assistant director in the early hours of the morning (as early as 3:00 a.m.), saying she either couldn't get to work the next day due to illness or would be late. Sometimes she would say she would be late but then not show up at all.

In the mid-1940s, working on a big-budget Technicolor musical like *The Harvey Girls* was very tough work for anyone. In a black-and-white drama or comedy, there was less stress and strain on the body due to not having to endure weeks of intensive and extensive singing and dancing rehearsals, followed by more hours in makeup and hair (including body makeup) to look right in front of the Technicolor cameras. As MGM star Ann Miller later noted, they were already worn out by the time they got to the set to begin the actual day of filming.[12] This was true to varying degrees for all of the on-camera talent, from the stars down to the extras. Technicolor was still a very cumbersome process. Many times, something would happen, and the film dailies would come back off color or in some other unusable state, necessitating retakes. The process was long. The pressure to perform, and perform perfectly with each take, was intense. For a performer like Garland, who already had a fragile psyche and personal insecurities about her talents, as well as fatigue, the thought of that daily grind could be torture, especially when the success of a film was resting on her shoulders.

In spite of Garland's bouts of bad behavior, production of *The Harvey Girls* still managed to move along without too many delays that wouldn't be experienced by any production (such as cast illnesses, accidents, etc.). Garland's last day on the production was June 14, 1945, just a little shy of six months of work.

The Harvey Girls cost a little over $2.5 million and grossed over $5.1 million.[13] It was another huge hit for Garland and the Freed Unit. It's no wonder. It's an enjoyable vintage MGM Technicolor musical treat featuring Garland at the top of her game, with strong support from Hodiak, Angela Lansbury, Marjorie Main, Ray Bolger, Virginia O'Brien, Chill Wills, and Cyd Charisse.

As history—which it purports, in a way, to be—"The Harvey Girls" . . . is probably a lot of malarkey, but who cares? As a musical show, it's way above average thanks to the tunes turned out by Johnny Mercer and Harry Warren and to the gaudy 1890-ish settings whipped up by Edwin B. Willis. Number 1 among these factors is Miss Judy Garland. Miss Garland, even though she is now a veteran, can still get over the impression that she is having more fun than anybody. She can still put over a song.
—Jim Billings, *Springfield Leader and Press*, Springfield, Missouri, February 16, 1946

Filmed in Technicolor against the picturesque frontier ground of New Mexico of the 1890s, "The Harvey Girls" offers unlimited scope for the dramatic, comic, and song-and-dance talents headed by Judy Garland, John Hodiak, Ray Boger, Angela Lansbury, Kenny Baker, Marjorie Main and Chill Wills.
—uncredited, *Sandusky Register*, Sandusky, Ohio, February 16, 1946

You've got to go back to "Meet Me in St. Louis" for an MGM musical with which to compare this one, and doubtless, you'll have to go back into your receipts ledger later on to decide, on a dollar basis, which is better of the two attractions. Like that one, this one has Judy Garland, one of the "Top Ten" Money-Making Stars of 1945, as its heroine and the singing leader of production numbers that make eye and ear happy to be present at the proceedings. It's a hit musical by any and all standards.
—William R. Weaver, *Motion Picture Herald*, January 5, 1946

Movie Songs magazine featuring *The Harvey Girls* (1946).
From the author's collection.

Inside the *Movie Songs* magazine featuring *The Harvey Girls* (1946). From the author's collection.

Another sign of the film's success was the various promotional campaigns put on by towns and cities across the country. Elaborate promotions for films were popular at this time due to the fact that television was practically nonexistent. Movies, radio, local plays, and phonographic records were the public's only sources of entertainment. As an example, in Topeka, Kansas, the manager of the Fox Atchison theatres had the Santa Fe Railway ship a scaled-down version of their trains to Atchison, Kansas, to "ballyhoo" the opening of the film there. He was even able to get a costume worn by Garland shipped to Atchison to display in "a special window display built around the costume."[14] Local newspapers ran multipage spreads, contests, and ads. The local radio stations played programs centered around the film. Retail stores featured elaborate window displays, with record stores focusing on the recent Decca Records album. As if that wasn't enough, both Atchison and Topeka had parades centered around the showing of the film. In Topeka, one of the original, real Harvey girls was "located and feted with resultant publicity."[15] The campaign worked. According to the local paper, the film broke all attendance records during its run "in spite of extremely cold weather."[16]

"On the Atchison, Topeka, and the Santa Fe" won the Oscar for Best Song for Harry Warren and Johnny Mercer. Lennie Hayton was nominated for Best Scoring of a Musical Motion Picture but lost to Morris Stoloff's score for *The Jolson Story*.

On a side note, in 1950, a railroad worker filed a lawsuit against MGM, claiming that the idea for *The Harvey Girls* was his. Clifford Funkhouser was a trainman for the Missouri-Kansas-Texas Railroad and had done research on the Harvey girls. He was seeking $2 million in damages. In 1952, a judge ruled against him. In his decision, the judge stated, "I think it is reasonable to assume any story of the Harvey girls, the Harvey system, or of the Santa Fe Railroad would necessarily have many parallels and many similar characters. Certainly, the stories of the Harvey girls have so long been in the public domain that no one can claim to have exclusive privilege in writing about them. They have long been the subject of many stories of fact and fiction."[17]

On June 15, 1945, just a day after her last day working on *The Harvey Girls*, Garland and Minnelli married at her mother's home. MGM studio boss Louis B. Mayer gave her away. Betty Asher was Garland's maid of honor. Ira Gershwin was the best man. In the wedding photos, Garland looks painfully thin but happy. The newlyweds left by train that night for their New York honeymoon. The honeymoon was a happy one. But even on her honeymoon, Garland had professional obligations, including two separate sessions at the Decca Records New York studios that produced four singles (see the Decca Records appendix), a few radio appearances, and that trip to Boston for the *Ziegfeld Follies* roadshow premiere. MGM was always looming in the background, just like New York City in *The Clock*, pulling the strings even on the couple's honeymoon.

MGM studio publicity still, 1945. From the author's collection.

A sign of Garland's natural positive outlook was what she did while walking along the Hudson River with Minnelli. She produced a bottle of pills and threw them into the river, exclaiming that she didn't need them anymore. Although these things are never that simple, she was no doubt sincere. The future looked bright to her. Garland had blossomed into a beautiful young woman, enjoying discovering what her talents were capable of and the success those talents were bringing to her. It was a happy and golden time. She was the top female musical star at the top studio in Hollywood. She was revered for her voice. She was popular on radio shows, performing with greats like Bing Crosby, Frank Sinatra, and many others while getting the chance to challenge herself vocally and stretch her natural comedic and dramatic gifts. She was a popular artist in Decca Records' roster of stars, giving her the chance to experiment by singing

October 5, 1945: Garland with Frank Sinatra, who was guest hosting *The Danny Kaye Show* on CBS Radio. From the author's collection.

songs she would never be allowed to sing on film at MGM. Most important, she soon discovered that she was pregnant.

When Garland and Minnelli returned to California and MGM, they announced that they were expecting. This time, the studio and Garland's mom took the news better than they previously had when she was married to David Rose. No abortion was needed. Unlike with the Rose marriage, Mayer (and almost everyone else at MGM) saw the Minnelli marriage as a positive thing for Garland and the studio. Minnelli was a company man, and he seemed to be able to keep Garland happy with minimal issues. Now she was married to their top musical director, which was a match made in MGM heaven.

Due to her pregnancy, the filming of Garland's guest appearance in *Till the Clouds Roll By* was moved up. Garland portrayed real-life Broadway legend Marilyn Miller in this highly fictional biopic about composer Jerome Kern. Garland plays a couple of dramatic scenes, including one with previous costar Lucille Bremer and one with previous costar Robert Walker. She gets to sing "Look for the Silver Lining" and "Who?" The former is performed on a mock-up of a Broadway stage, with Miller (Garland) as a dishwasher surrounded by seemingly endless piles of dishes. It's one of Garland's best vocals and one of MGM's best song arrangements. At one point, Garland hums over the music. Only Judy Garland could get away with humming over such a beautiful arrangement. People assumed that the dishes were a way to hide Garland's pregnancy, but, in fact, that is the way Miller originally performed the number on Broadway.

"Sunny/Who?" is Garland's big production number. The chorus performs the circus-themed "Sunny" opening with a silent Garland coming out as a bareback rider, and, with some clever editing, a stand-in does the actual riding around the ring while standing on the horse. In true Minnelli fashion, the number opens with a cacophony of activity featuring everything from a trapeze woman twirling around by her teeth to an array of clowns and even gold-painted live elephants. This sequence segues into "Who?" featuring Garland in a completely different setting, floating down a flight of stairs surrounded by formally attired chorus men and going into the song and dance. She's costumed in a beautiful yellow/gold gown with almost blonde auburn hair, which works perfectly against the backdrop of the male dancers all in black. Never was Garland more luminous than she is in this number (except in *Meet Me in St. Louis*). She's presented as a glamorous musical leading lady; plus she's at the right weight and in total command of her talents, singing and dancing with a grace and confidence that only a performer of her caliber could pull off. Additionally, Minnelli perfectly staged and filmed the sequence. According to legend, Garland was apparently quite amused to be singing "Who?" to a group of men while in her pregnant condition. "Who?" was originally planned to be much longer. It's unknown whether all of the extended sections heard in the complete audio prerecording were actually filmed; no footage has ever been found. Judging from the way the number fades in from "Sunny" and from surviving behind-the-scenes photos, it looks as though the unused intro chorus and some of the additional Garland vocals were possibly filmed but ultimately deleted for length and to allow for a smooth transition from "Sunny" to "Who?" due to the deletion of another number on the "Sunny" circus set, "D'Ya Love Me?"

Garland's last day on the film, November 7, 1945, was spent filming the ultimately deleted "D'Ya Love Me?" number on the circus set. The song was planned to follow "Sunny," with

1946: Garland is presented as the epitome of feminine beauty in this magazine ad for Max Factor lipstick. From the author's collection.

Garland still in her horseback costume. Surviving silent outtake footage shows her doing some comedy bits with two clowns, played by the famous clown team the Arnaut Brothers, before singing the song, followed by more comedy and then the rest of the song. The audio outtake for the song survives, and when paired with the footage, it's clear why it was cut. It's poorly staged and boring and would have ground the film to a halt. Even the great Minnelli didn't always hit a musical home run.

On November 8, 1945, Garland went on official maternity leave from MGM. She made one radio appearance afterward, participating in the Jerome Kern memorial show on CBS Radio on December 9, 1945. The *Command Performance* Christmas show she and other stars prerecorded on September 25 was broadcast on Christmas Day. On January 28, 1946, she had her last work before giving birth. She re-created her role in *The Clock* in an abridged version on the January 28, 1946, edition of the *Lux Radio Theatre*, costarring with her *Harvey Girls* costar, John Hodiak, who played the role that in the film is played by Robert Walker. Garland anticipated a bright future ahead. She was awaiting the birth of her new baby, she would continue her collaboration with her brilliant husband, and she would possibly be branching out via live performances and maybe even a Broadway show. Being MGM's top musical leading lady, it seemed as though all the previous years of hard work and sacrifice had been worth it because now everything looked rosy. Garland couldn't have known that the last half of the decade would end up being the opposite, and in just a few years, in 1950, she would be gone from MGM forever.

Gorgeous Garland. This studio portrait was taken of Garland in 1946, although she looks more like the Garland of 1941. From the author's collection.

CHAPTER *8*

MGM TREADMILL
THE PIRATE AND *EASTER PARADE*

In her column published on February 6, 1944, writer Inga Arvad told the story of Garland's rise to fame based partly on interviews with her. Garland said, "When my contract expires—by that time, I will have been here 12 years—I would like to do a show and maybe a couple of pictures each year. There is nothing like having an audience. You get immediate reaction; you know if your singing is good or not. In pictures, you have to wait for months before you are sure one way or the other."[1]

The fact that Garland was talking to a columnist in early 1944 about her desire to leave MGM indicates that it had been on her mind for a while and was important to her. Her current contract with MGM wasn't up for renewal for another three years. Garland was nothing if not brilliant in knowing herself when it came to her talent and her career. She might not have been able to successfully navigate affairs of the heart and finances, but she was always spot on about herself. She preferred performing in front of a live audience, and she intermittently got her fix via the audiences at the live radio shows in which she participated. Her film promotional tours also gave her some chances to connect with audiences. The recent triumphs of her solo concert at the Robin Hood Dell and the two USO tours that followed almost immediately, all in the summer and fall of 1943, no doubt helped Garland to realize that what she truly wanted wasn't just to be a movie star churning out movies but to be a live performer. She also most likely knew she had reached a level of success that should have given her more agency and control over her career.

Unfortunately, that didn't happen. Once MGM knew about her plans (and they would have known before any column was printed), they went to work to do anything and everything to keep her under contract.

Despite her reputation for being fragile, her abuse of drugs, and her propensity for destroying film schedules, there was no denying that Judy Garland was one of the few stars in Hollywood who could carry a film with just her name above the title (no costars) and generate big box office success. At this point, all of Garland's films had turned a profit; most turned big profits. Her recent blockbuster success with *Meet Me in St. Louis* and, to a lesser degree, *The Clock* had made her one of the biggest movie stars in Hollywood. She made the Gallup Poll for the fifth year in a row as one of the top five movie actresses alongside Ingrid Bergman, Betty Grable, Bette Davis, and fellow MGM star Greer Garson.[2] Both *The Harvey Girls* and *Till the Clouds Roll By* had yet to be

Garland with daughter Liza Minnelli, 1946. From the author's collection.

released, but every indication was that they would also be blockbusters (they were). Even the troubled and uneven *Ziegfeld Follies of 1946* turned a profit. MGM wasn't about to risk Judy Garland going independent, jeopardizing their bottom line.

In the meantime, Liza May Minnelli was born at Cedars of Lebanon Hospital in Los Angeles on March 12, 1946, at 7:58 a.m. She weighed six pounds, ten ounces. Some in Hollywood wondered whether the child was really a product of the union of Garland and Minnelli or Garland and one of her lovers. Due to the rumors and assumptions about Minnelli's homosexuality, some thought the baby might look like someone else, perhaps Joe Mankiewicz, but when Liza was born, it was obvious that she was her father's daughter.

Garland had managed to stay off the pills while she was pregnant, afraid they might hurt the unborn child or cause problems. After the birth, she suffered from postpartum depression and needed follow-up surgery due to issues with the cesarean birth. As late as mid-April 1946, Garland was still on bed rest at home, as noted by the newspaper columns. On April 16, Ethel arrived in St. Petersburg, Florida, to attend the funeral of Minnelli's father in Vincente's place so he could stay with Garland as she recuperated. Garland's weakness in those initial months after

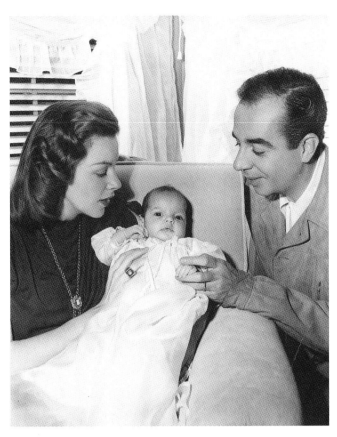

Garland and Vincente Minnelli with daughter Liza Minnelli, 1946. From the author's collection.

the birth didn't hinder her joy in being a mother and doting on Liza. She loved being a mom, and in later decades, all three of her children, Liza, Lorna Luft, and Joe Luft (the latter two were born in the 1950s while Garland was married to husband number three, Sid Luft)—plus anyone who knew the family—talked about her great love of her children. A good example of this is when Garland watched her son Joe sing "Where Is Love" on the Christmas episode of *The Judy Garland Show* in 1963. The look on Garland's face is pure motherly love and pride. In her later years, Garland was very open about how her own mother mistreated her, and she was determined not to repeat that behavior. She succeeded.

Four months after Liza's birth, Garland went back to work, not at MGM but on the radio. On July 17, 1946, she appeared on the *Bob Crosby Show* and sang "If I Had You" and "I Got the Sun in the Morning." The latter was from the recent Irving Berlin Broadway hit, *Annie Get Your Gun*, which MGM purchased for Garland to star in the film adaptation and would later become a legendary part of her downfall at the studio. Garland also took part in another tribute to Jerome Kern; this time, it was a partially live concert at the Hollywood Bowl on July 20, 1946. The concert is notable because it resulted in an unintentional Judy Garland MGM recording.

In February 1946, the Hollywood Bowl Association approached Arthur Freed to produce a Kern memorial concert for their summer season. Freed accepted. At the time of the request, the studio was finishing up production of the Kern biopic *Till the Clouds Roll By*. Most of the guest stars in the film also appeared on the broadcast, with Robert Walker narrating. Walker had the lead role in the film, portraying Kern. The concert was divided into three sections: The first featured the California Junior Symphony Orchestra playing a medley of Kern songs, followed by MGM's musical arranger and composer Johnny Green conducting the Hollywood Bowl Orchestra, with some of the stars from the film re-creating their numbers (including Garland singing "Look for the Silver Lining" and "Who?"), ending with the orchestra performing a "Mark Twain Suite" (a Kern eulogy written by Freed). The third section was a "Finale Medley," which was the same as in the film. However, at the concert, the performers sang live, accompanied by the orchestra-only tracks from the MGM prerecording sessions that were originally created for and used in the film. This approach was unusual in that it necessitated playing playback discs for the singers to sing along with.

Twenty minutes after the concert had started, word came that Lena Horne would not be able to appear. Since they were using the MGM prerecording discs for the finale medley section, which included Lena's "Why Was I Born?" solo, that section couldn't be cut at such short notice. At intermission, Roger Edens went to Garland's dressing room and persuaded her to step in for Lena. They quickly rehearsed the song at a "small, broken-down piano" in a "passageway leading to the dressing rooms backstage."[3] Garland came through with a beautiful performance. The end result was a "new" Judy Garland MGM recording. Over the years, collectors who knew the film and could compare the orchestra track in the film to the radio recording had wondered whether this Garland version of "Why Was I Born?" was a rare, unreleased prerecording that Garland recorded at the studio. It wasn't. Some thought she was originally slated to sing it in the film. She wasn't. The "new" recording was created by the last-minute marriage of Garland singing live on the air while backed by the MGM prerecording.

1946 movie magazine ad promoting *Till the Clouds Roll By*. From the author's collection.

Around this time, Garland's agents, Phil Berg and Bert Allenberg of the Berg-Allenberg talent agency, were negotiating a new contract for her with MGM. In January 1946, while she was still pregnant with Liza and on maternity leave, MGM raised her salary from $2,500 to $3,000 per week. This increase was in accordance with her September 26, 1940, contract, which superseded her previous contract, the first one she had signed for MGM in 1935 after her audition. As noted, Garland did not want to sign another multiyear contract with MGM or any other studio. However, since having made her desires known as far back as late 1943/early 1944, MGM had the time to do every-

214   CHAPTER 8

thing it could to entice her into staying. They got their wish.

Garland's new contract, typed on November 20, 1946, but not taking effect until the existing contract expired on January 2, 1947, was incredibly generous even by Hollywood standards. The terms included the following: Garland could continue to work with Minnelli; MGM would produce "lavish productions" starring Garland at no more than two films per year, and one could be a guest appearance, in which she would still get top billing; she could keep (and have first dibs on the services of) her favorite makeup artist, Dottie Ponedel, as long as Ponedel was "employed by the studio"; and she could still make "phonographic records" and appear on radio shows. For this, she would receive a weekly salary of $5,619.23 (at a 1947 dollar value), which was close to $1,000 a day for the six-day workweek with a guarantee of $300,000 per year ($150,000 per film). It was too good to pass up. However, Garland said later that after she signed the contract, she immediately regretted it and knew she had made a terrible, dreadful mistake.[4]

Just before signing the contract, on November 6, 1946, Garland was due back at MGM for her first work since going on maternity leave, a scheduled costume fitting for her next film, *The Pirate*, directed by Minnelli. Perhaps it was angst created by the contract negotiations, her postpartum depression, or simply the fear of beginning that studio grind again, but Garland had her secretary call in sick for her. On December 1, columnist Edith Gwyn reported, "There have been rumors all over town that Judy Garland wouldn't be re-signing M-G-M when her present contract expires. . . . But at this writing, the new deal is on paper, and Judy is poised, pen in hand, to sign her name to a new termer at M-G-M."[5] Gwyn's column is notable not only because its publication predated Garland's eventual return to the studio by one day but also because it was MGM's way to let the public (and the movie industry) know that they had the power to continue to control the great Garland career, despite her strong desire to leave. It was common practice for studios to give inside information to columnists in order to control a narrative to their benefit.

On December 2, 1946, Garland returned to MGM after thirteen months away and completed a short day of wardrobe tests and rehearsals. In a flashback to her schedule in the early 1940s, Garland didn't go home afterward; she instead appeared live that evening in another abridged adaptation of one of her movies for the *Lux Radio Theatre* radio show. This time, Garland, Margaret O'Brien, and Tom Drake re-created their roles in *Meet Me in St. Louis*.

THE PIRATE

Production on *The Pirate* began with high hopes and artistic aspirations but quickly turned into a waking nightmare, especially for Garland. The film was planned as her big return to the screen, with a witty script and featuring songs written specifically for the film by the equally witty Cole Porter, plus her good friend Gene Kelly as her costar. Naturally, her husband Minnelli was directing. The film was a pet project of Minnelli's, and he threw himself into creating a bright, Technicolor Caribbean world that was barely rooted in reality. Kelly, for his part, was thrilled at the chance to pay homage to one of his childhood idols, swashbuckling silent film legend Douglas Fairbanks, in his portrayal of Serafin, the traveling actor who pretends to be the fictional notorious pirate "Mack the Black." Two of his costumes in the film are based on what Fairbanks wears in the 1926 swashbuckler *The Black Pirate*. Kelly also saw *The Pirate* as a chance to advance the art of dance on film. Garland's role, however, wasn't as exciting, which could be part of why she wasn't as enthusiastic about the film once it began to take shape. Originally, Garland was as passionate about the project as Kelly and Minnelli were, seeing the film as a way to showcase her talents for sophisticated comedy. But in reality, her character, Manuela, wasn't much different from her previous ingenue roles. On paper, Manuela is a sheltered, innocent Caribbean country girl who lives in a fantasy world of stories about the fabled pirate "Mack the Black." She is forced into an arranged engagement with the town's less-than-desirable and much older mayor. Manuela is so innocent and sheltered that she hasn't even been to the seashore, even though she lives on an island. She begs her aunt to see the ocean just once before her marriage. Compared to Kelly's dashing actor Serafin, who gets to parade around as a combination campy and hypermasculine pirate, Garland's role is just another lovestruck innocent with nothing to do but to moon over her pirate fantasies.

The plot of *The Pirate* is based on the non-musical 1942 Broadway comedy of the same name written by S. N. Behrman and starring Alfred Lunt and Lynn Fontanne. MGM bought the film rights in 1943, planning to make a non-musical comedy film with William Powell, Hedy Lamarr, and Charles Laughton. Garland's lover at the time, Joe Mankiewicz, provided an early draft of a screenplay, envisioning it as a musical comedy starring Garland. However, due to his relationship with her and the resulting big blowout argument with both Garland's mom, Ethel, and MGM studio boss Louis B. Mayer, he left the studio. The project went through a few more writers before costume and scenic designer Lemuel Ayers, who designed the original Broadway show and was at MGM at the time (he was the art director for *Meet Me in St. Louis*), suggested a musical version of it to Freed with songs by Porter. Freed assigned Anita Loos and Joseph Than to write the screenplay. Garland, Kelly, Minnelli, Porter, and Edens gathered at Freed's home to hear the results. Contrary to previous reports, the Loos–Than screenplay did not present the pirate masquerading as an actor. Freed biographer Hugh Fordin put that story out in 1975 without supporting documentation, and it has been repeated ever since. The real problem with their screenplay was the addition of extra characters and subplots and an overall poorly executed storyline.[6] Fordin goes on to explain that at that reading at Freed's house, the group was stunned. Porter broke the ice by quipping, "Uh . . . it must have been an incredible amount of work for you."[7] Undeterred, Freed and Minnelli then engaged the husband-and-wife team of Frances Goodrich and Albert Hackett to fix the screenplay, and the film was back on track.

Garland's first notable work on the film was her first prerecording session on December 27, 1946. She recorded the ballad "Love of My Life," which was filmed and then cut after the first preview but included on the official MGM Records soundtrack album. The following day,

216   CHAPTER 8

Garland clowning on the set of *The Pirate* in 1947. From the author's collection.

Garland prerecorded the first version of "Mack the Black." This version also ended up on the cutting room floor, and, due to the rocky and unintentionally long production, the new version wasn't rerecorded until a year later, on December 15, 1947. This first version was incredibly noisy and over-arranged to the point that when Freed heard it, he complained to music coordinator Magdalene "Lela" Simone, "It sounds like a Chinese carnival!" To which she replied, "Well, I've never been to one, but I'm sure it must be terribly noisy, shrill and high-pitched."[8] A few takes from the prerecording session have survived and are, indeed, over-arranged and shrill. The idea behind the number was to open the film with Garland singing about her love of the exploits of the notorious pirate "Mack the Black Macoco" (Porter came up with the "Mack the Black" nickname). After that was cut and the rerecorded number was moved to a different section of the film, the result was that Garland did not sing a note in the film until thirty-one minutes had passed. A clip of part of the original version has survived in the film's trailer.

For the first half of 1947, Garland worked almost exclusively on *The Pirate*. The only other professional obligation she had was her appearance on the *Philco Radio Time Bing Crosby Show* recorded on February 4, 1947, which aired on February 19, 1947. One of Garland's songs in the show is a lovely rendition of "I've Got You Under My Skin," written by *The Pirate*'s composer, Cole Porter. She was scheduled to appear on the Academy Awards show on March 11, 1947, and sing "On the Atchison, Topeka, and the Santa Fe" from *The Harvey Girls* (1946), which was nominated for and won Best Song. Unfortunately, she had to cancel that engagement. By that point, it had been only a few months since production on *The Pirate* had begun, and Garland had already started to unravel. Physically, she was too thin and weak. Emotionally, she wasn't any better. She had managed to stay off the pills during her pregnancy, but she began to use them as a crutch again once production on *The Pirate* got rolling. She most likely assumed the pills would give her energy and help her through, as they always seemed to do. But this time, they didn't. Her actions were prompted at least in part by her insecurities and the pressure of living up to the stipulations of that new contract, which, although it was for only five years, seemed like an eternity of servitude to MGM. The success of each film resting firmly on her shoulders created a constant inner turbulence of stress and insecurity. She simply couldn't handle it. Garland was the type of performer who, if she thought she wasn't going to perform well, wouldn't go into the studio. She wasn't being a diva; she was acting on her own insecurities as a performer, as well as her razor-sharp theatrical instincts. Naturally, she, more than anyone, knew whether she would be good or great in front of the cameras. However, she was usually so great that her "good" was what most other performers would call "great." She could come in and be merely good in her own estimation and still be great to everyone else.

Garland had begun seeing a psychiatrist again, resuming sessions with Dr. Simmel, who had been her psychiatrist a few years earlier during her romance with Joe Mankiewicz. Minnelli or her makeup woman and good friend, Dottie Ponedel, would drive her to her sessions, which were usually at the beginning of the day. Studio boss Louis B. Mayer had previously been against psychiatry, but the situation with Garland was such that he acquiesced and hired another psychiatrist, Dr. Frederick Hacker, to be on the set with her to keep her steady. It didn't help much, mainly because Garland couldn't be open and honest with her psychiatrists and therapists. She had a difficult time when forced to delve into her own psyche and confront her personal demons. As she had done a few years earlier when her sister Virginia drove her to her early morning sessions, she would boast to Ponedel about the stories she made up:

> *At the time that Judy went to Dr. Simmel, she laid on the couch, and she came out to me and said "Well, Dottie, I lied today better than I've ever lied in my life." She said, "And I think he swallowed everything I said." I said, "Do you think he did, Judy?" And she said, "Yes, he did because he looked straight at me, and I looked straight at him while I was lying. I lied better than anybody on that couch the whole week there that he had." And so, I said, "Well Judy, you know Louis B. Mayer is paying 50 dollars every time you go in to see this doctor." She said, "Let them pay it," she said, "And they'll hear the best lies that ever was told in the world." She said, "I can think of the biggest ones and the best ones." I said, "Judy, you're only fooling yourself; you're not fooling this analyst at all." She said, "Well, I have nothing else to tell him but lies. Now let's go to the studio, and I'll tell Louis B. Mayer I had a wonderful session today."[9]*

Garland prerecorded "Voodoo" on April 10, 1947, and began filming the sequence a day later. The scene took place at night, although filmed during the day on a darkened sound stage, with fires lit, extras in place, and Kelly in full sexy Serafin mode. Serafin uses voodoo to hypnotize Manuela, and in her trance, she sings "Voodoo." The dance that Kelly and Garland had rehearsed in February and March and filmed in April has been described as so sensual that when

Mayer was alerted and viewed the rushes, he was horrified and demanded the film be burned. Allegedly, a new version was choreographed and rehearsed, and when the time came to reshoot it, Garland fell apart. She appeared on the set, looked into the fire, and completely broke down, screaming, "I'm going to burn to death! They want me to burn to death!" She then ran up to some of the extras and pleaded, "Do you have some Benzedrine?"[10] Garland had to be led off the set. That's the legend.

The story of Garland's breakdown during "Voodoo" has been repeated many times by many biographers (and endless clickbait articles). It's become one of the most well known of the Garland legends. However, it's probably not true, or, at best, it's an exaggerated version of what really happened. The production assistant's (Wallace "Wally" Worsley) daily production notes did not mention the incident. MGM was obsessive about noting the exact times and details of Garland's daily activities, so it's odd there isn't any reference to this debacle. The breakdown legend continues that Garland was off the film for two or more weeks. The production notes show that "Voodoo" and the surrounding scenes were filmed in mid- to late April, and Garland, while continuing her spotty attendance, wasn't out for more than three or four days at a time for the next few months. Either Worsley didn't want to report such a heartbreaking scene or it was a case of a minor incident being blown out of proportion when it spread through the rumor channels in Hollywood and beyond. The story about Mayer demanding the film be burned and the whole sequence being redone sounds more like "creative writing" than fact. Likewise, there was no second series of new rehearsals and no days of filming any alleged revamping of the number. The earliest report about the incident was in Hugh Fordin's 1975 book about the Freed Unit, *The World of Entertainment! Hollywood's Greatest Musicals*. Fordin doesn't give a source for the story. No one has provided a legitimate source since.

Although it's probably not entirely true, the fact that this story has been reported as such over the decades is a reflection of the lore associated with Garland's very real struggles during filming and how the fictional incident neatly reflects that situation. Considering her state of being at the time, it makes sense that Garland would eventually have a breakdown on the set and possibly be in full view of some of the cast and crew. Later, during rehearsals for the "Be a Clown" number in late June, Garland had that breakdown, which kept her off the film for two weeks. Columnist Hedda Hopper reported the incident: "Judy Garland had a complete nervous breakdown[,] I learned tonight, and is confined to her Bel Air home. . . . When I visited her on the set six weeks ago, she called me into her dressing room and confided that she was on the verge of a nervous collapse."[11] The same day the Hopper column was printed, columnist Jack Lait was a bit more blunt: "The Judy Garland breakdown may be charged to benzadrine [*sic*]. Always thin and active during the pre-birth months and since Judy took on weight. Then she started overdosing to reduce. Her constitution couldn't take it."[12] It's very possible the "Voodoo" legend is a combination of an incident during the filming of that number with this later breakdown.

After struggling through the filming of "Voodoo," Garland managed to prerecord the

"Be a Clown"—Garland and Gene Kelly, July 1947. From the author's collection.

reprise version of "Love of My Life" and another version of "You Can Do No Wrong," both on May 13, 1947. A previous attempt to record the latter on May 5 resulted in "no accepted takes—will do over again."[13] Porter was at the studio and attended that May 5 recording session. He and Garland got into a heated argument about her pronunciation of "caviar" in the song. He didn't like it, and Edens stepped in to convince Garland to sing it Porter's way.[14] The song was originally intended to be sung in a sarcastic tone, coming after Manuela realizes that Serafin as Macoco is really the actor who previously hypnotized her. She mocks him with "You Can Do No Wrong" before the manic scene where she throws everything in the adjoining room at him. But in the final film, she sings it after she knocks him out at the end of that scene, as a traditional ballad. As no recordings survive from that May 5 session, it's unknown how sarcastically she had originally sung it. If Garland had not been under the stress and fatigue she was currently experiencing, she wouldn't have gotten into such a heated spat with Porter.

Another issue Garland had during the filming was her jealousy of Minnelli and Kelly. Due to her absences, Minnelli shot around her, resulting in more collaboration between him and

Kelly. Garland went so far as to accuse the two of using her to get ahead and implying that they were sleeping together.[15] Once again, if Garland had been in her right mind, none of it would have been an issue.

Filming finally ended, or so everyone thought, on July 16, 1947, after the rousing "Be a Clown" finale number had been shot. Three days later, Garland made an unpublicized suicide attempt and was sent to the Las Campanas sanitarium in the Compton area of Los Angeles, followed by a few weeks at the Austen Riggs Center in Massachusetts. The suicide attempt is alleged to have been the result of Garland walking in on Minnelli in bed with one of their male servants. She reacted by running into her bathroom and cutting her wrists with a razor blade. Minnelli was able to stop her before any serious damage had been done, but it was clear that Garland needed serious professional help. This is the incident that future author Jacqueline Susann found out about and put in her book *Valley of the Dolls*, having a similar scenario happen to her character, Neely O'Hara, who was based on Garland.[16]

Garland turned her stay at the sanitarium into more of her funny, self-deprecating anecdotal stories. She said that when she was taken to the facility, it was at night, and she was sedated. Two sanitarium staff took a side and helped Garland to walk across the lawn to her room. She was conscious enough to realize that she kept stumbling, feeling like something kept grabbing at her feet. She thought she was truly losing her mind. The next morning, after the sedative had worn off, she looked out her window and saw what had caused the previous night's confusion: the lawn was littered with croquet wickets.[17] She was relieved she hadn't gone insane and got a big laugh out of it.

On her second day at the Las Campanas sanitarium, Garland ventured onto the lawn and realized that the other patients didn't seem "crazy" at all; rather, as she put it, "I met some of the most charming people there. Sensitive, intelligent, humorous people. As far as I could gather, not one of them was demented in the common sense. Most of them were just too highly strung and too sensitive for reality. . . . Many, in fact, most of them were people like me—desperately and impossibly exhausted. I realized that I had a great deal in common with them."[18]

Another story Garland liked to tell was how every morning at 5:00, a woman would come into her room and do a thorough search. As Garland described it:

One of my favorite and most disturbing characters was a nurse. Every morning, she came into my room very quietly at five o'clock. Because of my insomnia, I had generally just fallen asleep. She was just quiet enough to waken me. I would lie wide-eyed as she searched my room. Every bottle, every drawer, every stitch of clothes, every corner. It took me about five mornings to get up enough courage to ask her what she was looking for. The first time I asked her, she didn't even answer me. She just kept looking.

Finally, one morning, I got belligerent. "Look," I said, "I don't know what you're looking for, but it isn't here. I haven't got any pills, dope, money, or whisky. I don't mind you looking for them, because that's your job, but does it have to be at five o'clock in the morning? At these rates!"[19]

After convincing the facility to let daughter Liza visit and enduring a heart-wrenching farewell after Liza had to leave, her new psychiatrist, Dr. Herbert Kupper, decided that it would be best for Garland to travel to the Austen Riggs Center in Stockbridge, Massachusetts. It was perfect because it was far from Los Angeles, and she could ideally get better treatment. Oddly enough, Dr. Kupper allowed Garland to persuade him to accompany her to Austen Riggs. Kupper unwisely stayed at the same place Garland was staying, the Red Lion Inn across from Austen Riggs. Her treatment at the center was given by Dr. Robert P. Knight, who found himself at odds with Kupper, who seemed to be in the way more often than not. When Knight mentioned his concern, Kupper abruptly left for California. In another impetuous mistake, Garland quit her treatment and followed not long after. During her time in Massachusetts, Garland reportedly spent a day in Stockbridge and was seen "walking about and visiting the Stockbridge Golf Club," and she attended the Berkshire Festival at the Tanglewood Estate, also in Stockbridge.[20] She was quoted as saying, "I am thoroughly enjoying my first visit to the Berkshires."[21]

The time away and the ability to go around town whenever she wanted was probably therapeutic for Garland, but after all of the time with the psychiatrists, she wasn't much better mentally or emotionally, if at all. Whatever progress she might have made was short lived. When she returned to California, she returned to the same conditions that led to her breakdown in the first place.

EASTER PARADE

A rough cut of *The Pirate* was assembled, which Garland saw on August 29, not long after returning from Massachusetts. And rough it was. The film needed more work before it was ready for release. While those involved were determining what to do with it, Garland went into rehearsals for her next film, *Easter Parade*, again with costar Gene Kelly and Minnelli directing. This time, instead of the arty aspirations of *The Pirate*, *Easter Parade* was a more traditional movie musical with a backstage plot. The script, again provided by Hackett and Frances Goodrich, was centered around Irving Berlin's song catalog, who was happily involved in the preproduction process, giving input to the story and providing new songs. Berlin originally wrote the melody of "Easter Parade" in 1917 with different lyrics, titled "Smile and Show Your Dimple." That song was not a success, so Berlin kept it in his "trunk" and recycled the melody with new lyrics and a new title, "Easter Parade," for the 1933 Broadway musical *As Thousands Cheer*. This time, with the new lyrics, it was a success. Producer Arthur Freed purchased the song from Berlin with the understanding that a film musical would be made centered around the song and other Berlin songs, old and new.

Garland and Kelly began work on the film on September 22, 1947, rehearsing the new Berlin song, "A Couple of Swells." Just days into the rehearsals, Minnelli was replaced as director with Charles Walters. On her request, Garland's psychiatrist, Dr. Kupper, suggested to Freed that it would be to Garland's benefit and improve her state of mind if she didn't have to face Minnelli

222   CHAPTER 8

both at home and at work. After the strain of the production of *The Pirate* and the couple's current marital problems, it made sense. Minnelli was understandably disappointed, partly because he was taken off such a great project, but also because Garland never let her feelings be known to him. She basically went behind his back and then said nothing. It was another crack in their faltering relationship.

Walters was a good friend of Garland's, their friendship going back to his early days at MGM, dancing with her in both *Girl Crazy* (1943) and *Presenting Lily Mars* (1943). In late 1947, he had just completed his first assignment directing an entire film, *Good News*, starring June Allyson and Peter Lawford. Although the film had yet to premiere (December 1947), it was clear that Walters had a future as a director. The fact that he and Garland got along so well was probably another factor that helped Freed decide to assign such a big project to the new director. Walters was happy with the assignment but unhappy with the current script. The basics of the story were good, being a variation on Shaw's *Pygmalion*. The fictional song and dance team of Don Hewes and Nadine Hale (Kelly and Cyd Charisse) breaks up when Hale abruptly leaves to go out on her own. She tells him, "You can dance with anyone." In his dejected state, he decides to prove that he can do just that and picks the first chorus girl he sees, Hannah Brown (Garland), and proceeds to do so. In true musical comedy fashion, they end up in love. However, in Walters's words, the original script was too "mean,"[22] meaning that it was too harsh in tone for a musical comedy. The recent Oscar winner and future novelist Sidney Sheldon was brought in to, in his words, "[make] it into a musical comedy."[23]

After being assigned the film, Walters attended one of Garland and Kelly's rehearsals; she jokingly said to him, "Look, sweetie, I'm no June Allyson, you know. Don't get cute with me—none of that batting the eyelids big or fluffing the hair routine for me, buddy! I'm Judy Garland, and just you watch it."[24] Garland loved to joke, and this is a good indication that the recent rest she had enjoyed and the switch in directors had a positive impact on her enthusiasm for the project. The dark cloud that seemed to hover over the production of *The Pirate* had disappeared. *Easter Parade* was beginning on a very positive and sunny note.

Without warning, a couple of new dark clouds appeared on the production's horizon. Both Kelly and Charisse had accidents that took them off the film. Charisse tore a ligament in her knee, and then, on October 13, Kelly broke his ankle. Charisse was relatively easy to replace. Ann Miller stepped in and started a fantastic run as MGM's resident queen of tap (Charisse recovered and became one of MGM's most popular dancing leading ladies). Kelly's role wasn't so easy to replace. The only star of the same caliber who could costar with Garland was Fred Astaire, but he was in a self-imposed retirement. Freed called Astaire, who was getting bored with retirement and jumped at the chance to work with Garland. In just three days, on October 16, Astaire was at MGM beginning rehearsals. Like Miller, this was the start of a brilliant second film career for Astaire that lasted at MGM for ten years.

When Astaire began rehearsals, Garland was in rehearsals for the "Mr. Monotony" number. The song was a novelty number, and she performed it brilliantly. She recorded it on November 12 and filmed it on November 21 and 22. Garland sexily wore the top half of a man's tuxedo, capped by a fedora. It's the outfit she later wore to even greater effect in *Summer Stock* (1950) while singing "Get Happy." "Mr. Monotony" was cut from *Easter Parade* before the film was released, but the dailies for both days of filming have miraculously survived, allowing the number to be re-edited. Two versions with slightly different edits were premiered in the 1990s, one on a LaserDisc release of the film and one in the 1994 compilation film *That's Entertainment! III*. It's one of the best of the surviving Garland MGM outtakes.

On November 15, 1947, Garland's long association with Decca Records came to an end when she recorded "I Wish I Were in Love Again," "Nothing But You," and "Falling in Love with Love," accompanied by the two-piano team of Eadie (Griffith) and Rack (Godwin). In the two years prior to this last session, Garland's output of recordings for the label had dropped significantly. In 1946, she recorded five songs, compared to the fourteen she recorded in 1945. The decrease was due to her health issues and her inability to keep up with the grind at the studio, as well as her pregnancy with Liza, which resulted in postpartum depression. The contract Garland signed on April 1, 1944, was for three years and forty-eight songs, and although she hadn't made that number yet in November 1947, Decca let the contract lapse. MGM Records had entered the record market with a new subgenre: the soundtrack album. Songs from the soundtracks of Garland's films from 1946 through 1950 were released by the label, effectively ending any hopes Decca may have had of creating more studio cast albums of songs from Garland films. After Garland's big comeback at the Palace Theatre in 1951, Decca began rereleasing some of her recordings in new compilation albums, beginning in 1951 with the *Judy at the Palace* album that misled the record-buying public into thinking it was songs from the show. The songs were known Garland songs from the Decca Garland catalog, 1942 and prior. The cover art featured photos of Garland from the Palace engagement, which added to the misconception. Decca continued to release a variety of Garland compilation albums in every new audio format, from 78 to 45 to 10″ and 12″ long-playing records to eight-track to cassette and, finally, CD into the 1990s.

Meanwhile, Minnelli deemed that retakes were needed for *The Pirate* even before the film's first preview on October 10, 1947, at the Academy Theatre in nearby Inglewood. Contrary to some reports about the preview being a disaster, 84 percent of those who filled out preview cards after the showing stated they enjoyed the film, while only 16 percent did not.[25] Beginning on October 22, Garland began retakes on *The Pirate*, and, for a while, she shuffled back and forth between those retakes and the ongoing *Easter Parade* production, working on both films on the same day in a few instances. After some of those retakes had been completed, a second preview of *The Pirate* was again held at the Academy Theatre. This time, 57 percent of those who filled out preview cards rated the film as excellent, with 29 percent as "good" and 8 percent as "fair."[26] As with the first preview, both "Voodoo" and the opening "Mack the Black" numbers were the least favorite, as was the original version of "Love of My Life" that Manuela sings to

224   CHAPTER 8

her hat while mooning over Serafin. It was decided to remove the opening number completely and replace it with a dialog scene of Manuela reading from a book about Mack the Black. Only the opening chorus of the original song was retained for the main title sequence. The "Voodoo" sequence was cut completely, and a new, less noisy version of "Mack the Black" was rehearsed, prerecorded, and filmed to take its place. "Love of My Life" was also completely deleted. Only the reprise version remains in the final film. The retakes were finally done on December 19. Due to the long production schedule, the film cost more than most musicals at the time, going half a million dollars over budget. When it was released on May 20, 1948, at Radio City Music Hall, it grossed more at the theatre than any other MGM film up to that point.[27] When it went into general release on June 10, 1948, it made a respectable amount, but it wasn't enough. The final cost was $3,768,496, and it grossed $2,956,000. It was the only Garland MGM film to be considered a failure.

Time has been kind to *The Pirate*. It's a "cult film" in which the flaws in the narrative flow are still there, but, overall, it's thoroughly enjoyable, especially the performances of Garland and Kelly. The MGM ads promoted the film as a "Technicolor Treasure Chest," and it is. Since its restoration from the original Technicolor negatives, Minnelli's hyper-stylized vision of the Caribbean almost jumps off the screen. His use of color, along with the set design and fabulous costumes, are all spot on, and, for the most part, he succeeds in creating a fanciful Caribbean world in which many viewers wouldn't mind living. Amazingly, and despite her issues behind the scenes, Garland not only looks wonderful in most of the scenes but also gives one of her best comedic performances. And yet audiences at the time didn't warm up to the film. It was a little too arty and miles away from what they expected from an MGM musical, especially a Judy Garland musical. If you look at the movie musicals released in 1948, *The Pirate* is indeed very different from any of them.

MGM's golden musical trio—Gene Kelly, Fred Astaire, and Garland—on the set of *The Pirate* in December 1947. From the author's collection.

Garland seemed to be in great spirits during the filming of *Easter Parade*. She was thrilled to be working with Astaire and was on her best behavior. That didn't mean she had a perfect attendance record or didn't have bouts of struggling with herself, but those incidents were minor. It probably helped that, unlike *The Pirate*, the bulk of the responsibilities for making the film successful weren't resting solely on her or her costar's shoulders. *Easter Parade* is less a "Judy Garland Musical" and more an "MGM Musical starring Judy Garland." Garland and Astaire are the two big stars, of course, and they get ample time to shine, but the supporting cast does as well.

MGM Records collectible record album shopping bag, 1948.
From the author's collection.

Ann Miller and Peter Lawford provide solid support not just musically (even Lawford's limited vocal range is fine) but also with their own subplots. *Easter Parade*, with its backstage story, is also more in keeping with Garland's vaudevillian roots. It's the kind of role in which she excelled and could breeze through dramatically and musically. And breeze she did. The only quibble would be that in some scenes, she looks overly thin and unhealthy.

Garland was also happy to be working with songwriter Irving Berlin. She revered him as much as she revered Astaire. At one point during one of the prerecording sessions, Berlin was on hand and made a suggestion, and, to his amusement, Garland mock-sarcastically replied, "Listen buster. You write 'em, I sing 'em."[28] This was the second time in the past year that a film's songwriter suggested how Garland sing a song, but, unlike the bad incident with Cole Porter during *The Pirate*, this time Garland was amiable, an indication that she was in a much better place emotionally.

Another enduring Garland legend that's been told in many articles and books sprang out of her and Astaire's "A Couple of Swells." The story, as told by Garland's sister Jimmie in *Modern Screen* magazine, published in October 1948, was that Astaire, always a very dapper man, had trouble with his costume. He was so put together that it was almost impossible for him to be

MORE THAN 1,500 PERSONS saw these youngsters in Mrs. Kelly Grogran's third grade at Central break out in a rhythmic rendition of "We're a Couple of Swells" at the PTA Carnival Thursday. The children were dressed in dilapidated evening clothes which were decorated with varicolored patches. Much to the delight of the class, front teeth were blacked with chewing gum, and the youngsters had a chance to mock Fred Astaire and Judy Garland who featured the number in a recent movie. All classes in the school presented special programs and the PTA "sold out" in soft drinks and other refreshments. (Gazette photo by Marcus Orr).

In Chillicothe, Ohio, Mrs. Kelly Grogan's third grade class presented their own version of Garland and Astaire's already famous "A Couple of Swells" in *Easter Parade*. Published in the *Chillicothe Gazette* on November 16, 1948. From the author's collection.

a convincing dirty hobo. Each time he showed up in costume and asked, "Is this too much?" it broke everyone up because he couldn't look anything less than well dressed, even as a hobo. After this happened a few times, Garland got her costume together, which was appropriately over the top; she went to Astaire's dressing room, and when he opened the door, she sarcastically quipped, "Is this too much?"[29] This anecdote is amusing, but it should be taken with a big grain of salt coming from Garland's sister Jimmie, as told to her by Garland, who, it's been established, loved to embellish for comic effect. Generally, the costumes for films were carefully designed and executed (by the wonderful Irene) and tested on the stars before delivery to the soundstage (or their dressing rooms) for filming. It's possible that Garland and Astaire had some input, as stars sometimes did when it came to their image, but, in this case, it's not probable that they would design their own costumes to the extent indicated by this anecdote. The most logical scenario is that an amusing incident regarding the costumes and the two stars had occurred on the set, which

Garland spun into a funny story. But the idea that Garland and Astaire would have designed their own costumes for such a key number in the film sounds more like Garland's tall tales mixed with a bit of publicity fodder with a kernel of truth.

"A Couple of Swells" was the film's highlight for most audiences and critics, then and now. Garland and Astaire are magical together, and one can't help but smile while enjoying watching them enjoy themselves. It's an all-time movie musical classic. Garland had it in her stage repertoire from the beginning of her Concert Years, less than a year after leaving MGM. She even performed it solo on her TV series. After singing the lyric "That's the rub," she deadpanned, "That was Fred's part." Only the great Garland could take such an iconic song and dance duet and make it equally iconic as a solo while remembering the original dance steps from the film.

"A Couple of Swells"—Garland and Fred Astaire, December 1947. From the collection of Bruce Hanson.

Another amusing event occurred when Garland and Lawford were filming "A Fella with an Umbrella" on MGM's Lot 2. Obviously, the number takes place during a rainstorm. A corner of "Eastside Street" in the standing "New York Streets" section was tarped off, and "rain" was piped in. Everything seemed to go fine until it was discovered that the red dye in the feather in Garland's hat "bled" all over the place, including across Garland's face. Twenty years later, on August 9, 1968, Garland and Lawford were guests on Mike Douglas's TV show and reminisced about *Easter Parade*. Garland told the red feather story, joking that she had "blood" across her face, "and they had to reset and get more rain, and they couldn't figure out what to do with this bloody feather, and they put Vaseline on it, which I thought was kind of unattractive!" Lawford and Garland joked about "the elevator." As Lawford explained, the studio went to great expense to install a working sidewalk freight elevator that would come up at a certain point in the song. Garland and Lawford were to be startled by almost falling in. Lawford continued, "They had the wrong lens on, and [in the final film] you never saw the sidewalk and the elevator. . . . We'd been worrying all day long about falling down the shaft."[30] In the final cut of the film, the sidewalk elevator is, in fact, seen. However, it doesn't come up in the way Lawford described. It's already up, and the duo sees it just before the doors close. They're able to walk over it and then stop and do their double take. Twenty years later, on Douglas's show, it's an obvious anecdote shared by Garland and Lawford, who both remember that in the final film, it's not shown. They also remember that the elevator effect was much more complicated than it was. As with most of Garland's funny stories, it's half truth (or less) and half exaggeration (or more) for comic effect.

One of the funniest scenes in the film is Hannah's attempt to prove to Don that she can turn men's heads while walking down the street. Hannah begins to walk ahead, trying to figure out how to catch men's eyes. She walks out of camera range as the focus stays on Don. Suddenly, the men walking by are looking back at Hannah, all of them, some of them laughing. Don puzzlingly looks around at them. The camera pulls back to reveal that Hannah has been distorting her face to get the men to look at her. Don almost busts her ruse when he catches up to her. Garland used what her family called "the bloopface." She and her sisters would make faces at cars passing by during their road trips when they were kids. Garland's "bloopface" usually got the most reactions from the unsuspecting drivers.

The last number Garland filmed for *Easter Parade* was the title number, which she and Astaire prerecorded on January 26, 1948. The ending of the title number, which also ends the film, was shot on MGM's second backlot, Lot 3, on "Drumhead Road," behind the "St. Louis Street." Most people assume that the finale was filmed on "Fifth Avenue" in the "New York Streets" section of Lot 2. However, that street was too modern to accurately portray Fifth Avenue in New York in 1912. So MGM simply built a section of 1912 Fifth Avenue on "Drumhead Road," constructing the facades of the bottom ten feet of the buildings as shown in vintage photographs. A matte painting completed the effect. This is another great example of MGM's attention to detail. They could have easily created their own version of what they assumed was 1912 Fifth Avenue. However, they wanted it to be as accurate as possible. It was worth the effort. The final effect was breathtaking on the big screen, and in some showings it generated spontaneous applause as the shot pulled back and up to reveal the full view.

Filming on *Easter Parade* was completed on February 9, 1948, with some retakes done on March 12. The film amazingly came in under budget by $191,280, costing $2,503,654.[31] It premiered at New York City's Loew's State Theatre on June 30, 1848, with huge cutouts of the four stars above the marquee on "Broadway's largest theatre display. The figures are three and one-half stories high."[32] It broke all attendance records at Loew's to that date and was held over for more than seven weeks. It went into general release in cities around the United States beginning on July 8, 1948, and was (and still is) an instant classic and a huge hit with audiences and critics. In just a few short weeks, it was performing an average of 132 percent at the box office, with Minneapolis at an astounding 181.8 percent, according to the July 31, 1948, issue of the trade magazine *Motion Picture Herald*. The total box office tally for the film was $6,083,000 on its initial release, making it one of the year's top films. Everyone welcomed Astaire back to the screen, and

MGM TREADMILL

most critics singled out Garland as a worthy new partner for him.

During the summer of 1948, Garland had both *The Pirate* and *Easter Parade* in general release, making her one of the year's top stars. Because of this overlap, some reviewers compared the two films, with a few preferring the former to the latter. Even Walters's directing style was unfairly compared to Minnelli's. Aside from those minor critiques, the critics were almost unanimous in their praise. *Easter Parade* has remained an enduring classic and a favorite of movie lovers, especially during the Easter holiday season.

Metro has served us up with a luscious chunk of musical comedy. It smacks the eye and the ear with an abundance of splashy colors, bouncy rhythms and pleasant romance and is a highly diverting piece of entertainment for anybody's theatre. Charles Walters keeps it rolling smoothly enough. Robert Alton did a great job in staging the musical numbers and the Technicolor work is generally fine.
—uncredited, *The Exhibitor's Film Bulletin* trade magazine, June 7, 1948

As long as Judy Garland is in this gay musical in Technicolor, the rest of the cast, and even the music, don't matter much to me. But it must be admitted that they're all good, too. . . . Judy has a pleasing voice, though not as wonderful as her fascinating face and provocative variety of expressions. There should be a better word for her than cute.
—Phil Barney, *Tampa Tribune*, Tampa, Florida, August 9, 1948

Perhaps it's a pity "Easter Parade" follows so fast on "The Pirate's" heels since almost every score, including plot, tints, and music, suffers by comparison. Even so, and although Charles Walters' direction lacks both freshness and imagination, it is ingratiating entertainment with only occasional dull interludes. . . . Miss Garland not only plays Hannah with appealing naturalness, but sings and dances with Astaire in a fashion that makes her his best partner since Ginger Rogers.
—Mildred Martin, *Philadelphia Inquirer*, Philadelphia, Pennsylvania, July 10, 1948

Miss Garland, too, is gifted, and her personality is of distinctive appeal. Again, she displays notable talent in "selling" a song, but she outdoes her past accomplishments as an actress and a dancer. She strikes effective dramatic notes here, and she proves that she can dance with Astaire as well as the best of them. Their romantic dancing is delightful, and their comedy tramp number is a special treat.
—George L. David, *Democrat and Chronicle*, Rochester, New York, July 16, 1948

Everybody sings—Judy Garland, 11 times; Fred Astaire, 9 times; Ann Miller, once; Richard Beavers, once; and Peter Lawford, once, thank heavens. . . . Judy shows some of the wistful appeal that harks back almost to her "Wizard of Oz" days, and is photographed prettier than usually.
—Betty French, *Akron Beacon Journal*, Akron, Ohio, July 19, 1948

MGM promotional portrait, 1948. From the author's collection.

A Gallup poll would probably place "A Couple of Swells" at the top of the Astaire-Garland numbers. Dressed like a couple of rag-tailed hoboes, they kid their tattered pants off the rich and the mighty in a solid piece of vaudeville that will long remain among your movie souvenirs. . . . Any partner is quite the same to Miss Garland, she is all-trouper and a yard wide, and her performance here in every department has the sleek polish of a young lady who knows all there is to know about the music halls.
—Harold V. Cohen, *Pittsburgh Post-Gazette*, Pittsburgh, Pennsylvania, July 30, 1948

At the twenty-first Academy Awards on March 24, 1949 (honoring the films of 1948), both *The Pirate* and *Easter Parade* received one nomination each, competing in the same category, Scoring of a Musical Picture: Lennie Hayton for *The Pirate* and Johnny Green and Roger Edens for *Easter Parade*. Green and Edens were the winners.

Easter Parade ended up being Garland's last starring role for the Freed Unit, but only by chance. The next two years would prove to be incredibly difficult for her, bringing home the fact that she was right about signing that new contract in 1946. It was, indeed, one of her biggest mistakes.

August 1948 edition of the *Screen Guide* fan magazine. From the author's collection.

C H A P T E R   *9*

VINTAGE MGM

IN THE GOOD OLD SUMMERTIME

Despite Garland's mostly positive experiences during the production of *Easter Parade*, when it was over, she was, once again, completely worn out and too thin. With the Garland–Astaire follow-up (*The Barkleys of Broadway*) not scheduled to begin for a few months, Garland looked forward to some time off to rest and try to get her health back. Two months, to be exact. Her only major professional obligation was a notable appearance with Fred Astaire and Perry Como on the NBC Radio show *The Chesterfield Supper Club* singing songs from *Easter Parade*.

Arthur Freed decided that he wanted her for a guest spot in his all-star biopic about the songwriting team of Richard Rodgers and Lorenz Hart titled *Words and Music*. Tom Drake and Mickey Rooney starred as Rodgers and Hart, respectively. Garland would be playing herself in a party sequence.

Garland took the role mainly because she was financially broke. MGM had withheld much of her salary due to her absences during the productions of *The Pirate* and *Easter Parade*, a little over fourteen weeks of total "suspension" time. Garland never paid attention to her finances. Like most women of her time, she was brought up and conditioned to leave financial matters up to someone else, usually "the man." Being in show business only encouraged that ignorance. Garland was the one singing for her supper (and the suppers of her family); others worried about the money. Throughout her life, a series of agents, representatives, and even her mother and stepfather mismanaged Garland's money. The financial situation prompted a return to the studio that was earlier than it should have been.

Garland's new manager and good friend Carlton Alsop went to see studio head Louis B. Mayer, who said that if Garland could get better, they would pay her $50,000 for her to perform one song in the film (half of what they withheld from her salary). Garland was at home on an intravenous glucose drip in an effort to gain weight and strength. Alsop gave Garland MGM's request, to which she responded, "Pa [her nickname for Alsop], get that fucking needle out of my arm. I'm going out there. I can sing, or I'll find out if I can still sing."[1] That's according to biographer Gerold Frank, who got the sequence of events mixed, reporting that "Johnny One Note" was the first song filmed, not "I Wish I Were in Love Again." Garland rallied to rehearse, record, and film "I Wish I Were in Love Again" with Rooney,

In the Good Old Summertime (1949). From the collection of Bruce Hanson.

which became their final on-screen appearance together and their only time in Technicolor. In the many photos taken during the prerecording session on May 28, 1948, with Garland's daughter Liza visiting, Garland doesn't look well at all. She's obviously thin and fatigued. Her eyes are hollow. The short filming schedule for the number started a few days later. Even for this short assignment, her attendance was bad. She was late, kept everyone waiting, or didn't show up. But when she was ready, she delivered, and, in spite of everything, she sparkled on screen in the short scene preceding the song and with Rooney when performing it. In hindsight, knowing what we know now, it's easy to see some of the fatigue on her face on film because we're looking for it, but while unsuspecting audiences of the time may have noticed that she was thin, they saw no hint of the extent of the struggles behind the scenes.

Garland's next assignment was *The Barkleys of Broadway*. The film was originally titled *You Made Me Love You* with the intent of having Garland reprise her early song hit of the same name. However, Garland's time off from mid-March through mid-May 1948 (with only one radio appearance) did not give her the strength she needed to endure the demands and strains of another big-budget musical. She had been on basically good behavior during *Easter Parade* due mostly to her awe of Astaire, but this time, she just couldn't do it. She seemed to do fine for the first two

Garland's daughter Liza Minnelli visits the MGM recording stage to watch Garland and Mickey Rooney prerecord "I Wish I Were in Love Again" for *Words and Music*, May 28, 1948. From the author's collection.

weeks, but by early July, she began to call in sick again almost daily. On one day, June 30, she called in sick but kept an evening radio obligation, appearing with Astaire on *The Tex and Jinx Show*, duetting on "It Only Happens When I Dance with You" and soloing other Irving Berlin songs. From July 7 through July 12, Garland called in sick for at least four days, prompting Freed to call her physician on July 12. He noted in a memo, "[Garland's physician] said that she could possibly work four or five days, always under medication and possibly blow up for a period and then work again for a few days. He was of the opinion that if she didn't have to work for a while it might not be too difficult to make a complete cure but that her knowledge of having to report every morning would cause such a mental disturbance within her that the results would be in jeopardy."[2] A few days later, on July 18, the studio cowardly sent Garland a registered letter firing her from the film and putting her on suspension without pay. The next day, Ginger Rogers took over Garland's role. The swiftness of this replacement indicates that although they were allegedly trying to help Garland, MGM was also working on finding a replacement. Immediately after Garland was fired, Freed had a script flown to Rogers at her Oregon ranch, where she had been enjoying some time off. Freed offered her $12,500 per week, which was over double what they were paying Garland.[3] In all, the studio spent $23,077 (at 1948 dollar value) on Garland's time on the film.[4] Years later, Garland remembered the cold indifference of the studio:

I missed one day, then two, and then three. Finally, I was fired from Barkleys of Broadway. They didn't even give me the courtesy of a call or a meeting or a discussion. They sent me a telegram.

The natural thing followed. The publicity department had to make me the "heavy." I had been fired because I was "ungrateful," "temperamental." No one said "exhausted" or "sick."

I became frantic. I tried to call someone, but the producer "wasn't on the lot." Mr. Mayer was "out of town." The other executives were "in conference." I stopped calling when I read in the paper that Ginger Rogers had replaced me. No one called me, either. Hollywood is a strange place when you're in trouble. Everyone is afraid it's contagious.

Out of sheer force of habit, I went to my analyst. He talked to me for a long time, but I became even more confused and despondent. I finally told him that I thought it was all a waste of time.

The doctor thought it over for a few minutes and said, "All right, Judy, if that's the way you feel, you should stop. It's up to you. But I want to tell you something. I only give you six months to live."

Just like that.

"What do you mean?" I asked him.

"Because you're suicidal. Definitely."

That had never occurred to me. But I did think about it from then on.[5]

Garland's recollections fifteen years later (and after a lot of water under the bridge) are slightly suspect. There is some truth to what she says, but, as with memories long after the fact, details can get muddied—especially details of a time when someone was in a mental fog like Garland. Considering she had been suicidal before, the conversation with her therapist about that possibility being new to her probably took place during a session a couple of years prior. What's important is the fact that Garland felt completely alone throughout the ordeal, with an unforgiving MGM shutting her out. Additionally, she and Minnelli continued having marital troubles; she couldn't go to him. She did have her new manager, Carlton Alsop, and his wife, actress Sylvia Sidney (known more now as the afterlife caseworker "Juno" in *Beetlejuice*). Both Alsop and Sidney were a great help to Garland. They, like a few others around her, offered support and sincerely tried to help her. But when, according to Garland, she got up the courage to speak out in her defense at MGM, she was stifled and told that she was "an ungrateful little girl. They had made me a star. Mr. Mayer thought that he knew how to bring up his own child."[6] Unfortunately for Garland, the depths of MGM's callousness would become even deeper over the next two years.

Notably, at one point after Garland had been fired from *Barkleys*, she returned to the set in full costume, parading around and acting as if nothing had happened, socializing with the cast and crew while, depending on which book one reads, she either ignored Rogers or chatted with her and *Barkleys* costar Oscar Levant. An unnerved Rogers went to her dressing room and refused to do any filming until Garland left. The stunt ended with Garland either forcibly being led from the soundstage, yelling insults at Rogers, or angrily storming out on her own after director Charles Walters asked her to leave. It's unclear whether the story is true. While there is a photo of Garland with Levant allegedly taken on this day, there is also a photo of Garland on the *Barkleys* set in costume for *Words and Music*. The two photos have puzzled Garland fans. In the latter pic, she's in conversation with Astaire and Rogers (both in full costume as well), who look like they are laughing with her. In both photos, she's heavy, but more so in the photo with Levant.

236   CHAPTER 9

Garland during a break in filming on the set of *In the Good Old Summertime*, January 8, 1949. From the author's collection.

Since the story of Garland's vengeful surprise visit notes that Astaire came on set as Garland was leaving, then, if it happened at all, it must have been after Garland returned to the studio after her weight gain.

During the break after *The Barkleys of Broadway*, Garland was able to again withdraw from her dependency on the pills. She gained some more weight and began to regain her health. In late September, she went back to work, prerecording an appearance on Bing Crosby's radio series, *Philco Radio Time*. The two sang "For Me and My Gal" and "Embraceable You," and Garland soloed on "Over the Rainbow." The show aired on October 6, a week after her return to MGM on September 24. Her only other non-MGM work at the time was her sole team-up with legendary stage and screen performer Al Jolson on the NBC Radio show *Kraft Music Hall* on September 30, 1948, and an appearance on Louella Parsons's radio show in the fall of 1948. The Parsons show is notable because it's one of the very few times Garland sang the opening verse of "Over the Rainbow."

While Garland was convalescing, *Words and Music* previewed, and audiences wanted a Garland encore to "I Wish I Were in Love Again." MGM paid her the remaining $50,000 from that earlier suspension, and she went into rehearsals and costume fittings for her reprise song, "Johnny One Note." Due to her weight gain, the costume she wore during "I Wish I Were in Love Again" didn't fit, so a duplicate was made to accommodate her now robust figure, with some minor changes noticeable in the film, such as the removal of the belt. In the film's narrative, both songs are performed at the same party, with "Johnny One Note" as an immediate encore. Critics and audiences noticed the sudden weight change (mere seconds in the film), but it didn't matter. The Garland aura once again worked its magic. She was singled out as one of the highlights in a film that is, at best, average. As a biopic, it's laughably fictional. The only reason to endure it today is for the great Rodgers and Hart songs performed to perfection by the MGM

Studio Orchestra and Chorus and a host of guest stars such as Betty Garrett, Lena Horne, June Allyson, Gene Kelly, Vera-Ellen, Ann Sothern, Perry Como, and Cyd Charisse. *Words and Music* was the last time Garland successfully completed a role for the Freed Unit.

Although Garland has just one scene and two songs in her brief guest appearance, she received top billing (or close to the top) in most of the ads and was one of the main stars listed alphabetically in the official posters. Some newspaper ads made it look like a "Gene Kelly/Judy Garland" movie the way the stars were listed. Rooney took issue with the fact that his costar Drake, whose role was as large as Rooney's, was relegated to the smaller print billing under the title, specifically pointing out Garland's small role in his complaints to MGM. They were, after all, playing the team of Rodgers and Hart, whom the film was about. There's no word about what the studio

On-set costume, hair, and makeup photo for *In the Good Old Summertime*, December 20, 1948. From the author's collection.

thought or whether Rooney really went to the studio with his complaints, but his grievances were enough to be picked up by the columnists and published throughout the summer of 1948. Considering what close friends he and Garland were, it's odd that he would single her out this way.

Garland didn't have much time to rest. The Freed Unit might have had their fill of her (for the time being), but MGM's other big musical producer, Joe Pasternak, was more than happy to have Garland in the lead role of his musical remake of the Ernst Lubitsch classic *The Shop Around the Corner* (1940), titled *The Girl from Chicago*. Pasternak adored Garland, and to lure her back, he didn't require her to lose weight or put undue pressure on her to be glamorous. He and the rest of the cast and crew did everything they could to make her feel loved and welcomed. Her costar, Van Johnson, was another Garland fan who went on record in interviews talking about how much he revered her and how they helped get her through the filming. He told the story many times about Mayer asking him how they were able to get a relatively stress-free performance out of Garland. His response was "We made her feel needed; we joked with her and kept her happy."[7] Pasternak had a single red rose delivered to Garland's dressing room every morn-

Liza Minnelli's screen debut with her mom, Garland, in *In the Good Old Summertime*, December 6, 1948.
From the author's collection.

ing with an anonymous card that read, "Happy day, Judy." She dispatched Dottie Ponedel to try to find out who this secret admirer was, to no avail. But it did its job; it helped lift her spirits. Pasternak later said, "There was never a word uttered in recrimination when she was late, didn't show up, or couldn't go on. Those of us who worked with her knew her magical genius and respected it."[8]

Garland's current suspension (and withholding of salary) by MGM ended on October 11, 1948, which was her first day of work on *The Girl from Chicago*. The day consisted of rehearsals and costume fittings. According to the *Daily Music Reports*, the title of the film was changed at some point between November 12 and November 16, 1948, from *The Girl from Chicago* to *In the Good Old Summertime*. The latter date was the first of two consecutive days Garland spent prerecording her songs. In a sign of her good health and positive attitude, on the first day she successfully recorded four of her six major solos, never needing more than three takes to get it letter-perfect, in styles ranging from light and airy ("Put Your Arms Around Me, Honey") to heart-wrenching ("Last Night When We Were Young"). The latter song was cut from the film for that reason—it was too serious. The surviving footage shows Garland performing the song flawlessly, but it's much too intense to be in an otherwise upbeat, sprightly musical. It was one of Garland's favorite songs, and she recorded it again on March 31, 1956, for the Capitol Records *Judy* album with almost the same arrangement and even more intense delivery, and she performed it live on her TV series in 1964.

The following day, November 17, 1948, Garland completed her prerecording duties for the film by breezing through "I Don't Care," "Play That Barbershop Chord," and the ultimately deleted finale version of the title song. Garland's voice in all the songs is at her most robust and lovely late 1940s tone. The recent rest and lightening of pressures seemed to have allowed her to relax her voice. The resulting MGM Records soundtrack album is notable because, even though it was originally just four songs on two 12″ 78 rpm discs, it was all Garland solos (with an assist from the King's Men on "Play That Barbershop Chord"). The holiday song written for the film, "Merry Christmas," was left off the soundtrack album and was not released until 1952 when it was included in the label's Christmas compilation record titled *Merry Christmas*. The outtake of "Last Night When We Were Young" first appeared on the label's 1951 compilation *Judy Garland Sings*. All of the songs would not appear together as a "complete" soundtrack until the label's series of soundtracks titled *Those Glorious MGM Musicals* was released in 1974. In 2001, the soundtrack was expanded by Rhino Records on compact disc and included the addition of the "Main Title," background music, the deleted finale, and more. The soundtrack album continues to be a favorite of Garland fans.

Garland posed for more MGM promotion photos on November 8, 1948. From the author's collection.

Initially, Garland was unhappy with the assignment. On the one hand, she knew she had to prove to the studio that she could be reliable, but, on the other hand, the role was a letdown after she had been given (and lost) the more glamorous role of Dinah Barkley in the higher-profile *The Barkleys of Broadway*. Meanwhile, her husband Vincente Minnelli was directing a high-profile film of his own, his adaptation of Flaubert's *Madame Bovary*. Garland was jealous of Minnelli because, in her mind, she was relegated to playing an insignificant shopgirl in an insignificant small-budget musical.[9] But thanks to the Pasternak Unit's crew and the film's cast, she ended up enjoying herself and gave one of her most charming performances. *In the Good Old Summertime* might not have been a splashy big-budget MGM musical like *Easter Parade*, but with Garland and Johnson's chemistry, and particularly Garland's performance, it's every bit the equal. Supporting players S. Z. "Cuddles" Sakall, Spring Byington, Buster Keaton, and Clinton Sundberg shine as well. Garland also looks much healthier than she was during *Easter Parade*, thanks that recent weight gain. Garland might have thought it insignificant, but, in reality, *In the Good Old Summertime* turned out to be one of her best and most enjoyable MGM films, featuring a relaxed and less strident light comedic performance from her.

Another aspect of the filming that brightened Garland's spirits was the screen debut of her two-and-a-half-year-old daughter, Liza Minnelli. On November 6, 1948, mother and daughter were on MGM's famous Lot 2 in front of the standing "Southern Mansion" set, which was disguised and used for the bandstand-in-the-park scenes that open and close the film. Liza has a cameo as the toddler daughter of Garland and Johnson's characters in the film's final shot. The event was heavily photographed and promoted in newspaper and magazine stories over the next year.

Filming on *In the Good Old Summertime* ended five days earlier than scheduled (a rarity for a Garland film at this time) on January 27, 1949.[10] It opened in theatres on July 26, 1949, and at New York's prestigious Radio City Music Hall on August 4, 1949. The Radio City engagement is an indication of MGM's confidence in the film's quality, as it was usually the bigger-budgeted, higher-profile films that played Radio City, but Garland's name was such a big box-office draw that MGM was assured of its success. During its initial release, *In the Good Old Summertime* grossed over $3.5 million on a budget of $1,576,635. In spite of what she had recently been through, Garland's performance on that big screen again had a magical effect on audiences. Once more, the strain behind the camera didn't show. At Radio City, audiences applauded spontaneously after "I Don't Care" as if it were a live stage performance, something unusual at the movies.[11] Some of the reviews:

> Good-natured ribbing, lilting song hits of yesteryear, plus Judy and Van combine to make this a most engaging Technicolor treat for the entire family. Your Reviewer Says: Full of melody and mirth.
> —uncredited, *Photoplay* magazine, September 1949

> Looking much sturdier than she did in her last screen appearance, Judy performs the role of the ambitious heroine with some of her old-time verve. She also sings the title song, and several old favorites with usual effectiveness.
> —Kate Cameron, *Daily News*, New York City, August 5, 1949

> It's romantic, it's intimate, it's compact, it's simple. Judy is at her magnificent tops. Sings in it, too.
> —Walter Winchell, "Winchell in New York," syndicated column, August 7, 1949

> Judy Garland follows up her big success in "Easter Parade" with another delicious romantic comedy, "In The Good Old Summertime," this time costarred with Van Johnson. The initial teaming of Miss Garland and Johnson should prove a forerunner to more films starring the popular stars who are ideally cast together, whether it be in a romantic spat or in a melody duet.
> —uncredited, *Terre Haute Tribune*, Terre Haute, Indiana, August 7, 1949

The MGM Records soundtrack album, which was two discs with four songs, also received positive reviews, such as this one:

VINTAGE MGM

Judy Garland, MGM's vivacious songstress, salutes the summer months, with an appropriate album for MGM Records, "In The Good Old Summertime." This MGM set is typical Judy Garland music, and she surely gives it her all. She's got personality-plus, infectious style, and lively interpretations. Judy Garland scores a winner with this two-pocket MGM record jacket!
—Jinny Constance, *Miami News*, Miami, Florida, August 21, 1949

The wonderful reviews and audience acceptance for *In the Good Old Summertime* was something Garland needed in July 1949. At the time of the film's release, she was on the East Coast undergoing treatment to cure her drug habit at the Peter Bent Brigham Hospital in Boston, Massachusetts. The long treatment was the result of the previous months of working herself into another total emotional and physical breakdown from gamely trying to play Annie Oakley in *Annie Get Your Gun*.

Mexican lobby card for *In the Good Old Summertime* (1949). From the author's collection.

CHAPTER *10*

NIGHTMARE AT MGM

ANNIE GET YOUR GUN

Annie Get Your Gun began its journey to the screen on Broadway. The fictionalized story of the very real Annie Oakley was a successful film in 1935 starring Barbara Stanwyck as Annie. The musical version, based in part on the film, was the brainchild of lyricist and librettist Dorothy Fields. Fields and her brother, Herbert, wrote the book of the musical, which was produced by Richard Rodgers and Oscar Hammerstein II, who, after their mega-hit *Oklahoma!*, had decided to go into producing Broadway shows while continuing to write songs and, sometimes, write the book or portions thereof. For *Annie*, Rodgers and Hammerstein hired Jerome Kern to write the score, with Fields providing the lyrics. But just after beginning work on the show, Kern died. They turned to Irving Berlin, who always wrote both the music and the lyrics, and Fields happily stepped aside as lyricist.

Berlin was apprehensive. He was used to writing songs for revues and peppering films that highlighted his catalog of songs with added new ones. *Annie* would be a solid book musical with songs integrated into the plot. He ended up writing one of the best scores ever written for a Broadway show, including the songs "There's No Business Like Show Business," "I Got the Sun in the Morning," "They Say It's Wonderful," "Anything You Can Do," "Doin' What Comes Natur'lly," and "You Can't Get a Man with a Gun," all of which were perfect for Garland, who gave the public a preview when she performed "I Got the Sun in the Morning" a couple of times on the radio in 1946. *Annie Get Your Gun* opened on Broadway on May 16, 1946, with Ethel Merman triumphing as Annie Oakley. It ran for 1,147 performances.

Almost before the curtain went down on opening night, every studio in Hollywood wanted to purchase the film rights for their resident musical leading ladies. MGM's Arthur Freed won out, purchasing the rights for Garland, who, with her earthy vulnerability, was perfect for the role. It was seen as a likely Garland mega-hit and instant classic, as *Meet Me in St. Louis* (1944) and *Easter Parade* (1948) had been before. Unfortunately, by the time the film went into production, Garland was in no shape to endure another big-budget Arthur Freed musical production.

Things seemed to start on a positive note. Garland's first day of work on *Annie* was March 7, 1949. She arrived on time at 10:00 a.m. for wardrobe work and then had a song rehearsal, being dismissed at 2:40 p.m. For the next several days of song rehearsals with her costar Howard Keel, she was late, but not by much;

Costume test for *Annie Get Your Gun* (1949). From the author's collection.

thirty-five minutes was the latest, until March 10, when she called the production assistant, Al Jennings, at 10:00 a.m. to say she was ill and wouldn't be able to get to the studio until later in the day, so her start time was moved to 2:00 p.m., for which she was on time. Garland didn't call in sick until March 18 and 19, which resulted in the rest of the production being halted for the day. March 25 was Garland's first prerecording session for the film. She recorded "Doin' What Comes Natur'lly" and "You Can't Get a Man with a Gun." Musical supervisor Lela Simone recalled a day that she and Roger Edens were present as Judy recorded some of the songs (which recording date is unknown): "In the monitor booth, for the first time Roger and I smiled each other into a more or less artificial enthusiasm, 'that was very nice, wasn't it?' we said. 'Nice' was a term we had never used for Judy before."[1] The implication was that the session grossly lacked the excitement and electric energy that usually accompanied a Garland recording session.

Garland prerecorded "Let's Go West Again," and Howard Keel prerecorded "My Defenses Are Down," both with the same male chorus, for *Annie Get Your Gun* on March 30, 1949. From the author's collection.

During the next few days of prerecording sessions, Garland also filed for divorce from her husband, Vincente Minnelli (on March 28). The couple publicly announced their separation on March 30, the same day Garland prerecorded "Let's Go West Again," a new song written by Berlin specifically for her to sing in the film.

The Garland–Minnelli marriage had been in trouble for some time. It had become so bad that the couple rented a second home on Sunset Boulevard so Garland or Minnelli would have a place to go after one of their fights.[2] Both allegedly had multiple affairs. The assumption was that Minnelli's affairs were with men, and after walking in on him with a man on at least one occasion, Garland's trust eroded. That's not something that's easy to move on from, especially in the late 1940s. Garland supposedly had an affair with the young Yul Brynner during the filming of *The Pirate* in 1947. However, considering her state of mind at the time and her physical frailty, not to mention her drug issues, it's difficult to imagine that she could sustain an affair or ongoing sexual relationship with anyone. But then again, it wouldn't have been impossible. The main point here is that although in the beginning Garland and Minnelli did love each other, or thought they loved each other, in the long term, their differences got in the way. At another time, if the circumstances of their lives and careers had been different, they might have had a longer, more positive marriage. But the more Garland faltered, the less it seemed Minnelli was equipped to be the solid rock of support she needed. It didn't help that he was also working at the same place she was, and, in her eyes, he increasingly represented the studio, so, in effect, even at home, she felt the studio hovering over her. By March 1949, as Garland was in the early weeks of *Annie Get Your Gun*, her renewed drug abuse had gotten so bad that Minnelli literally "snatched away her pills" in an effort (however misguided) to stop her.[3] Their divorce wasn't final until the early 1950s, after Garland had left MGM, but the two remained friends and continued to respect each other's talents. They also had daughter Liza, keeping their lives forever entwined.

After she completed *In the Good Old Summertime*, Garland had planned to take a vacation;

instead, MGM enticed her to start work on *Annie*. It was a monumental mistake. In hindsight, it is baffling that MGM was so quick to push Garland into *Annie Get Your Gun*. It's doubtful there was any real malice behind the decision; no one would have wanted to harm her intentionally. But harm her, they did. Her drug intake became as bad as it had been in 1947, if not worse. This time, her hair began to fall out, and one of her new doctors, Dr. Fred Pobirs (suggested to help her by family friend and doctor Marc Rabwin), took inventory of her medicines and her personal issues and suggested that she take shock treatments. She endured six of them.

Another person who stepped in to help Garland was Harry Anslinger. Anslinger was the head of the US Bureau of Narcotics. The story of Anslinger going to MGM to intervene on Garland's behalf, only to be shot down with "We've got 14 million dollars tied up in her," has become a huge part of the Garland legend. Over the years, biographers have misrepresented the facts of Anslinger's story, having relied on what others had copied from his newspaper interview in 1969.

Not long after Garland's death in 1969, Anslinger revealed that his experiences trying to help a major movie star with her addiction, as told in his 1961 book *The Murderers: The Story of the Narcotic Gangs*, were a thinly veiled account of his attempts to help Garland. According to him, in 1949 (possibly 1948) he and the agency were investigating drug use in Hollywood. He was tipped off about Garland's dilemma (which wasn't a big secret in Hollywood) and met with her. In 1969, he reported, "She said she was exhausted from a heavy schedule of movie-making," and she told him that "she was taking amphetamines (pep pills) when she got out of bed in the morning, minor stimulants during the day, a shot of morphine before fulfilling night-time engagements and finally, a sleeping pill to help her sleep."[4] In his 1961 book, he said that he "conducted a running battle for months with a famous producer in an effort to save one of our loveliest screen stars [Garland]." He found out that an unethical doctor known in Hollywood as "the Croaker" had Garland on "drugs and stimulants almost every hour of her waking life."

> *She started at six a.m. with amphetamines to get her pretty eyes open so that she could be down at the studio by seven-thirty to begin rehearsing. She would take minor stimulants during the day, but by two p.m., neither her body nor her voice had the strength called for to perform as the director required for his shooting script. The physician would take care of her with a "bang" in the arm, employing a strong narcotic drug. At the close of the day, she required phenobarbital to steady her nerves. Then, in the evening—because of publicity demands—she had to be seen at various restaurants and night clubs. By the end of her long day, her nerves were in such a state that she could sleep only by taking an enormous dose of paraldehyde.[5]*

Anslinger doesn't mention morphine in his 1961 account, but he does note that he believed Garland to be "a fine woman caught in a situation that could only destroy her." He called the stars in Hollywood who were addicts the victims of "a bevy of leeches," the leeches being the studios that created the kind of workload that pushed stars to addiction and then callously turned a blind eye to their problems. Anslinger went to New York to talk to the head of the

246   CHAPTER 10

studio. That was Nicholas Schenck, the head of Loew's Inc., which was MGM's parent company. Anslinger told Schenck that Garland needed a full year off in a sanitarium to get well, to which Schenck replied, "Simply unthinkable. I've got fourteen million dollars invested in her. I couldn't afford your plan. She's at the top of her box office right this minute."[6] In the 1969 version, Anslinger said he went to a "high MGM official" and told the official that she needed a full year off to rest and get over her addictions. The reply was "We have $14,000,000 tied up in her, and she is the studio's biggest asset."[7] That article is the source of the popular label for Garland as "MGM's Biggest Asset." Over the decades, it's been assumed that Mayer or MGM's new vice president in charge of production, Dore Schary, gave the heartless responses. If his 1961 book is to be believed, it was Schenck who had the heartless exchange with Anslinger, which is believable considering the sequence of events when Garland was fired from *Annie Get Your Gun*. As Anslinger reported about one of his meetings:

> *"Suppose," I asked [the MGM official], "she takes her life, as she has already tried to several times? Or merely makes a mistake and swallows too many of her pills. What happens to your fourteen million?"*
>
> *"We'll have to take that chance."*
>
> *"There's one other factor," I said. "In her condition, she may blow her top at any time. If she does—there goes your picture and your millions."*
>
> *That, in fact, is exactly what happened. In a state of almost complete uncontrol, she walked out on her next film. . . . Another star had to be brought in and the entire film remade.[8]*

During one of the conversations Anslinger had with Schenck about Garland, Schenck told him to go after "the big peddlers and leave my stars alone." Anslinger had found out that the source of Garland's supply, "the Croaker," was also an addict. He couldn't get her to stop seeing him, so he pleaded with Schenck, "Get her out of the hands of that doctor and under the care of a reliable physician. If you do, you may save her life." Schenck's response was "You can't dictate to these big stars. They're too emotional and temperamental. Besides, she can use any doctor she damn feels like. Telling her what doctor to use is not in her contract, and we couldn't get a clause like that even if we wanted to." Anslinger left the meeting, in his own words, speechless. He was able to force the doctor to stop giving Garland the illegal drugs and said that she accepted his advice and hired a "good physician," who, according to Anslinger, was successful in curing her. "Ultimately, she returned to starring roles. More than once, she has gone out of her way to let me know her gratitude."[9]

Although Anslinger wasn't aware of Garland's issues until 1949 (according to the 1969 article), she had already been using the combination of drugs she had told him about (or a similar regime) off and on for the previous two years, judging from her repeated yo-yo cycle of drug abuse—breakdowns, rest, withdrawal, and repeat. Each time she went back to the drugs, thinking they would help her, the results were worse than before. It had happened. Her habit, her crutch, had become her illness, and Garland found herself suffering an addiction that immobilized her more often than not. It must be noted that although Garland was experiencing the effects of addiction, she wasn't acting out negatively on purpose. As Anslinger noted, she was caught in a situation in which she was steered into the use of illegal drugs by the doctor Anslinger mentioned (and probably others), but she had no one to help guide her out of her predicament. There were those around her who tried, but no one was qualified because few (if any) could have understood what she was going through. Her husband, Vincente Minnelli, certainly wasn't sure of what to do. Her psychiatrists and medical doctors were also stymied in one way or another. Garland was indeed caught on "a treadmill" and didn't know how to get off. She knew she had to get off the drugs, but she was also insecure in her abilities, thinking that the only way to make it through each day and the pressures it wrought was what had worked before—her chemical crutches. She probably innocently assumed, "This time, it'll help me."

Much has been written about MGM's alleged intentional malice toward Garland, with most of the ire directed at studio boss Louis B. Mayer. Although Mayer would, at times, take an interest in the day-to-day workings of a production, he usually didn't get involved, leaving that up to the producers. In Garland's case, he tried to help her on multiple occasions. During her short time on *The Barkleys of Broadway*, he personally went to her home to talk to her and try to help.[10] He also ended up loaning her money to pay for hospital stays. Whether it was out of kindness or guilt regarding what had happened to her since that audition in 1935, the true motivations behind Mayer's support will never be known. People want to find a villain to blame for Garland's fall at MGM because it's easy to blame one person rather than to delve into the nuances of her career at the studio, her relationships with those who ran it, her personal demons, and her own culpability. Mayer was the head of the studio and ultimately was responsible for what happened there, generally speaking. But he can't be solely blamed for her problems any more than any-one else. It's not as black and white as "Mayer [or MGM] worked her to death" or "Mayer [or MGM] abused her." Schary certainly didn't show any patience or compassion toward Garland or her troubles, as would soon be seen during the production of *Annie Get Your Gun*.

Another aspect to consider in all of this speculation is the action taken by producer Arthur Freed or, rather, his apparent inaction. In spite of his brilliance in producing movie mu-sicals, Freed was known for being crude in manner and speech. Reportedly, he wasn't the most tactful or empathetic person, with most people seeing Roger Edens as the one who really drove the Freed Unit, at least artistically. If anyone is a villain in this scenario, albeit an unknowing one, it would be Freed. He should have given Garland time off before *Annie Get Your Gun*, and, most important, he shouldn't have assigned Busby Berkeley as the director. Berkeley was the complete opposite of the kind of director needed to guide Garland through the film not just emotionally but also in helping her get a handle on how to portray the character. Berkeley was past his prime and a severe alcoholic. He and Garland hadn't worked together since the big blowup over "I Got

Costume test for *Annie Get Your Gun* (1949). From the author's collection.

Rhythm" in 1943's *Girl Crazy*. She despised him. Freed's choice of Berkeley as the director was reckless and showed a complete lack of compassion and understanding of Garland's present problems. He seemed to turn a blind eye. In the list of those around Garland who really did try to help her in the late 1940s, Freed's name isn't included; Mayer's is.

Garland's first day of filming on *Annie Get Your Gun* was April 6, 1949, on the "Exterior Wilson Hotel" set, the "Doin' What Comes Natur'lly" song and its surrounding scenes. She tried to deliver, and on this first day, she had a call to be in makeup at 8:00 a.m., arriving at 9:25 a.m.—late, but not bad. She joined Freed in a projection room to view a wardrobe test; then she was back on the soundstage and ready on set at 11:25 a.m. The number was completed the following day. The production then moved on to filming some of the non-musical scenes.[11] Unfortunately, Garland's costar, Howard Keel, broke his leg on the second day of filming and was off the film until it healed. This added more pressure on Garland to carry the film, pressure she couldn't handle. Unlike *Easter Parade*, in which the two supporting roles, played by Ann Miller and Peter Lawford, have large amounts of screen time, *Annie Get Your Gun* is all about Annie Oakley and Frank Butler, meaning more time on screen and more demands on Garland.

Freed biographer Hugh Fordin reported that Garland didn't work on the Wilson Hotel set until the end of the first week and a half of shooting, at which point Berkeley shouted at the crew, which threw Garland into a kind of PTSD from her previous films with him, and she walked off the set. Fordin doesn't give a source for his information or for his claim that when viewing the dailies, she was so discouraged she went over to the water cooler and downed a handful of Benzedrine pills. The production notes by Al Jennings show that Garland did not leave early on either of the days they filmed on the Wilson Hotel set. In fact, for the next several days, Garland was on the set around 11:00 a.m. or so and stayed until the end of the shooting day. She first called in sick on April 11 but was back the next day.

The footage of the ensuing non-musical scenes shot on the Exterior NY Pier, Interior Pullman Car, and the US and European Travel Montage sets does not exist, but the song and surrounding scenes for "Doin' What Comes Natur'lly" do and have been released. The footage is fascinating to watch for a couple of reasons. First, Garland is fine and isn't outwardly showing any of the signs that she's not up to par, aside from some very tired-looking eyes and the fact that the special Garland magical sparkle isn't there. Although it's not as bad as the legend built it up to be in the decades before the footage was released, it's not great or even very good either; it's just fine. When director Charles Walters was called in to look at the footage, he later said that Garland was at her worst and that she "couldn't decide whether she was Ethel Merman, Mary Martin, Martha Raye or herself."[12] Walters was being overly dramatic. Garland's delivery of the dialog before and after the song shows that while she really didn't have a clue of how to play the character, she wasn't imitating any of those other ladies, either. She wasn't imitating anyone at all. She was reading the lines and performing the songs almost as if it were a rehearsal. Second, Berkeley's filming is all wrong. It's an obvious soundstage and not really outside like it's supposed to look; the filming doesn't try to hide that, and the staging of the scenes and the song are very boring. It looks more like a stage show than a film, as has been commented over the decades. Berkeley clearly didn't know what he was doing. Finally, Garland's wig and makeup are terrible. While Annie Oakley is supposed to be a backwoods country girl, the wig they gave Garland is an obvious wig and more unflattering than it needs to be. Her makeup is practically nonexistent, so her face, like the wig, is also more severe than it needs to be. Garland obviously wasn't the only person who didn't have a grasp of how to present the character. The makeup and hair department didn't either.

After more filming of various non-musical scenes, Garland went into rehearsals on April 18 for the "I'm an Indian, Too" production number, prerecording the song on April 25. Filming the now infamous "I'm an Indian, Too" production number began on April 27, this time under the direction of the film's dance director, Robert Alton, not Berkeley. Garland was on time for a 10:30 a.m. call to be on the set, and filming lasted until 5:30 p.m. Footage survives from this and the next four days of filming, making it possible to piece together a representation of the original concept for the number. The concept is much more elaborate than in the final version of the film, with the "Indians" doing a Hollywood version of a "native" dance, and after emerging from a teepee, Annie is put through her paces in an effort to become "an Indian, too." After over four minutes of this back-and-forth, she's finally made an Indian and then goes into the song. Sadly, this footage doesn't present Garland at her best, either. At one point in the raw footage, she faints into the dancers behind her. It's unclear whether it was part of the choreography or if Garland actually fainted. Alton's assistant, Alex Romero, who was one of the dancers in the scene, said that at times he had to hold Garland up because she was "so intoxicated on drugs."[13] On one

250   CHAPTER 10

of the days, Freed was visiting the set, and Garland slid or fell to the floor (from either fatigue or the drugs, or perhaps from both). Freed began to scream and berate her in front of the cast and crew: "What's the matter with you? Get up off your ass, and let's film this scene!"[14] Freed wasn't the only one yelling at Garland. The assistant director, Al Jennings, noted that in the early days of filming Garland would come in feeling fine, but "Buzz would see her, and he would start screaming and yelling and hollering the way Buzz did. Ten minutes later, I would be called to her dressing room. 'I'm sick,' she would say. 'I can't stand it. I've got to go home.' And that would be the end of that."[15]

The "I'm an Indian, Too" footage was judiciously edited into an abridged version and presented in *That's Entertainment! III* in 1994 and on the subsequent home media releases of the film on disc. In its edited form, like "Doin' What Comes Natur'lly," it's serviceable. It's not as bad as the entire sequence put together or when looking at the raw footage before the edits were made, but, like Garland's performance, it's not great, either. That fourth day of filming was the last on the number, for the time being. On the following day, Garland and Berkeley had a "serious blowup" on the set, presumably another day of planned filming on the montage scenes, which Garland filmed the next day, but she left early, sick again.[16] Garland felt bad about leaving early on May 4, so she called the production manager, Walter Strohm, and apologized, offering to relinquish her pay for the day, as detailed in Strohm's memo dated the same day.[17]

Berkeley was finally fired from the film at this time, and Charles Walters came on board to take over. After looking at the footage, he decided it all had to be reshot. He met with Garland for three hours on May 5, at which point she said, "It's too late, Chuck; I haven't got the energy or the nerve anymore."[18] Three days later, Garland was back in rehearsals for the new Walters version of "Doin' What Comes Natur'lly," which was a short day. She was on time for a 2:00 p.m. call and then dismissed at 3:25 p.m. Two days later, on May 10, all hell broke loose.

Behind the scenes was Dore Schary, a man who not only didn't care much for musicals but also wasn't sympathetic to Garland's situation in any form. After he had been hired by MGM in 1948, he had a meeting with Garland, during which she angrily railed against the studio, used four-letter words, and complained about how overworked she was. Now, with the problems with *Annie Get Your Gun*, he called Schenck in New York to discuss the situation. Schary noted that Garland obviously couldn't continue, the implication being that she would eventually fall apart completely. He told Schenck that at that point, the company would have spent a lot of money but would not have a film to release. Schary was told to do what he had to do.[19] So the decision to fire Garland from the film was made. But rather than simply going to Garland and removing her, they waited for her inevitable next slip-up.

Schary's callousness is puzzling. When Garland was romancing Joe Mankiewicz in the early 1940s, Schary was part of their inner circle, spending a lot of time at her home playing games, making records, and socializing. At that time, he was the head of the "B" unit at MGM, and, according to Garland, he was in her house weeping because he was the lowly head of "the

NIGHTMARE AT MGM

Bs," as they were called. However, since taking over as head of all production at MGM, he couldn't (or wouldn't) offer a helping hand.

There are conflicting stories about the sequence of events on May 10, 1949, when Garland was fired from *Annie Get Your Gun*. She had called the assistant director, Al Jennings, at 7:30 a.m. to say that she might not be in because she had had a bad night and wasn't feeling well. He talked to her for fifteen minutes. She felt better and was at the studio at 10:10 a.m., in her dressing room, made up but not in costume, for the planned filming of "I'm an Indian, Too." She arrived on the set at 11:18 a.m., and waiting for her was a letter from MGM vice president Louis K. Sidney:

> *You must be aware of the fact that your contract with us requires you to be prompt in complying with our instructions and to perform your services conscientiously and to the full extent of your ability and as instructed by us. We desire to call your attention to the fact that on a great many occasions since the commencement of your services on "ANNIE GET YOUR GUN," you were either late in arriving on the set in the morning, late in arriving on the set after lunch, or were otherwise responsible for substantial delays or curtailed production, all without our consent.[20]*

The memo warned Garland that if she was late again, she would be put on suspension. Gerold Frank's 1975 biography described Garland's business manager, Carlton Alsop, walking onto the *Annie* set to find it a scene of pandemonium, with Garland waving the letter, "screaming epithets," and bursting into tears, crying to him, "I never lost anybody any money in my life!"[21] Garland's makeup artist and good friend, Dottie Ponedel, told the story differently, per Frank. She said that she was with Garland when the letter was delivered, and Garland was at first incredulous: "Dottie, they can't do that to me, can they?" Dottie told her that yes, they could. Garland became angry and indignant. "Not me," she said.[22] In his 2002 book detailing Garland's life on a day-by-day basis, Scott Schechter writes that Garland did not get the letter until after she returned from lunch; it was hand-delivered to her at 1:30 p.m., after which she refused to take the blame and got MGM to apologize. But when she returned to the set, she discovered the production had been shut down at 2:10 p.m., and she was officially fired "later that afternoon."[23]

Hugh Fordin's 1975 book about the Freed Unit tells the same basic story as Schechter, including Garland returning to the set after the company had been dismissed, with Dottie exclaiming, "Where is everybody? Get them all back, Judy is on her way." But when Garland came out, everyone was gone.[24] Gerald Clarke's biography noted that Garland received that first letter in the morning and was "considerably chastened" and that she rushed to the set from her dressing room and rehearsed until lunch; then, when she came back from lunch, whoever was watching her assumed that since she wasn't actually on the set but in her dressing room, it meant she was late and they delivered the second letter, which fired her from the production.[25] Both Fordin and Clarke noted that Strohm tried to stop the second letter from being delivered: "Oh, they weren't supposed to deliver that letter yet."[26] All of these stories are relayed here as an example of how details about important events can be clouded due to the number of people involved and how they remember any given sequence of events, especially a day of a whirlwind of events as this one was. This is why there are so many misconceptions, legends, and even myths regarding Garland's life and career, especially her time on *Annie Get Your Gun.*

As best as can be gleaned, MGM delivered a warning letter to Garland for being late that morning. After lunch, at approximately 1:30 p.m., the second letter was delivered, allegedly by the MGM aide Lester Peterson, which explained that due to her refusal "to comply with our instruction to report on the set" (a reference to that first letter), MGM "shall refuse to pay you any compensation commencing as of May 10, 1949, and continuing until the expiration of the time which would have been reasonably require to complete the role of 'ANNIE' in the photoplay 'ANNIE GET YOUR GUN' or until completion of such role by such other person [a replacement]."[27] Garland became hysterical, which is possibly the scene that Alsop walked in on. Although the second letter had been delivered, either Strohm or Mayer (most likely Strohm) told Jennings to call Garland back to the set at 2:00 p.m. in an apparent effort to smooth things over since she wasn't actually late after lunch and that second letter shouldn't have been delivered. Her response was "I shall never come back—now or ever."[28] Later she had a change of heart, and that's when Dottie went to the set and told Jennings that Garland was on her way, only to find that everyone was leaving. The production was closed at 2:10 p.m., allegedly on Mayer's orders.[29] "Well, get them back, Judy's on her way." Jennings replied, "Too late."[30] Quite a lot had happened between 1:30 p.m., when everyone came back from lunch, and 2:10 p.m., when the production was shut down. Later that afternoon, MGM sent a third memo to those affected stating that Garland's contract had been suspended and that she "is not to be called or requested to render services of any kind whatsoever unless the matter is cleared with Mr. Mannix or Mr. Schary."[31]

The debacle of *Annie Get Your Gun* was completely unnecessary, callous (at best) to Garland, and a total waste of time and money for MGM. In a mind-numbingly epic lapse in judgment and common sense, Freed was unthinking to believe that after everything that had come before, Garland would be able to complete the film without proper rest while under the direction of the tyrannical Busby Berkeley. In the time it took for all of this to play out, Garland could have had proper rest and treatment for her addictions and been healthy enough to make the role a truly great one for her and the studio. Walters was removed from the project as well, with George Sidney replacing him and finishing the film. In another example of the disorganization and miscommunication around the project at this time, Walters found out about being taken off the film not from the studio but by reading about it in columnist Hedda Hopper's latest column. When he called Hopper to find out her source, she told him, "Oh my God! You didn't know? I'm sorry, it's true, I got it from L. B. [Mayer]."[32] Betty Hutton was borrowed from Paramount to play Annie, and while the film was a hit when it was released, it has remained a pleasant, serviceable MGM musical, much like a good "B" musical rather than the "A" musical it should be. The entire film

NIGHTMARE AT MGM

253

seems rushed, perhaps due to the time and money spent before it was back on track with Hutton in the lead role. Hutton's performance is out of control. She's allowed to engage in too much of her manic mugging, which she was famous for, making the Annie character cartoonish. If Garland had been at her best, she would have delivered a more nuanced performance. The switching from scenes shot outdoors to soundstages that are meant to be outdoor scenes but don't look like anything other than soundstages also hurts the flow of the film. Irving Berlin was one of the most disappointed in the film's outcome. He wanted Garland to play Annie, and in the 1970s, the film went out of circulation due to the Berlin estate. It resurfaced on home media in 2000. In the end, it's one of the great missed opportunities of Garland's career and in the history of the great MGM musicals.

BACK TO BOSTON

The recent events made it clear that Garland needed serious professional help to withdraw completely from her medications. Mayer and Garland's manager, Carlton Alsop, met and decided, on advice from Garland's family doctor, Dr. Marc Rabwin, as well as Garland's psychiatrist and even Mayer's personal doctor, that she should be sent to the Peter Bent Brigham Hospital in Boston, Massachusetts. All agreed, including Garland, that she couldn't be treated in Los Angeles. Mayer offered to have the studio pay for her stay, telling Garland it was the least the studio could do. Garland later told the story that while she was in Mayer's office, he called Schenck in New York. Schenck refused, suggested coldly that she go to a charity hospital, and even more coldly stated that MGM wasn't in the money-lending business. Mayer offered to pay for her stay out of his own money, saying to Garland, "If they'll do this to you, they'll do this to me." However, the truth is that MGM did pay Garland's hospital bills while she was in Boston ($40,000). They also noted that the studio would not force her into another film until the physician-in-chief at Peter Bent, Dr. George W. Thorn, provided a statement that he believed she was ready.[33]

Garland waves at reporters after giving a press conference during which she admitted her addiction to prescription medicine, June 9, 1949. From the author's collection.

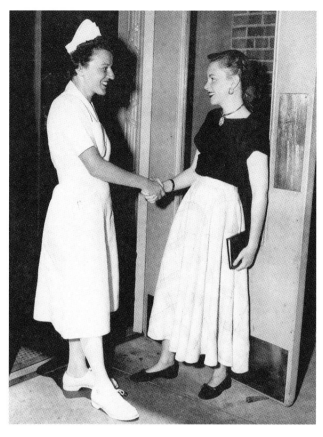

While at rehab at Peter Bent Brigham Hospital in Boston, Massachusetts, Garland (accompanied by nurse Lillian Goodman) gave a press conference admitting her addiction to prescription medicine, June 9, 1949.
From the author's collection.

Alsop accompanied the frail, ninety-pound Garland to the Peter Bent Brigham Hospital, where she began treatment and the very painful, very agonizing withdrawal from her addictions under the care of the physician assigned to her, Dr. Augustus Rose.

On June 6, Garland held a press conference at the Ritz-Carlton Hotel in Boston, Massachusetts, in which she announced her addiction to prescription medications. She told reporters that she was "learning to sleep all over again—without sleeping pills," adding, "What can you do? You get so exhausted working on a picture that you can't sleep. But you know you've got to sleep because you have to face that camera in the morning."[34] Photos of Garland posing with her nurse were published in papers around the country. The public had no idea about the extent of Garland's addictions; the official story was that it was simply an addiction to sleeping pills. The fact that a star of her caliber announced any kind of addiction while entering a hospital for treatment was a rare and major development in the relationship between movie stars and the public. Today, it's normal.

In about four weeks, Garland had improved amazingly, was drug free, and was eating properly. She was allowed to move to outpatient status and took a suite at the Ritz-Carlton, where she had announced her addiction to the public just a few weeks prior. Alsop, who diligently visited and helped as much as he was allowed to while she was at the hospital, provided much-needed support at the hotel and a watchful eye to keep her on track. Others were also supportive, including Frank Sinatra, who called her each day and sent gifts. He visited when he was allowed to and actually took her out for the evening on her doctor's approval. Mayer visited as well. The biggest boost to Garland's well-being was the visit by her daughter, three-year-old Liza Minnelli (and nurse), arriving on Garland's birthday, June 10. The mother/daughter reunion at the train station was photographed and published in papers around the country.

NIGHTMARE AT MGM

Dr. Rose began to get through to Garland, but not by much. Garland was so used to being "Judy Garland" and getting her way via her voice and her very persuasive manner that she hadn't reconciled that she was really Frances Gumm living in a Judy Garland fantasy world. Even before she was "Judy Garland," her source of acceptance was her stage persona, her voice, and her talent. The vaudeville world she grew up in, the one that had trained and honed her superhuman talent and ability to connect with and dazzle audiences, was also the vaudeville world that was the foundation of the fantasy world she currently lived in. The on-stage Frances made everyone love her, and she loved them back. That fantasy became her reality when she was just two and a half years old, and it had continued ever since. She had been to many psychiatrists over the years, and they hadn't been much help because she could not or would not truly look deep into herself. She tried to charm them like she charmed everyone else, not wanting to really see what her issues were. Now, with Dr. Rose in Boston, she found someone who wasn't as easily swayed, and although, in the end, he wasn't able to get her to see as deep into herself as she should have, he at least got further than most. In a display of her effect on people, an apparent attempt to show Dr. Rose the fantasy world she lived in was real, she opened the windows of his office and sang to her fans below, who would be there each day to see her come and go and hopefully get a few seconds with her. She sang for them, and the applause and cheers flowed into Dr. Rose's office. He flatly told her, "Look, we can't do this, Judy. . . . You're trying to make me into one of your fans. I can't help you in that way. We shall have to meet somewhere else."[35]

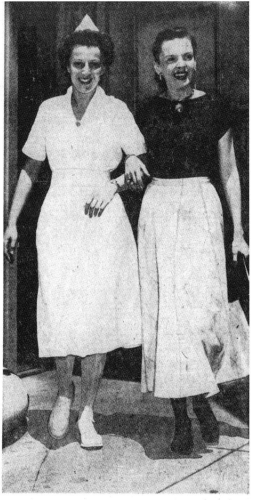

Newspaper clipping of Garland with nurse Lillian Goodman at the press conference in which Garland admitted her addiction to prescription medicine, June 9, 1949. From the author's collection.

On another occasion, Garland had apparently gotten hold of some pills and ended up under her bed at the hotel, kicking and screaming, refusing to come out. Rose was called, and when he showed up, he sent the attending nurse out and crawled under Garland's bed to talk to her. He finally convinced her to come out and talk with him.[36]

Aside from those setbacks, Garland progressed so well overall that she was allowed to go to Cape Cod with Liza and Alsop to spend the Fourth of July holiday there with Alsop's wife, actress Sylvia Sidney, and her son from a previous marriage. The time in Cape Cod did Garland even more good, as did a detour to see a show at a summer theatre on the cape. At the show, a cast member announced that she was in the audience, and he was able to coax her up to sing. She sang her heart out to the cheers and approval of the audience before going back to her seat and enjoying the show. The audience's acceptance of her was therapeutic, although, again, it was for "Judy Garland" and not Frances Gumm.

On August 5, 1949, either Dr. Rose or Dr. Thorn approved Garland temporarily returning to Los Angeles and MGM to discuss the upcoming production of *Summer Stock*. Columnist Patricia Clary, reporting on Garland's return to Los Angeles, was notably harsh about Garland and her problems, stating that "a fat and sunburned Judy Garland bounced back to movietown today." Since Garland's weight was always gossip fodder, Clary quotes Alsop as saying, "The first thing they'll tell her is to get that weight off. I think it looks good, and it's good for her."[37] While she was in Hollywood, Garland was photographed with other stars, including Katharine Hepburn and Billie Burke, celebrating Ethel Barrymore's seventieth birthday. Contrary to what Clary wrote, Garland does not look "fat" in the photos at all. She's thicker than her "camera-thin" weight, but she's very radiant and healthy looking. The time at Peter Bent seemed to be working.

In late August, Garland returned to Boston to finish her treatment. She was judged healthy enough to return to Los Angeles and resume her life in early September, accompanied by Dr. Rose. One event that happened before she left Peter Bent was notably therapeutic for her. She had bonded with the young patients at the children's hospital near Peter Bent. She first visited the hospital early in her treatment when she had to go there for some tests. Most of the children were special needs or had rheumatic fever and, after learning that she was coming, were excited to see her. They mostly knew her from *The Wizard of Oz*, which was enjoying its first theatrical rerelease that same summer. Unsure of herself at first, Alsop told her to give the children what the sign on the end of each bed said: "TLC" (Tender Loving Care). Garland spent time at each bedside chatting with the children. It was a thrill for the children, but it also did Garland more good than anyone assumed. She returned almost daily. There was a particular five-year-old girl who had been so abused by her family that she wouldn't speak to anyone, not even the nurses. Garland nevertheless stopped and spoke to her each time she visited. When it was time for Garland to leave for good and return to Los Angeles, she went to the hospital one last time.

Finally, I arrived at the last ward, where my little silent child was. The whole ward followed me, holding my hands and clinging to me. I was so grateful to them, because they had really made me well again. They really had. I walked over to the corner and sat down on the bed of my little silent friend. She just looked at me with her great, beautiful heartbreaking eyes.

I tried to be as casual as possible. "Well, my friend, I'm going now, and I want to thank you for all you've done for me. I'm going to miss you. Be a good girl, and take care of yourself and if you need anything, don't forget to write." I started to lean over to kiss her.

Suddenly she sprang forward on her knees and screamed at the top of her lungs, "Judy!" The first sound that had come out of her mouth in years. Then she threw her arms around my neck and started to talk and talk and talk and talk. What she said didn't make a bit of sense: "My mother— don't leave—Judy—going away." Wild talks, just everything. She kept saying, "Don't leave, don't leave." I was holding onto her and rocking her. The other children were crying. I was crying. The nurses were crying.[38]

Garland missed her train and stayed with the girl until she calmed down, gently making the girl promise to talk to the nurses and having her talk to each nurse before she went to sleep. Garland said, "If I was cured at Peter Bent Brigham, it was only because of those children."[39] The event had a profound effect on Garland. She had already loved children, but from this point forward, children's charities were always a priority for her, and she freely gave of her time and talent whenever possible. What made it so profound was the fact that when visiting the children, although they saw her as "Judy Garland," she wasn't singing or performing or using her charm to get their approval. She was herself, stripped of the trappings of her superstardom, but still a woman who was a loving, empathic person who genuinely cared about them.

On returning to Los Angeles, Garland didn't go immediately to MGM. Her first professional engagement was on Bing Crosby's radio show. The show was, like all of Crosby's shows were, prerecorded, this time in late September for an October 1 air date. Garland sang "I Don't Care" from *In the Good Old Summertime* and duetted with Crosby on "Ma, He's Making Eyes at Me" and "Maybe It's Because." The chemistry with Crosby was palpable, and Garland seemed to be healthier than she had been in a long time. She seemed ready to restart her career.

CHAPTER *11*

GOODBYE MGM

SUMMER STOCK AND *ROYAL WEDDING*

On her return to Los Angeles from the Peter Bent Brigham Hospital in Boston in early September 1949, Garland was healthier than she had been in a long, long time—at least physically. She had gained weight and was completely off the drugs that had plagued her off and on for the past several years. Her doctor in Boston, Dr. Augustus Rose, had misgivings about the fact that she still had not effectively resolved her issues with her inner demons. He wasn't happy that Garland had accepted the assignment to star in *Summer Stock* without his blessing. But it was probably obvious even to him that she couldn't stay away from her family and her life for much longer. In the end, Judy Garland went to her grave without truly resolving her issues with those inner demons.

For the time being, things were looking up, and once again producer Joe Pasternak had come to the rescue, so to speak, with this starring role in *Summer Stock*, and, again, there was no pressure to be bone thin for the camera. Garland had already had early discussions about the film at MGM while on a two-week break from Brigham. After she returned for good, she went into rehearsals in the first week of October 1949.

Summer Stock wasn't the kind of role Garland normally would have considered taking, but since no one else (that is, the Freed Unit) seemed to want her, she accepted. She told her husband, Vincente Minnelli, "If I can just get one great number across, I won't mind the story too much."[1] The plot is about a troupe of New York actors led by an unknown singer/actor/director

(Gene Kelly) who descend on a rural farm (run by Garland) to put on their show in the barn as an out-of-town tryout in order to get it seen and ideally produced on Broadway. It was Judy and Mickey putting on a show all over again. Pasternak originally planned to reunite Garland and Rooney in the film, but Rooney's contract with MGM had not been renewed despite his solid performance in 1948's *Words and Music* portraying a fictionalized version of the tortured yet brilliant lyricist Lorenz Hart. Rooney's attachment to *Summer Stock* was fleeting at best. As early as December 1948, it was reported in the columns that Pasternak was producing *Summer Stock* and that Garland and Kelly would star.[2] At the same time, Hedda Hopper noted that writer Cy Gomberg had been given a "Christmas present" when he was given the green light to adapt his story "Summer Stock" into "a big musical, with the usual Culver City [MGM] stars as the musical group."[3] By February 2, 1949, columnists, including Sheilah Graham, reported that Kelly would star with June Allyson in the film, along with Gloria DeHaven (who

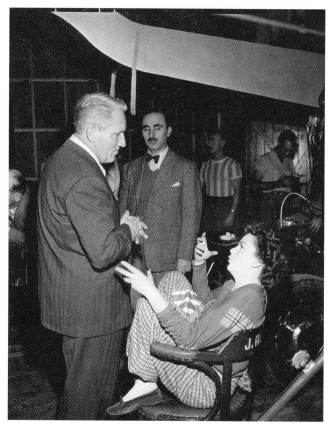

Garland chats with Spencer Tracy on the set of her husband's film *Father of the Bride*. Garland is in costume for the "Heavenly Music" number in *Summer Stock*, January 23, 1950. She ultimately opted out of the number. From the author's collection.

stayed attached to the film, playing the sister of Garland's character, Jane).[4] As an example of the musical chairs being played with the casting, at least in the columns, Betty Jaynes, who had a large supporting role in *Babes in Arms* (1939), duetting with Garland on another "opera vs. jazz" medley, was mentioned as also being cast in *Summer Stock*, although what role she would have played is unknown.

When *Summer Stock* went into production in late 1949, Kelly was riding high with the twin successes of *Take Me Out to the Ball Game* and *On the Town* (both released in 1949). The latter had yet to be released when Kelly took the role in *Summer Stock*, but anyone at the studio who had already seen it knew it was a huge step forward in the advancement of dance on film and would be a big hit (it was). Doing *Summer Stock* was a backward step for Kelly. Dr. Rose had accompanied Garland back to Los Angeles (paid for by MGM on orders from Louis B. Mayer) and accompanied her to the set once filming began, helping her make the transition back into moviemaking. Rose told Kelly, "If you don't do this picture, Judy will be in great trouble. She has serious problems, and she needs someone whom she trusts implicitly."[5] It probably didn't take much convincing. Kelly was a good friend to Garland and, along with the film's director, Charles Walters, adored her and her unique talent. Both men felt compelled to help support and guide her through the film after everything she had recently been through. Kelly never forgot how much she championed him when he first came to MGM and helped guide him on his first film, costarring with her in 1942's *For Me and My Gal*. He was happy to pay some of that back.

On October 13, 1949, Garland had her first prerecording session for the film. She recorded two of the new songs written by Harry Warren and Mack David: "If You Feel Like Singing, Sing" and "(Howdy Neighbor) Happy Harvest." Two weeks later, on October 27, she prerecorded "Friendly Star." Garland's voice had grown immensely during the interim between the *Annie Get Your Gun* prerecordings and these, displaying a newfound maturity. The full-throttled power behind her vocals was new, especially in "Friendly Star," which is a preview of her intensely robust, multilayered voice in *A Star Is Born* (Warner Bros., 1954). "Friendly Star" is one of Garland's best MGM vocals, but it's rarely singled out due to the attention usually accorded (justifiably so) to the even more dazzling "Get Happy."

Garland received a warning letter from MGM on October 31, just a few weeks after beginning work on the film, chastising her for missing six out of the previous twenty days of preproduction. She then met with studio boss Louis B. Mayer and asked to be released from the film and her contract with MGM. He persuaded her to stay and complete the film. The MGM rumor mill worked fast with this hot topic. The following day, articles appeared in multiple papers across the United States claiming that Garland was in jeopardy of losing the role due to her weight gain. "Judy Garland to Lose Role if She Doesn't Reduce," read one headline; "Excess Baggage Banned—Poundage Nearly Costs Judy Garland a Role," read another. One article was simply titled "Ultimatum." The ultimatum was that she had to lose "6 to 8 pounds" or face a possible suspension: "The MGM top brass had a noon meeting to discuss the possible removal of the 27-year-old singing star and even a possible suspension because she

On the set still of Garland filming the "If You Feel Like Singing, Sing" number for *Summer Stock*, November 1949. From the collection of Bruce Hanson.

reportedly had ignored a previous order to reduce." That detailed article went on to state that "a publicist" (the name was not given) noted that "Judy needs the weight, but the studio wants her down to scale for the picture. They plan to start shooting in November." Garland missed a Saturday rehearsal (on October 29) that kept a "large cast" waiting, though "spokesmen" (again, no names were given) "denied the report, but admitted that Miss Garland had been absent one day last week because of 'a cold.'"[6] Other articles reported that Garland "pleaded for 'just one more chance' and it was given to her."[7]

Garland was still drug free, receiving only glucose injections administered by and with the approval of, presumably, Dr. Rose.[8] The injections helped give her energy, but without the perils of the barbiturates. Despite her efforts and sincerity in wanting to stay healthy, the progress Garland had made at Peter Bent Brigham soon began to erode. Her insecurities, especially about her weight, were destroying any shred of confidence she might have had when she first returned from Peter Bent Brigham. Pasternak and Walters were not after her to lose weight, but the studio was harping at her, and the newspaper columns and magazines added another layer of pressure. She reached for the pills again. Dr. Rose complained to MGM executive Benny Thau that people were giving Garland pills as early as 5:00 a.m., something he said he couldn't compete with.[9] A decade later, Garland remembered:

> *I continued with "Summer Stock." Every day I got "get the weight off, Judy. You're still too fat." Too fat at a hundred and five. They kept telling me the rushes looked awful. So, I started to get ill again. The only way to get weight off for me was more Benzedrine and no food. Not less food, but no food. The less I ate, the more nervous I became and then the migraines started to come back and the no sleep. It was like a bad dream that I thought I'd put away. Boston was finished. All the good work. All the high hopes. I was in the trap again.[10]*

The entire production crew did everything they could to keep Garland happy and comfortable. It wasn't out of pity; it was out of their love for her and her talents. In the ensuing decades, everyone who was interviewed about working on the film spoke of how much they adored Garland and did what they could to help her out. Not only Pasternak, Walters, and Kelly but also Gloria DeHaven, Eddie Bracken, and Carleton Carpenter (among others) spoke in awe of her incredible talents and how wonderful she was as a person. They considered it a privilege to be working with her. They understood the pressures and (as much as they could) her inner struggles. They knew that Garland's actions were not malicious because Garland wasn't a malicious person by nature. Garland had, to her credit, a usually upbeat and positive personality. It's one of the aspects of her nature that helped her get through the struggles. Although it seems as if the production of *Summer Stock* was all bad days, there were also good days, days when Garland's wit and humor shone through. While Garland could be unreliable in getting onto the set in makeup and costume, ready to go, she was still a professional, usually keeping her bad behavior in her dressing room. When she was on the set and ready to go, she was brilliant, and the cast and crew recognized that.

262   CHAPTER 11

Garland's daughter Liza Minnelli visits the set of *Summer Stock*. From the author's collection.

Garland was also sensitive to the needs of her fellow performers and crew. This was partly due to her vaudeville training and partly due to her need to please everyone. Eddie Bracken, who kept Garland laughing on and off screen thanks to his comedic talents, later took credit for helping Garland finish the film. In his story, Bracken was under contract for an upcoming Broadway show, and with *Summer Stock* dragging on, he was afraid he'd be in breach of that contract. He mentioned his concerns to Dore Schary, who coldly said, "There's nothing wrong with her; she's just being obstinate." Bracken told Schary he would call Garland. Bracken then called her and told her his dilemma, and right away, she rallied to help him. Authors David Fantle and Tom Johnson, in their excellent book *C'mon, Get Happy: The Making of* Summer Stock, note that Bracken did not have any looming Broadway show at the time, so his memory is a bit faulty; however, since he told the story multiple times, it's possible that the basics of the story are true. As Bracken stated, "[The studio was] using the wrong tactics. They were making demands and saying she had to do this, she had to do that, and she told them what to do with themselves. But when you do it [his way], she's an old vaudevillian; naturally, she'd do it for another actor."[11] Schary's remark that Garland wasn't sick but was "just being obstinate" is a clear reflection of his heartlessness toward her and the studio's indifference. Judging from this and his actions toward her during *Annie Get Your Gun*, Schary was unable or unwilling to understand what she was going through. He thought of her as a spoiled star and had zero sympathy for her. Bracken later said, "She just fought with the upper echelon, the authority, the people that were yelling at her, telling her to do this, telling her to do that, and she refused to do it. If someone had asked her nicely, it would have been done in one second. That was the difference with Judy Garland."[12] Comedian Phil Silvers, who played Kelly's sidekick in the film, also helped to keep the atmosphere light and to lift Garland's spirits. In his autobiography, Silvers commented that the studio regarded Garland's issues as "spoiled self-indulgence."[13]

It was clear that things would be different with the new regime at the studio headed by Schary. Schary was hired by Nicholas Schenck, the head of Loew's in New York, who owned and ran MGM. Mayer ran the studio (now with Schary), and Schenck ran the company. Mayer and Schary were polar opposites in their tastes in films and their ideas for the future of the studio. MGM, like all of Hollywood, was having a hard time due to the growing popularity of television and the 1948 court ruling (*United States v. Paramount*) that split the theatres from the studios. Previously, the studios owned the theatres where their films played, dictating what was shown. The case claimed that the studios violated anti-trust laws. The case had been going on for a long time, but the ruling didn't come until 1948. It hurt the entire structure of the studio system and brought about the demise of that system. Although MGM was one of the last to comply with the ruling, by 1949, every penny counted. In the Garland version of *A Star Is Born* (1954), Charles Bickford (playing a studio boss) tells James Mason (as fading star Norman Maine) that his time at the studio is over: "They can't afford you anymore, Norman, you're too big a risk. Those big, fat, lush days when a star could get drunk and disappear and hold up production for two weeks are over. Even if you hadn't slipped a little, they still wouldn't take the chance. Your record's too bad. No one can afford it anymore." The dialog could have been lifted straight out of what was happening to Garland and the studios at this time. As Bickford's studio boss was sympathetic to Maine, Mayer was sympathetic to Garland. One of the film's songwriters, Harry Warren, recalled that Mayer sent Garland flowers when she called in sick.[14] Schary was not sympathetic. By all appearances, Schary leaned back and waited for Garland to falter again, which he knew she eventually would.

If there was one person who was the savior of *Summer Stock*, it had to be director Charles Walters. When he was given the assignment, Walters worked diligently with the writers to improve the quality of the script so that it would be worthy of not just Garland and Kelly but also an MGM musical. He also knew how to keep Garland happy, which was crucial to her during this tough time. Walters stated, "Judy needed more reassurance than anyone I've ever known . . . professionally mainly, but even as a person."[15] Walters had been a close friend to Garland since his early days at the studio. Now, after directing and helping her through *Easter Parade* in 1947 and 1948, he was adept at coaxing that Garland magic from her, even when she wasn't in the mood at all and let him know it. On one occasion, Garland told Walters, "Listen, buster, if you think I'm going to act today, you're out of your fucking mind. I'm heading for the hills." He called her bluff and said he'd go with her: "I'll go with you because I feel just as much like making you act as you feel like acting." That did the trick. Garland was, as she had been with Bracken, instantly concerned and wanted to help. "We got to do it. We got to," she said. "Can't we get the crew?"[16] Walters also knew that heaping praise and accolades on Garland while she was performing helped to assuage her insecurities.

Although he handled Garland well, that didn't save Walters from her early morning phone calls. In the mid-1940s, Garland developed a habit of calling people, usually a director or assistant director attached to the film she was working on, at 2:00 or 3:00 a.m. She would vent her insecurities, or list a litany of phobias, or complain that she wasn't sleeping and didn't think

264   CHAPTER 11

she'd be at the studio in the morning. The assistant director's notes for her films are littered with documentation about her many early morning calls. If she couldn't get hold of a director or someone else associated with one of her films, Garland would call up friends, people she thought would be sympathetic to her plight. One of the main people she called was her manager, Carlton Alsop. Alsop spent many sleepless nights either on the phone or with her in person, helping her to calm down. Garland developed another pattern of behavior when, due to the pressures from the studio to "get the weight off," she resorted to the pills again. Garland begged friends for just one Seconal or Dexamyl tablet, asking them (unbeknownst to each other) to put the tablet in an envelope and leave it in their mailbox. Someone (probably Garland) would come by in the middle of the night to pick it up. It wasn't long before the friends found out they weren't the only ones "helping" Garland by putting an envelope with one pill in their mailboxes. This scenario could be what Dr. Rose was referring to when he said that people were giving Garland pills at 5:00 a.m.

The trials and tribulations of filming *Summer Stock* did not go unnoticed by the press. Garland's issues were probably "the worst kept secret" in Hollywood. On December 9, 1949, columnist Jimmie Fidler reported in his column that MGM would buy Garland a $160,000 mansion if she behaved.

Miss Garland, whether her actions have been prompted by poor health, foolish habits, or just plain nasty disposition, has been a Grade AAA pain in the neck to her studio bosses (not to mention the company's stockholders) for the last two or three years. According to the testimony of key MGM workers, her tantrums and her general refusal to co-operate have cost the studio hundreds of thousands of dollars in production delays.

Judy's salary is big enough, and her contractual obligations are clear enough, that she shouldn't need bribes to behave herself. . . . To give a $160,000 bonus for good behavior doesn't make sense.[17]

The story about the mansion isn't true, but Fidler's angry column is an example of the line the studio gave to columnists. Garland was portrayed as an ungrateful, spoiled star. On the same date, an uncredited syndicated Associated Press article noted that "Judy Garland isn't going to risk another breakdown from overwork," stating that she planned to take four months off between films. Garland is quoted from the set of *Summer Stock*: "I think it's important to have a rest between pictures. And it's important to get away from Hollywood. I plan to take a trip after every picture—to Europe or someplace else." She also said that she would return to Boston after *Summer Stock* was finished: "It will just be a visit to report my progress—which is considerable."[18]

The production dragged on, with columnists continuing to report on the film's slow progress, Garland's weight, and her spotty attendance record causing delays. Erksine Johnson reported, "The new leaf turned over by Judy Garland is very becoming. For a while there, Judy was playing her big scenes in sanitariums and in the MGM doghouse instead of on the screen. Now she's back in front of a camera for 'Summer Stock' and anxious to do a good job. 'I've lost 10 pounds, and I have to lose a few more. I gained weight because I'm so healthy. I've learned how

GOODBYE MGM

265

to eat, and for the first time in my life, I can sleep at night.'"[19] Famed columnist Hedda Hopper came to Garland's defense with "Judy Garland has been out of 'Summer Stock' for the past few days due to illness. So, before those rumors get rolling again, here are the facts. I checked with other members of the cast, and they told me that Judy couldn't have been more cooperative during the entire picture. A series of strenuous dance routines has been draining her energies. She contracted laryngitis and a virus infection."[20]

MGM publicity portrait of Garland in costume for *Summer Stock*, February 1950. From the author's collection.

By early February, Garland seemed to have recovered. On February 2, 1950, Garland and Kelly prerecorded "All for You" and "(Howdy Neighbor) Happy Harvest" (the finale version); the next day, they prerecorded "You Wonderful You," and then, on February 13, they prerecorded the song's reprise. Between the prerecording sessions was the filming of the songs recorded just a couple of days prior, which was fast by MGM standards. In just a few more weeks, Garland's work on the film was finished. She left to rest in nearby Carmel, California.

After just a couple of weeks, MGM came calling again. It was decided that another number was needed for the film's finale sequence. There was no big "Judy Garland number" in the film. As Walters stated,

> *When we finished* Summer Stock, *Judy went away to lose some weight. And we realized we didn't really have a finish to the picture. She hadn't done her big last number. And in the two weeks she was away, she lost 20 pounds and looked absolutely great. So an awful lot of people thought when we did "Get Happy," we'd taken a number out of an older picture, something that hadn't been used in another picture. But it wasn't; it was only two weeks later, and we did "Get Happy."*[21]

"Get Happy" was Garland's idea. She had been reminded of the song (written in 1930 by Harold Arlen and Ted Koehler) when Arlen played it at a recent party. She said to Walters, "Chuck, you get 'Get Happy' for me; we build the dance around that, and I'll do it. I'll give you a week—otherwise, forget it."[22] Saul Chaplin provided the arrangement, saying that he and Walters went to Garland's home and played the arrangement for her. True to her genius, Garland only mouthed along with Chaplin but didn't sing it because she wasn't feeling well. Six days later, she was on the MGM recording stage with just a lyric sheet in front of her. Chaplin claimed that she made a perfect take on the third try.[23] Whether that third take was "perfect" or not, we'll never know. The surviving *Daily Music Report* notes only one take was printed (kept for use in the film), and that was Take 12; no other take was listed or printed for use in the film.

During her short time away in Carmel, Garland lost at least twenty pounds thanks to a hypnotist or "mystic," depending on which biography you read. She looked and acted like the old Garland, again in total command of her talents. Walters staged and rehearsed Garland's group of male backup dancers for three days, using the cloud backdrop that is briefly seen earlier in the film; Garland came in, she watched Walters do her part, and the number was shot in two days. She wore the same outfit she wore in the deleted "Mr. Monotony" number in *Easter Parade*, the top half of a men's tuxedo with a fedora sexily tilted on her head. The look was created by *Easter Parade*'s costumer, Irene, as an homage to Marlene Dietrich, whom Irene had been on the phone with the day before she designed the costume. Walters and producer Arthur Freed asked her to create a sexy costume for Garland's solo, and Irene thought of Dietrich.[24] Garland looked so good that when she arrived on the "Get Happy" set, her appearance elicited catcalls from the crew. This response no doubt boosted her confidence.

The quick shoot went well, with just a minor hiccup when, on the first take, Walters yelled, "Cut!" and told Garland that she was "too tentative." This angered her, and she retreated to her dressing room. After following her, Walters was able to smooth things over. He later said that to help Garland get an idea of how to perform the number, he told her to "be Lena Horne."[25] It's interesting that Walters would say that. If it's true—and there's no reason to doubt it, considering that Walters said he had used similar references with Garland before—then it's a testament to Garland's genius that there's no hint of Ms. Horne in her performance. In the decades since "Get Happy" was filmed, in all the times it's been analyzed, celebrated, and copied, never has anyone ever gotten "Lena Horne" out of Garland's performance. "Get Happy" is Judy Garland at her very best as Judy Garland. No slight to Ms. Horne, who was amazing in her own right, but "Get Happy" is all Garland. She's presenting herself as sexy, chic, and mature, the Garland of every fan's dreams. It's one of the best numbers she ever put on film and one of the most iconic, right up there with "Over the Rainbow," "The Trolley Song," and "The Man That Got Away." Ask any Garland fan or movie musical fan to name Garland's best film performances, and "Get Happy" is near the top of their list, if not at the very top. Even people who don't know a thing about Garland recognize the imagery. Without Garland's unique performing genius, "Get Happy" wouldn't have become the mini masterpiece that it is. It's been imitated often by all manner of performers, but it's never been equaled, not by a long shot.

Summer Stock premiered on August 31, 1950, and was another success for Garland and MGM. At a final cost of $2,024,848, it grossed over $3.3 million on its initial release. After all of

GOODBYE MGM

the ups and downs of the production, what ended up on the screen turned out to be a thoroughly entertaining light lark of a film. Like *In the Good Old Summertime*, Garland's performance and the film itself have aged well. With decades between the film's release and now, its breezy, fun entertainment is a glowing example of an original movie musical of the golden age—in beautiful three-strip Technicolor. It's nostalgia at its finest and most charming. It also helps that Garland's performance, in spite of her issues, is a happy one. She sings beautifully and dances gloriously, and her added weight isn't the issue it was in 1950. She looks healthy and beautiful. Then she comes out and knocks "Get Happy" out of the park with the singular effortlessness that was her special magic. Even director Walters recognized how bright and cheery the film was while in the editing room. He later said that he thought

"Get Happy." From the author's collection.

to himself, "How dare this look like a happy picture!"[26] None of the drama behind the scenes showed up in the film. His frustration is understandable, considering what he was going through. Little did Walters, Garland, or anyone else suspect that *Summer Stock* would be Garland's MGM swan song.

THE LAST STRAW

After her dazzling work on "Get Happy," Garland went back to Carmel, planning to rest for at least six months. But after just a few weeks, MGM came calling yet again. This time, Arthur Freed wanted her back to replace the pregnant June Allyson in *Royal Wedding*. Allyson remembered, "'Oh no,' she [Garland] said, 'How dare you do this to me. My first vacation in my entire life and you (I can't use the word she used), but you have to go and get pregnant.' And I was almost sorry I was there for a few minutes!"[27] Charles Walters was again the director, but after his experience with *Summer Stock*, he told Freed, "I'm terribly sorry, but I cannot go through it again. I've just spent a year and a half of my life with her, and I'm ready for a mental institution. Take

The November 29, 1950, edition of the *Columbus Telegram* (Columbus, Nebraska) amusingly used a ten-year-old photo of Garland as the centerpiece of its ad artwork for *Summer Stock*.
From the author's collection.

me off!"[28] Freed assigned the film to Gene Kelly's frequent collaborator Stanley Donen and told Garland that Walters was taken off due to his ulcer (which Walters claimed she had given him).

According to biographer Gerold Frank, an amusing sequence of events was put in motion. Garland called and then went to visit Walters, who was relaxing in Malibu, California, and became a kind of Florence Nightingale, attempting to nurse him back to health. She called in the "mystic" doctor from Carmel who had helped her shed the weight just prior to "Get Happy" to help. In just three days, Garland's hovering had gotten to the point that she planned to move in temporarily, even sending her secretary, Myrtle Tully, over with some clothes and incidentals. Walters panicked, sent the secretary back, and called Freed, who told him to leave town. Walters then called Roger Edens, and the two came up with a scheme. Walters would drive to Robert Alton's place overlooking the ocean in the Pacific Palisades, park his car, and walk over to Edens's house. The ruse seemed to work until Garland made one of her 2:00 a.m. phone calls, this time to Alton, panicking that she hadn't heard from Walters. Alton, unaware of the ruse, told her that he didn't know what was going on but that he just noticed that Walter's car had "been parked in front of my house for the last two days, and you know I'm only a block from the cliff." That sent Garland into a frenzy; she went to Edens's place (where Walters was hiding), worried that Walters had thrown himself off the cliff. Edens realized his mistake in not letting Alton in on the ruse. Everything was fine after Walters appeared, safe and sound.[29] If anything, this anecdote speaks to Garland's loyalty to her friends and her willingness to always help when needed. Keeping up with the studio's expectations was different. It was one thing for Garland to decide to do something of her own volition, but being ordered what to do by the studio made her automatically resist.

Once again, it's unconscionable that Freed would think that Garland could handle the pressures of another high-profile Freed Unit "A" musical after her recent track record. There was a tug-of-war being played out, one that had been playing out for the last couple of years. On one side was Loew's Inc. and the executives (Schary and Schenck), who saw Garland as an emotional, temperamental, spoiled star who refused to honor her contractual obligations. In their view, they had given her everything, and now she was ungrateful. It probably didn't help that what appeared on screen (a happy-go-lucky Garland without a care in the world) was the opposite of what played out during the productions (tardiness, absenteeism, emotional outbursts). Seeing a seemingly fine Garland on screen conflicted with her behavior and her complaints. It's more than probable that Schary and Schenck felt that if she appeared so well on screen, then she must be okay, with her issues being merely temperament. Garland also sang her heart out all night at Hollywood parties. Her impromptu performances are now part of Hollywood lore. She was a welcome guest and usually ended up singing late into the night, sometimes calling in sick the next day. Or the scenario would be that she would call in sick to the studio, then sing all night, and then be sick again the following day. Schary and Schenck probably felt that if she could sing all night, she should be able to perform at the studio. In spite of not being able to lose the weight the studio wanted her to lose, the still unreleased *Summer Stock* was seen as another success, especially "Get Happy," which dazzled everyone, and once again, Garland's genius worked against her. The studio assumed the healthy, fabulous Garland was back and ready to go.

On the other side was Garland, stuck on a seesaw of extreme physical and mental highs and lows that neither she nor anyone seemed to understand, nor were they able to stop it and find a permanent, healthy solution. Her stay at the Peter Bent Brigham facility in the summer of 1949 was, in hindsight, too short. When she returned from that stay, she was healthy and drug free. But she returned too early. She hadn't resolved the issues she needed to resolve, and when the studio pressures mounted, she reached for the solution that she always thought would help: the drugs to help her get through the days. She truly needed, as Harry Anslinger had previously suggested, a year off. Obviously, a year away from the studio would be an eternity for MGM and hurt their bottom line, and thanks to the callous attitude of the executives, Garland was expected to deliver. Still, Freed, who was closer to Garland than most due to his association with her going back to that 1935 audition, should have been more sympathetic and understanding. When Allyson announced her pregnancy, Freed's call to have Garland come back is inexcusable. Garland could have declined, but she needed the money and couldn't afford another suspension. She also needed to prove, both to herself and to the studio, that she could deliver.

Garland's first day of work on *Royal Wedding* was a rehearsal on May 24, 1950. As had happened before, things started out well enough, with Garland coming in on time or close to it for rehearsals and wardrobe fittings. On June 9, the production celebrated her twenty-eighth birthday (which was on June 10, her day off), presenting her with a big cake. Photos were taken of Garland rehearsing and chatting with visitors, including her husband, Vincente Minnelli, Gene Kelly, and the film's producer, Arthur Freed. Garland is also seen with her makeup woman and friend, Dottie Ponedel. From all appearances, it appeared as though the high-profile visitors were there to provide moral support. From June 11 through June 16, Garland wasn't required to

During rehearsals for *Royal Wedding*, a birthday cake was brought in for Garland on June 9, 1949 (her birthday was June 10). She and her husband, Vincente Minnelli (on the left), along with producer Arthur Freed, posed for photos. *Photofest.*

be at the studio until 10:30 a.m. or later, as late as 1:00 and 2:00 p.m. on a couple of days. On June 16, she posed with Astaire for a costume test photo for the novelty number "How Could You Believe Me When I Said I Loved You When You Know I've Been a Liar All My Life?" It turned out to be the last day that Garland worked on an MGM film. On June 17, she was due in rehearsals at 1:00 p.m. At 11:25 a.m., she called to cancel the day due to waking up with a migraine.[30] That was the last straw for MGM. They dropped her from the film and put her on suspension. On June 19, a memo was sent from F. L. Hendrickson to the executives, including Schenck and Freed, telling them that Garland's contract had been suspended on June 17 and that "no requests of any kind to render services are to be made of her unless advised otherwise by Mr. Thau."[31] The news of Garland's suspension was in the newspapers that day.

This time, Garland's reaction to her suspension was different. On June 19, the same day as Hendrickson's memo, Garland was at her and Minnelli's home, just above the Sunset Strip, with Minnelli, her secretary, Myrtle Tully, and her manager, Carlton Alsop, discussing what to do next when, at approximately 6:00 p.m., she suddenly ran to her bathroom screaming, "Leave me alone; I want to die!"[32] She locked the door, broke a drinking glass, and scratched her throat with it. Pandemonium ensued. Minnelli and Tully banged on the door. Garland, in a moment of clarity, unlocked the door, but Minnelli had already grabbed a chair and broke it down anyway. He saw her throat bleeding and became hysterical. Alsop had to slug Minnelli to get him to come to his senses. Alsop then put Garland in his car and drove her to the couple's main residence on Sunset Boulevard. Their doctor, Dr. Francis Ballard, treated Garland at the home and later described her injuries as "superficial lacerations."[33]

At lightning speed (apparently the press had been keeping an eye on the main house due to Garland's recent struggles), the press was outside the home. MGM police chief Whitey Hendry (MGM was big enough to have its own in-house police force) told the press that he had a dozen studio police guarding Garland's home, "shooing away the curious and watching maids tiptoe upstairs where the actress lay sleeping."[34] This wasn't Garland's first suicide attempt, but it was the first to make the papers. It was first reported the next day (June 20) in the early afternoon editions of the Los Angeles papers and became front-page news across the United States later that afternoon and evening.

At the Minnelli home, a flurry of people came and went. According to Alsop, MGM representative Ralph Wheelwright walked out after seeing Garland, and when asked by the press what had happened, he motioned across his throat with a finger. Alsop saw it and tackled him, screaming at him. Wheelwright's response was "We will withdraw all MGM support."[35] Katharine Hepburn was one of the first on the scene, refusing to speak to reporters. She told Garland, "You're one of the two greatest living talents we have. Now you get your ass up. The world needs you." On her way out, to avoid the press, she jumped over a back fence.[36] Other reports claim Hepburn said Garland was one of the three greatest talents in the world, with "Your ass has hit the gutter. There's no place to go but up. Now, Goddamnit, do it!"[37] Mayer's secretary and Garland champion from 1934 onward, Ida Koverman, also visited. When she left, she wouldn't give a statement to the reporters, only saying, "You have your job to do, and I have mine."[38]

Wheelwright and fellow MGM representative Jack Atlas gave the initial studio reports about what had happened. Atlas noted that right after it happened, "[Garland] said she was sorry she had done it." Wheelwright told the press he saw Garland that morning (June 20) and said, "She was sleeping, so I didn't disturb her. Her throat was bandaged, but it was a very small bandage. It didn't look like anything serious."[39] Columnist Bob Thomas reported that Dr. Ballard said the cut was minor "and attributed it to an impulsive, hysterical act. . . . I saw her, and she has a slight bandage on her neck. No stitches were taken."[40]

The initial studio line was that Garland had been suspended for failure to report to the studio for a rehearsal. Alsop was quoted in one article: "The rehearsal was only for an hour. The picture isn't scheduled to start until July 15. I don't see how an hour's absence at this stage can be so important." Minnelli had initially denied the report. The studio told the press that Minnelli initially denied it because "Vincent [*sic*] was so upset. He didn't know what to do or say. When we got there, we advised him that it would be best to tell the facts just as they happened." When asked why the denial, he said, "He's her husband, you can understand, can't you?"[41] MGM no doubt would have preferred that the story not be known at all, but since there was nothing they could do about it, they decided to get in front of it. The studio released a statement that said that the suspension was "the final and last resort, arrived at after all other means have failed and arrived at with greatest regret. Several times, against our better judgment, at her insistence, we have started films with her, and her consequent illness had caused us embarrassment, delay, inconvenience, and a loss of morale to co-workers."[42] MGM was attempting to make the incident all Garland's fault, claiming that she was insistent on returning to work when she wasn't ready. To make things worse, the *Los Angeles Times* published a photo of Wheelwright soberly and melodramatically making that throat-cutting motion with his finger, with the caption, "At the Minnelli home Ralph Wheelwright, film publicist, shows how Judy Garland cut throat."[43] It's

272　　　　　　　　　　　　　　　　　　　　　　　　　　　CHAPTER 11

unclear whether the photo was actually taken at the Minnelli home. The article does not mention Wheelwright being tackled by Alsop, so it was most likely staged later, but it's tacky and heartless nonetheless.

What MGM hadn't yet realized was just how loyal Garland's fans were and how beloved she was by the public. As the dust began to settle in the days after the event, the sympathy began to pour in. Some of the articles noted that for the past few years, she had been "pale and sickly," with one noting, when talking about her career, how the studio initially wanted her to lose weight and then wanted her to gain weight, then lose weight. One article noted, "One thing is certain: The 'little girl with the big voice' has almost everybody's sympathy."[44]

Oddly enough, just two days after the suicide attempt and while the fallout was still reverberating, MGM drafted a "recording royalty" contract for the MGM Records soundtrack album to *Summer Stock*, dated June 21, which began,

> *Pursuant to the rights granted to us under your contract of employment with us dated November 21, 1946, it is our intention to produce from the sound track of our photoplay presently entitled "SUMMER STOCK" and to sell phonograph records of one or more compositions performed and recorded by you in the rendition of your services for us in connection with said photoplay. These records may be sold and disposed of by us as single records and/or as part of an album and/or albums and/ or on long playing records and/or otherwise. Such albums may include records which do not embody recordings from sound track made by you and such long playing records may also embody compositions not recorded by you.*

The songs referenced were listed in this order: "Friendly Star," "(Howdy Neighbor) Happy Harvest," "If You Feel Like Singing, Sing," and "Get Happy." Garland was granted a royalty of 2.5 percent of 90 percent of the sales price for each solo side, 5 percent of 90 percent of the retail sales price for solos on both sides, and 5 percent of 90 percent of the retail sales price of long-play records, "divided by total number of compositions contained in such record." Among other stipulations, the contract noted that Garland could not make any other recordings of the songs "for a period of five (5) years following the date of this agreement." It also stipulated that if Garland were in breach of the contract, she would automatically be "deemed to have waived all future royalties with respect to the composition recorded by you for the other person, firm or corporation." The contract was sent to Alsop, and Garland signed it on June 21, 1950. The contract was standard for the Records Division of MGM for their soundtrack releases, and it's more than a little tone-deaf for MGM to bother Garland with it just two days after her suicide attempt. They could have waited.

In the ensuing weeks after the suicide attempt, things quieted down as Garland got a grip on her situation. She was seen out on the town with Minnelli, although, for all intents and purposes, the marriage was over and had been for a long time in spite of the random reconciliations mentioned in the papers. Garland, accompanied by daughter Liza, went to Sun Valley for more

GOODBYE MGM

rest in late July, allegedly on the advice of Louis B. Mayer, where she was photographed fishing for trout with Joe Burgy, a local sports director. Photos of Garland proudly showing off her trout were published, and most of the captions and articles noted she had attempted suicide, but almost in passing. After Sun Valley, Garland and Liza went to Lake Tahoe on the California/Nevada border. On August 11, Garland was involved in a minor fender bender that made the news. Bob Scott, the owner of several power launches at Tahoe, was driving Garland from the Cal-Neva Lodge (the site of her "discovery" in 1935) to the North Shore Club when the car hit a rock, blowing out a tire. Garland was thrown into the windshield but suffered only a minor laceration on her nose that was treated privately. She left Tahoe the following day, purportedly because there was "too much excitement" there.

Columnist Aline Mosby reported on August 6 that a recent preview of *Summer Stock* for critics and the public was a smashing success, noting that "a crowd of hard-boiled Hollywood press folks gave Judy the kind of ovation that any big star dreams of getting. After every song she sang, the applause was deafening. . . . She looked so happy in the picture that the audience, if it hadn't read all about it in the papers, never would have guessed about the tough time she had working in 'Summer Stock.'" Mosby noted that "Friendly Star" and "Get Happy" had the audience whispering. About the latter, she reported, "When she sang the lines about singing all those blues away, the audience cheered."[45]

Harold Heffernan wrote about the preview at the Academy Theatre in Hollywood, taking aim at Schary for not being as sensitive to Garland's needs as he should have been:

> *"Summer Stock" was lifted above average by the ingratiating personality, acting and singing ability of the girl who has proved one of the greatest enigmas in Hollywood's fantastic experiences with scores of neurotics.*
>
> *One thing remains certain after a look at this actress in "Summer Stock." There's a lot of wonderful entertainment and rich box-office profits to be salvaged from Judy Garland, and it seems a downright shame she cannot get the proper understanding and handling from the big bosses who have been in charge of her at the studio.*
>
> *What Dore Schary did so quietly and effectively in rehabilitating the mentally mixed-up Robert Walker two years ago, after other executives on the MGM lot had thrown up their hands, remains an outstanding example of human relations. Maybe this same "doctor" Schary could take over the guidance of the very confused Judy and get her back on an even keel, both on and off stage.*
>
> *How about a consultation, Dr. Schary?[46]*

Heffernan was right. The studio seemed to have a double standard. It appeared that Garland was a victim of the studio's misogyny. Alsop confronted the studio, telling them they seemed willing to spend all the time and money available helping certain troublesome actors (all men) with everything from alcohol binges to hiding one's running around with a variety of young men.

But with Garland, they seemed only to assume that she was being emotional and nothing was really wrong with her.

When *Summer Stock* opened in August 1950 and snaked its way around the country in the ensuing months, it was a personal triumph for Garland. Contrary to what MGM assumed, audiences everywhere thought the robust Garland was perfectly fine. Garland's confidence got a boost from showman Billy Rose. He penned an adoring open letter to Garland in his column "Pitching Horseshoes" titled "Love Letter to a National Asset." Rose went to a private showing of the film and said, in part,

> *You see, Judy, I hadn't seen you on the screen in quite a while, and I had almost forgotten how all-fired good you are. I found your portrayal of a farm girl in "Summer Stock" as convincing as a twenty-dollar gold piece, and when you leveled on Harold Arlen's old song, "Get Happy"—well, it was Al Jolson in lace panties, Maurice Chevalier in opera pumps! . . . It gets down to this, Judy: In an oblique and daffy sort of way, you are as much a national asset as our coal reserves—both of you help warm up our insides. And the day you stop making pictures, you're going to take a lot of warmth out of the lives of millions. . . . One thing more: Next time you're down in the dumps—if there has to be a next time—it might help you to remember that you're only feeling the way most of us feel a good part of the time. Unfortunately, we're in no position to ease your headache. You, on the other hand, through the medium of the neighborhood theatre, can do more than a million boxes of aspirin to ease ours.[47]*

Dorothy Kilgallen followed Rose's lead and wrote a fan letter as well, which was published in her syndicated column in August 1950 and read in part,

> *Dear Judy: You have had a bad time in your private life recently, but take a look at your latest picture and cheer up. . . . You could not sit through that picture without realizing the girl up there on the screen—warm, vivid, vital, tremendously appealing—has a combination of qualities no other actress in Hollywood can match. . . . But there is more than that. The big extra, which has always been there, is [your] great personality. . . . It is a rare, rare thing to own, Judy. Cherish it. Take care of yourself.[48]*

The film received mostly glowing, sometimes stellar reviews. Everyone agreed that although the plot was corny, the cast's performances, especially Garland's, elevated it. Garland was singled out; Erksine Johnson noted she had "a new Helen Hayes quality in her emoting."[49] Wanda Hale of the *Daily News* in New York noted that Garland and Kelly "brought hearty applause from enthusiastic spectators attending the first showing . . . at the Capitol Theatre."[50]

Instead of alienating her fans, Garland's recent problems rallied public support. Garland saw this adulation firsthand. She and Dottie Ponedel were in New York, and on September 5, Garland slipped into a late-night screening of *Summer Stock* at the Capitol Theatre. After the screening was over, she was spotted by the audience; the crowd broke out with screams of "We love you, Judy!" The event was such that the press covered it. Earl Wilson wrote in his column that the crowd shouted, "We love you," "We're all for you," "Keep making pictures," and "Keep your chin up!" Garland broke down in tears and called to the crowd, "God love you all!" and later told Wilson, who interviewed her at her hotel,

> *I didn't know anybody knew I was there, but when the picture was over, the whole balcony seemed to rise and start to applaud. Then, the main floor became a sea of people cheering. Then they came out into the street and over to the car. It wasn't like a mob, but like a lot of friends. I've been weeping every minute since—with joy. It's so encouraging.*[51]

When Wilson asked about her plans for her next film, she replied, "There are no plans, but I think this thing tonight was the greatest thing in my life. It was so astonishing and so wonderful." The manager of the Capitol Theatre said, "It was the biggest ovation I've ever seen. The whole world seemed to be cheering the little lady on—but I guess really it was only a couple of thousand people."[52]

While she was in New York, it was reported that Garland was in talks with Rodgers and Hammerstein about possibly replacing Mary Martin in *South Pacific* on Broadway. Rodgers and Hammerstein also allegedly wanted to write a stage or film musical version of *Alice Adams* for her. Neither project happened. Garland would not have been up to carrying a full Broadway musical five nights a week, twice on Saturday. She was also on Arthur Freed's initial list to play Julie in his upcoming remake of *Show Boat*. She had been since Freed convinced MGM to purchase the property and finance a Broadway revival in 1946, the same year the show was featured in an extended sequence in *Till the Clouds Roll By*. Garland wasn't Julie in that film (Lena Horne was, and she was great), instead being given the lofty and more glamorous role of Broadway superstar Marilyn Miller. After Schary arrived at the studio, he wanted singer Dinah Shore to play it. She was all wrong for the part. By the time the film went into production, Garland had left MGM, and Freed had decided that Ava Gardner was right for it, and she went for it, even singing her own vocals quite convincingly (which were still dubbed but included on the MGM Records soundtrack album). Due to the Hollywood Production Code and its racism, Lena Horne was not allowed to portray a woman of mixed race in a relationship with a white man.

The accolades flowing in for Garland and *Summer Stock* didn't go unnoticed by MGM. Garland's fan mail increased so much that a lengthy article was syndicated explaining that 90 percent of the flood of fan mail for her was sympathetic. Her fan mail jumped 50 percent, and she was receiving fifteen hundred letters per week. As a result, MGM decided to engage in an all-out promotional campaign. The tone had changed. Now an unnamed studio "official" was quoted as saying that Garland was recently "a victim of the monster—Hollywood." Another "spokesman" for the studio said that between their recording, publishing, and radio affiliates, they were giving Garland "the greatest promotional campaign we have ever given any star." "We're not only interested in sales. We want to give Judy the big buildup so she'll know we have confidence in her and will regain confidence in herself. We all feel Judy came up the hard way and that she's a good, clean girl. Hollywood killed her. It was too much for her. She deserves all the feeling we can give her. We've got to let people know how we feel about her."[53] The folks at MGM Records noted that the sales of the soundtrack album were ahead of *Annie Get Your Gun*, which had been the top seller of the last three years.

When Garland returned to Hollywood in mid-September 1950, she didn't go directly to the studio to make another film. She was still under suspension, and MGM was still figuring out what to do with her. Garland's good friend Bing Crosby, another peer who idolized her, ignored the recent troubles and asked her to return to his radio show. In the past couple of years, due to her struggles, Garland hadn't appeared on the radio with any regularity. Crosby's shows were always recorded a week or two prior to the scheduled air dates, and Crosby kept things casual. It was the perfect atmosphere for Garland and the ideal way for her to show the public she was recovering and doing well. Her first appearance was taped on September 20, 1950. She sang "Get Happy" and duetted with Crosby on "Sam's Song," and, with fellow guest Bob Hope, the three sang "Goodnight Irene." Garland returned five days later for another appearance, this time singing "Friendly Star" and another duet with Crosby, "Tzena, Tzena, Tzena." The recordings survive and are still enjoyable thanks to the chemistry between Garland and Crosby and their wonderful vocals. Both shows aired in mid-October. By that point, Garland and MGM had parted ways for good.

By September 29, 1950, Garland had been in talks with MGM, off and on, about her future with the studio for weeks. MGM considered giving her another chance, especially after *Summer Stock* was a surprise hit and the studio saw that Garland's public was loyal. Even after a suicide attempt, which would have ruined anyone else's career, Garland's cachet increased. It helped that *Summer Stock* came out when it did, giving audiences a look at the Garland they loved and not the victim in the news reports. Due to her unique aura of vulnerability mixed with her genius (an overused word but apropos here), people were sympathetic to her problems. Once again, she "was one of us," struggling through personal troubles just like anyone else, regardless of her talent and fame. On this day (September 29, 1950), MGM agreed to let Garland out of her contract. Fifteen years to the month after her audition in 1935, Judy Garland was no longer an MGM employee.

On the same day she was free from MGM, Garland signed a standard boilerplate "Artist's Manager Contract" with the William Morris Agency, which outlined her agreement to have four different agents work on her behalf, including John Hyde. Hyde was known as "Johnny" and became famous for helping a struggling Marilyn Monroe become a star. The contract was signed by Garland and her primary agent, Abe Lastfogel. Lastfogel signed Garland for over a dozen radio performances from November 1950 through March 1951 with a fee of $1,500 per appearance. These included more Crosby show appearances, a radio adaptation of the Katharine Hepburn film *Alice Adams*, and, on Christmas Day 1950, Garland's only reprise of her role as Dorothy in *The Wizard of Oz*, in the abridged sixty-minute radio version for the *Lux Radio Theatre* program.

Goodbye MGM

Although most people assume that September 29 was the last time Garland was on the MGM lot, it wasn't. She returned to the studio as a visitor a couple of months later, on December 6, to see her husband, Vincente Minnelli, filming part of the ballet sequence for *An American in Paris*, starring Gene Kelly. There's no word about whether she visited anyone else, any other film set, or even how long she stayed.

At the same time, Garland's final (and this time legal) separation from Minnelli was announced in early December. Their divorce wouldn't be final until March 1952, but this separation was another aspect of her transition from her life and career at MGM to whatever lay ahead.

It was the end of an era. Garland had been the muse and biggest star of the MGM musical. Her star blazed so strong and bright it's no wonder that after fifteen years of shooting across movie screens, it burned out—for the time being. The year 1951 brought a new decade, a new life, and a new career for Garland. No one, not even Garland, could have known that an entirely new, dazzling career lay ahead, in which she would become a true living legend and the World's Greatest Entertainer.

One of Garland's last promotional photos for MGM, 1950. From the author's collection.

CHAPTER *12*

Post-MGM Highlights

Judy Garland's legendary post-MGM life and career can be properly covered only by a separate book. But since it was greatly infused and influenced by her MGM years, this chapter briefly covers the highlights in the hope that it'll properly convey just why Garland became a living legend and was known as the "World's Greatest Entertainer" during her lifetime (and after).

Once Garland had been set free from MGM, she was most likely the happiest star in Hollywood. The previous few years of her up-and-down struggles with the studio were now a thing of the past. She was a free agent and could do what she wanted. She was probably also nervous. Nervous about the unknown. She had no clear path. After fifteen years of growing up in a studio that took care of things for her, twenty-eight-year-old Garland was like someone leaving home for the first time.

Considering the incredible achievements of Judy Garland's post-MGM career, it began rather quietly. After her break with the studio in late 1950, Garland continued to make radio appearances, mostly on Bing Crosby's show. He ignored all the naysayers claiming she was washed up, and insisted she be a guest on his show. It did wonders for her confidence and kept her in the public consciousness. Audiences were treated to a wonderful variety of songs sung in that special Garland manner, including "How Deep Is the Ocean," "You're Just in Love" (with Vic Damone), the then-new "Rudolph the Red-Nosed Reindeer" (with Crosby), "(I'm in Love with) a Wonderful Guy," "Mean to Me," and a sizzling adult version of "You Made Me Love You" (minus the teen-aged fan letter to Clark Gable). She also premiered her versions of two songs that would become staples of her concerts: "Rock-a-Bye Your Baby with a Dixie Melody" and "When You're Smiling." She and Crosby likewise duetted on the novelty song she was supposed to perform with Fred Astaire in *Royal Wedding*, "How Could You Believe Me When I Said I Love You When You Know I've Been a Liar All My Life." The film had just been released, and during their usual banter, Crosby asked Garland about *Royal Wedding*, "Were you going to be in Royal Wedding out at MGM?" and Garland quipped, referencing MGM's lion logo, "I was before Leo the Lion BIT ME!" Crosby replied, "He's an old lion, Leo, his teeth are all gone." Garland joked, "He sure has got sharp gums!"

Almost immediately after Garland's break with MGM, columnists and just about everyone else in Hollywood speculated about who would fill the void she left. Debbie Reynolds was the top contender. However, it should be noted that Reynolds was currently an ingenue, and if she had played any of Garland's roles, they would have been the type that Garland played in the early 1940s. By this time in late 1950, if Garland had stayed at MGM, she would have been given the high-profile and more mature leading lady roles, not the ingenue roles. The truth is that Garland was so unique that no one could fill her shoes.

Garland enjoying some down time in Hollister, California, 1952. From the collection of Michael Siewert.

MGM had several other musical leading ladies on hand, but aside from the Pasternak Unit's musicals that usually featured the classical singers Jane Powell and Kathryn Grayson, the MGM musicals, especially those produced by the Freed Unit, moved into more male-centered, dance-heavy fare. Gene Kelly and Fred Astaire mainly alternated between two leading ladies, the dancers Cyd Charisse and Vera-Ellen (both of whom had to have their vocals dubbed). Other musical leading ladies/ingenues at MGM in the early 1950s included dancer Leslie Caron (who usually was dubbed); June Allyson, although, after dropping out of *Royal Wedding*, she was never the female lead in another MGM musical, though she sang in an almost musical, the comedy *The Opposite Sex* (1956); and Debbie Reynolds. Reynolds was closest in spirit to Garland, with a similarly fresh-faced girl-next-door image, and she usually sang her own songs in a nice voice. She was also, like Garland, a natural dancer who was not professionally trained but still able to keep up with the pros. By the mid-1950s, the movie musical was losing its luster and falling out of favor with audiences, while, at the same time, the studios were tightening their budgets and fighting to survive. The era of the big-budget movie musical was coming to an end. Garland's exit was, unintentionally, just in time.

THE PALACE COMEBACK

While in New York in September 1950, Garland again met Sid Luft, the man who would become her husband and the father of her daughter Lorna Luft and son Joe Luft. He also became her manager and was responsible for some of her biggest successes. The two hit it off, having briefly crossed paths twice when Garland was much younger. Luft was the opposite of her currently estranged husband, Vincente Minnelli. He was a brash, tough man, whereas Minnelli was quiet and introspective. Later, while he was in Los Angeles, Luft joined Garland and her agent at the Brown Derby, discussing what to do with the great Garland career. In light of recent events, the movies didn't want her. She was too big of a star to stay on the radio in her own series and too big to move to television. Garland's agents suggested appearing at the Palladium. The idea wasn't totally off base. The Palladium had previously approached Garland and MGM to have her perform there, but that didn't happen. Now the time was right.

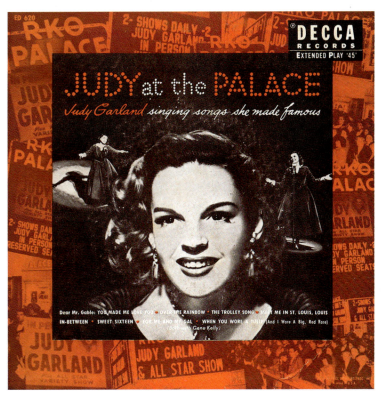

Decca Records capitalized on Garland's success at the Palace Theatre by releasing a compilation of her most well-known songs from their catalog. From the author's collection.

Whether she knew it or not, when Garland left MGM, she left with a body of work, a repertoire, and name recognition that other performers can only dream of—then or now. She also had a very loyal and ardent fan base who were (and are) always ready to be there, giving their unwavering support.

Garland left for London on the Île-de-France on March 30, 1951. On April 9, 1951, Garland opened her show at the London Palladium. She was a smash hit. Her Concert Years had begun. Garland stayed in concert at the Palladium through May 5, 1951. After a brief vacation in Paris, France, Garland embarked on a two-month tour of England, Scotland, and Ireland. Everywhere she

POST-MGM HIGHLIGHTS

went, the public loved her. When she returned to London at the end of the tour, she spent a week giving her show at the Hippodrome in Birmingham.

The show biz folks in the United States took notice of her success, and there was talk about film projects, although nothing was concrete. While in New York, Luft was walking down Broadway and looked up at the Palace Theatre. He hit on the idea of Garland re-opening the theatre as a vaudeville house. He thought of Garland's films, especially *For Me and My Gal*, in which the epitome of success in vaudeville was to "play the Palace."

The Palace was renovated in 1949, bringing stage acts back to the stage to accompany the films being shown. After more renova-

Another snapshot of Garland enjoying some down time in Hollister, California, 1952. From the collection of Michael Siewert.

tion, Garland brought vaudeville back to the Palace in a vaudeville show (no movies) on October 16, 1951. She was an even bigger smash than she had been at the Palladium. The reviews were the best of her career to date, and the original four-week run was extended ultimately to nineteen record-breaking weeks. Garland won a special Tony Award for the concert.

After the Palace, Garland and Luft vacationed in Palm Beach, Florida. His divorce from his wife, actress Lynn Bari, was finalized in late 1950, and Garland's divorce from Vincente Minnelli became final in March 1952 while she was in Palm Beach.

In April 1952, Garland returned to Los Angeles for the first time in a year. It was a triumphant return and important because this was "home," where her peers were, many of whom had counted her out. She opened her concert at the Los Angeles Philharmonic on April 21, 1952, for a four-week run. The new "Concert Judy" was someone they hadn't seen before. Her voice was bigger and stronger than ever and had a new maturity. The audience was a who's who of Hollywood, and they all cheered, sobbed, and were mesmerized. Judy Garland's aura on stage was undeniable. At a Garland concert, everyone became a part of "the cult," even for just a few hours.

Garland appeared on a few more Crosby radio shows and then took her concert to the Curran Theatre in San Francisco for a month. It was the final stop of her "Palace Tour." While

Promotional photo for Garland's short tenure with Columbia Records, 1953. From the author's collection.

in San Francisco, Garland and Luft drove south to a friend's ranch in Hollister, California. They were married at the ranch on June 8, 1952, returning to San Francisco the next day for Garland to keep her obligation to the Curran. Daughter Lorna Luft was born in Los Angeles on December 21, 1952. Like her older half-sister, Liza Minnelli, Lorna followed their mother into a show business career of her own.

On January 5, 1953, Garland's mom, Ethel Gumm, passed away in Santa Monica, California. Garland and Ethel had a complicated relationship. There's no denying that Ethel was a stage mother in the stereotypical sense of the title. Whether the abusive events that Garland attributed to Ethel really happened or were exaggerated in her memories is something we'll never know. Ethel certainly worked Garland and her sisters too hard and introduced them to pills (whether caffeine or barbiturates is unknown). Garland's great success and career were the result of Ethel's drive, but so were much of Garland's inner turmoil and personal issues. Garland was devastated by Ethel's death, which is an indication of just how deeply complicated their relationship was.

Later, in 1953, Garland recorded her first studio recordings in five and a half years—four tracks for Columbia Records: "Heartbroken," "Go Home, Joe," "Without a Memory," and "Send My Baby Back to Me." The singles didn't make much of an impact, and Garland didn't record anything else for the label, although the label did get to release the soundtrack album for *A Star Is Born* (1954), which to date has never been out of print in one audio format or another.

A STAR IS BORN

The biggest event in Garland's "Concert Years" in the 1950s wasn't a concert at all, but rather her triumphant return to the movies in 1954's *A Star Is Born*. Garland had been out of films for three years when production began in August 1953. Her return to films was not at MGM. Garland and Luft had formed their own production company, Transcona Enterprises, in 1952 and had signed a nine-film deal with Warner Bros. *A Star Is Born* was a film Garland had wanted to make since she played the lead role of Esther Blodgett (Vicki Lester) in a radio adaptation in 1942. At that time, MGM had no interest in making a musical remake of a film about a starlet's relationship with an alcoholic husband. It was too serious for what they perceived as Garland's squeaky-clean girl-next-door image. Now the time was right. George Cukor was brought in as director (it was his first musical), and Harold Arlen and Leonard Gershe wrote the original songs, including a new Garland standard, the Oscar-nominated "The Man That Got Away." Garland's performance of the song in the film is another of her very best. Her full-throttled delivery is mesmerizing and spine tingling. Garland's other tour de force in the film is the delightful "Someone at Last," in which she spoofs the movie musical's "production number to end all production numbers." It's performed by Vicki for her husband Norman Maine (the brilliant James Mason) in

Garland and an unnamed dancer during the filming of the "Black Bottom" number in *A Star Is Born* (1954). From the author's collection.

284   CHAPTER 12

The great Garland comeback, and ever the vaudevillian, "Swanee" in *A Star Is Born* (1954).
From the author's collection.

their home, with Vicki lip-synching to a playback record to show him all the facets of the number they're shooting at the (fictional) studio.

After filming was completed, it was decided that a new production number was needed to show what makes Vicki the overnight sensation portrayed in the film. Roger Edens came up with the lengthy "Born in a Trunk" number that traded in on Garland's image of being "born in a trunk" in vaudeville, showing Vicki playing an unnamed star who explains and narrates her rise to fame. The sequence ends with a rousing rendition of the Al Jolson favorite, "Swanee." After *A Star Is Born* was released, "Swanee" became another Garland standard.

Filming was finally completed in late July 1954, almost a full year after it began. The previews of the original rough cut that ran three hours and sixteen minutes were successes. Just before the premiere, fifteen minutes were cut, bringing the running time down to three hours and one minute. That version premiered at the Pantages Theatre in Hollywood on September 29, 1954. The premiere was the biggest Hollywood had seen in a long time, attended by a seemingly endless parade of stars, big and small. NBC-TV televised the premiere with Jack Carson (who played "Libby") as the host, quickly interviewing some of the stars. The premiere and the reviews of the film couldn't have been greater successes. Judy Garland was back in films in a role that im-

POST-MGM HIGHLIGHTS

mediately put her in the front of the Oscar race for Best Actress. Everyone agreed that Garland was a shoo-in to win. *A Star Is Born* was lauded as a masterpiece.

In mid-October 1954, Jack Warner (one of the Warner Brothers and head of the studio) ordered that the film be cut even more to allow for more showings per day, attempting to maximize the earning potential. It had the opposite effect. Unfortunately, the cuts were made arbitrarily, without Cukor's input or approval (he was out of the country at the time). Two of Garland's songs were removed (but remained on the soundtrack album), and entire chunks of the scenario were also cut. The popularity of the film suffered. Some theatre owners requested the original version be made available for them to have the ability to choose. Despite the cuts, Garland was the front-runner for the Oscar for Best Actress. The film was also nominated for Best Actor (Mason), Best Song ("The Man That Got Away," Arlen and Gershe), Best Art Direction—Color (Malcolm Bert, Gene Allen, Irene Sharaff, George James Hopkins), Best Costume Design—Color (Jean Louis, Mary Ann Nybert, Irene Sharaff), and Best Scoring of a Musical Picture (Ray Heindorf). The film didn't receive Best Picture or Best Director nominations, an indication of the film's reputation as unsuccessful and the lack of support from Warner Bros., which, by that point, had effectively written it off.

George Jessell (*center*) with Garland and costar Jack Carson at the star-studded gala premiere of *A Star Is Born* on September 29, 1954, at the Pantages Theatre in Los Angeles. From the author's collection.

On the night of the Oscar telecast (March 30, 1955), Garland was in the hospital, having just given birth to her third child, Joseph Luft. NBC, which broadcast the event, was so sure Garland would win that they went to a lot of expense and trouble rigging her hospital room to be able to broadcast, live, her acceptance speech. When Grace Kelly was announced as the winner, it sent shockwaves throughout the entertainment industry. The TV crew in Garland's hospital immediately took everything down without saying a word. Garland turned the sequence of events into another funny anecdotal story about the flurry of activity before the winner was announced contrasted with the complete silence of everyone after she lost.

Naturally, Garland was disappointed at having lost the Oscar. To the outside world, she took the high road and said that she was awarded something greater than the Oscar: her son Joe. That's true. Sadly, the loss effec-

Garland and costar James Mason in *A Star Is Born* (1954). From the author's collection.

tively ended any long-term film comeback plans. Warner ruined the film's chances of success when he hacked it out of greed and then wouldn't support it with an Oscar campaign. Garland came away from the experience with the feeling that Hollywood didn't want her back. But she got the last laugh, at least posthumously. In 1983, the restored 176-minute version of the film premiered, spearheaded by Ronald Haver for the American Film Institute. The musical numbers were reinstated, as were most of the cut scenes, and, in place of the bits with missing footage, a montage of stills was shown over the rediscovered complete stereo soundtrack. When the TV channel Turner Classic Movies (TCM) gave its first TCM Film Festival, a recently remastered print of the restored film was the centerpiece at the screening. The film has endured as a true film masterpiece. When watching it today and comparing it with the other movie musicals released in the same year, it's clear that it was ahead of its time. It has a unique look, using the new CinemaScope process to great advantage. Garland and Mason's performances, and the performances of the supporting cast, are as real and fresh as when it first premiered.

THE WIZARD OF OZ ON TELEVISION

On November 3, 1956, *The Wizard of Oz* premiered on television, broadcast in color by CBS-TV. The film, already considered a classic, had previously had its first theatrical rerelease in 1949 as an "MGM Masterpiece Reprint" and a second rerelease in 1955. The rereleases were successful, which was part of what prompted CBS to purchase the film as a special-event one-time broadcast. CBS allegedly had wanted *Gone with the Wind*, but MGM gave a flat "no" on that and offered *Oz* as an alternative.

The premiere broadcast in 1956, hosted by the Cowardly Lion, Bert Lahr, and Garland's daughter Liza Minnelli was a big success. However, it wasn't shown again until December 13,

1959, which was the first of the annual broadcasts that lasted until the final network broadcast in 1998, at which point it switched permanently to cable and, in the twenty-first century, to streaming. In those intervening four decades, the film became a cultural touchstone. It was the kid event of the year, rivaled only by the Christmas holiday season and Halloween. In the decades prior to the home media revolution of the early 1980s, the only way to see the film (aside from some random theatrical showings and a major theatrical rerelease in the early 1970s) was via the annual broadcasts. It was a special event that was anticipated for weeks, and the shared experience of watching the film on TV at the same time created a special sense of shared community.

To capitalize on that first broadcast, MGM Records finally released the first soundtrack album for the film. The album was unique. It featured songs and dialog taken directly from the soundtrack of the film, edited down to fit the 12″ LP time constraints (also released on three 7″ 45 rpm "extended play" records). The intent was to create a listening experience similar to watching the film. It was

The world television premiere of *The Wizard of Oz* on CBS-TV on November 3, 1956. From the author's collection.

the only official soundtrack album until an expanded version was released on compact disc and cassette in 1989 by CBS Special Products. Since that time, the complete soundtrack taken from the surviving prerecording sessions has been released in multiple versions and formats.

As far as Garland's legacy is concerned, the annual broadcasts gave her, as Ray Bolger noted, a kind of immortality. It was because of these broadcasts that more than a few people became lifelong *Oz* and Garland fans.

THE LATE 1950s

After the disappointment over *A Star Is Born* and some rest after giving birth to her son, Joe, Garland returned to the stage, embarking on a planned seven-city tour that included triumphs in San

Label of the 1956 MGM Records soundtrack album featuring songs and dialog from *The Wizard of Oz*. From the author's collection.

Diego and Long Beach, California. The tour was cut short when Garland was offered a contract with CBS-TV for her TV debut. At the same time, she signed a five-year contract with Capitol Records. It was her first long-term contract with a label since her time with Decca Records in the 1930s and 1940s. The contract ended up lasting ten years and included some of her greatest recordings. The CBS-TV special, the premiere of *The Ford Star Jubilee* series, was a success, as was her debut Capitol album, *Miss Show Business*, which was released to coincide with the TV special.

Garland continued her concerts throughout the last half of the decade, interspersed with making albums for Capitol under the musical direction of greats such as Nelson Riddle and Gordon Jenkins. In 1956, she made her nightclub debut in Las Vegas, Nevada (she had several successful Vegas engagements in the late 1950s and early 1960s), made another TV special, and ended the year with a triumphant return to the Palace Theatre in New York, which, like her 1951 comeback, was extended, this time to a total of seventeen weeks. Garland's 1958 engagement at the Cocoanut Grove in Hollywood was another smash hit. Capitol Records recorded the final night's show, resulting in the first-ever Judy Garland concert album.

The end of the decade brought Garland more success with a newly revamped show for a tour of opera houses, including the Metropolitan Opera House in New York, the Chicago Opera House, and the War Memorial Opera House in San Francisco. But by the end of 1959, Garland had ballooned to more than 180 pounds. When she entered Doctor's Hospital in New York City on November 18, 1959, she was near death. She was treated for hepatitis and told that she would be a "semi-invalid for the rest of her life" and wouldn't be able to work again.[1]

POST-MGM HIGHLIGHTS

THE 1960s

In January 1960, Garland signed a deal with Random House Publishing to write her autobiography. She began work on it with Fred Finklehoffe (the same Finklehoffe who wrote the screenplays for some of her big MGM hits). The book never happened, but the recordings she made with Finklehoffe and the sixty-five-page unfinished manuscript have survived and give some insight into Garland's life as she saw it (or as she saw it at that time). Garland's memories were usually clouded a bit by her current frame of mind.

Although Garland had been told she would never work again, the rest was so good that she entered a dazzling career renaissance. Her first work was recording "The Far Away Part of Town" for the film *Pepe* (1960). Garland did not appear in the film; the song played during a dance by Shirley Jones and Dan Daily. The song was nominated for the Best Song Oscar that year (losing to "Never on Sunday" from the film of the same name). Garland began recording tracks for the Capitol album *Judy: That's Entertainment!*, which has remained one of her best albums. In August 1960, while in London, Garland went to the EMI studios and recorded tracks for a new album. The album was put on hold, and before it had a chance to be released, *Judy at Carnegie Hall* happened, featuring most of the same songs on the live album of the same name. Six of the unreleased recordings popped up on the 1962 Capitol compilation album *The Garland Touch*. All of the recordings from the session were finally released together in 1972. The recordings are arguably her best studio versions of the songs.

On August 28, 1960, Garland returned to the London Palladium. She premiered her new, two-act, one-woman concert format, which was the first known two-act, solo, one-woman concert by a female pop vocalist—a format still in use today. It was just Garland and the band. There were no dancers, sets, or other extraneous gags or even costumes. It worked. Thanks to her recent rest and renewed health, Garland was better than ever. Her voice was beyond compare, and she was at the top of her game. The Palladium engagement was the first of a new tour that took her to several cities in England

Garland with her daughter Lorna Luft and son Joe Luft, November 27, 1957. From the author's collection.

Garland with Richard Widmark and Howard Caine in *Judgment at Nuremberg* (1961). From the author's collection.

and then to Paris (two engagements) and Amsterdam. This was followed by a return to the United States, where she briefly toured before filming her return to the movies, playing Irene Hoffman in the film adaptation of the "Playhouse 90" TV drama special *Judgment at Nuremberg*. Garland was nominated for the Oscar for Best Supporting Actress but lost to Rita Moreno in *West Side Story*. After filming *Judgment at Nuremberg*, Garland returned to her concert tour, culminating in her once-in-a-lifetime triumph at New York's Carnegie Hall.

"Judy at Carnegie Hall" took place on April 23, 1961, and immediately became an entertainment legend. Garland was on fire. She mesmerized the packed house, which included some of the biggest names in show business at the time (apparently tipped off that Garland was in peak form), including Harold Arlen, Ethel Merman, Rock Hudson, Bette Davis, Debbie Reynolds, Julie Andrews, Carol Channing, Myrna Loy, Richard Burton, Jerry Herman, Phil Silvers, Maurice Chevalier, and many more. Also in attendance were Garland's family, her husband Sid Luft and her children, Liza Minnelli and Lorna and Joe Luft. Toward the end of the concert, the audience of three thousand (including the celebrities, who were every bit as awed by Garland as everyone else) spontaneously rushed to the stage to touch her as if she were a goddess (she kind of was at this point). Garland sang a total of twenty-six songs split by one intermission and in a voice as strong at the end as it was in the beginning. Capitol Records recorded the event, and their two-record set became the fastest-selling double LP in history at that time. It won five Grammy Awards: Album of the Year (the first time for a female artist and a concert album), Best Solo Vocal Performance (female), Best Album Cover (Jim Silke), Best Engineering Contribution, Popular Recording (Robert Arnold), and a special Artists and Repertoire Award to the set's producer, Andy Wiswell. The album has never been out of print.

The Carnegie Hall concert and album added a new layer of mystique and legend to Garland that is unique to Garland and Garland only. It is still referred to as the "Greatest Night in Show Business History." Some of Garland's chatter between songs on the original album has also passed into legend: "Do you really want more? Aren't you tired?" and "I know, I'll sing them all, and we'll stay all night!" Subsequent releases of the album on CD include the complete concert as recorded, adding in the chatter and stories missing from the original album, which focused on presenting all of the songs due to the LP time constraints of the time. The concert has also been given anniversary tributes and even misguided attempts at re-creation by performers who needed the help of other singers to try to copy what Garland had accomplished solo.

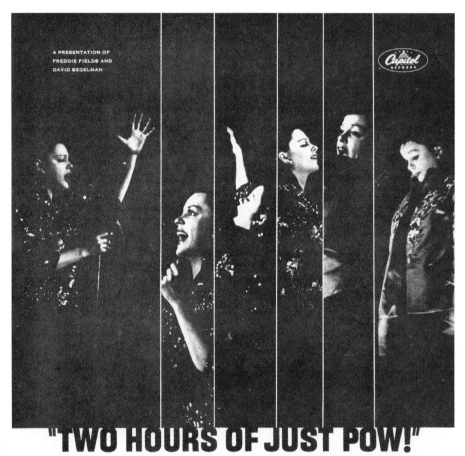

The historic "Judy at Carnegie Hall" concert on April 23, 1961, was immortalized on the two-disc Capitol Records release. From the author's collection.

292   CHAPTER 12

Garland's final film, *I Could Go on Singing* (1963). From the author's collection.

After the success of the Carnegie Hall concert and before the album was released, Garland continued her tour across the United States and into Canada. Seeing Judy Garland in concert became an event. She triumphed everywhere she went. At the end of 1961, she recorded her songs and dialog for the animated film *Gay Purr-ee*, which reunited her with the songwriters of *The Wizard of Oz*, Harold Arlen and E. Y. Harburg, who wrote new songs for this film. Garland had a busy 1962. She returned to television for the CBS special *The Judy Garland Show* (a.k.a. "Judy, Frank, and Dean") featuring her with Frank Sinatra and Dean Martin. She filmed her role in *A Child Is Waiting*, costarring Burt Lancaster and directed by Stanley Kramer. Capitol Records attempted to re-create the Carnegie Hall success by having Garland record a live show at the Manhattan Center in New York, to be titled "Judy Takes Broadway." Marilyn Monroe and the young pre-stardom Barbra Streisand were in attendance. Garland was suffering from laryngitis and struggled through some of the songs, unable to complete the concert. It was planned for her to return and finish the album, but that never happened. The recordings were not released until most of them were released on Capitol in 1989 on *Judy Garland Live!*, which, although posthumous, became the last original Judy Garland album released by the label.

Garland returned to London just days after the Manhattan Center session to begin filming what became her final musical and final film, *I Could Go on Singing*, released in 1963. Garland plays an American concert hall singer attempting to reconnect with the son she left in the care of the boy's father, played by Dirk Bogarde. Arlen and Harburg wrote the new title song. The film features Garland on stage at the London Palladium, giving audiences an idea of how Garland was in concert. Although the film received mixed reviews, Garland's performance is one of her better ones and has grown in stature over the years.

After Garland returned to the United States, she continued her concerts and made a

POST-MGM HIGHLIGHTS

memorable appearance on Jack Paar's talk show, telling funny stories about her vaudeville years and life at MGM. Robert Goulet, who was her voice costar in *Gay Purr-ee*, joined her, and the two sang a couple of songs from the film. The success of the Paar show is part of what convinced CBS to sign Garland for a weekly TV show. On January 30, 1963, Garland began taping another TV special for CBS, titled *Judy Garland and Her Guests Phil Silvers and Robert Goulet*. The special was another success.

Garland returned to touring and attended the London premiere of *I Could Go on Singing* before returning to Los Angeles to begin taping her TV series *The Judy Garland Show*. The first episode was taped on June 24, 1963, and a wide variety of stars were in attendance to offer support. Garland's first guest, at her request, was her best friend, Mickey Rooney. Much like Warner Bros. had done with *A Star Is Born*, CBS went into the project gung-ho and then washed their hands of it when it began to falter. The show was a success with the critics and the public, but CBS scheduled it opposite the wildly popular ratings champ *Bonanza*. The initial format was wonky, prompting viewers to write to CBS to let Judy be "Judy." The change in personnel and format helped, but by that time, CBS had already decided the show would not be renewed after its first year. *The Judy Garland Show* did not provide Garland with the financial stability she thought it would, but it added greatly to her legacy. The show is now considered a classic, and it's no wonder. Garland gave her all, giving brilliant and electrifying performances that have stood the test of time, such as "A Cottage for Sale," "Ol' Man River," "As Long as He Needs Me," and "The Battle Hymn of the Republic." She also had a who's who of great performers as guests, including Lena Horne, Peggy Lee, Tony Bennett, Ethel Merman, Count Basie, Vic Damone, Diahann Carroll, Martha Raye, and a young Barbra Streisand. She also had daughter Liza Minnelli on a couple of times, and all of her children (Liza, Lorna, and Joe) on the Christmas edition. The show aired its last episode on March 26, 1964.

THE BEGINNING OF THE END

Not long after *The Judy Garland Show* ended, Garland and her new companion, Mark Herron (Garland had been separated and filed for divorce from her husband Sid Luft), took a vacation in Hawaii prior to embarking on a concert tour in Australia. The Australian tour turned out to be a debacle that garnered Garland some of the worst press of her career. She was a success in Sydney, where she gave two concerts on May 13 and 16, 1964. She then went to Melbourne, where, due to fatigue and vocal issues, she was sixty-five minutes late. The results were disastrous. The audience was brutally nasty to her, and she got through only half of her show before leaving the stage. For a trouper of Garland's stature to walk off the stage, it had to be really bad. Regardless of the great concerts in Sydney, the tabloid press was brutal, making the whole tour seem like a disaster, with Garland portrayed as an intoxicated mess.

Garland and Herron then went to Hong Kong, where, while Typhoon Viola battered the city on May 28, 1964, Garland overdosed on pills and was rushed to a hospital through the typhoon. She was so close to death that the news spread that she had passed away, although it was corrected quickly. Garland had pleurisy in both lungs, and her heart and throat were damaged. To make matters worse, the tubes in her throat damaged her vocal cords. She was told not to sing for a year, but by July 23, 1964, she had another "comeback" at the "Night of 100 Stars" at the London Palladium. She was such a hit that she even upstaged the Beatles, getting the biggest response from the audience and the critics.

Garland's next big project was returning to the London Palladium for another concert, this time sharing the bill with her eighteen-year-old daughter, Liza Minnelli, who was already making a name for herself in the entertainment world. Garland announced the shows in spite of Liza's initial resistance. Originally scheduled for one concert on November 8, 1964, the demand was so great, that a second concert, on November 15, was added. That second concert was also videotaped by ITV British Television, which broadcasted just 55 minutes of the 150-minute concert, and only those 55 minutes survived. Garland's voice wasn't up to par for the concerts, which was partly a result of the vocal damage in Hong Kong. Capitol Records recorded both shows for a planned concert album, but the recording for the second show was marred by the hum of the ITV cameras. Garland and Liza recorded new vocals to the orchestra tracks from the second concert on November 23, but only a fraction was used on the resulting double-disc album. The concert album was released in July 1965 but, unfortunately, wasn't nearly as successful as the Carnegie Hall album, with an odd lineup of songs placing "The Man That Got Away" as Garland's opening number, a song she never opened with.

Garland spent the next few years in concert, highlighted by successful concerts at the O'Keefe Center in Toronto, Canada; the Arie Crown Theatre in Chicago, Illinois; and the Forest Hills Stadium in Forest Hills, New York, where she broke the record for longest standing ovation—thirty minutes at the end of her concert. She also made mostly successful guest appearances on many TV variety shows, including returning to Jack Paar's program with more funny stories. Garland almost appeared in one of two competing film biographies of Jean Harlow, the Electrovision version starring Carol Lynley as Harlow. Garland would have played Harlow's mother. When she left, Garland allegedly told Lynley, "Honey, I'm not drunk, I'm not on drugs, and I'm telling you this is a piece of junk, and I'm getting out!"[2]

After thirteen years of marriage, Garland's divorce from her third husband, Sid Luft, was finalized on May 19, 1965. Garland had been spending her time with Herron, who had become her constant companion. The two married in Las Vegas on November 14, 1965. The marriage wasn't successful; the couple separated in April 1966.

Garland's last film work occurred when she signed on to play Helen Lawson in the 20th Century Fox adaptation of Jacqueline Susann's best seller *Valley of the Dolls*. The show business roman à clef, about three young women working their way up the show business ladder, featured a character, Neely O'Hara, who was clearly based on Garland, being a young singer with a one-

POST-MGM HIGHLIGHTS

295

in-a-million voice who becomes a great film star addicted to pills (the "dolls" in the title). The Lawson character was based mostly on Ethel Merman. Garland began work on the film in March 1967, prerecording her solo "I'll Plant My Own Tree." It was the last time Garland recorded a song for a film. Once filming began, Garland tried to make the best of the role in spite of a rocky start. But, according to Patty Duke, who played Neely in the film, the director, Mark Robson, treated Garland deplorably, making her arrive early but not calling on her until late in the day, at which point her insecurities and "self-medicating" had gotten the best of her and she was in no shape to perform. After filming some scenes, Garland was fired. Both sides blamed the other, and it became another blight on Garland's public image. The one good thing to come out of the debacle was that Garland kept her gold pantsuit (and an all-white version, too), which became her last great iconic look, symbolizing "Judy in Concert."

Garland in costume for *Valley of the Dolls* (1967), which she was unable to complete. From the author's collection.

As usual, Garland followed the failure of *Valley of the Dolls* with another great comeback, hitting the concert stage again, highlighted by her third and final engagement at the Palace Theatre in New York, opening on July 31, 1967. This time, her daughter Lorna and son Joe were part of the act, as was Charlie Bubbles. The engagement was another triumph. The first three nights of the engagement were recorded by ABC Records, who quickly put out a single-disc record, *Judy Garland: At Home at the Palace—Opening Night*, which actually consisted of tracks from those first three nights. It was the last original Judy Garland album released during her lifetime. After the Palace run ended on August 26, 1967, Garland took her concert on the road again, where she was generally a hit. It was her last big concert tour.

THE END OF THE ROAD

For the next two years, Garland's life was mostly a series of ups and downs. Her health was beginning to fail her, and she began to look frail. She managed a few notable concerts, giving her last concert in the United States on July 20, 1968, at the J. F. K. Stadium in Philadelphia, Pennsylvania. Philadelphia was the site of Garland's first concert in July 1943. Garland stayed mostly in New York City, singing in nightclubs and appearing on TV talk shows. One memorable talk show appearance was *The Tonight Show* with Johnny Carson on December 17, 1968. Garland touchingly sang "It's All for You" and "Till After the Holidays," which were written by her latest companion, John Meyer. Meyer took care of Garland at the time, as she was basically homeless. She soon was reacquainted with Mickey Deans, a nightclub manager. Deans took over managing Garland, accompanying her to London for an engagement at the Talk of the Town cabaret that lasted from December 30, 1968, to February 1, 1969. The engagement was mostly a success. Garland's divorce from Mark Herron became final on February 11, 1969 (the two hadn't been together since April 1966), and Garland then married Deans on March 15, 1969. He was her fifth and last husband.

After their marriage, Garland and Deans flew to Stockholm, Sweden, for the start of a brief Scandinavian tour. Her final concert took place at the Falkoner Centre in Copenhagen, Denmark, on March 25, 1969. By this point, Garland seemed to be living on borrowed time. She was incredibly thin and frail. Overall, her voice was a shadow of what it had been, although she could still rally and give some great performances. To those around her, it seemed as though her body was shutting down. After the tour, Garland and Deans traveled back to London before returning to New York for a brief time, and then they went back to London on June 17. Garland spent the next few days relaxing and doing a little bit of socializing. In the early morning hours of June 22, 1969, Garland quietly passed away in the bathroom of the mews cottage at 4 Cadogan Lane in London that she and Deans were renting. She was forty-seven years old.

Garland's death was front-page news around the world. Many articles were printed about her life, her tragedies, her successes—but mostly her tragedies. The myth of Garland as the eternal victim had been a part of her image for years prior to her death. Garland was keenly aware of it; she was also aware that there wasn't anything she could do about it. After her death, the myth of Garland's life as a series of tragedies, illnesses, bad marriages, bad agents, and a tragic death continued and continues to this day. On June 25, 1969, the hospital pathologist ruled that Garland's death was "an accidental death by incautious overdose of barbiturates." Her body was flown to New York, and her funeral was held at Campbell's Funeral Home. More than twenty-two thousand people came to pay their last respects at the funeral, held on Friday, June 27, 1969. The press reports at the time seemed to marvel at the diversity of the crowd, being surprised that Garland's appeal transcended age, class, and race.

THE LEGACY

At the time of Garland's death, she was known to the general public more for her recent ups and downs than her great body of work. In the early morning hours of Saturday, June 28, 1969, the day after her funeral, a popular gay bar, the Stonewall Inn, was raided by the police. This time, the patrons and the local gay community fought back, beginning the modern gay rights movement. One of the myths around that event was that the patrons were bereft with grief over Garland's death and had had enough, prompting the riots. Whether this story is entirely true is open to debate. There's no doubt that many of the patrons had been to the funeral and were grieving the loss of their icon. That grief most likely played a part in the will to fight back, but it's also true that the community had already been pushed to the breaking point. Garland's death and subsequent funeral might not have been the spark that lit the fire of the gay rights movement, but it was definitely part of it.

At the time of Garland's death, her films had been relegated to the world of late-night "Late Late Show" or "Afternoon Matinee" broadcasts on local TV stations. Usually, the films were trimmed and broken up by endless commercial breaks. The quality of the prints was poor. Only the hardcore Garland or old movie fans were willing to stay up and sit through the broadcasts. Many fans would set their alarm clocks to wake up in time for early morning broadcasts, those being the only way to see many of her films. Most fans had no other options, aside from purchasing 8 mm or 30 mm film prints when available. The "home media" market was still years away.

Less than a year after Garland's death, in May 1970, MGM held its now legendary auction of props, costumes, and just about anything that wasn't nailed down. It was the final nail in the coffin of Old Hollywood and the Studio System, which "New Hollywood" seemed eager to bury and forget. Many of Garland's costumes, as well as costumes and props from her films, were auctioned. The highlight of the auction, and the one that got most of the press, was the auction of the Ruby Slippers from *The Wizard of Oz*. Since that time, the slippers have generated a mythology of their own.

The slippers that were auctioned in 1970 went for an unheard sum of $15,000 to an anonymous buyer. They were thought to be the only surviving pair. However, the auction's costume and prop curator, Kent Warner, found four pairs (including an Arabian-styled test pair) and wisely (some would say deviously) kept the best pairs to sell on his own secretly. It soon became known that at least one other pair of slippers survived when a woman from Tennessee, Roberta Bauman, came forward with her pair. She had won the pair in an MGM contest in 1939 and had kept them ever since. The pair sold at the 1970 auction was later donated by the owner to the Smithsonian in Washington, DC, where they have remained. Bauman's pair have been auctioned twice. One of the pairs that Warner kept was sold to collector Michael Shaw, who generously shared them at various events until they were stolen in 2005 from the Judy Garland Museum in Grand Rapids, Minnesota. They were recovered by the FBI in 2018. That pair is mismatched, the mates being the pair at the Smithsonian. Due to the extensive restoration done by the Smithsonian, the two pairs could not be matched. The final pair Warner kept was the most pristine, assumed to be the pair used for close-ups and the "tapping" scene. He put them up for auction

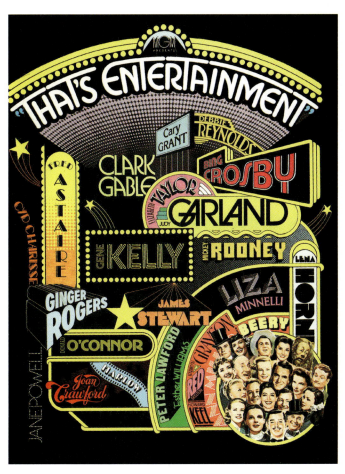

That's Entertainment! (1974) introduced a new generation of fans to Garland's MGM filmography. From the author's collection.

in 1981. The new owner then put them up for auction in 2011, but the reserve price was not met, so the pair stayed in storage until 2012 when actor Leonardo DiCaprio, director Steven Spielberg, and allegedly other unknown donors purchased the pair for an undisclosed price. They donated the slippers to the Academy of Motion Picture Arts and Sciences as one of the main attractions in the new Academy Museum of Motion Pictures that opened in 2021. The Arabian pair was purchased from Warner by another MGM legend, Debbie Reynolds, and added to her immense collection of costumes and props in the hopes that they would be part of a planned museum. The museum never happened, and the pair was sold in 2011 when Reynolds auctioned her entire collection.

In the mid-1970s, Garland's reputation and legacy began to turn around. The surprise hit of the 1974 summer movie box office was the compilation film *That's Entertainment!* Garland was featured in two segments, the only star to be given that honor. For Garland's legacy, *That's Entertainment!* introduced audiences to her film performances, cementing her status as the greatest female movie musical star of the golden era. It had been just five years since her untimely death. The negative headlines and seemingly endless tabloid tragedies and comebacks that dominated her final years had begun to fade. People began to recognize and appreciate her for her incredible versatility and talent and not as a victim of those tabloid dramas. *That's Entertainment!* came along at the right time. It tapped into and almost single-handedly legitimized the nostalgia market. In September 1973, eight months before the premiere of *That's Entertainment!*, the MGM Records label repackaged its classic-era soundtracks in a series of six two-record sets titled *Those Glorious MGM Musicals*. The series was so popular that six more two-record sets were released in February 1974. All of the previously released MGM Records soundtracks to Garland's films were part of the series. A sequel, *That's Entertainment! Part 2*, was released in 1976. A third installment, *That's Entertainment! III*, was released in 1994. Even more Garland treasures were included in the sequels, the last one famously featuring previously unreleased outtakes such as "I'm an Indian, Too," and "Doin' What Comes Natur'lly" from *Annie Get Your Gun* (1949) and "Mr. Monotony" from *Easter Parade* (1948). The series was initiated by producer Jack Haley Jr., the son of the "Tin Man," Jack Haley. In an odd twist of fate, the son of the Tin Man married Dorothy's daughter. Haley Jr. married Liza Minnelli in 1974; their marriage lasted until 1979.

In May 1975, *Judy* by Gerold Frank was published. The book was heavily promoted as the first comprehensive biography about Garland, with an added layer of legitimacy as Frank had the cooperation of Garland's family, most notably Garland's third husband, Sid Luft. Two more Garland biographies were published in 1975, each excellent in different ways: *Rainbow: The Stormy Life of Judy Garland* by Christopher Finch (well balanced, with a focus on her MGM years) and *Young Judy* by authors David Dahl and Barry Kehoe (chronicling Garland's life up to and just after her 1935 MGM audition). A third biography, simply titled *Judy Garland*, by Anne Edwards, was also published in 1975. Garland had become a hot topic in the publishing industry. In 1977, the first serious book about the making of *The Wizard of Oz* was published, written by Aljean Harmetz. It was the first time many of the behind-the-scenes details and photos had been published. Unfortunately, Harmetz perpetuated the incorrect urban myth that the film was a flop when initially released in 1939, among other mistakes that have since been corrected in subsequent and more thoroughly researched books about the film.

The Garland masterpiece *A Star Is Born* was the first major film to be restored. The reconstruction was spearheaded by the Academy of Motion Picture Arts and Sciences and historian Ronald Haver, who scoured the vaults searching for any and all missing footage. The star-studded re-premiere of the nearly complete version on July 7, 1983, at New York's Radio City Music Hall was a success, followed by screenings in major cities across the United States and subsequent home media releases. The film is now finally recognized as a true film masterpiece.

In the early 1980s, the burgeoning home media market took off when VHS videotapes and videotape recorders/players became popular. VHS sales and rental stores popped up, and studios were more than happy to rerelease classic films along with recent films in a new and lucrative market. *The Wizard of Oz* was always one of the first films to be released in every new format—first in the early "videodisc" market (a precursor to LaserDiscs) and then videotape, LaserDisc, DVD, Blu-ray, and 4K-UltraHD. Film restoration became popular, with LaserDisc becoming the format of choice for serious film fans and collectors due to its superior image quality and ability to hold media content such as alternate audio tracks and bonus features. The 1993 LaserDisc boxed set *The Ultimate Oz* led the way. The deluxe boxed set featured previously unreleased recording session audio on the alternate audio tracks, surviving special effects footage, interviews, outtake footage, and much more. The set was so successful that the Disney company used the format for collector's editions of some of its classic films.

PBS-TV premiered the documentary *Judy Garland: The Concert Years* on March 22, 1985, which presented many of Garland's performances from her TV series for the first time in years.

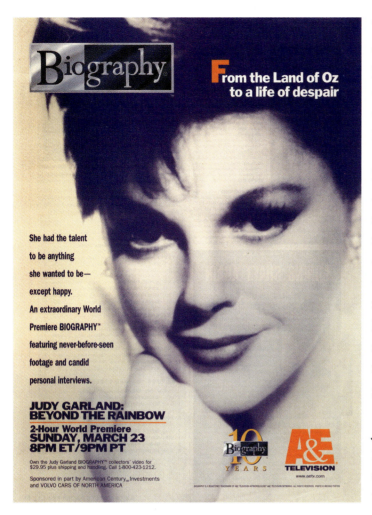

Promotional ad for the 1997 biography special about Garland produced and broadcast by A&E (the Arts and Entertainment Channel).

The special was well written and introduced Garland's incredible talent and performance to a new audience. The entire twenty-six-episode series (plus outtakes) was later remastered and released on DVD beginning in 1999.

Multiple anniversary events highlighted the ensuing decades. The fiftieth anniversary of *The Wizard of Oz* featured many products and celebrations, including the first of many upgraded versions of the film on home media. Over the years, more anniversary editions were released in the latest home media format. It got to the point that every five years, a new anniversary set was released, flooding the market with too many "money grab" releases of the film.

The A&E TV documentary *Judy Garland: Beyond the Rainbow* premiered on March 23, 1997, and was a critical and ratings success. It was the first comprehensive and balanced documentary about Garland's life and career, featuring new and archival interviews with those who knew and worked with Garland.

The hundredth anniversary of the film industry in 1998 was marked by the American Film Institute presenting the first in a series of annual lists. *The Wizard of Oz* was named the sixth greatest film (and the third greatest musical) of the previous one hundred years. Garland was named the eighth greatest female star, "Over the Rainbow" was named the number 1 song, and several other other Garland films were included in the other lists. Several of Garland's recordings have been inducted into the Grammy Hall of Fame. Likewise, several of her films have been selected for preservation in the National Film Registry at the Library of Congress. Additionally, there have been many more tributes, anniversaries, celebrations, and discoveries of more recordings and film footage over the decades since her untimely death.

The ABC-TV miniseries titled *Life with Judy Garland: Me and My Shadows*, based in part on the memoir of Garland's second daughter, Lorna Luft, premiered on February 25, 2001. Aired in

POST-MGM HIGHLIGHTS

two parts on consecutive nights, it was the first dramatic presentation of Garland's life and career. It was a critical and ratings success featuring Emmy-winning performances by Tammy Blanchard (as the young Garland) and Judy Davis (as the adult Garland). The miniseries won a total of five Emmy awards. It introduced Garland and her legacy of work to a new generation. This was followed just a few years later by the PBS *American Masters* documentary *Judy Garland: By Myself*, which premiered on February 25, 2004, and was another ratings and critical success, this time putting the focus on Garland's own words to tell her story, along with archival film footage.

By the turn of the twenty-first century, Judy Garland had become one of the few icons of the golden age of Hollywood still instantly recognizable to the general public. This is in large part due to *The Wizard of Oz* having become so entrenched in our cultural experience. Many writers have noted how many of the lines from the film have become a part of our societal lexicon as a shorthand for a variety of emotions. This unique legendary status is a reflection of Garland's talent, which is consistently recognized by not just the public but also those in the current entertainment industry, most of whom revere her. Despite the clickbait tabloid articles online and in print and the negative mythology that sometimes plagues her story, Judy Garland remains a true entertainment legend. MGM provided Garland with the means to become an enduring legend, but it was her voice and her talent that made it possible. It's fitting that she has become the voice of MGM. Without Judy Garland, the mystique of MGM wouldn't be as lustrous as it is.

APPENDIX A

JUDY GARLAND'S
MGM FILMOGRAPHY

The following is a list of the films Judy Garland made during her tenure at MGM, including the official shorts. All films were produced by MGM unless otherwise noted. The pre-MGM shorts are not included, nor are the films that she made after she left MGM. The songs listed here are all of Garland's songs in the films, including outtakes, and are solos unless otherwise noted. The main credits and cast are listed. Complete lists of all the songs, casts, and credits for all of Garland's films can be found online at TheJudyRoom.com.

LA FIESTA DE SANTA BARBARA (short) (1935)
Producer: Lewis Lewyn
Release Date: December 7, 1935

Garland and her sisters filmed this short in the summer of 1935, just prior to Garland's audition for (and subsequent signing with) MGM. This is also the last performance of the Garland Sisters as a trio. Although the film was released by MGM, it was an independent production made outside of the studio. This is the first time Garland was filmed in (the then-new) three-strip Technicolor.

Song: "La Cucaracha" (The Garland Sisters—each sister gets a short solo in the song). It's amusing to see (hear) Garland and her sisters sing about marijuana!

EVERY SUNDAY (short) (1936)
Director: Felix E. Feist
Screenplay: Mauri Grashin

This was Garland's first official film for MGM, costarring Deanna Durbin.

Garland Songs: "Opera vs. Jazz" (duet with Durbin), "Americana" (both songs music by Con Conrad, lyrics by Herb Magidson)

PIGSKIN PARADE (1936—produced and released by 20th Century Fox)
Producer: Bogart Rogers
Director: David Butler
Screenplay: Harry Tugend, Jack Yellen, and William Conselman; from a story by Arthur Sheekman, Jack Yellen, and Mark Kelly

Main Cast: Stuart Erwin as Amos Dodd, Jack Haley as Slug, Patsy Kelly as Bessie, Arline Judge as Sally Saxon, Grady Sutton as Mortimer, Johnny Downs as Chip Carson, Tony Martin as Tommy, Dixie Dunbar as Ginger Jones, Betty Grable as Laura Watson, Judy Garland as Sairy Dodd, Fred Kohler Jr. as Biff, the Yacht Club Boys (as themselves)

Songs (all written by Lew Pollack [music] and Sidney D. Mitchell [lyrics]): "The Balboa" (with Dixie Dunbar, Johnny Downs, Betty Grable, Judy Garland, Jack Haley, Patsy Kelly, and the Yacht Club Boys), "The Texas Tornado," "It's Love I'm After," "Hold That Bulldog" (outtake)

BROADWAY MELODY OF 1938 (1937)
Producer: Jack Cummings
Director: Roy Del Ruth
Screenplay: Jack McGowan; original story by Jack McGowan and Sid Silvers

Main Cast: Robert Taylor as Steve Raleigh, Eleanor Powell as Sally Lee, George Murphy as Sonny Ledford, Binnie Barnes as Caroline Whipple, Buddy Ebsen as Peter Trot, Sophie Tucker as Alice Clayton, Judy Garland as Betty Clayton, Charles Igor Gorin as Nicki Papaloapas, Raymond Walburn as Herman Whipple, Robert Benchley as Duffy, Willie Howard as Waiter, Charley Grapewin as James K. Blakely, Robert Wildhack as the sneezer, Billy Gilbert as George Papaloapas, Barnett Parker as Jerry Jason, Helen Troy as Emma Snipe

Garland Songs: All songs written by Nacio Herb Brown (music) and Arthur Freed (lyrics) except "You Made Me Love You." "Yours and Mine" (partial Garland solo behind the main titles), "Everybody Sing" (with Sophie Tucker, Barnett Parker, and the MGM Studio Chorus), "(Dear Mr. Gable) You Made Me Love You" ("You Made Me Love You" music by James V. Monaco, lyrics by Joe McCarthy, "Dear Mr. Gable" music and lyrics by Roger Edens), "Your Broadway and My

Broadway" (dance by Garland and Buddy Ebsen), "Your Broadway and My Broadway" (outtake), "Yours and Mine" (outtake) (with Eloise Rawitzer and the St. Brendan's Boys Choir), "I'm Feelin' Like a Million" (outtake)

THOROUGHBREDS DON'T CRY (1937)
Producer: Harry Rapf
Director: Alfred E. Green
Screenplay: Lawrence Hazard; from an original story by Eleanore Griffin and J. Walter Ruben
Music and Lyrics: Nacio Herb Brown and Arthur Freed

Main Cast: Judy Garland as Cricket West, Mickey Rooney as Timmy Donovan, Sophie Tucker as Mother Ralph, C. Aubrey Smith as Sir Peter Calverton, Ronald Sinclair as Roger Calverton, Forrester Harvey as Wilkins, Charles D. Brown as "Click" Donovan, Frankie Darro as "Dink" Reid, Henry Kolker as "Doc" Godfrey, Helen Troy as Hilda

Garland Songs: Both songs written by Nacio Herb Brown (music) and Arthur Freed (lyrics). "Got a Pair of New Shoes" (solo and with Mickey Rooney and Ronald Sinclair), "Sun Showers" (outtake)

SILENT NIGHT (short) (1937)

Garland rehearsed, recorded, and filmed the short from November 6 through November 8, 1937.

This charming short, MGM's Christmas trailer for 1937, features Garland singing "Silent Night" backed by the St. Luke's Episcopal Church Choristers of Long Beach. Conductor William Ripley Dorr later stated that "she told me she had sung in a church choir since she was very small and loved church music."

EVERYBODY SING (1938)
Director: Edwin L. Marin
Original Story and Screenplay: Florence Ryerson and Edgar Allan Woolf; additional dialog by James Gruen

Main Cast: Allan Jones as Ricky Saboni, Judy Garland as Judy Bellaire, Fanny Brice as Olga Chekaloff, Reginald Owen as Hillary Bellaire, Billie Burke as Diana Bellaire, Reginald Gardiner as Jerrold Hope, Lynne Carver as Sylvia Bellaire, Helen Troy as Hillary's Secretary, Monty Woolley as John Fleming

Garland Songs: "Swing Mr. Mendelssohn" (with the St. Brendan's Boys Choir dubbing for school girls) (music by Bronislau Kaper and Walter Jurmann, lyrics by Gus Kahn), "Melody Farm" (music by Bronislau Kaper and Walter Jurmann, lyrics by Gus Kahn), "Bus Sequence (Melody Farm)" (with Allan Jones, Reginald Gardiner, Mildred Rogers for Lynne Carver, and Adia

JUDY GARLAND'S MGM FILMOGRAPHY   305

Kuznetzoff) (music by Bronislau Kaper and Walter Jurmann, lyrics by Gus Kahn), "Swing Low, Sweet Chariot" (words and music by Wallace Willis, special material by Roger Edens), "Why? Because!" (with Fanny Brice) (music and lyrics by Bert Kalmar and Harry Ruby), "Ever Since the World Began/Shall I Sing a Melody?" (music and lyrics by Roger Edens), "Melody Farm" (finale reprise) (with Allan Jones, Fanny Brice, and the MGM Studio Chorus)

LOVE FINDS ANDY HARDY (1938)
Producer: Carey Wilson
Director: George B. Seitz
Screenplay: William Ludwig; based on stories by Vivian B. Bretherton and characters by Aurania Rouverol

Main Cast: Lewis Stone as Judge James K. Hardy, Mickey Rooney as Andrew Hardy, Cecilia Parker as Marian Hardy, Fay Holden as Mrs. Hardy, Judy Garland as Betsy Booth, Lana Turner as Cynthia Potter, Ann Rutherford as Polly Benedict, Gene Reynolds as Jimmy MacMahon

Garland Songs: "In-Between" (music and lyrics by Roger Edens), "Meet the Beat of My Heart," "It Never Rains, But What It Pours" (music and lyrics by Harry Revel and Mack Gordon), "Bei Mir Bist Du Schoen" (outtake) (music by Sholom Secunda, lyrics by Jacob Jacobs, English lyrics by Sammy Cahn and Saul Chaplin, special material by Roger Edens)

MARCH OF DIMES (independent short, circa 1938)

Most likely filmed on the MGM backlot, on the "New England" (Andy Hardy) Street, Garland and Mickey Rooney provide a public service announcement encouraging people to send in money to help fight polio.

LISTEN, DARLING (1938)
Producer: Jack Cummings
Director: Edwin L. Marin
Screenplay: Elaine Ryan and Anne Morrison Chapin; from the story by Katherine Brush

Main Cast: Freddie Bartholomew as Buzz Mitchell, Judy Garland as Pinkie Wingate, Mary Astor as Dottie Wingate, Walter Pidgeon as Richard Thurlow, Alan Hale as J. J. Slattery, Scotty Beckett as Billie Wingate

Garland Songs: "Zing! Went the Strings of My Heart" (James F. Hanley), "Ten Pins in the Sky" (Joseph McCarthy and Milton Ager), "On the Bumpy Road to Love" (Al Hoffman, Al Lewis, and Murray Mencher) (with Freddie Bartholomew, Mary Astor, and Scotty Beckett), "On the Bumpy Road to Love" (reprise) (with Freddie Bartholomew, Mary Astor, Walter Pidgeon, and Scotty Beckett)

THE WIZARD OF OZ (1939)

Producer: Mervyn LeRoy

Production Assistant: Arthur Freed

Director: Victor Fleming; uncredited: George Cukor, Norman Taurog, Richard Thorpe, King Vidor

Screenplay: Noel Langley, Florence Ryerson, Edgar Allan Woolf; uncredited: Irving Brecher, William Cannon, Herbert Fields, Arthur Freed, E. Y. Harburg, Samuel Hoffenstein, John Lee Mahin, Herman Mankiewicz, Jack Mintz, Ogden Nash, and Sid Silvers

Score: Herbert Stothart

Main Cast: Judy Garland as Dorothy Gale, Frank Morgan as Professor Marvel, Doorman, Cabby, Guard, and the Wizard of Oz, Ray Bolger as Hunk Andrews/Scarecrow, Bert Lahr as Zeke/Cowardly Lion, Jack Haley as Hickory Twicker/Tin Woodman, Margaret Hamilton as Miss Almira Gulch/Wicked Witch of the West, Billie Burke as Glinda, the Good Witch of the North, Charley Grapewin as Uncle Henry, Clara Blandick as Aunt Em, Pat Walshe as Nikko, the Singer Midgets as the Munchkins, Terry the dog as Toto

Garland Songs: All songs written by Harold Arlen (music) and E. Y. "Yip" Harburg. "Over the Rainbow," "The Wind Began to Switch," "If I Only Had a Brain" (with Ray Bolger), "We're Off to See the Wizard" (with Ray Bolger, Jack Haley, and Buddy Ebsen), "If I Only Had the Nerve" (with Bert Lahr, Ray Bolger, and Jack Haley), "The Merry Old Land of Oz" (with Frank Morgan, Ray Bolger, Jack Haley, Bert Lahr, and MGM Studio Chorus), "If I Were King of the Forest" (with Bert Lahr, Ray Bolger, and Jack Haley), "The Jitterbug" (outtake) (with Ray Bolger, Jack Haley, and Bert Lahr), "Over the Rainbow" (reprise) (outtake)

BABES IN ARMS (1939)

Producer: Arthur Freed

Director: Busby Berkeley

Screenplay: Jack McGowan and Kay Van Riper; screenplay contributors: Florence Ryerson, Edgar Allan Woolf, Joe Laurie, John Meehan, Walter DeLeon, Irving Brecher, Ben Freedman, and Anita Loos; based on the musical by Richard Rodgers and Lorenz Hart

Music and Lyrics: "Babes in Arms," "Where or When" (music by Richard Rodgers, lyrics by Lorenz Hart), "Good Morning" (music by Nacio Herb Brown, lyrics by Arthur Freed), "God's Country" (music by Harold Arlen, lyrics by E. Y. Harburg), "I Cried for You" (music by Gus Arnheim and Abe Lyman, lyrics by Arthur Freed)

Main Cast: Mickey Rooney as Mickey Moran, Judy Garland as Patsy Barton, Charles Winninger as Joe Moran, Guy Kibbee as Judge Black, June Preisser as Rosalie Essex (Baby Rosalie), Grace Hayes as Florrie Moran, Betty Jaynes as Molly Moran, Douglas McPhail as Don Bricek, Ann Shoemaker as Mrs. Barton, Margaret Hamilton as Martha Steele

Garland Songs: "Good Morning" (with Mickey Rooney) (music by Nacio Herb Brown, lyrics by Arthur Freed), "Opera vs. Jazz" (with Betty Jaynes and Mickey Rooney), "Babes in Arms" (with Douglas McPhail, Mickey Rooney, Betty Jaynes, and the MGM Studio Chorus) (music by Richard Rodgers, lyrics by Lorenz Hart), "Where or When" (music by Richard Rodgers, lyrics by Lorenz Hart), "I Cried for You (Now It's Your Turn to Cry over Me)" (music by Gus Arnheim and Abe Lyman, lyrics by Arthur Freed), "Minstrel Show Sequence" (includes "Minstrel Show," "Oh! Suzanna," and "I'm Just Wild about Harry") (with Mickey Rooney, Douglas McPhail, and the Crinoline Choir) ("Minstrel Show" music and lyrics by Roger Edens, "Oh! Susanna" music and lyrics by Stephen Foster, "I'm Just Wild about Harry" music by Eubie Black, lyrics by Percy Wenrich), "Finale Sequence" (includes "God's Country" and "My Day") (with Mickey Rooney, Douglas McPhail, Betty Jaynes, Sally Mueller, Helen Pacino, Betty Rome, Irene Crane, Albert Mahler, Bob Priester, Ralph Leon, N. Nielsen, John Moss, Charles Schroeder, Allan Watson, J. D. Jewles, and the MGM Studio Chorus) (music by Harold Arlen, lyrics by E. Y. "Yip" Harburg, special material by Roger Edens)

IF I FORGET YOU (independent short, 1940)

In early 1940, Garland recorded and filmed "If I Forget You" for the Will Rogers Memorial Fund. It's a beautiful number showing off Garland's range when she jumps a full octave toward the end. The short was created for the annual Will Rogers National Theatre Week," which began on April 25, 1940. Although the short is titled "If I Forget You," the lyrics that Garland sings are all "If *we* forget . . ."

This short is a good example of the several shorts and newsreels Garland appeared in during the 1940s, ranging from public service announcements for causes like the March of Dimes to brief shots featuring her and stars entertaining and working for the troops or arriving at film premieres.

ANDY HARDY MEETS DEBUTANTE (1940)

Producer: Carey Wilson
Director: George B. Seitz
Screenplay: William Ludwig; based on stories by Vivian B. Bretherton and characters by Aurania Rouverol

Main Cast: Lewis Stone as Judge James K. Hardy, Mickey Rooney as Andy Hardy, Cecilia Parker as Marian Hardy, Fay Holden as Mrs. Hardy, Judy Garland as Betsy Booth, Ann Rutherford as Polly Benedict, Diana Lewis as Daphne Fowler, George Breakston as Beezy, Sara Haden as Aunt Milly

Garland Songs: "I'm Nobody's Baby" (music by Milton Ager, lyrics by Benny Davis and Lester A. Santly, "Alone" and "All I Do Is Dream of You" (music by Nacio Herb Brown, lyrics by Arthur

308   APPENDIX A

Freed), "Buds Won't Bud" (outtake) (music by Harold Arlen, lyrics by E. Y. "Yip" Harburg and Ted Koehler), "All I Do Is Dream of You" (outtake) (music by Nacio Herb Brown, lyrics by Arthur Freed)

STRIKE UP THE BAND (1940)

Producer: Arthur Freed

Director: Busby Berkeley

Original Screenplay: John Monks Jr. and Fred Finklehoffe

Music and Lyrics: "Strike Up the Band" (music by George Gershwin, lyrics by Ira Gershwin), "Our Love Affair," "Do the La Conga," "Nobody," and "Drummer Boy" (music and lyrics by Roger Edens)

Musical Director: Georgie Stoll

Main Cast: Mickey Rooney as Jimmy Connors, Judy Garland as Mary Holden, Paul Whiteman as Himself, June Preisser as Barbara Frances Morgan, William Tracy as Phillip Turner, Larry Nunn as Willie Brewster, Margaret Early as Annie, Ann Shoemaker as Mrs. Connors

Garland Songs: "Our Love Affair" (with Mickey Rooney) (music by Roger Edens, lyrics by Arthur Freed), "Do the La Conga" (with Mickey Rooney, Six Hits and a Miss, and the MGM Studio Chorus) (music and lyrics by Roger Edens), "Nobody" (music and lyrics by Roger Edens), "Nell of New Rochelle Routine" (includes "Gay Nineties" and "Heaven Will Protect the Working Girl") (with Mickey Rooney, June Preisser, William Tracy, Larry Nunn, Margaret Early, and the MGM Studio Chorus), "Gay Nineties" (music and lyrics by Roger Edens), "Heaven Will Protect the Working Girl" (music by A. Baldwin Sloane, lyrics by Edgar Smith), "Drummer Boy" (with Six Hits and a Miss and the MGM Studio Orchestra featuring Mickey Rooney on drums and vibraphone), "Finale" (includes "Strike Up the Band," "Do the La Conga," "Our Love Affair," and "Drummer Boy") (with Mickey Rooney, Six Hits and a Miss and the MGM Studio Orchestra and Chorus), "The Curse of an Aching Heart" (music by Al Piantadosi, lyrics by Henry Fink) (outtake)

LITTLE NELLIE KELLY (1940)

Producer: Arthur Freed

Director: Norman Taurog

Screenplay: Jack McGowan; based on the musical comedy written, composed, and produced by George M. Cohan

Main Cast: Judy Garland as Nellie Kelly/Little Nellie Kelly, George Murphy as Jerry Kelly, Charles Winninger as Michael Noonan, Douglas McPhail as Dennis Fogarty, Arthur Shields as Timothy Fogarty

Garland Songs: "A Pretty Girl Milking Her Cow" (and reprise) (traditional Irish folk song, English lyrics by Thomas Moore, additional material by Roger Edens), "It's a Great Day for the Irish" (with Doug McPhail and the MGM Studio Chorus) (music and lyrics by Roger Edens), "Singin' in the Rain" (music by Nacio Herb Brown, lyrics by Arthur Freed), "Nellie Kelly, I Love You" (with Doug McPhail, George Murphy, and the MGM Studio Chorus) (music and lyrics by George M. Cohan), "Nellie Kelly, I Love You" (reprise) (with Doug McPhail, George Murphy, and Charles Winninger) (music and lyrics by George M. Cohan), "Danny Boy" (outtake) (traditional Irish melody, lyrics by Frederic Weatherly)

ZIEGFELD GIRL (1941)
Producer: Pandro S. Berman
Director: Robert Z. Leonard
Screenplay: Marguerite Roberts and Sonya Levien; original story by William Anthony McGuire
Musical Numbers: directed by Busby Berkeley

Main Cast: James Stewart as Gilbert Young, Judy Garland as Susan Gallagher, Hedy Lamarr as Sandra Kolter, Lana Turner as Sheila Regan, Tony Martin as Frank Merron, Jackie Cooper as Jerry Regan, Charles Winninger as "Pop" Gallagher, Edward Everett Horton as Noble Sage, Philip Dorn as Franz Kolter, Paul Kelly as John Slayton, Eve Arden as Patsy Dixon, Dan Dailey Jr. as Jimmy Walters, Al Shean as Al, Fay Holden as Mrs. Regan

Garland Songs: "Laugh? I Thought I'd Split My Sides" (with Charles Winninger) (music and lyrics by Roger Edens), "I'm Always Chasing Rainbows" (music by Harry Carroll, lyrics by Joseph McCarthy) "Minnie from Trinidad" (with the MGM Studio Chorus) (music by Harry Carroll, lyrics by Joseph McCarthy), "Finale" (with Tony Martin and the MGM Studio Chorus) (includes "Ziegfeld Girls" [music and lyrics by Roger Edens] and "You Gotta Pull Strings" [music by Walter Donaldson, lyrics by Harold Adamson], "We Must Have Music" [outtake] [music by Nacio Herb Brown, lyrics by Gus Kahn], "Special Material/I'm Always Chasing Rainbows" [outtake] [music and lytrics by Roger Edens], "You Never Looked So Beautiful Before" [music by Walter Donaldson, lyrics by Harold Adamson])

LIFE BEGINS FOR ANDY HARDY (1941)
Producer: Carey Wilson
Director: George B. Seitz
Screenplay: Agnes Christine Johnson; based on the characters created by Aurania Rouverol

Main Cast: Lewis Stone as Judge James K. Hardy, Mickey Rooney as Andy Hardy, Judy Garland as Betsy Booth, Fay Holden as Mrs. Hardy, Ann Rutherford as Polly Benedict, Sara Haden as Aunt Milly, Patricia Dane as Jennitt Hicks ("The Wolfess"), Ray McDonald as Jimmy Frobisher, George Breakston as Beezy

Garland Songs: All songs are not in the final film. "America (My Country 'Tis of Thee)" (melody adopted from "God Save the Queen," lyrics by Samuel Francis Smith), "Easy to Love" (words and music by Cole Porter), "Abide with Me" (music by Felix Mendelssohn, lyrics by Henry Francis Lyte), "The Rosary" (music by Ethelbert Nevin, lyrics by Robert Cameron Rogers)

BABES ON BROADWAY (1941)

Producer: Arthur Freed
Director: Busby Berkeley
Screenplay: Fred Finklehoffe and Elaine Ryan; original story by Fred Finklehoffe

Main Cast: Mickey Rooney as Tommy Williams, Judy Garland as Penny Morris, Fay Bainter as Miss Jones ("Jonesy"), Virginia Weidler as Barbara Jo Conway, Ray McDonald as Ray Lambert, Richard Quine as Morton Hammond ("Hammy"), Donald Meek as Mr. Stone, Alexander Woollcott as Himself, James Gleason as Thornton Reed, Annie Rooney as the third girl opposite Hammy; uncredited: Donna Reed as Jonesy's Secretary (her film debut), Joe Yule (Mickey Rooney's real-life father) as Mason, Reed's Aid, Margaret O'Brien as Child Auditioner (her film debut)

Garland Songs: "How about You?" (with Mickey Rooney) (music by Burton Lane, lyrics by Ralph Freed), "Hoe Down" (with Mickey Rooney, Six Hits and a Miss, the Five Musical Maids, and MGM Studio Chorus) (music by Roger Edens, lyrics by Ralph Freed), "Chin Up! Cheerio! Carry On!" (with the St. Luke's Episcopal Church Choristers and the MGM Studio Chorus) (music by Burton Lane, lyrics by E. Y. Harburg), "Ghost Theater Sequence" (with Mickey Rooney, the Stafford Quartet, the Debutantes, the Notables, and the Uptowners) (includes "Mary's a Grand Old Name" [music and lyrics by George M. Cohan], "I've Got Rings on My Fingers" [music by Maurice Scott, lyrics by R. P. Weston and F. J. Barns], and "Yankee Doodle Boy" [music and lyrics by George M. Cohan]), "Bombshell from Brazil" (with Mickey Rooney, Richard Quine, Ray McDonald, Virginia Weidler, Annie Rooney, Robert Bradford, and the MGM Studio Chorus) (music and lyrics by Roger Edens), "Minstrel Show Sequence" (with Mickey Rooney, Ray McDonald, Virginia Weidler, Richard Quine, Annie Rooney, and the MGM Studio Chorus) (includes "Minstrel Show" [music and lyrics by Roger Edens], "Blackout over Broadway" [music by Burton Lane, lyrics by Ralph Freed], "F. D. R. Jones" [music and lyrics by Harold J. Rome, additional material by Roger Edens], "Waiting for the Robert E. Lee" [music by Lewis F. Muir, lyrics by L. Wolfe Gilbert], and "Babes on Broadway" [music by Burton Lane, lyrics by Ralph Freed])

WE MUST HAVE MUSIC (1942)

This lengthy short was made to show audiences the inner workings of the MGM Music Department. The title is taken from the Garland song that opens the short, "We Must Have Music," which she and Tony Martin had recorded on December 22, 1940, and filmed for the finale to 1941's *Ziegfeld Girl*. The song was replaced by a much grander finale, and MGM cleverly used the outtake for this short. This is the only known existing footage of the cut number. Also included in the short is some behind-the-scenes footage of a rehearsal of "Hoe Down" from Garland and Rooney's *Babes on Broadway*, followed by a clip of the number from the film.

FOR ME AND MY GAL (1942)

Producer: Arthur Freed
Director: Busby Berkeley
Screenplay: Richard Sherman, Fred Finklehoffe, and Sid Silvers; original story by Howard Emmett Rogers ("The Big Time")

Main Cast: Judy Garland as Jo Hayden, George Murphy as Jimmy K. Metcalfe, Gene Kelly as Harry Palmer (his screen debut), Marta Eggerth as Eve Minard, Ben Blue as Sid Simms, Richard Quine as Danny Hayden, Keenan Wynn as Eddie Melton, Horace (Stephen) McNally as Mr. Waring, Lucille Norman as Lily Duncan

Garland Songs: "Jimmy K. Metcalfe & Co." Sequence (includes "The Doll Shop" [music and lyrics by Roger Edens], "Don't Leave Me Daddy" [music and lyrics by Joe Verges], and "By the Beautiful Sea" [music by Harry Carroll, lyrics by Harold Atteridge]) (with George Murphy and Lucille Norman), "For Me and My Gal" (with Gene Kelly) (music by George W. Meyer, lyrics by Edgar Leslie and E. Ray Goetz, additional material by Roger Edens), "When You Wore a Tulip" (with Gene Kelly) (music by Percy Wenrich, lyrics by Jack Mahoney), "After You've Gone" (music by Turner Layton, lyrics by Henry Creamer), "'Till We Meet Again" (partial) (music by Richard A. Whiting, lyrics by Raymond B. Egan), "Ballin' the Jack" (with Gene Kelly) (music by Chris Smith, lyrics by James Henry Burris), "How You Gonna Keep 'Em Down on the Farm?" (music by Walter Donaldson, lyrics by Sam M. Lewis and Joe Young), "Where Do We Go from Here?" (with the King's Men and the MGM Studio Chorus) (music by Percy Wenrich, lyrics by Howard Johnson), "YMCA Montage" (includes "It's a Long Way to Tipperary" [music by Jack Judge, lyrics by Harry Williams], "Smiles" [music by Lee M. Roberts, lyrics by J. Will Callahan], and "Pack Up Your Troubles in Your Old Kit Bag" [music by Felix Powell, lyrics by George Asaf]), "When Johnny Comes Marching Home (with the MGM Studio Chorus) (music and lyrics by Louis Lambert, additional material by Roger Edens), "For Me and My Gal" (finale) (with Gene Kelly and the MGM Studio Chorus) (music by George W. Meyer, lyrics by Edgar Leslie and E. Ray Goetz, additional material by Roger Edens), "Don't Bite the Hand That's Feeding You" (outtake) (music by James Morgan, lyrics by Thomas Holer), "Three Cheers for the Yanks" (with Six Hits and a Miss and the MGM Studio Chorus) (music by Hugh Martin, lyrics by Ralph Blane), "For Me and My Gal (original finale) (with George Murphy, Gene Kelly, and the MGM Studio Chorus) (music by George W. Meyer, lyrics by Edgar Leslie and E. Ray Goetz, additional material by Roger Edens)

PRESENTING LILY MARS (1943)

Producer: Joseph Pasternak
Director: Norman Taurog
Screenplay: Richard Connell and Gladys Lehman; based on the novel by Booth Tarkington

Main Cast: Judy Garland as Lily Mars, Van Heflin as John ("Thorny") Thornway, Fay Bainter as Mrs. Thornway, Richard Carlson as Owen Vail, Spring Byington as Mrs. Mars, Marta Eggerth as Isobel Rekay, Connie Gilchrist as Frankie, Leonid Kinskey as Leo, Patricia Barker as Poppy, Janet Chapman as Violet, Annabelle Logan Rosie, Douglas Croft as Davey, Ray McDonald as Charlie Potter, Tommy Dorsey and His Orchestra as Themselves, Bob Crosby and His Orchestra as Themselves, the Wilde Twins as Themselves, Charles Walters as Specialty Dancer (Garland's dance partner in the finale), Joe Yule (Mickey Rooney's real-life father) as Mike the Stage Doorman

Garland Songs: "Tom, the Piper's Son" (music by Burton Lane, lyrics by E. Y. Harburg), "Every Little Movement Has a Meaning of Its Own" (with Mary Kent for Connie Gilchrist) (music by K. Hoscnha, lyrics by Otto Harbach), "When I Look at You" (music by Walter Jurmann, lyrics by Paul Francis Webster), "When I Look at You" (Comedy Version, a.k.a. Caro Mona) (music by Walter Jurmann, lyrics by Paul Francis Webster, additional material by Roger Edens), "A Russian Rhapsody," "Finale" (with Charles Walters, Tommy Dorsey and His Orchestra, and the MGM Studio Chorus) (includes "Where There's Music" [music and lyrics by Roger Edens], "Its Three O'Clock in the Morning" [music by Julian Robledo, lyrics by Dorothy Terris], "Broadway Rhythm" [music by Nacio Herb Brown, lyrics by Arthur Freed]), "Paging Mr. Greenback" (outtake) (with the MGM Studio Chorus) (music by Sammy Fain, lyrics by E. Y. Harburg), Unused Medley (cut from finale sequence) (with the MGM Studio Chorus) (includes "St. Louis Blues" [music and lyrics by W. C. Handy], "It's a Long Way to Tipperary" [music by Jack Judge, lyrics by Harry Williams], "In the Shade of the Old Apple Tree" [music by Edward Van Astyne, lyrics by Harry Williams])

GIRL CRAZY (1943)

Producer: Arthur Freed
Director: Norman Taurog
Screenplay: Fred Finklehoffe
Music: George Gershwin
Lyrics by: Ira Gershwin
Based on musical play *Girl Crazy* by Guy Bolton and Jack McGowan
"I Got Rhythm" number directed by Busby Berkeley

Main Cast: Mickey Rooney as Danny Churchill Jr., Judy Garland as Ginger Gray, Gil Stratton as Bud Livermore, Robert E. Strickland as Henry Lathrop, Rags Ragland as Rags, June Allyson as

Specialty Number, Nancy Walker as Polly Williams, Guy Kibbee as Dean Phineas Armour, Frances Rafferty as Marjorie Tait, Henry O'Neill as Mr. Churchill Sr., Howard Freeman as Governor Tait, Tommy Dorsey and His Orchestra as Themselves

Garland Songs: All music and lyrics by George and Ira Gershwin. "Bidin' My Time" (with the King's Men and the MGM Studio Chorus), "Could You Use Me?" (with Mickey Rooney), "Embraceable You" (with Henry Kruze, P. Hanna, G. Mershon, H. Stanton, E. Newton, Tommy Dorsey and His Orchestra, and the MGM Studio Chorus), "But Not for Me," "I Got Rhythm" (with Mickey Rooney, Six Hits and a Miss, the Music Maids, Hal Hopper, Trudy Erwin, Bobbie Canvin, Tommy Dorsey and His Orchestra, and the MGM Studio Chorus), "Bronco Busters" (outtake) (with Mickey Rooney, Nancy Walker, and the MGM Studio Orchestra and Chorus), "Embraceable You" (deleted reprise/outtake) (with Mickey Rooney)

THOUSANDS CHEER (1943)
Producer: Joe Pasternak
Director: George Sidney
Original Screenplay: Paul Jarrico and Richard Collins; based on their story "Private Miss Jones"

Garland guest starred as herself in the "All-Star MGM Parade" of performers that came toward the end of the film. This was Garland's first appearance in Technicolor since *The Wizard of Oz* in 1939.

Main Cast: Kathryn Grayson as Kathryn Jones, Gene Kelly as Eddie Marsh, Mary Astor as Hyllary Jones, John Boles as Colonel William Jones, Ben Blue as Chuck Polansky, Frances Rafferty as Marie Corbino, Jose Iturbi as Himself; Guest Stars: Judy Garland, Mickey Rooney, Red Skelton, Eleanor Powell, Lucille Ball, Ann Sothern, Virginia O'Brien, Frank Morgan, Lena Horne, Marsha Hunt, Marilyn Maxwell, Donna Reed, Margaret O'Brien, June Allyson, Gloria DeHaven, John Conte, Sara Haden, Don Loper, Maxine Barrat, Kay Kyser and His Orchestra, Bob Crosby and His Orchestra, Benny Carter and His Band

Garland Song: "The Joint Is Really Jumpin' Down at Carnegie Hall" (with Jose Iturbi at the piano) (music by Hugh Martin, lyrics by Ralph Blane, additional material by Roger Edens)

MEET ME IN ST. LOUIS (1944)
Producer: Arthur Freed
Director: Vincente Minnelli
Assistant Director: Wallace Worsley
Screenplay: Irving Brecher, Fred Finklehoffe; from the novel by Sally Benson; uncredited script contributions: Sally Benson, Doris Gilbert, Sarah Y. Mason, Victor Heerman, William Ludwig

Main Cast: Judy Garland as Esther Smith, Margaret O'Brien as "Tootie" Smith, Mary Astor as Mrs. Anna Smith, Lucille Bremer as Rose Smith, Leon Ames as Alonzo Smith, Tom Drake as John Truett, Marjorie Main as Katie the maid, Harry Davenport as Grandpa, June Lockhart as Lucille Ballard, Henry H. Daniels Jr. as Lon Smith Jr., Joan Carroll as Agnes Smith, Chill Wills as Mr. Neely

Garland Songs: "Meet Me In St. Louis, Louis" (with Lucille Bremer, Joan Carroll, Harry Davenport, and the MGM Studio Chorus) (music by Kerry Mills, lyrics by Andrew B. Sterling), "The Boy Next Door" (music by Hugh Martin, lyrics by Ralph Blane), "Skip to My Lou" (with Lucille Bremer and the MGM Studio Chorus) (traditional with new music and lyrics by Hugh Martin and Ralph Blane), "Under the Bamboo Tree" (with Margaret O'Brien) (music and lyrics by Bob Cole), "Over the Bannister" (music by Conrad Salinger, lyrics by Roger Edens), "The Trolley Song" (with the MGM Studio Chorus) (music by Hugh Martin, lyrics by Ralph Blane), "Have Yourself a Merry Little Christmas" (music by Hugh Martin, lyrics by Ralph Blane), "Boys and Girls Like You and Me" (outtake) (music by Richard Rodgers, lyrics by Oscar Hammerstein II)

COMMAND PERFORMANCE (US Army Signal Corps—1944)

This edition of the radio show *Command Performance* was filmed on March 5, 1944, and released as "Army-Navy Screen Magazine No. 20" by the US Army Signal Corps for broadcast both in the states and for the troops overseas. It features emcee Bob Hope introducing a host of performers, including Betty Hutton and Lana Turner (who takes a soldier's request to sizzle a steak in front of the microphone so they could hear it!), as well as Garland engaging in some quick banter with Hope and then singing "Over the Rainbow."

This is the only known footage of Garland performing her signature song as she sang it in dozens of radio shows and other live performances throughout the 1940s. She's radiant. The look on her face and in her eyes when she hits that last note is pure magic. For this reason, it's included here even though it wasn't filmed by or at MGM.

THE CLOCK (1945)
Producer: Arthur Freed
Director: Vincente Minnelli
Assistant Director: Al Shenberg
Screenplay: Robert Nathan and Joseph Schrank; based on a story by Paul Gallico and Pauline Gallico

This was Garland's dramatic debut.

Main Cast: Judy Garland as Alice Mayberry, Robert Walker as Corporal Joe Allen, James Gleason as Al Henry, Keenan Wynn as the Drunk, Marshall Thompson as Bill, Lucille Gleason as Mrs. Al Henry, Ruth Brady as Helen; uncredited: Moyna MacGill as Woman in Restaurant, Arthur Freed, Roger Edens, Robert Nathan, Terry Moore, Ruby Dandridge

THE HARVEY GIRLS (1946)
Producer: Arthur Freed
Associate Producer: Roger Edens
Director: George Sidney
Screenplay: Edmund Beloin, Nathaniel Curtis, Harry Crane, James O'Hanlon, and Samson Raphaelson; additional dialogue by Kay Van Riper; based on the book by Samuel Hopkins Adams; original story by Eleanore Griffin and William Rankin

Main Cast: Judy Garland as Susan Bradley, John Hodiak as Ned Trent, Ray Bolger as Chris Maule, Preston Foster as Judge Sam Purvis, Virginia O'Brien as Alma, Angela Lansbury as Em, Marjorie Main as Sonora Cassidy, Chill Wills as H. H. Hartsey, Kenny Baker as Terry O'Halloran, Selena Royle as Miss Bliss, Cyd Charisse as Deborah

Garland Songs: Unless otherwise noted, all music by Harry Warren, lyrics by Johnny Mercer. "In the Valley Where the Evening Sun Goes Down," "On the Atchison, Topeka, and the Santa Fe" (with Cyd Charisse, Virginia O'Brien, Marjorie Main, Ray Bolger, Benny Carter, the Seckler Group, the Williams Brothers [Andy, Bob, and Don], and the MGM Studio Chorus) (additional music and lyrics by Kay Thompson and Ralph Blane), "Training Montage" (The Train Must Be Fed) (with Edward Earle, Selena Royle, Marjorie Main, Joe Karnes, Elva Kellogg, Virginia O'Brien, Cyd Charisse, and the MGM Studio Chorus) (music and lyrics by Harry Warren, Conrad Salinger, and Roger Edens), "It's a Great Big World" (with Virginia O'Brien and Marion Doenges for Cyd Charisse), "Swing Your Partner Round and Round" (with Marjorie Main and the MGM Studio Chorus), "In the Valley Where the Evening Sun Goes Down" (deleted reprise) (with Kenny Baker and the MGM Studio Chorus), "March of the Doagies" (outtake) (with Joe Karnes, Frank Laine, Don Ellis, Eugene Dorian, Ralph Blane, Don Williams, and the MGM Studio Chorus), "March of the Doagies" (outtake reprise) (with the MGM Studio Chorus), "Hayride" (outtake/deleted) (Ray Bolger, Judy Garland, and the MGM Studio Chorus), "My Intuition" (outtake) (with John Hodiak)

ZIEGFELD FOLLIES OF 1946
Producer: Arthur Freed
Associate Producer: Roger Edens
Directors: Vincente Minnelli, George Sidney, Lemuel Ayres, Roy Del Ruth, Merrill Pye, and Norman Taurog
Screenplay: Robert Alton, John Murray Anderson, Lemuel Ayers, Ralph Blane, Guy Bolton, Allen Boretz, Irving Brecher, Eddie Cantor, Erik Charell, Harry Crane, Roger Edens, Joseph Erons,

David Freedman, Devery Freeman, Everett Freeman, E. Y. Harburg, Lou Holtz, Cal Howard, Al Lewis, Robert Lewis, Max Liebman, Don Loper, Eugene Loring, Wilkie Mahoney, Hugh Martin, Jack McGowan, William Noble, James O'Hanlon, Samson Raphaelson, Philip Rapp, Bill Schorr, Joseph Schrank, Frank Sullivan, Kay Thompson, Charles Walters, and Edgar Allan Woolf

Another guest spot for Garland. She played the "great lady" in the "A Great Lady Has an Interview" musical segment written by Kay Thompson and Roger Edens, commonly known as "Madame Crematante." Garland recorded, rehearsed, and filmed her sequence from July 6, 1944, to July 21, 1944 (after completing *Meet Me in St. Louis*). The film was given a quick roadshow engagement on August 13, 1945, but didn't go into general release until April 8, 1946.

TILL THE CLOUDS ROLL BY (1946)
Producer: Arthur Freed
Director: Richard Whorf (Judy Garland's numbers directed by Vincente Minnelli)
Screenplay: Myles Connolly and Jean Holloway; story by Guy Bolton, adapted by George Wells; based on the life and music of Jerome Kern

Garland had a small guest spot playing the real-life Broadway legend Marilyn Miller. In this guest spot, she gets a couple of dramatic scenes as well as three numbers.

Main Cast: Robert Walker as Jerome Kern, Judy Garland as Marilyn Miller, Lucille Bremer as Sally Hessler, Joan Wells as Sally as a young girl, Van Heflin as James I. Hessler, Paul Langton as Oscar Hammerstein; Guest Stars: June Allyson, Kathryn Grayson, Lena Horne, Van Johnson, Tony Martin, Dinah Shore, Frank Sinatra, Gower Champion, Cyd Charisse, Angela Lansbury, Ray McDonald, Virginia O'Brien, Caleb Peterson, William "Bill" Phillips, Wilde Twins (Lyn and Lee), Cameo by Esther Williams

Garland Songs: Music for all songs composed by Jerome Kern. "Look for the Silver Lining" (lyrics by Buddy DeSylva), "Sunny"/"Who?" (with the MGM Studio Chorus) (lyrics by Otto Harbach and Oscar Hammerstein II), "D'Ye Love Me" (outtake) (lyrics by Otto Harbach and Oscar Hammerstein II)

THE PIRATE (1948)
Producer: Arthur Freed
Director: Vincente Minnelli
Screenplay: Albert Hackett and Frances Goodrich; based on the play by S. N. Behrman as produced by the Playwrights Producing Company and the Theatre Guild (some sources also credit Lillian Braun, Anita Loos, Joseph L. Mankiewicz, Joseph Than, and Wilkie Mahoney as having contributed to the writing)

Main Cast: Judy Garland as Manuela Alva, Gene Kelly as Serafin, Walter Slezak as Don Pedro Vargas, Gladys Cooper as Aunt Inez, Reginald Owen as the Advocate, George Zucco as the Viceroy, the Nicholas Brothers as Specialty Dancers

Garland Songs: All songs written by Cole Porter. "Mack the Black," "You Can Do No Wrong," "Love of My Life," "Be a Clown" (with Gene Kelly), "Voodoo" (outtake)

EASTER PARADE (1948)
Producer: Arthur Freed
Director: Charles Walters
Screenplay: Sidney Shelton, Frances Goodrich, and Albert Hackett; based on a story by Frances Goodrich and Albert Hackett

Main Cast: Judy Garland as Hannah Brown, Fred Astaire as Don Hewes, Peter Lawford as Jonathan Harrow III, Ann Miller as Natine Hale, Jules Munshin as Francois, the Heat Waiter, Clinton Sundberg as Mike the Bartender

Garland Songs: All songs written by Irving Berlin. "I Want to Go Back to Michigan," "A Fella with an Umbrella" (with Peter Lawford), "Medley" (with Fred Astaire) ("I Love a Piano," "Snooky Ookums," "When the Midnight Choo Chho Leaves for Alabam"), "It Only Happens When I Dance with You," "A Couple of Swells" (with Fred Astaire), "Better Luck Next Time," "Easter Parade" (with Fred Astaire and the MGM Studio Chorus), "Mr. Monotony" (outtake)

WORDS AND MUSIC (1948)
Producer: Arthur Freed
Director: Norman Taurog
Screenplay: Fred Finklehoffe; story by Guy Bolton and Jean Holloway; adaptation by Ben Feiner Jr. (with Jean Holloway, Guy Bolton, Isabel Lennart, and Jack Mintz); based on the lives and music of Richard Rodgers and Lorenz Hart

Garland made another guest appearance, playing herself in a party scene and singing "I Wish I Were in Love Again" with Mickey Rooney and "Johnny One Note." Both songs written by Richard Rodgers (music) and Lorenz Hart (lyrics).

Main Cast: Mickey Rooney as Lorenz Hart, Perry Como as Eddie Lorrison Anders, Ann Sothern as Joyce Harmon, Tom Drake as Richard Rodgers, Betty Garrett as Peggy McNeil, Janet Leigh as Dorothy Feiner, Marshall Thompson as Herbert Fields; Guest Stars: June Allyson, Judy Garland, Lena Horne, Gene Kelly, Cyd Charisse, Mel Torme, Vera-Ellen, Dee Turnell, Emory Parnell, Helen Spring, Edward Earl, Allyn McLerie, The Blackburn Twins

IN THE GOOD OLD SUMMERTIME (1949)

Producer: Joe Pasternak

Director: Robert Z. Leonard

Screenplay: Albert Hackett, Frances Goodrich, and Ivan Tors; from a screenplay by Samson Raphaelson and a play by Miklós László (*The Shop around the Corner*)

Main Cast: Judy Garland as Veronica Fisher, Van Johnson as Andrew Larkin, S. Z. ("Cuddles") Sakall as Otto Oberkugen, Spring Byington as Nellie Burke, Buster Keaton as Hickey, Marcia Van Dyke as Louise Parkson, Clinton Sundberg as Rudy Hansen

Garland Songs: "Meet Me Tonight in Dreamland" (music by Leo Friedman, lyrics by Beth Slater Whitson), "Put Your Arms Around Me, Honey" (music by Albert Von Tilzer, lyrics by June McRee), "Play That Barbershop Chord" (with the King's Men) (music by Lewis Muir, lyrics by William Tracy and Ballard MacDonald), "I Don't Care" (music by Harry Sutton, lyrics by Jean Lenox), "Merry Christmas" (music by Fred Spielman, lyrics by Janice Torre), "Finale" ("In the Good Old Summertime") (outtake) (with Van Johnson and the King's Men) (music by George Evans, lyrics by Ren Shields), "Last Night When We Were Young" (outtake) (music by Harold Arlen, lyrics by E. Y. Harburg)

ANNIE GET YOUR GUN (1949)

Garland did not complete the film, but it's listed here because it's the only film that Garland was unable to complete and yet had recorded the complete score and filmed two musical numbers and some dramatic scenes prior to her departure.

Garland Songs: All songs written by Irving Berlin. "Doin' What Comes Natur'lly" (with Peter Price, Sharon McManus, Carol Sue Sherwood, and Jeanette Williams), "You Can't Get a Man with a Gun," "There's No Business Like Show Business" (with Howard Keel, Frank Morgan, Keenan Wynn, Bill Seclar, and Mac McLain), "They Say It's Wonderful" (with Howard Keel), "There's No Business Like Show Business" (reprise), "I'm an Indian, Too" (with the MGM Studio Chorus), "The Girl That I Marry" (reprise), "I Got the Sun in the Morning," "Anything You Can Do (I Can Do Better)" (with Howard Keel), "Let's Go West Again" (outtake)

SUMMER STOCK (1950)

Producer: Joe Pasternak

Director: Charles Walters

Screenplay: George Wells and Sy Gomberg; story by Sy Gomberg

Main Cast: Judy Garland as Jane Falbury, Gene Kelly as Joe Ross, Eddie Bracken as Orville Wingait, Gloria DeHaven as Abigail Falbury, Marjorie Main as Esmé, Phil Silvers as Herb Blake, Ray Collins as Jasper Wingait, Nita Bieber as Sarah Higgins, Carleton Carpenter as Artie, Hans Conried as Harrison Keath

JUDY GARLAND'S MGM FILMOGRAPHY

Garland Songs: All songs written by Harry Warren (music) and Mack Gordon (lyrics) unless otherwise noted. "If You Feel Like Singing, Sing," "(Howdy Neighbor) Happy Harvest" (with the MGM Studio Chorus), "You Wonderful You" (with Gene Kelly) (lyrics by Saul Chaplin and Jack Brooks), "Friendly Star," "All for You" (with Gene Kelly and the MGM Studio Chorus) (music and lyrics by Saul Chaplin), "You Wonderful You" (reprise) (with Gene Kelly) (lyrics by Saul Chaplin and Jack Brooks), "Get Happy" (music by Harold Arlen, lyrics by Ted Koheler), "Finale" ([Howdy Neighbor] Happy Harvest) (with Gene Kelly, Phil Silvers, and the MGM Studio Chorus)

OTHER FILM PROJECTS

Judy Garland was considered, even in passing, for every musical made in Hollywood during the Golden Age. That's an exaggeration, but her talent was so revered that she was always in demand and usually at the top of most wish lists. At MGM she was regularly the first choice for the latest musical, especially in the Freed Unit (which she helped create). Everyone wanted to work with her. Songwriters Oscar Hammerstein II and Jerry Herman both exclaimed that when they wrote a song, they would imagine how "Judy Garland would sing it." As a result, Garland's name was attached to many projects that either did not get past the planning stages or were eventually made with other stars. Columnists Hedda Hopper and Louella Parsons regularly mentioned Garland's name in news blurbs about a variety of film projects. Some of the mentions are most likely the product of the MGM publicity department. So, while many projects were, in fact, legitimate, many were fictitious.

THIS TIME IT'S LOVE/BORN TO DANCE (1935/1936)

This is the first known film project that Garland was considered for after signing with MGM in September 1935. The 1975 book *Young Judy* by David Dahl and Barry Kehoe features the contents of a letter from October 1935 in which Garland's father, Frank Gumm, relayed to their family friend John Perkins in Lancaster, California, that Garland was to start production on *This Time It's Love* in January 1936 with an April 1936 release date. The film would star Robert Montgomery and Jessie Matthews, with Garland playing opposite Buddy Ebsen. *This Time It's Love* eventually became *Born to Dance*, starring Eleanor Powell, and was released in 1936. On March 10, 1936, Cole Porter noted in his diary that to his "great joy," *Born to Dance* would include "Buddy Ebsen and Judy Garland." Garland's part was written out before she would have begun any work on the film.

LA BELLE DOLLY (1935/1936)

In *Variety*'s December 18, 1935, issue, there is a short blurb (dated December 17) that MGM was preparing an adaptation of Edgar Allan Woolf's *La Belle Dolly* as Garland's first film, costarring the seventy-four-year-old opera diva Madame (Ernestine) Schumann-Heink. Schumann-Heink was a legendary opera star who was forced out of retirement when she lost everything in the Crash of 1929; she worked as a coach and, of course, singer. Harold W. Cohen picked up the story for his column "The Drama Desk" on December 24, 1935, but mentioned only Mme. Schumann-Heink and Woolf's names. It's unknown whether the intent was to have Garland sing in a more operatic style. This role sounds more like the kind that would be played by Deanna Durbin rather than Garland. The property had been at MGM for at least a few years. In 1933, *Variety* noted that the film would be made starring the young Jackie Cooper with the older actress Marie Dressler. Details about the plot are unknown, although it appears that it was probably a typical story about an older mentor with a younger performer and/or relative.

THE GREAT ZIEGFELD (1935)

Universal originally owned the rights to this screen adaptation of Florenz Ziegfeld's amazing life. In 1934, Garland and her sisters were noted as one of the acts that would appear in the film. There are no records of any studio contracts being signed with Universal for either Garland alone or with her sisters. If a contract were created, it would have been for a one-picture deal and not the standard long-term contract for new contract players. An article in *Variety* on January 29, 1935, about vaudeville acts in Hollywood noted, "Francis [*sic*] Garland landed a part in Universal's 'Great Ziegfeld.' In *Variety*'s November 20, 1935, issue, Garland's connection to the film was mentioned again. By this time, she had been signed by MGM. The notice reported that producer Sam Katz was looking for a story to star Garland and went on to claim that Garland went to MGM with the Ziegfeld project when it was transferred from Universal, that Universal had changed her name to Garland, and that "the studio paid little attention to her until some of the execs heard her sing at a night spot several months after she came on the lot." This *Variety* notice was obviously given to the paper by MGM, probably to get some press out about their upcoming Ziegfeld film and Garland, who was already making waves with her radio and personal appearances. MGM released their version of *The Great Ziegfeld* in 1936 to critical and financial acclaim, becoming the second musical to win the Oscar for Best Picture (the first was MGM's *The Broadway Melody* in 1929).

YOURS AND MINE (1935)

In his introduction of Garland for the November 15, 1935, broadcast of the radio show *The Shell Chateau Hour*, Wallace Beery mentions that since her first appearance on the same show in October, she had been signed by MGM (in reality, she signed with MGM in September) and Sam Katz had "written her into his next picture *Yours and Mine*." This was probably more studio PR than actual plans, created to build up Judy's importance to an audience still fairly unaware of her existence.

OUR GANG FOLLIES (a.k.a. OUR GANG FOLLIES OF 1936) (1935)

In December 1935, MGM planned to loan Garland to the Hal Roach Studios for an *Our Gang Follies* film. The studio changed its mind at the last minute, possibly because *This Time It's Love* had become *Born to Dance* with Garland still attached to it in March 1936. She ended up working on a test short (with Deanna Durbin) for MGM's exhibitor's convention in Chicago, Illinois, in May 1936, which was followed by work on the short *Every Sunday* in June 1936, also with Durbin. In the summer of 1936, the deal to loan her to Fox for *Pigskin Parade* came along, which was a better showcase for her talents than an *Our Gang* film would have been.

GONE WITH THE WIND (1939)

Producer David O. Selznick originally wanted Garland to play the role of Scarlett O'Hara's younger sister, Colleen. Garland, however, was busy making that other masterpiece of 1939: *The Wizard of Oz*. The part of Colleen went to Garland's fellow MGM contract player and Andy Hardy's girlfriend, Ann Rutherford.

GOOD NEWS (1939)

Arthur Freed planned a remake of the 1930 MGM college musical *Good News* (based on the popular 1927 Broadway musical of the same name) as Garland and Rooney's follow-up to *Babes in Arms* (1939). MGM studio chief Louis B. Mayer suggested he build a new musical around the Gershwin song "Strike Up the Band" because it "sounded patriotic." *Good News* was again suggested for Garland and Rooney in 1943, but that didn't pan out either. Eventually, it was made by the Freed Unit in 1947, starring June Allyson and Peter Lawford.

VERY WARM FOR MAY (1942)

After *Babes on Broadway* and just prior to *For Me and My Gal*, producer Arthur Freed wanted to film the Oscar Hammerstein/Jerome Kern show "Very Warm for May" starring Garland with Ray McDonald and Marta Eggerth or Kathryn Grayson. But the plot was too similar to the three previous "Let's Put on a Show!" films. Freed wanted to keep moving forward with the advancement of the film musical, and this plot would be a step backward. He eventually turned it over to fellow MGM producer Jack Cummings, and it became 1944's *Broadway Rhythm* starring Ginny Sims and George Murphy.

THE BELLE OF NEW YORK (1943/1945)

Garland's involvement in this project dates back to at least 1943. In an October 14, 1943, letter to Oscar Hammerstein, producer Arthur Freed mentions, "Regarding the Belle of New York. We have a fine outline for the story and I am still counting on you and Dick [Richard] Rodgers to do the score." Hammerstein replied on June 7, 1943: "Regarding the Judy Garland picture you spoke to Dick and me about, we are looking forward to receiving a story layout whenever you have one."

Freed put *The Belle of New York* on the production schedule in 1945, starring Garland and Fred Astaire. In his book about the Freed Unit, *The World of Entertainment! Hollywood's Greatest Musicals*, Hugh Fordin states, "At one time the project had to be aborted during rehearsals because Judy Garland, Astaire's costar, dropped out." No mention of any time period is made, although it was most likely in 1945 when Astaire was on the MGM lot filming *Ziegfeld Follies*. Freed finally made *The Belle of New York* in 1952 with Astaire and Vera-Ellen.

THE RAZOR'S EDGE (1945)

Garland really wanted the role of Sophie (eventually played by Anne Baxter) in the 1946 version of the W. Somerset Maugham novel. Baxter won a Supporting Actress Oscar for the role. 20th Century Fox wanted Garland as well, but in 1945 there was no way MGM would loan their top star to a rival studio for a gritty drama, especially when that star was Hollywood's singing sweetheart, Judy Garland. One of Garland's former lovers, Tyrone Power, also stars in the film. It would have been fascinating to see the two together in a film. Perhaps Garland would have been nominated for, and maybe even won, the Supporting Oscar as well?

YOLANDA AND THE THIEF (1947)

Garland was never seriously in the running for this film. It was planned for production at the same time as *The Harvey Girls*. Because *Yolanda* was being directed by her husband, Vincente Minnelli, and was to star Fred Astaire, Garland wanted to be in it rather than *The Harvey Girls* and tried to persuade producer Arthur Freed to switch the roles. He convinced her that *The Harvey Girls* was a better showcase of her talents. He was right.

ROMANCE ON THE HIGH SEAS (1948)

Garland was allegedly on the Warner Bros. list of possible replacements for the film's original lead, Betty Hutton. The film's director, Michael Curtiz, instead auditioned and hired then band singer Doris Day, which marked the beginning of her dazzling film career. One wonders what magic Garland could have brought to Day's big hit song from the film, "It's Magic."

TAKE ME OUT TO THE BALL GAME (1948)

Gene Kelly and Stanley Donen had turned in a story idea to producer Arthur Freed that included Kathryn Grayson as the lead. Freed swapped out Grayson with Garland. Garland had recently had a tough time filming her numbers for *Words and Music* and beginning (and then being taken out of) the production of *The Barkleys of Broadway*, so Freed replaced her with Esther Williams. The Rodgers and Hammerstein song "Boys and Girls Like You and Me," which was deleted from *Meet Me in St. Louis*, was here sung by Frank Sinatra to Betty Garrett but also deleted.

JUDY GARLAND'S MGM FILMOGRAPHY

SHOW BOAT (1940s/1951)

This is another film that had been earmarked for Garland for several years during her tenure at MGM. Producer Arthur Freed had wanted to remake the Oscar Hammerstein/Jerome Kern milestone since becoming a producer in 1939 (and probably before). He had the studio finance a 1946 revival on Broadway after purchasing the rights from Universal, which previously had made an early 1929 part-talkie film and a well-loved 1936 version. Freed wanted Garland to play the supporting role of the tragic singer Julie. The Freed version wouldn't get made until 1951, after Garland had left the studio. Garland fans have always speculated on how different the role and the film would have been if Garland had the chance to play the role. It had also been argued (with some validity) that if Garland had stayed at MGM, her status as the studio's premier musical leading lady would most likely have prevented her from being cast in a secondary role that disappears from most of the last half of the story.

APPENDIX B

MGM PRERECORDINGS AND RECORDS

The following is a list of the recordings Garland made for her MGM films, including outtakes. It's a minor miracle that only a few sessions are lost. At least a few takes, if not all, that were "printed" (saved for use by the MGM audio technicians) are extant. Beginning in the early 1930s, MGM began recording the music for their films in an early version of what is now called "multitrack" recording. They placed microphones around the recording stage to create what they called "stems," which were separate tracks that they then mixed to make a balanced mono track. The recordings were transferred from optical film to tape in the late 1940s and then saved again after an edict came down to destroy them; most of the recordings have been restored and, where all of the stems survived, remixed into stereo. Only *Meet Me in St. Louis* (1944) and *Ziegfeld Follies of 1946* (1946) have been made available on home media with all of the music (songs and background scoring) in full stereo. Most of the information here was taken from the surviving *Daily Music Report* sheets that detail all of the recording sessions for the films. Note that some of the titles are different from what the official titles became. In those instances, both the original title and the final titles are noted.

Recording Date	Title	Film
June 30, 1936	Americana	*Every Sunday* (1936)
June 30, 1936	Opera vs. Jazz	*Every Sunday* (1936)
March 5, 1937	Everybody Sing	*Broadway Melody of 1938* (1937)
March 14, 1937	Your Broadway and My Broadway	*Broadway Melody of 1938* (1937)
April 16, 1937	Yours and Mine (outtake)	*Broadway Melody of 1938* (1937)
May 7, 1937	(Dear Mr. Gable) You Made Me Love You	*Broadway Melody of 1938* (1937)
August 1, 1937	Feelin' Like a Million	Rehearsal Recording
August 26, 1937	Swing, Mr. Mendelssohn	*Everybody Sing* (1938)
August 27, 1937	Who Knows? (Garland never appeared in *Rosalie*, but the MGM music department records note that she recorded this song for the film on this date. The recording has not survived. Nelson Eddy sings the song in the final film.)	*Rosalie* (1937)
September 11, 1937	Sun Showers (outtake)	*Thoroughbreds Don't Cry* (1937)
September 20, 1937	Got a Pair of New Shoes	*Thoroughbreds Don't Cry* (1937)
October 4, 1937	Melody Farm (Down on Melody Farm)	*Everybody Sing* (1938)
October 21, 1937	Bus Sequence	*Everybody Sing* (1938)
October 24, 1937	Got a Pair of New Shoes (thirty-second "walk" version)	*Thoroughbreds Don't Cry* (1937)
November 6, 1937	Silent Night (recorded and filmed November 6 through 8, 1937)	*Silent Night* (1937)
November 8, 1937	Sweet Chariot (Swing Low, Sweet Chariot)	*Everybody Sing* (1938)
December 13, 1937	Finale Ultimo (Shall I Sing a Melody?)	*Everybody Sing* (1938)
December 21, 1937	Why? Because! ("Snooks" number)	*Everybody Sing* (1938)

June 21, 1938	It Never Rains, But What It Pours (first known surviving Garland recording in stereo)	*Love Finds Andy Hardy* (1938)
June 21, 1938	Bei Mir Bist Du Schoen (outtake)	*Love Finds Andy Hardy* (1938)
June 24, 1938	In Between	*Love Finds Andy Hardy* (1938)
June 24, 1938	Meet the Beat of My Heart (partial outtake)	*Love Finds Andy Hardy* (1938)
July 28, 1938	Ten Pins in the Sky	*Listen, Darling* (1938)
September 16, 1938	Zing! Went the Strings of My Heart	*Listen, Darling* (1938)
September 26, 1938	On the Bumpy Road to Love	*Listen, Darling* (1938)
September 30, 1938	If I Only Had a Brain	*The Wizard of Oz* (1939)
September 30, 1938	If I Only Had the Nerve	*The Wizard of Oz* (1939)
September 30, 1938	Wonderful Wizard of Oz (We're Off to See the Wizard) (duo)	*The Wizard of Oz* (1939)
September 30, 1938	Wonderful Wizard of Oz (We're Off to See the Wizard) (trio)	*The Wizard of Oz* (1939)
September 30, 1938	Wonderful Wizard of Oz (We're Off to See the Wizard) (quartet)	*The Wizard of Oz* (1939)
October 6, 1938	The Jitterbug (outtake)	*The Wizard of Oz* (1939)
October 7, 1938	Over the Rainbow	*The Wizard of Oz* (1939)
October 11, 1938	We're Off to See the Wizard (duo) (alternate lyric) (subheaded as "Wonderful Wizard of Oz" and "Lyric")	*The Wizard of Oz* (1939)
October 11, 1938	We're Off to See the Wizard (trio) (alternate lyric) (subheaded as "Wonderful Wizard of Oz" and "Lyric")	*The Wizard of Oz* (1939)
October 11, 1938	We're Off to See the Wizard (quartet) (alternate lyric) (subheaded as "Wonderful Wizard of Oz" and "Lyric")	*The Wizard of Oz* (1939)
October 11, 1938	If I Were King of the Forest	*The Wizard of Oz* (1939)

MGM PRERECORDINGS AND RECORDS

October 17, 1938	Over the Rainbow (deleted reprise—sung live on set; orchestra was recorded on May 6, 1939)	*The Wizard of Oz* (1939)
October 30, 1938	The Merry Old Land of Oz (first session)	*The Wizard of Oz* (1939)
December 14, 1938	Munchkin Musical Sequence	*The Wizard of Oz* (1939)
December 22, 1938	Follow the Yellow Brick Road/You're Off to See the Wizard	*The Wizard of Oz* (1939)
December 22, 1938	The Jitterbug (outtake—new opening chorus with Jack Haley replacing Buddy Ebsen's earlier vocals)	*The Wizard of Oz* (1939)
December 28, 1938	The Merry Old Land of Oz (second session)	*The Wizard of Oz* (1939)
December 30, 1938	The Merry Old Land of Oz (third session)	*The Wizard of Oz* (1939)
January 3, 1939	The Merry Old Land of Oz (fourth session)	*The Wizard of Oz* (1939)
February 28, 1939	If I Only Had a Brain	*The Wizard of Oz* (1939)
May 15, 1939	Good Morning	*Babes in Arms* (1939)
May 15, 1939	Where or When (reprise)	*Babes in Arms* (1939)
May 15, 1939	Opera vs. Jazz	*Babes in Arms* (1939)
May 23, 1939	Babes in Arms	*Babes in Arms* (1939)
May 23, 1939	I Cried for You	*Babes in Arms* (1939)
June 27, 1939	Mistral Show Sequence (including "I'm Just Wild about Harry")	*Babes in Arms* (1939)
June 27, 1939	Finale Sequence (including "God's Country")	*Babes in Arms* (1939)
March 14, 1940	I'm Nobody's Baby	*Andy Hardy Meets Debutante* (1940)
March 14, 1940	Buds Won't Bud (outtake)	*Andy Hardy Meets Debutante* (1940)
April 1, 1940	If I Forget You	Will Rogers Tribute Film (circa 1940)
April 12, 1940	Our Love Affair	*Strike Up the Band* (1940)
April 12, 1940	Nobody	*Strike Up the Band* (1940)
April 23, 1940	Nell of New Rochelle Routine	*Strike Up the Band* (1940)

April 23, 1940	Curse of the Aching Heart (outtake)	*Strike Up the Band* (1940)
May 8, 1940	Alone (only one take was printed and went unused; it was recorded again on May 10, 1940—this May 8 take is not known to exist)	*Andy Hardy Meets Debutante* (1940)
May 10, 1940	All I Do Is Dream of You (outtake)	*Andy Hardy Meets Debutante* (1940)
May 10, 1940	Alone	*Andy Hardy Meets Debutante* (1940)
June 8, 1940	Drummer Boy	*Strike Up the Band* (1940)
June 27, 1940	La Conga	*Strike Up the Band* (1940)
July 10, 1940	Strike Up the Band—Finale	*Strike Up the Band* (1940)
July 10, 1940	Curse of the Aching Heart (outtake) (this was handwritten at the end of this day's report, noting the scene number as 2061 and that Take 4 was kept for use)	*Strike Up the Band* (1940)
August 9, 1940	It's a Great Day for the Irish	*Little Nellie Kelly* (1940)
August 9, 1940	Hansom Cab—Nellie Kelly (Nellie Kelly I Love You)	*Little Nellie Kelly* (1940)
September 9, 1940	Singin' in the Rain	*Little Nellie Kelly* (1940)
September 9, 1940	A Pretty Girl Milking Her Cow (second version in the film)	*Little Nellie Kelly* (1940)
September 9, 1940	Nellie Kelly Waltz (Nellie Kelly I Love You)	*Little Nellie Kelly* (1940)
September 10, 1940	Danny Boy (outtake)	*Little Nellie Kelly* (1940)
September 10, 1940	A Pretty Girl Milking Her Cow (first version in the film)	*Little Nellie Kelly* (1940)
November 13, 1940	I'm Always Chasing Rainbows	*Ziegfeld Girl* (1941)
November 13, 1940	I'm Always Chasing Rainbows—Audition (forty-two-second track)	*Ziegfeld Girl* (1941)
November 13, 1940	Laugh? I Thought I'd Split My Sides	*Ziegfeld Girl* (1941)
December 22, 1940	Finale (includes We Must Have Music outtake and I'm Always Chasing Rainbows outtake)	*Ziegfeld Girl* (1941)

MGM Prerecordings and Records

January 14, 1941	Minnie from Trinidad	*Ziegfeld Girl* (1941)
February 24, 1941	Minnie from Trinidad "new ending" (prerecordings made on this date were just forty-eight seconds)	*Ziegfeld Girl* (1941)
March 19, 1941	The Ziegfeld Girl—Finale (new finale)	*Ziegfeld Girl* (1941)
May 19, 1941	America (outtake)	*Life Begins for Andy Hardy* (1941)
June 4, 1941	Easy to Love (outtake)	*Life Begins for Andy Hardy* (1941)
June 4, 1941	Abide with Me (outtake)	*Life Begins for Andy Hardy* (1941)
June 4, 1941	The Rosary (outtake)	*Life Begins for Andy Hardy* (1941)
June 25, 1941	Easy to Love (partial/outtake)	*Life Begins for Andy Hardy* (1941)
July 18, 1941	How about You?	*Babes on Broadway* (1941)
July 23, 1941	The Rosary (outtake/second session)	*Life Begins for Andy Hardy* (1941)
August 11, 1941	Bombshell from Brazil	*Babes on Broadway* (1941)
August 29, 1941	Hoe Down	*Babes on Broadway* (1941)
September 10, 1941	Chin Up! Cheerio! Carry On!	*Babes on Broadway* (1941)
September 23, 1941	Minstrel Show (including F. D. R. Jones)	*Babes on Broadway* (1941)
September 24, 1941	Babes on Broadway	*Babes on Broadway* (1941)
October 10, 1941	Ghost Theatre Sequence	*Babes on Broadway* (1941)
March 20, 1942	Doll Shop (a.k.a. Jimmy K. Metcalfe & Co. Medley)	*For Me and My Gal* (1942)
March 21, 1942	Ballin' the Jack	*For Me and My Gal* (1942)
March 21, 1942	For Me and My Gal	*For Me and My Gal* (1942)
March 24, 1942	After You've Gone	*For Me and My Gal* (1942)
March 27, 1942	Till We Meet Again	*For Me and My Gal* (1942)
March 27, 1942	Where Do We Go from Here?	*For Me and My Gal* (1942)
March 27, 1942	How You Gonna Keep 'Em Down on the Farm?	*For Me and My Gal* (1942)
March 27, 1942	For Me and My Gal (outtake/original finale)	*For Me and My Gal* (1942)

May 26, 1942	YMCA Montage, includes Smiles, It's a Long Way to Tipperary, and Pack Up Your Troubles in Your Old Kit Bag and Smile, Smile, Smile	*For Me and My Gal* (1942)
May 26, 1942	Vaudeville Montage, includes When You Wore a Tulip and Don't Bite the Hand That's Feeding You (outtake)	*For Me and My Gal* (1942)
May 27, 1942	Three Cheers for the Yanks (outtake)	*For Me and My Gal* (1942)
June 25, 1942	When Johnny Comes Marching Home/For Me and My Gal	*For Me and My Gal* (1942)
June 25, 1942	YMCA Montage Insert (36 and 39 second unnamed Garland vocals)	*For Me and My Gal* (1942)
June 28, 1942	Every Little Movement Has a Meaning of Its Own	*Presenting Lily Mars* (1943)
June 28, 1942	Tom, Tom, the Piper's Son	*Presenting Lily Mars* (1943)
September 18, 1942	When I Look at You	*Presenting Lily Mars* (1943)
September 18, 1942	Caro Mona (When I Look at You parody)	*Presenting Lily Mars* (1943)
October 16, 1942	Paging Mr. Greenback (outtake)	*Presenting Lily Mars* (1943)
December 22, 1942	The Joint Is Really Jumpin' Down at Carnegie Hall	*Thousands Cheer* (1943)
December 29, 1942	I Got Rhythm	*Girl Crazy* (1943)
January 2, 1943	Bronco Busters (outtake)	*Girl Crazy* (1943)
March 4, 1943	Finale Broadway Rhythm	*Presenting Lily Mars* (1943)
March 5, 1943	Finale Routine (Where There's Music medley)	*Presenting Lily Mars* (1943)
March 29, 1943	But Not for Me	*Girl Crazy* (1943)
April 14, 1943	Bidin' My Time	*Girl Crazy* (1943)
April 15, 1943	Embraceable You	*Girl Crazy* (1943)
April 15, 1943	End Title (Embraceable You outtake)	*Girl Crazy* (1943)
April 28, 1943	Could You Use Me?	*Girl Crazy* (1943)
June 9, 1943	Walking in the Garden (Garland humming only)	*Girl Crazy* (1943)

MGM PRERECORDINGS AND RECORDS

November 30, 1943	Boys and Girls Like You and Me (outtake)	*Meet Me in St. Louis* (1944)
November 30, 1943	Over the Bannister	*Meet Me in St. Louis* (1944)
December 1, 1943	Meet Me in St. Louis, Louis	*Meet Me in St. Louis* (1944)
December 2, 1943	Clang Clang Clang Went the Trolley (The Trolley Song)	*Meet Me in St. Louis* (1944)
December 3, 1943	Meet Me in St. Louis, Louis (Esther and Rose duet version)	*Meet Me in St. Louis* (1944)
December 3, 1943	Skip to My Lou	*Meet Me in St. Louis* (1944)
December 4, 1943	The Boy Next Door	*Meet Me in St. Louis* (1944)
December 4, 1943	Have Yourself a Merry Little Christmas	*Meet Me in St. Louis* (1944)
December 17, 1943	Under the Bamboo Tree	*Meet Me in St. Louis* (1944)
July 17, 1944	Madame Crematante (a.k.a. A Great Lady Has an Interview)	*Ziegfeld Follies of 1946* (1946)
January 5, 1944	It's a Great Big World	*The Harvey Girls* (1946)
January 8, 1945	On the Atchison, Topeka, and the Santa Fe	*The Harvey Girls* (1946)
January 13, 1945	Harvey Girls Training Sequence (The Train Must Be Fed)	*The Harvey Girls* (1946)
February 15, 1945	In the Valley (Where the Evening Sun Goes Down) (impromptu recording with Kay Thompson)	*The Harvey Girls* (1946)
February 16, 1945	In the Valley (Where the Evening Sun Goes Down)	*The Harvey Girls* (1946)
February 16, 1945	My Intuition (outtake)	*The Harvey Girls* (1946)
February 17, 1945	In the Valley (Where the Evening Sun Goes Down) (second recording)	*The Harvey Girls* (1946)
February 17, 1945	March of the Doagies (outtake)	*The Harvey Girls* (1946)
February 17, 1945	March of the Doagies (outtake reprise)	*The Harvey Girls* (1946)

February 19, 1945	Hayride (outtake)	*The Harvey Girls* (1946)
February 19, 1945	Swing Your Partner	*The Harvey Girls* (1946)
October 2, 1945	Look for the Silver Lining	*Till the Clouds Roll By* (1946)
October 9, 1945	Who?	*Till the Clouds Roll By* (1946)
October 15, 1945	D'Ye Love Me? (outtake)	*Till the Clouds Roll By* (1946)
December 27, 1946	Love of My Life (outtake)	*The Pirate* (1948)
December 28, 1946	Mack the Black (outtake)	*The Pirate* (1948)
February 12, 1947	Mack the Black (temporary track ending/outtake)	*The Pirate* (1948)
March 28, 1947	Nin (Garland is listed with Gene Kelly as providing vocals for at least eight takes listed as "Pt 2—Revised"; this recording is not known to exist)	*The Pirate* (1948)
April 10, 1947	Voodoo (outtake)	*The Pirate* (1948)
May 5, 1947	You Can Do No Wrong (the *Daily Music Report* states "no accepted takes—will do over again"; the song was rerecorded on May 13, 1945)	*The Pirate* (1948)
May 13, 1947	Love of My Life (reprise/final version as heard in the film)	*The Pirate* (1948)
May 13, 1947	You Can Do No Wrong	*The Pirate* (1948)
July 14, 1947	Be a Clown	*The Pirate* (1948)
November 12, 1947	Mr. Monotony (outtake)	*Easter Parade* (1948)
November 12, 1947	I Want to Go Back to Michigan	*Easter Parade* (1948)
November 13, 1947	A Couple of Swells	*Easter Parade* (1948)
November 17, 1947	Vaudeville Montage	*Easter Parade* (1948)
November 15, 1947	Mack the Black (final version used in the film)	*The Pirate* (1948)
January 7, 1948	A Fella with an Umbrella	*Easter Parade* (1948)

MGM PRERECORDINGS AND RECORDS

January 7, 1948	It Only Happens When I Dance with You	*Easter Parade* (1948)
January 7, 1948	Better Luck Next Time	*Easter Parade* (1948)
January 26, 1948	Easter Parade	*Easter Parade* (1948)
March 10, 1948	A Fella with an Umbrella (this session consisted of a short twenty-second vocal with the note "Sync voice to track")	*Easter Parade* (1948)
May 28, 1948	I Wish I Were in Love Again	*Words and Music* (1948)
September 30, 1948	Johnny One Note	*Words and Music* (1948)
November 16, 1948	Last Night When We Were Young	*In the Good Old Summertime* (1949)
November 16, 1948	Merry Christmas	*In the Good Old Summertime* (1949)
November 16, 1948	Put Your Arms Around Me, Honey	*In the Good Old Summertime* (1949)
November 16, 1948	Meet Me Tonight in Dreamland	*In the Good Old Summertime* (1949)
November 17, 1948	Play That Barbershop Chord	*In the Good Old Summertime* (1949)
November 17, 1948	I Don't Care	*In the Good Old Summertime* (1949)
November 17, 1948	In the Good Old Summertime (finale version/outtake)	*In the Good Old Summertime* (1949)
March 25, 1949	Doin' What Comes Natur'lly	*Annie Get Your Gun* (1949)
March 25, 1949	You Can't Get a Man with a Gun	*Annie Get Your Gun* (1949)
March 28, 1949	They Say That Falling in Love (They Say It's Wonderful)	*Annie Get Your Gun* (1949)
March 28, 1949	The Girl That I Marry (reprise)	*Annie Get Your Gun* (1949)
March 30, 1949	Let's Go West Again (outtake)	*Annie Get Your Gun* (1949)
March 31, 1949	There's No Business Like Show Business	*Annie Get Your Gun* (1949)
March 31, 1949	There's No Business Like Show Business (reprise)	*Annie Get Your Gun* (1949)
April 1, 1949	I've Got the Sun in the Morning	*Annie Get Your Gun* (1949)

April 1, 1949	Anything You Can Do	*Annie Get Your Gun* (1949)
April 25, 1949	I'm an Indian, Too	*Annie Get Your Gun* (1949)
October 13, 1949	If You Feel Like Singing, Sing	*Summer Stock* (1950)
October 13, 1949	Happy Harvest	*Summer Stock* (1950)
October 27, 1949	Friendly Star	*Summer Stock* (1950)
February 2, 1950	All for You	*Summer Stock* (1950)
February 2, 1950	Happy Harvest (finale)	*Summer Stock* (1950)
February 3, 1950	You Wonderful You	*Summer Stock* (1950)
February 13, 1950	You Wonderful You (reprise)	*Summer Stock* (1950)
March 15, 1950	Get Happy	*Summer Stock* (1950)

MGM Records flyer circa 1948. From the collection of Bruce Hanson.

MGM PRERECORDINGS AND RECORDS

MGM Records released their first soundtrack album in 1947, MGM-1, which was the soundtrack album for *Till the Clouds Roll By* (1946). The soundtrack market was a new one, and MGM took full advantage of this new source of revenue. Initially, the soundtracks were just eight heavily edited songs spread over four 78 rpm discs. The soundtrack album eventually expanded when the long-playing format came along, allowing for more music and longer tracks. MGM Records, though, reissued their limited soundtracks in the new formats without expanding the tracks. MGM Records went defunct in the early 1990s; at the same time, Rhino Records was contracted by Turner Entertainment (which owned the MGM library) and began to release newly remastered and expanded editions of the MGM soundtracks. The following list includes all of the Judy Garland MGM Records soundtracks released in the United States, both soundtracks and compilations. The various international versions are not listed (including the UK and Japanese imports), as that would require another book. Fittingly, and in another example that Judy Garland was "The Voice of MGM," the final two soundtrack releases from MGM Records bearing the MGM Records logo before the label went defunct in the 1990s were new-to-CD Garland film soundtracks (*Meet Me in St. Louis* and *Ziegfeld Follies of 1946*).

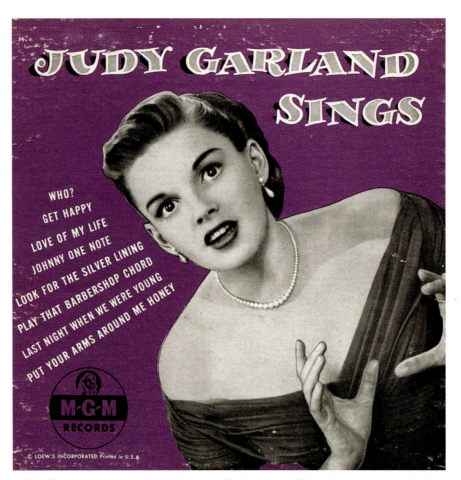

MGM Records 7" 45 rpm boxed set compilation (1951). From the author's collection.

Year	Type	Title	Catalog	Notes
1946	78 Album	Till the Clouds Roll By	MGM-1	Reissued as E-501, X-1, and K-1
1948	78 Album	The Pirate	MGM-21	Reissued as E-21. No corresponding 45 or EP issue is known.
1948	78 Album	Words and Music	MGM-37	Reissued as E-504 and K-17. No corresponding EP issue is known.
1949	78 Album	Easter Parade	MGM-40	Reissued as E-502 and X-40. No corresponding EP issue is known.
1949	78 Set	In the Good Old Summertime	MGM L-11	Special 2-record 78 rpm "gatefold" release.
1949	78 Album	MGM's Silver Anniversary	MGM-42	
1950	10″ LP	Till the Clouds Roll By	MGM E-501	
1950	4ea 45s	Till the Clouds Roll By	MGM K-1	Boxed edition
1953	2 EP 45s	Till the Clouds Roll By	MGM X-1	
1950	10″ LP	Easter Parade	MGM E-502	
1950	10″ LP	Summer Stock	MGM E-519	
1950	4ea 45s	Words and Music	MGM K-37	Boxed edition
1950	4 EP 45s	Summer Stock	MGM K-56	Boxed edition
1950	78 Album	Summer Stock	MGM-56	Reissued as E-519 and K-56. No corresponding EP issue is known.
1950	10″ LP	Words and Music	MGM E-505	
1951	10″ LP	Judy Garland Sings	MGM E-82	

1951	4 EP 45s	Judy Garland Sings	MGM K-82	Boxed edition
1951	78 Album	Judy Garland Sings	MGM-82	Reissued as E-82 and K-82. No corresponding EP issue is known.
1951	10″ LP	The Pirate	MGM E-21	
1951	10″ LP	Merry Christmas	MGM E-169	
1953	2 EP 45s	Easter Parade	MGM X-40/X-60	Gatefold edition
1953	4 EP 45s	Easter Parade	MGM X4062/3	Boxed edition
1953	Single EP 45	Get Happy	MGM X1038	
1954	12″ LP	If You Feel Like Singing, Sing	MGM E-3149	
1954	Single EP 45	Judy Garland	MGM X1122	
1954	Single EP 45	Look for the Silver Lining	MGM X1116	
1954	10″ LP	MGM's 30th Anniversary Album	MGM E-240	
1954	12″ LP	MGM's 30th Anniversary Album	MGM E-3118	
1954	2 EP 45s	MGM's 30th Anniversary Album	MGM X-240	Gatefold edition
1954	2 EP 45s	MGM's 30th Anniversary Album	MGM X4104/5	Boxed edition
1955	12″ LP	Annie Get Your Gun/Easter Parade	MGM E-3227	
1955	12″ LP	Gentlemen Prefer Blondes/ Till the Clouds Roll By	MGM E-3231	
1955	2 EP 45s	If You Feel Like Singing, Sing	MGM X 268	Gatefold edition

1955	2 EP 45s	If You Feel Like Singing, Sing	MGM X4175/6	Boxed edition
1955	12″ LP	In the Good Old Summertime/An American in Paris	MGM E-3232	
1955	12″ LP	The Pirate/Summer Stock	MGM E-3234	
1955	12″ LP	Two Weeks with Love/ Words and Music	MGM E-3233	
1956	12″ LP	The Wizard of Oz	MGM E-3464ST	
1956	2 EP 45s	The Wizard of Oz	MGM X4413/4/5	Boxed edition
1956	3 EP 45s	The Wizard of Oz	MGM X3464	
1959	12″ LP	Girls and More Girls	MGM L-70118	
	12″ LP	Star Spectacular	MGM PM-10	Special Promo LP; Garland song: Singin' in the Rain
1960	12″ LP	Words and Music/Good News	MGM E-3771ST	
1960	12″ LP	Singin' in the Rain/Till the Clouds Roll By	MGM E-3770ST	
1961	12″ LP	The Judy Garland Story Volume 1: The Star Years	MGM E-3989P	Reissue of MGM E-3149
1962	12″ LP	The Judy Garland Story Volume 2: The Hollywood Years	MGM E-4005P	
1962	12″ LP	Magnificent Moments from MGM Movies	MGM E/SE-4017	Garland songs: Johnny One Note, Over the Rainbow
1962	12″ LP	The Wizard of Oz	MGM E/SE-3996ST	
1963	12″ LP	The Very Best of Motion Picture Musicals	MGM E/SE-4171	Reissue of E-4017; Garland songs: Johnny One Note, Over the Rainbow

1963	12″ LP	The Wizard of Oz/Babes in Toyland	MGM CH/CHS-510	The MGM Children's Label CH-500 Series
1964	12″ LP	The Very Best of Judy Garland	MGM E/SE-4204	
1964	12″ LP	An All Star Salute: The Very Best of Gershwin	MGM E/SE-4242	Garland song: But Not for Me
1964	12″ LP	An All Star Salute: The Very Best of Berlin	MGM E/SE-4240	Garland songs: Better Luck Next Time, You Can't Get a Man with a Gun
1964	12″ LP	An All Star Salute: The Very Best of Jerome Kern	MGM E/SE-4241	Garland song: Look for the Silver Lining
1964	12″ LP	An All Star Salute: The Very Best of Rodgers and Hart	MGM E/SE-4238	Garland song: Johnny One Note
1965	12″ LP	Judy Garland	M/MS-505	"Metro" label
1966	12″ LP	Judy Garland in Song	M/MS-581	"Metro" label
1966	12″ LP	Till the Clouds Roll By: The Music of Jerome Kern	M/MS-578	"Metro" label
1966	12″ LP	Words and Music	M/MS-580	"Metro" label
1968	12″ LP	24 Karat Gold from the Sound Stage	MGM SE 242-2	Garland song: Over the Rainbow
1969	12″ LP	Forever Judy	MGM PX-102	
1969	12″ LP	The Golden Years at MGM	MGM SDP-1/2	
1969	12″ LP	The Wizard of Oz	PX-104	Licensed to the Singer Sewing Company
1969	12″ LP	Happy Anniversary	PX-105	Limited edition compilation for the International Silver Company; Garland song: The Boy Next Door
1970	12″ LP	Judy Garland	GAS-113	"Golden Archive Series"
1972	12″ LP	The Golden Age of Movie Musicals	MGM SQBO-93890	

340   APPENDIX B

1973	12″ LP	Those Glorious MGM Musicals: Good News/In the Good Old Summertime/Two Weeks with Love	MGM 2SES-49ST	
1973	12″ LP	Those Glorious MGM Musicals: Singin' in the Rain/Easter Parade	MGM 2SES-40ST	
1973	12″ LP	Those Glorious MGM Musicals: The Pirate/Pagan Love Song/Hit the Deck	MGM 2SES-43ST	
1973	12″ LP	Those Glorious MGM Musicals: Till the Clouds Roll By/ Three Little Words	MGM 2SES-45ST	
1973	12″ LP— Set	The M-G-M Years	P6S 5878	Six-record compilation of MGM Records soundtracks; released "in cooperation with Columbia House"
1974	12″ LP	That's Entertainment	MCA 2SE-50ST	
1974	12″ LP	Those Glorious MGM Musicals: Deep in My Heart/Words and Music	MGM 2SES-54ST	
1974	12″ LP	Those Glorious MGM Musicals: Everything I Have Is Yours/Summer Stock/I Love Melvin	MGM 2SES-52ST	
1976	12″ LP	That's Entertainment, Part Two	MG-1-5301	
1986	12″ LP	Easter Parade	MCA-1459	
1986	12″ LP	The Wizard of Oz	MCA-39046	

Year	Format	Title	Catalog No.	Notes
1986	12″ LP	Good News/In the Good Old Summertime	MCA-39083	
1986	12″ LP	Summer Stock/Lovely to Look At	MCA-39084	
1986	12″ LP	Words and Music	MCA-25029	
1986	12″ LP	Great Music from MGM Volume 1	MSM-35072	MCA Records, Inc.; Turner Broadcasting System, Inc.
1986	12″ LP	Great Music from MGM Volume 2	MSM-35072	MCA Records, Inc.; Turner Broadcasting System, Inc.
1987	12″ LP	Till the Clouds Roll By	MCA-25000	
1987	12″ LP	The Pirate/Pagan Love Song	MCA-39080	
1987	CD	Summer Stock/Everything I Have Is Yours/I Love Melvin	MCAD-5948	CD version of the 1986 MCA Records LP
1987	CD	The Pirate/Hit the Deck/Pagan Love Song	MCAD-5950	CD version of the 1987 MCA Records LP
1987	CD	In the Good Old Summertime/Good News/Two Weeks with Love	MCAD-5952	CD version of the 1986 MCA Records LP
1987	12″ LP CD	The Best of Judy Garland from MGM Classic Films	MCAD-31176	Includes MGM Records tracks as well as Decca recordings
1994	CD	That's Entertainment! III	CDQ 5 55215 2 1	Angel/MGM Records release
1994	CD	Meet Me in St. Louis	MGM 305123	Reissued by Rhino Records in 1995. This and *Ziegfeld Follies* are the last two official MGM Records soundtracks ever issued.
1994	CD	Ziegfeld Follies of 1946	MGM 305124	Reissued by Rhino Records in 1995

The Original MGM Records 78 rpm release of "Get Happy" from the *Summer Stock* soundtrack album (1950).
From the author's collection.

If You Feel Like Singing (the title for *Summer Stock* in the United Kingdom), 1970s soundtrack album reissue. From the author's collection.

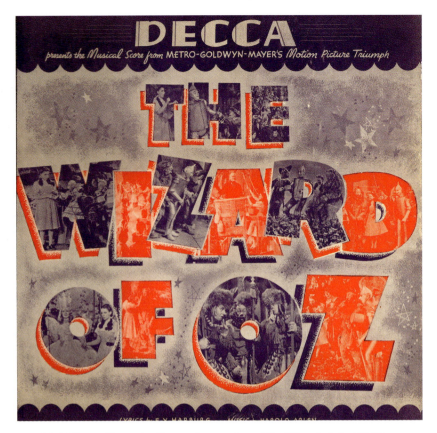

1940 Decca Records album of songs from *The Wizard of Oz* (1939).
From the author's collection.

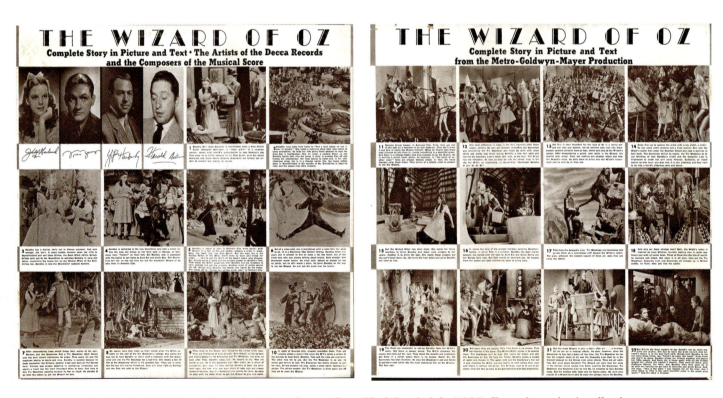

Inside the 1940 Decca Records album of songs from *The Wizard of Oz* (1939). From the author's collection.

APPENDIX C

DECCA RECORDS

Judy Garland's association with Decca Records predated her association with MGM. On March 29, 1935, the "Garland Sisters" (twelve-year-old Garland and her two older sisters, Virginia and Mary Jane) recorded test records for the label accompanied on the piano by their mother, Ethel Gumm. The trio sang "Moonglow," and Garland (listed as Francis [*sic*] Garland) soloed on "Bill" and a medley of "On the Good Ship Lollipop/The Object of My Affection/Dinah."

Although the label's Los Angeles representative, Joe Perry, was enthusiastic and even sent "Bill" to his colleagues in New York, the tests were rejected. They were thought lost until 2004, when the two Garland solos surfaced. The owner of the two records provided the story of how they were hidden and then rediscovered in an email to this author in 2004:

My mother's brother (also my Godfather) took us (me, my Mom, my younger sister, and my Aunt) to Judy's home which had just been sold and was no longer occupied. His landlord at the time had a "clean up business" and told my Uncle to come see this house. The house was 2 story and I remember lots of red carpeting going up the stars, and especially a room with nothing but mirrors (for dance practice I would guess). There was also a "train" in the backyard. This train left a big impression on me as it was like something you'd see at Knott's Berry Farm.

On our way to the car we came upon this trash, a big pile (I can see it in my head) and my Mom and her brother started to rummage through it. My Mom ended up with 5 albums, a wooden cane, and a script "Man O'War." The significance of these did not seem too great. Who would want them? They were just beat up records and were lying in a pile of trash. They sat in my Mom's closet for years and years and years. If it was 1960 I was only 6 years old at the time, but I have a memory like an elephant and can see this like it was yesterday. My Dad just told me the other day that he also had a metal box with receipts for gardeners, etc., and that he threw that out a long, long time ago.

After trying to sell them to Capitol Records and MCA Music (which owned the Decca catalog) and getting turned down (Decca's attitude was "Why should we pay you for recordings that are already ours?"), the family put the records (which remained unknown to the public) up for auction in 2006. The winning bid did not meet the reserve price, so the discs went back to the family and again disappeared from the public until 2010, when they were remastered and released on the JSP Records CD boxed set "Judy Garland—Lost Tracks." At last, a happy ending, although "Moonglow" (the only studio recording made by Garland with her sisters) remains lost.

When Garland signed with Decca Records, she was the youngest singer ever signed to a contract by a major record label. Garland remained with Decca for a full decade, recording her last singles on November 15, 1947. This association gave her a chance to sing a variety of song genres that she wouldn't necessarily have had the chance to sing at MGM. Much like her radio performances, she was able to experiment and sing with people not on the MGM roster, such as Bing Crosby and Dick Haymes. In addition to the studio versions of songs from her films (such as "Over the Rainbow" and "The Trolley Song"), Garland's Decca catalog includes such popular songs as "Stompin' at the Savoy," "Blues in the Night," "That Old Black Magic," "Love," "Oceans Apart," "Smilin' Through," and "You'll Never Walk Alone."

The following is a chart of all of Garland's Decca recordings, including notes about alternates and unused tracks.

Date Recorded	Title	Matrix Number	Record Number	Release Date
March 29, 1935	Moonglow (The Garland Sisters) This recording has not survived.	N/A (probably DLA-157 OR 160)	N/A	N/A
March 29, 1935	Bill (as "Francis [*sic*] Garland")	DLA-158-A	N/A	N/A
March 29, 1935	Medley: On the Good Ship Lollipop/The Object of My Affection/Dinah (as "Francis [*sic*] Garland")	DLA-159-A	N/A	N/A
November 27, 1935	No Other One This recording has not survived.	DLA-280	N/A	N/A
November 27, 1935	All's Well This recording has not survived.	DLA-283	N/A	N/A
June 12, 1936	Stompin' at the Savoy This and "Swing, Mr. Charlie" were recorded with the popular jazz band Bob Crosby and His Orchestra. When the record was released, no orchestra accompaniment was given. The band's manager, Gil Rodin, told Decca that they didn't want to use their name associated with "this unknown girl."	61165-A	848 A	July 1936

June 12, 1936	Swing, Mr. Charlie	61166-A	848 B	July 1936
August 30, 1937	Everybody Sing The alternate, or "B" take, was mistakenly issued instead of the "A" take when Decca released its two-LP set "Collector's Items" in 1973. This error would not be corrected until the "A" side was included in the 1994 CD boxed set *Judy Garland—The Complete Decca Masters* (plus).	DLA-860-A	1432 A	September 1937
August 30, 1937	All God's Chillun Got Rhythm The alternate, or "B" take, was mistakenly issued instead of the "A" take when Decca released its two-LP set "Collector's Items" in 1973. This error would not be corrected until the A-side was included in the 1994 CD boxed set *Judy Garland—The Complete Decca Masters* (plus).	DLA-861-A	1432 B	September 1937

September 24, 1937	Dear Mr. Gable (You Made Me Love You The alternate, or "B" take, was mistakenly issued instead of the "A" take when Decca released its two-LP set "The Best of Judy Garland" in 1963, which was subsequently released as the 1989 Japanese two-CD called *The Best of Judy Garland* (MCA Records/Warner-Pioneer Corporation 27P2-2839). This error would not be corrected until the "A" side was included in the 1994 CD boxed set *Judy Garland— The Complete Decca Masters* (plus).	DLA-967-A	1463 A	October 1937
September 24, 1937	You Can't Have Everything	DLA-968-A	1463-B	October 1937

April 25, 1938	Cry, Baby, Cry The alternate, or "B" take, was mistakenly issued instead of the "A" take when Decca released its two-LP set "Collector's Items" in 1973 but would not make its CD debut until the 2011 JSP Records four-CD release *Smilin' Through: The Singles Collection, 1936–1947.*	DLA-1285-A	1796 A	May 1938
April 25, 1938	Sleep My Baby Sleep	DLA-1284-A	1796 B	May 1938
August 21, 1938	It Never Rains, But What It Pours	DLA-1437-A	2017 A	October 1938
August 21, 1938	Ten Pins in the Sky This is the only instance of Decca using the "C" take instead of the "A" or "B" takes as the official release version.	DLA-1436-C	2017 B	October 1938
July 28, 1939	Over the Rainbow No. 5 on Billboard in Sept. 1939	DLA-1840-A	2672 A	September 1939
July 28, 1939	The Jitterbug	DLA-1841-A	2672 B	September 1939
July 28, 1939	In-Between	DLA-1842-A	15045 A	March 1940

July 28, 1939	Sweet Sixteen	DLA-1843-A	10545 B	March 1940
July 29, 1939	Zing! Went the Strings of My Heart According to the 1975 British book *Directory of Popular Music: 1900–1965*, compiled by Leslie Lowe, "Zing!" and "I'm Just Wild about Harry" were released in England on Decca's Brunswick label in the spring of 1940. "Zing!" was not released in the United States until 1943.	DLA-1850-A	UK: Brunswick 02969 B US: Decca 18543 A	UK: Spring 1940 US: May 20, 1943
July 29, 1939	I'm Just Wild about Harry This recording was released in the United Kingdom under the "Brunswick" label in 1940. It was not re-leased in the United States until 1984, when it was included on the MCA Records LP *Judy Garland—From the Decca Vaults*.	DLA-1851-A	02969 B (Brunswick)	Spring 1940 (UK)

July 29, 1939	Swanee Note: Only the "A" take was cut on this date, and it was rejected. Judy rerecorded the song on October 16, 1939. This rejected "A" take is not known to exist.	DLA-1852-A	N/A	N/A
July 29, 1939	Fascinating Rhythm	DLA-1853-A	18543 B	May 20, 1943
October 16, 1939	Oceans Apart	DLA-1868-A	2873 A	March 1940
October 16, 1939	Figaro The "B" take was mistakenly issued instead of the "A" take when it was released on the LP "More Than a Memory" in 1974. It made its CD debut on the 2011 JSP Records 4-CD release *Smilin' Through: The Singles Collection, 1936–1947*.	DLA-1871-A	2873 B	March 1940
October 16, 1939	Embraceable You	DLA-1869-A	2881 A	April 1940
October 16, 1939	Swanee	DLA-1870-A	2881 B	April 1940

April 10, 1940	I'm Nobody's Baby No. 3 on Billboard in mid-1940	DLA-1972-A	3174 B	June 1940
April 10, 1940	(Can This Be) The End of the Rainbow	DLA-1971-A	3231 A 4081 B	September 1940, November 1941
April 10, 1940	Buds Won't Bud	DLA-1973-A	3174 A	June 1940
April 10, 1940	Wearing of the Green	DLA-1974-A	3165 B	August 1940
April 15, 1940	Friendship (duet with Johnny Mercer) An alternate take [DLA 1987-B] has survived and is available on the 2011 JSP Records four-CD release *Smilin' Through: The Singles Collection, 1936–1947.*	DLA-1987-A	3165 A	August 1940
December 18, 1940	I'm Always Chasing Rainbow An alternate take (DLA-2282-C) has survived and was first released on the 1984 MCA Records LP *Judy Garland—From the Decca Vaults.*	DLA-2282-A	3593-B	January 1941

December 18, 1940	Our Love Affair	DLA-2283-A	3593-A	January 1941
December 18, 1940	A Pretty Girl Milking Her Cow	DLA-2284-A	3604-B	January 1941
December 18, 1940	It's a Great Day for the Irish	DLA-2285-A	3604 A	January 1941
July 20, 1941	The Birthday of a King	DLA-2578-A	4050 A	December 1941
July 20, 1941	The Star of the East	DLA-2579-A	4050 B	December 1941
October 24, 1941	How about You?	DLA-2798-A	4072 A	November 1941
October 24, 1941	Blues in the Night An alternate take (DLA-2799-B) has survived and is available on the 2011 JSP Records four-CD release *Smilin' Through: The Singles Collection, 1936–1947.*	DLA-2799-A	4081 A	November 1941
October 24, 1941	F. D. R. Jones	DLA-2800-A	4072 B	November 1941

April 3, 1942	The Last Call for Love An alternate take [DLA 1987-B] has survived and is available on the 2011 JSP Records four-CD release *Smilin' Through: The Singles Collection, 1936–1947*.	DLA-2968-A	18320 B	June 1942
April 3, 1942	Poor You An alternate take [DLA 1987-B] has survived and is available on the 2011 JSP Records four-CD release *Smilin' Through: The Singles Collection, 1936–1947*.	DLA-2969-A	18320 A	June 1942
April 3, 1942	On the Sunny Side of the Street	DLA-2970-A	18524 B	May 20, 1943
April 3, 1942	Poor Little Rich Girl	DLA-2971-A	18540 B	May 20, 1943
July 26, 1942	For Me and My Gal (duet with Gene Kelly) No. 5 on Billboard in 1943	DLA-3140-A	18480 A	January 1943
July 26, 1942	When You Wore a Tulip (duet with Gene Kelly)	DLA-3141-A	18480 B	January 1943
July 26, 1942	That Old Black Magic	DLA-3142-A	18540 A	May 20, 1943

DECCA RECORDS

July 26, 1942	I Never Knew (I Could Love Anybody Like I'm Loving You)	DLA-3143-A	18524 A	May 20, 1943
November 2, 1943	But Not for Me	L-3250-A	23309 A	April 6, 1944
November 2, 1943	I Got Rhythm An alternate take (L-3252-B) has survived and is available on the 2011 JSP Records four-CD release *Smilin' Through: The Singles Collection, 1936–1947.*	L-3252-A	23310 B	April 6, 1944
November 4, 1943	Embraceable You An alternate take (L-3253-B) has survived and is available on the 2011 JSP Records four-CD release *Smilin' Through: The Singles Collection, 1936–1947.*	L-3253-A	23308 A	April 6, 1944
November 4, 1943	Could You Use Me? (duet with Mickey Rooney)	L-3254-A	23308 B	April 6, 1944
November 4, 1943	Biden' My Time (Featuring the Leo Diamond Harmonica Quintet)	L-3255-A	23310 A	April 6, 1944

December 22, 1943	No Love, No Nothin'	DLA-3264-A	18584 A	January 27, 1944
December 22, 1943	A Journey to a Star	DLA-3265-A	18584 B	January 27, 1944
April 20, 1944	The Boy Next Door	L-3385-A	23362 B	November 2, 1944
April 20, 1944	Boys and Girls Like You and Me	L-3386-A	23362 B	November 2, 1944
April 20, 1944	Have Yourself a Merry Little Christmas An alternate take (L-3387-C) has survived and was first released on the MCA (Decca) 1992 CD *Judy Garland: Changing My Tune—The Best of the Decca Years, Vol. Two.*	L-3387-A	23362 A	November 2, 1944
April 21, 1944	The Trolley Song No. 3 on Billboard in 1944	L-3388-A	23361 A	November 2, 1944
April 21, 1944	Skip to My Lou	L-3389-A	23360 B	November 2, 1944
April 21, 1944	Meet Me in St. Louis, Louis	L-3390-A	23361 B	November 2, 1944
July 31, 1944	You're Got Me Where You Want Me (duet with Bing Crosby)	L-3485-A	23410 B	April 19, 1947

July 31, 1944	Mine (duet with Bing Crosby) An additional "C" take has also survived.	L-3486-A	23804-B	January 20, 1947
January 26, 1945	This Heart of Mine An alternate take (DLA-3727-B) has survived and was first released on the MCA (Decca) 1992 CD *Judy Garland: Changing My Tune—The Best of the Decca Years, Vol. Two.*	DLA-3727-A	18660 A	March 22, 1945
January 26, 1945	Love	DLA-3728-A	18660 B	March 22, 1945
March 9, 1945	Connecticut (duet with Bing Crosby) An alternate take (L-3750-B) has survived was first released on the MCA (Decca) 1992 CD *Judy Garland: Changing My Tune—The Best of the Decca Years, Vol. Two.*	L-3750-A	23804 A	January 20, 1947

March 9, 1945	Yah-Ta-Ta, Yah-Ta-Ta (Talk, Talk, Talk) (duet with Bing Crosby) No. 5 on Billboard in late 1945 An alternate take (L-51085/L-3751-T) has survived and was first released on the 1984 MCA Records LP *Judy Garland—From the Decca Vaults*. An additional "B" take has also survived.	L-3751-A	23410 A	April 19, 1945
May 14, 1945	March of the Doagies (with Kenny Baker and the Kay Thompson Chorus) This recording was not given a record number because the song was cut from the film *The Harvey Girls* prior to the release of the film and the Decca cast album of songs from the film. It had its official US release in 1984 on the MCA Records LP *Judy Garland—From the Decca Vaults*.	L-3858-A	(see note)	November 12, 1984
May 14, 1945	Swing Your Partner Round and Round	L-3859-A	23459 B	November 1, 1945

| May 15, 1945 | On the Atchison, Topeka, and the Santa Fe (full orchestra and chorus version; repeat tag at end)

This is the complete original version, Parts 1 and 2. Part 1 (chorus intro) had its debut on the 1994 CD boxed set *Judy Garland—The Complete Decca Masters* (plus).

Part 2 (Garland's entrance and vocal) of this song was rerecorded on September 10, 1945, and that is the version heard on the original 78 album. When Decca began rereleasing these recordings on LP in the 1950s, they mistakenly released this May 1945 rejected version of Part 2. It begins with Judy singing "What a lovely trip" as she does in the film and ends with the repeat of the song title three times at the end (again as in the film). The recording made on September 10 changes the lyric from "trip" to "day" for continuity, and the end coda was shortened. | L-3861-A | (see note) | 1950s/1994 |

July 7, 1945	On the Atchison, Topeka, and the Santa Fe (with the Merry Macs) No. 10 on Billboard in 1945 Garland recorded this pop version of the song while on her honeymoon with Vincente Minnelli in New York City.	W-72967-A	23436 A	November 9, 1945
July 7, 1945	If I Had You (with the Merry Macs) The second song Garland recorded while on her honeymoon with Vincente Minnelli in New York City. An alternate take (W-72968-B) has survived and was first released on the 1984 MCA Records LP *Judy Garland—From the Decca Vaults*.	W-72968-A	23436 B	September 9, 1945
July 10, 1945	You'll Never Walk Alone The third song Garland recorded while on her honeymoon with Vincente Minnelli in New York City.	W-72973-A	23539 B	April 15, 1946

DECCA RECORDS

July 10, 1945	Smilin' Through The fourth song Garland recorded while on her honeymoon with Vincente Minnelli in New York City.	W-72974-A	23539 A	April 15, 1946
September 7, 1945	It's a Great Big World (with Virginia O'Brien and Betty Russell)	L-3956-A	23460 A	November 1, 1945
September 7, 1945	In the Valley (Where the Evening Sun Goes Down)	L-3957-A	23458 B	November 1, 1945
September 10, 1945	On the Atchison, Topeka, and the Santa Fe (short version; minus the choral intro; short ending) This is the version that was originally released on 78 as part of the original Decca cast album. When the cast album was released on LP in the 1950s, Decca mistakenly used the rejected version of Part 2 recorded on May 15, 1945. See the notes for May 15, 1945, for further details.	L-3958-A	23458 A	November 1, 1945

September 11, 1946	Arent's You Kind of Glad We Did? (with Dick Haymes)	L-4294-A	23687 B	October 21, 1946
September 11, 1946	For You, For Me, Forevermore (with Dick Haymes)	L-4295-A	23687 A	October 21, 1946
September 11, 1946	Changing My Tune	L-4296-A	23688 A	October 21, 1946
October 1, 1946	Don't Tell Me That Story An alternate take (L-4318-T) has survived and was first released on the 1984 MCA Records LP *Judy Garland—From the Decca Vaults*.	L-4318-A	23756 B	December 2, 1946
October 1, 1946	There Is No Breeze (To Cool the Flame of Love)	L-4319-A	23756 A	December 2, 1946
November 15, 1947	Nothing But You	L-4564-A	24469 B	July 19, 1948

November 15, 1947	I Wish I Were in Love Again (with Two Piano Accompaniment by Eadie Griffith and Rack Goodwin) An alternate take (L-4565-B) has survived was first released on the MCA (Decca) 1992 CD *Judy Garland: Changing My Tune—The Best of the Decca Years, Vol. Two*. It is also available on the 2011 JSP Records four-CD release *Smilin' Through: The Singles Collection, 1936–1947*.	L-4565-A	24469 A	July 19, 1948
November 15, 1947	Falling in Love with Love (with Two Piano Accompaniment by Eadie Griffith and Rack Goodwin) This recording was evidently made as an afterthought at the end of the recording session. It was not discovered until 1992, when the producers of the MCA (Decca) CD *Judy Garland: Changing My Tune—The Best of the Decca Years, Vol. Two* found it and included it in that CD. It is also available on the 2011 JSP Records four-CD release *Smilin' Through: The Singles Collection, 1936–1947*.	(see note)	MCAD-10504	July 1992

Acknowledgments

I want to give a special thanks to Steven Bingen, who guided me through the process of writing this book and has given his unwavering support. Thank you to Mike Siewert, Hisato Masuyama, and Bruce Hanson, whose friendships I treasure and who contributed some of the photos in this book.

A special thanks to Brian Stamp, Mark Rivard, and Rick and Steve for being such great long-term friends and for all the frivolity and jokes along the way.

Another special thanks to John Haley and Raphael Geroni for their technical and creative expertise and their friendship, plus Yannek Cansino, who was a big help with details about Deanna Durbin's time at MGM.

In addition to their support, the following folks have shared so many great images and data with *The Judy Room* website (in alphabetical order): David Alp, Kim Lundgreen, and Bobby Waters.

There are many great people who have supported me, the website, and the social media outlets over the years in a variety of ways. These selfless folks have given ongoing encouragement, lively conversations, and fun. In alphabetical order: Richard Anthony, Don C. Berry, Armand DiNucci, Joseph Ebneth, Elias Eliadis, David Fantle, Jaymee Filline, Jack Garcia, Robert Gold, Scott Hedley, Fred Hough, Sam Irvin, Ryan Jay, Tom Johnson, Walter Krueger, Peter Mac, Stuart Main, Nolan McCormick, Cynthia Meader, Shimoda Miwa, Kaoru Nakajima, Meredith Ponedel, Ranse Ransome, Sharon Ray, Bobby Rivers, Michelle Russell, D. J. Schaefer, Randy Schmidt, Joe Shipbaugh, Richard Skipper, Art Smith, Rick Smith, Tom Struble, John David

Thomas, Robert Welch, and Don Woodie. To all of the members of The *Judy Room*'s social media outlets and to my family I thank you for everything.

In loving memory of the late Scott Schechter.

Last but not least, to Judy Garland for giving so much of herself to us all.

MGM promotional photo, 1938. From the author's collection.

NOTES

CHAPTER 1—THE ROAD TO MGM

1. Clarke, *Get Happy: The Life of Judy Garland.*

2. Russell, *From Tennessee to Oz, Part 2.*

3. Dahl and Kehoe, *Young Judy.*

4. Russell, *From Tennessee to Oz, Part 2.*

5. Russell, *From Tennessee to Oz, Part 2.*

6. Clarke, *Get Happy: The Life of Judy Garland.*

7. Ibid.

8. Frank, *Judy.*

9. Ibid.

10. Dahl and Kehoe, *Young Judy.*

11. Garland, "The Real Me," *McCall's,* April 1957.

12. Dahl and Kehoe, *Young Judy.*

13. Russell, *From Tennessee to Oz, Part 2.*

14. Ibid.

15. Dahl and Kehoe, *Young Judy*.

16. Russell, *From Tennessee to Oz, Part 2*.

17. Garland, 1960 Audiotape.

18. Ibid.

19. Garland, *The Jack Paar Show*, December 2, 1962.

20. Schechter, *Judy Garland: The Day-by-Day Chronicle of a Legend*.

21. Russell, *From Tennessee to Oz, Part 2*.

22. Dahl and Kehoe, *Young Judy*.

23. Russell, *From Tennessee to Oz, Part 2*.

24. Dahl and Kehoe, *Young Judy*.

25. Russell, *From Tennessee to Oz, Part 2*.

26. Finch, *Rainbow: The Stormy Life of Judy Garland*.

27. Dahl and Kehoe, *Young Judy*.

28. Garland, 1960 Audiotape.

29. Ibid.

30. Ibid.

31. Uncredited, *Los Angeles Times*, December 24, 1928.

32. Schechter, *Judy Garland: The Day-by-Day Chronicle of a Legend*.

33. Uncredited, *Ledger-Gazette*, Lancaster, California, March 1, 1929.

34. Dahl and Kehoe, *Young Judy*.

35. Ibid.

36. Call, *Variety*, August 30, 1932.

37. Schechter, *Judy Garland: The Day-by-Day Chronicle of a Legend*.

38. Bock, *Variety*, August 8, 1933.

39. Schechter, *Judy Garland: The Day-by-Day Chronicle of a Legend*.

40. Frame, *Long Beach Sun*, August 10, 1933.

41. Uncredited, *Long Beach Sun*, August 12, 1933.

42. Edwa, *Variety*, September 5, 1933.

43. Hegyi, *Hollywood Citizen News*, August 25, 1933.

44. Cary, *Hollywood's Children.*

45. Uncredited, *Spokesman-Review*, Spokane, WA, March 2, 1934.

46. Schechter, *Judy Garland: The Day-by-Day Chronicle of a Legend.*

47. Gumm, *Rutherford Courier*, Murfreesboro, TN, April 27, 1934.

48. Frank, *Judy.*

49. Dahl and Kehoe, *Young Judy.*

50. Ibid.

51. Frank, *Judy.*

52. Lyons, syndicated column, August 20, 1954.

53. Uncredited, *St. Joseph News-Press Gazette*, St. Joseph, MO, October 5, 1934.

54. Uncredited, *St. Joseph News-Press Gazette*, St. Joseph, MO, October 6, 1934.

55. Uncredited, *Kansas City Star*, Kansas City, MO, September 30, 1934.

56. Call, *Variety*, November 6, 1934.

57. Schechter, *Judy Garland: The Day-by-Day Chronicle of a Legend.*

58. Oliver, *Los Angeles Herald-Express*, December 10, 1934.

59. Combs, *Hollywood Citizen News*, Hollywood, CA, December 10, 1934.

60. Soanes, *Oakland Tribune*, Oakland, CA, December 27, 1934.

61. Edwa, *Variety*, March 13, 1935.

62. Dahl and Kehoe, *Young Judy.*

63. Hanifin, *San Francisco Chronicle*, May 4, 1935.

64. Edwa, *Variety*, May 22, 1935.

65. Frank, *Judy.*

66. Ibid.

67. Uncredited, *Los Angeles Times*, August 9, 1935.

68. Uncredited, *Los Angeles Times*, August 15, 1935.

69. Fordin, *The World of Entertainment! Hollywood's Greatest Musicals.*

70. Ibid.

71. Goode, *Show Business Illustrated*, October 31, 1961.

72. Frank, *Judy.*

73. Dahl and Kehoe, *Young Judy*.

74. Ibid.

75. Johnson, "Conversation with Roger Edens," *Sight and Sound*, 1958.

76. Clarke, *Get Happy: The Life of Judy Garland*.

77. Sidney, Commentary Track, "Judy Garland: The Golden Years at M-G-M," 1994 LaserDisc, MGM/UA Home Video.

78. Finch, *Rainbow: The Stormy Life of Judy Garland*.

79. Soanes, *Oakland Tribune*, Oakland, CA, November 1, 1935.

CHAPTER 2—MGM's NEWEST CONTRACT PLAYER

1. Garland, *The Jack Paar Show*, December 2, 1962.

2. Fordin, *The World of Entertainment! Hollywood's Greatest Musicals*.

3. Skolsky, *Photoplay*, July 1943.

4. Schechter, *Judy Garland: The Day-by-Day Chronicle of a Legend*.

5. Dahl and Kehoe, *Young Judy*.

6. Schechter, *Judy Garland: The Day-by-Day Chronicle of a Legend*.

7. Ibid.

8. Finch, *Rainbow: The Stormy Life of Judy Garland*.

9. Uncredited, *Variety*, December 4, 1935.

10. Parsons, syndicated, March 5, 1936.

11. Martin, *Hollywood Citizen News*, Hollywood, CA, December 19, 1935.

12. Uncredited, *Indianapolis News*, Indianapolis, IN, January 1, 1936.

13. Uncredited, *Hollywood Citizen News*, Hollywood, CA, April 3, 1936.

14. Uncredited, *Hollywood Citizen News*, Hollywood, CA, May 20, 1936.

15. Skolsky, syndicated, May 29, 1936.

16. O'Brien, Liner Notes, *Judy Garland—The Complete Decca Recordings* (plus), MCA Records, 1994.

17. Hopper and Brough, *Chicago Tribune*, Chicago, IL, March 2, 1963.

18. Author's correspondence with Durbin biographer Yannek Cansino.

19. Uncredited, *Variety*, March 9, 1938.

20. Frank, *Judy*.

21. Pastos, *Pin-Up: The Tragedy of Betty Grable*.

22. Uncredited, *Film Daily* (trade magazine), October 20, 1936.

23. Lusk, *Picture Play*, January 1, 1937.

24. McPherson, *St. Louis Post Dispatch*, St. Louis, MO, October 25, 1936.

25. T. H. C., *Kossuth County Advance*, Kossuth, OH, November 26, 1936.

26. Clarke, *Get Happy: The Life of Judy Garland*.

27. Transcript, *Jack Oakie's College* (radio show), April 20, 1937.

28. Frank, *Judy*.

29. Ibid.

30. Clarke, *Get Happy: The Life of Judy Garland*.

31. Garland, *The Dick Cavett Show*, December 13, 1968.

32. Truesdell, "Part in Broadway Play," Syndicated, February 8, 1942.

33. Arvad, "Judy Garland Hopes to Sing in Big Show," syndicated, February 6, 1944.

34. Garland, "The Real Me," *McCall's*, April 1957.

35. Uncredited, *Morning Herald*, Uniontown, PA, March 5, 1938.

36. Irwin, "Sweet Sixteen," syndicated, November 21, 1939.

37. Stokes, "That Garland Gang," syndicated, March 27, 1938.

38. Uncredited, *Film Daily* (trade magazine), November 18, 1940.

39. Uncredited, *Deseret News*, Stalk Lake City, UT, November 29, 1940.

40. Uncredited, *Variety*, February 9, 1938.

41. Uncredited, *Pensacola News Journal*, Pensacola, FL, January 24, 1938.

42. Cohen, *Miami News*, Miami, FL, January 25, 1938.

43. Uncredited, *Variety*, February 2, 1938.

44. Hobe, *Variety*, February 16, 1938.

45. Winchell, syndicated, February 16, 1938.

46. Uncredited, *Variety*, February 16, 1938.

47. Monahan, *Pittsburgh Press*, Pittsburgh, PA, February 28, 1938.

48. Cohen, *Variety*, March 3, 1938.

49. Uncredited, *Pittsburgh Post-Gazette*, Pittsburgh, PA, February 26, 1938.

50. Otis, *Variety*, March 9, 1938.

51. Garland, Letter to Perry Frank, March 28, 1938.

52. Holst, *Detroit Free Press*, March 22, 1938.

53. Uncredited, *Variety*, March 30, 1938.

54. Uncredited, *Albuquerque Journal*, Albuquerque, NM, April 4, 1938.

CHAPTER 3—MGM MAGIC

1. Wilcox, "For Women Only," syndicated, January 1, 1939.

2. Fordin, *The World of Entertainment! Hollywood's Greatest Musicals.*

3. Finch, *Rainbow: The Stormy Life of Judy Garland.*

4. Parsons, syndicated, February 28, 1938.

5. Uncredited, *The Exhibitor* (trade magazine), August 23, 1939.

6. McKelvey, *Green Bay Gazette*, Green Bay, WI, August 12, 1939.

7. Garland, *The Jack Paar Show*, May 7, 1967.

8. Ibid.

9. Uncredited, *The Robesonian*, Lumberton, NC, March 20, 1977.

10. Uncredited, *Daily News*, New York, NY, April 9, 1939.

11. Newspaper Advertisement, *Daily News*, New York, NY, April 10, 1939.

12. Newspaper Advertisement, *Daily News*, New York, NY, April 11, 1939.

13. Gilbert, *Bergen Evening Record*, Hackensack, NJ, April 14, 1939.

14. Newspaper Advertisement, *Daily News*, New York, NY, April 13, 1939.

15. Winchell, syndicated, April 1939.

16. Clarke, *Get Happy: The Life of Judy Garland.*

17. Fordin, *The World of Entertainment! Hollywood's Greatest Musicals.*

18. Clarke, *Get Happy: The Life of Judy Garland.*

19. Uncredited, *Evening News*, Harrisburg, PA, November 10, 1939.

20. Peak, *Boston Globe*, Boston, MA, November 13, 1939.

21. Schechter, *Judy Garland: The Day-by-Day Chronicle of a Legend.*

22. Ibid.

23. Ibid.

24. Graham, syndicated, November 22, 1939.

25. Frank, *Judy*.

26. Clarke, *Get Happy: The Life of Judy Garland*.

27. Ibid.

28. Frank, *Judy*.

29. Ibid.

30. Clarke, *Get Happy: The Life of Judy Garland*.

31. Ibid.

32. Peak, *Boston Globe*, Boston, MA, November 13, 1939.

33. Frank, *Judy*.

34. Ibid.

CHAPTER 4—MGM'S SINGING SWEETHEART

1. Laird, *Kansas City Times*, February 17, 1940.

2. Clarke, *Get Happy: The Life of Judy Garland*.

3. Uncredited, Associated Press, March 8, 1940.

4. Schechter, *Judy Garland: The Day-by-Day Chronicle of a Legend*.

5. Fordin, *The World of Entertainment! Hollywood's Greatest Musicals*.

6. Minnelli, *I Remember It Well*.

7. Fordin, *The World of Entertainment! Hollywood's Greatest Musicals*.

8. Johnson, "Conversation with Roger Edens," *Sight and Sound*, 1958.

9. Shipman, *Judy Garland: The Secret Life of an American Legend*.

10. Uncredited, *Detroit Free Press*, Detroit, MI, December 3, 1940.

11. Garland, *The Judy Garland Show*, December 13, 1963.

12. Uncredited, "Just Among Friends," *Los Angeles Evening Citizen News*, January 24, 1940.

13. Edwards, *Judy Garland*.

14. Clarke, *Get Happy: The Life of Judy Garland*.

15. Frank, *Judy*.

16. Ibid.

17. Ibid.

18. Ibid.

19. Frank, *Judy*.

20. Vale, "Star Dust," syndicated column, February 1941.

21. Schechter, *Judy Garland: The Day-by-Day Chronicle of a Legend*.

22. Ibid.

23. Carroll, syndicated column, January 1942.

24. Uncredited, Associated Press syndicated article, May 16, 1943.

25. Vale, "Star Dust," syndicated column, May 1943.

26. Uncredited, *Rolla Herald*, Rolla, MO, January 29, 1942.

27. Schechter, *Judy Garland: The Day-by-Day Chronicle of a Legend*.

28. Uncredited, *Battle Creek Enquirer*, Battle Creek, MI, January 22, 1942.

29. Ibid.

30. Ibid.

31. Uncredited, *St. Louis Star and Times*, St. Louis, MO, January 26, 1942.

32. Uncredited, *Decatur Daily Review*, Decatur, IL, January 26, 1942.

33. Hicks, *Fort Worth Star-Telegram*, Fort Worth, TX, January 30, 1942.

34. Uncredited, *Weatherford Democrat*, Weatherford, TX, November 23, 2009.

35. Uncredited, *Austin American*, Austin, TX, January 30, 1942.

36. Uncredited, *Fort Worth Star-Telegram*, Fort Worth, TX, January 28, 1942.

37. Uncredited, *Evening News*, Harrisburg, PA, February 3, 1942.

38. Truesdell, syndicated column, February 1942.

39. Frank, *Judy*.

40. Ibid.

41. Reid, *Photoplay*, November 1942.

42. Uncredited, *Atlanta Constitution*, Atlanta, GA, February 7, 1943.

CHAPTER 5—MGM'S SINGING SWEETHEART GROWS UP

1. Fantle and Johnson, *C'mon, Get Happy: The Making of* Summer Stock.

2. Murphy and Lasky, *"Say . . . Didn't You Used to Be George Murphy?"*

3. Kelly, Archival Interview, "MGM When the Lion Roars," 1992.

4. Uncredited, syndicated article, May 1942.

5. Uncredited, "Child of Former Citizen Stands High in Contest," *Daily News Journal*, Murfreesboro, TN, March 27, 1930.

6. Ibid.

7. Uncredited, "Child Known Here Wins in Contest," *Home Journal*, Murfreesboro, TN, March 28, 1930.

8. Fordin, *The World of Entertainment! Hollywood's Greatest Musicals*.

9. Uncredited, *Showmen's Trade Review* (trade magazine), October 24, 1942.

10. Uncredited, *Showmen's Trade Review* (trade magazine), December 19, 1942.

11. Uncredited, *Showmen's Trade Review* (trade magazine), December 12, 1942.

12. Pasternak, *Easy the Hard Way*.

13. Frank, *Judy*.

14. Clarke, *Get Happy: The Life of Judy Garland*.

15. Johnson, "Conversation with Roger Edens," *Sight and Sound*, 1958.

16. Phillips, *Charles Walters: The Director Who Made Hollywood Dance*.

17. Hirschorn, *The Hollywood Musical*.

18. Phillips, *Charles Walters: The Director Who Made Hollywood Dance*.

19. Garland, "The Real Me," *McCall's*, April 1957.

20. Frank, *Judy*.

21. Ibid.

22. Ponedel, Archival Interview, *Impressions of Garland*, 1972 TV documentary.

23. Fleming, *The Fixers*.

24. Ibid.

25. Garland, "The Real Me," *McCall's*, April 1957.

26. Clake, *Get Happy: The Life of Judy Garland*.

27. Frank, *Judy*.

28. Ibid.

29. Mankiewicz, Archival Interview, 1978.

30. Uncredited, *Philadelphia Inquirer*, Philadelphia, PA, June 27, 1943.

31. Singer, "Judy Garland Enraptures Dell Throng," *Philadelphia Inquirer*, Philadelphia, PA, July 2, 1943.

32. Uncredited, "Judy Garland Sets New Record at Dell," *Mount Carmel Item*, Mount Carmel, PA, July 2, 1943.

33. Uncredited, *Motion Picture Daily*, July 1, 1943.

34. Uncredited, *Variety*, July 14, 1943.

35. Uncredited, *Courier News*, Bridgewater, NJ, July 8, 1943.

36. Uncredited, *Asbury Park Press*, Asbury Park, NJ, July 11, 1943.

37. McCarthy, *Daily News*, New York, NY, July 21, 1943.

38. Uncredited, *The Sentinel*, Carlisle, PA, July 20, 1943.

39. Uncredited, *Harrisburg Telegraph*, Harrisburg, PA, July 19, 1943.

40. Uncredited, *The Sentinel*, Carlisle, PA, July 20, 1943.

41. Uncredited, *Lebanon Daily News*, Lebanon, PA, July 22, 1943.

42. Walker, *Harrisburg Telegraph*, Harrisburg, PA, July 25, 1943.

43. Uncredited, *New Castle News*, New Castle, PA, July 19, 1943.

44. Uncredited, *News Herald*, Franklin, PA, July 23, 1943.

45. Uncredited, *Star Press*, Muncie, IN, July 25, 1943.

46. Uncredited, *Des Moines Register*, Des Moines, IA, September 10, 1943.

47. Uncredited, *Showmen's Trade Review* (trade magazine), September 15, 1943.

48. Ibid.

49. Safford, *Minneapolis Star*, Minneapolis, MN, September 9, 1943.

50. Mawhinney, "Buyers Star as Third Loan Drive Begins," *Philadelphia Inquirer*, Philadelphia, PA, September 10, 1943.

51. Uncredited, *News Herald*, Franklin, PA, September 11, 1943.

52. Uncredited, *The Exhibitor* (trade magazine), September 1, 1943.

53. Ibid.

54. Cutler, "Movie 'Greats' Parade Here This Afternoon," *Boston Globe*, September 10, 1943.

55. Uncredited, *The Exhibitor* (trade magazine), September 15, 1943.

56. Cutler, "Film Stars Pack Boston Garden," *Boston Globe*, September 10, 1943.

57. Uncredited, *Daily News*, New York, NY, September 12, 1943.

58. Uncredited, *Salt Lake Tribune*, Salk Lake City, September 13, 1943.

59. Uncredited, *Daily News*, New York, NY, September 12, 1943.

60. Uncredited, *Showmen's Trade Review* (trade magazine), September 18, 1943.

61. Ibid.

62. Uncredited, *The Exhibitor* (trade magazine), September 22, 1943.

63. Uncredited, *Windsor Star*, Windsor, Ontario, Canada, September 15, 1943.

64. Lanning, "Personal Appearances," *Cincinnati Enquirer*, Cincinnati, OH, September 12, 1943.

65. Uncredited, *Minneapolis Star*, September 17, 1943; uncredited, *The Exhibitor* (trade magazine), September 29, 1943.

66. Murphy, "Oh, Dmitri! Did You Ever Get That Phone Call?" *Minneapolis Star*, Minneapolis, MN, September 18, 1943.

67. Uncredited, *St. Louis Star and Times*, St. Louis, MO, September 18, 1943.

68. Uncredited, *The Exhibitor* (trade magazine), September 29, 1943.

69. Edwards, "Hollywood Bond Cavalcade Show Is Success Despite Illness of Most of Cast," *Fort Worth Star-Telegram*, September 22, 1943.

70. Uncredited, *The Exhibitor* (trade magazine), September 29, 1943.

71. Ibid.

CHAPTER 6—MORE MGM MAGIC

1. Fordin, *The World of Entertainment! Hollywood's Greatest Musicals*.

2. Kaufman, *Meet Me in St. Louis*.

3. Ibid.

4. Fordin, *The World of Entertainment! Hollywood's Greatest Musicals*.

5. Ibid.

6. Ibid.

7. Ibid.

8. Griffin, *A Hundred or More Hidden Things: The Life and Films of Vincente Minnelli*.

9. Fordin, *The World of Entertainment! Hollywood's Greatest Musicals*.

10. Hirschorn, *The Hollywood Musical*.

11. Astor, *A Life on Film*.

12. Finch, *Rainbow: The Stormy Life of Judy Garland*.

13. Ponedel and Ponedel, *About Face*.

14. Schechter, *Judy Garland: The Day-by-Day Chronicle of a Legend*.

15. Ibid.

16. Kaufman, *Meet Me in St. Louis*.

17. Griffin, *A Hundred or More Hidden Things: The Life and Films of Vincente Minnelli*.

18. Ibid.

19. Minnelli, Archival Interview, "MGM When the Lion Roars," 1992.

20. Griffin, *A Hundred or More Hidden Things: The Life and Films of Vincente Minnelli*.

21. Mann, *Wisecracker: The Life and Times of Willliam Haines*.

22. Inge, "*Meet Me in St. Louis* Is Captivating," *St. Louis Star and Times*, November 22, 1944.

CHAPTER 7—MGM's GREATEST ASSET

1. Anslinger and Oursler, *The Murderers: The Story of the Narcotic Gangs*.

2. Fordin, *The World of Entertainment! Hollywood's Greatest Musicals*.

3. Ibid.

4. Ibid.

5. Finch, *Rainbow: The Stormy Life of Judy Garland*.

6. Zinnemann, Letter to Vincente Minnelli, August 28, 1944.

7. Clarke, *Get Happy: The Life of Judy Garland*.

8. Fordin, *The World of Entertainment! Hollywood's Greatest Musicals*.

9. Ibid.

10. Tuttle, Archival Interview, *MGM: When the Lion Roars*, 1992.

11. Feltenstein, Archival Interview, "*That's Entertainment! III:* Behind the Screen," 1994.

12. Miller, Archival Interview, "*That's Entertainment! III:* Behind the Screen," 1994.

13. Fordin, *The World of Entertainment! Hollywood's Greatest Musicals*.

14. Uncredited, *Motion Picture Herald* (trade magazine), February 23, 1946.

15. Ibid.

16. Uncredited, *Atchison Daily Globe*, Atchison, KS, January 31, 1946.

17. Uncredited, "Film Story Is Not His," *Kansas City Times*, Kansas City, MO, August 1, 1952.

CHAPTER 8—MGM TREADMILL

1. Arvad, syndicated column, February 1944.

2. Frank, *Judy*.

3. Fordin, *The World of Entertainment! Hollywood's Greatest Musicals*.

4. Schechter, *Judy Garland: The Day-by-Day Chronicle of a Legend*.

5. Gwyn, "Hollywood in Review," *Philadelphia Inquirer*, December 1, 1946.

6. Hess and Dabholkar, *The Cinematic Voyage of* The Pirate.

7. Fordin, *The World of Entertainment! Hollywood's Greatest Musicals*.

8. Ibid.

9. Ponedel, Archival Interview, *Impressions of Garland*, 1972 TV documentary.

10. Fordin, *The World of Entertainment! Hollywood's Greatest Musicals*.

11. Hopper, syndicated column, July 1947.

12. Lait, syndicated column, July 1947.

13. MGM *Daily Music Report*, May 5, 1947.

14. Hess and Dabholkar, *The Cinematic Voyage of* The Pirate.

15. Griffin, *A Hundred or More Hidden Things: The Life and Films of Vincente Minnelli*.

16. Clarke, *Get Happy: The Life of Judy Garland*.

17. Finch, *Rainbow: The Stormy Life of Judy Garland*.

18. Garland, "There'll Always Be an Encore," *McCall's*, January 1964.

19. Ibid.

20. Uncredited, *Berkshire Eagle*, Pittsfield, MA, August 7, 1947.

21. Uncredited, *Berkshire Eagle*, Pittsfield, MA, August 11, 1947.

22. Fordin, *The World of Entertainment! Hollywood's Greatest Musicals*.

23. Ibid.

24. Ibid.

25. Hess and Dabholkar, *The Cinematic Voyage of* The Pirate.

26. Ibid.

27. Ibid.

28. Finch, *Rainbow: The Stormy Life of Judy Garland*.

29. Ibid.

30. Garland and Lawford, *The Mike Douglas Show*, August 9, 1968.

31. Schechter, *Judy Garland: The Day-by-Day Chronicle of a Legend*.

32. Uncredited, *Motion Picture Herald* (trade magazine), July 10, 1948.

CHAPTER 9—VINTAGE MGM

1. Frank, *Judy*.

2. Clarke, *Get Happy: The Life of Judy Garland*.

3. Ibid.

4. Schechter, *Judy Garland: The Day-by-Day Chronicle of a Legend*.

5. Garland, "There'll Always Be an Encore," *McCall's*, January 1964.

6. Ibid.

7. Clarke, *Get Happy: The Life of Judy Garland*.

8. Ibid.

9. Finch, *Rainbow: The Stormy Life of Judy Garland*.

10. Schechter, *Judy Garland: The Day-by-Day Chronicle of a Legend*.

11. Clarke, *Get Happy: The Life of Judy Garland*.

CHAPTER 10—NIGHTMARE AT MGM

1. Fordin, *The World of Entertainment! Hollywood's Greatest Musicals*.

2. Clarke, *Get Happy: The Life of Judy Garland*.

3. Ibid.

4. Petacque, syndicated column, July 1969.

5. Anslinger and Oursler, *The Murderers: The Story of the Narcotic Gangs*.

6. Ibid.

7. Petacque, syndicated column, July 1969.

8. Anslinger and Oursler, *The Murderers: The Story of the Narcotic Gangs*.

9. Ibid.

10. Clarke, *Get Happy: The Life of Judy Garland.*

11. Schechter, *Judy Garland: The Day-by-Day Chronicle of a Legend.*

12. Fordin, *The World of Entertainment! Hollywood's Greatest Musicals.*

13. Ibid.

14. Clarke, *Get Happy: The Life of Judy Garland.*

15. Ibid.

16. Schechter, *Judy Garland: The Day-by-Day Chronicle of a Legend.*

17. Fordin, *The World of Entertainment! Hollywood's Greatest Musicals.*

18. Clarke, *Get Happy: The Life of Judy Garland.*

19. Frank, *Judy.*

20. Ibid.

21. Ibid.

22. Ibid.

23. Schechter, *Judy Garland: The Day-by-Day Chronicle of a Legend.*

24. Fordin, *The World of Entertainment! Hollywood's Greatest Musicals.*

25. Clarke, *Get Happy: The Life of Judy Garland.*

26. Ibid.

27. Frank, *Judy.*

28. Fordin, *The World of Entertainment! Hollywood's Greatest Musicals.*

29. Schechter, *Judy Garland: The Day-by-Day Chronicle of a Legend.*

30. Clarke, *Get Happy: The Life of Judy Garland.*

31. Fordin, *The World of Entertainment! Hollywood's Greatest Musicals.*

32. Ibid.

33. Frank, *Judy.*

34. Uncredited, United Press syndicated article, June 1949.

35. Frank, *Judy.*

36. Ibid.

37. Clary, *The Dispatch*, Moline, IL, August 5, 1949.

38. Garland, "There'll Always Be an Encore," *McCall's*, January 1964.

39. Ibid.

CHAPTER 11—GOODBYE MGM

1. Minnelli, *I Remember It Well*.

2. French, syndicated column, December 1948.

3. Hopper, syndicated column, December 1948.

4. Graham, syndicated column, February 1949.

5. Frank, *Judy*.

6. Uncredited, *Los Angeles Times*, Los Angeles, CA, November 1, 1949.

7. Uncredited, Associated Press syndicated column, "Judy Garland to Lose Role if She Doesn't Reduce," November 1949.

8. Minnelli, *I Remember It Well*.

9. Frank, *Judy*.

10. Garland, 1960 Audiotape.

11. Fantle and Johnson, *C'mon, Get Happy: The Making of* Summer Stock.

12. Bracken, Archival Interview, *Judy Garland: Beyond the Rainbow*, A&E TV (1997).

13. Fantle and Johnson, *C'mon, Get Happy: The Making of* Summer Stock.

14. Ibid.

15. Ponedel, Archival Interview, *Impressions of Garland*, 1972 TV documentary.

16. Frank, *Judy*.

17. Fidler, syndicated column, December 1949.

18. Uncredited, *Vancouver Sun*, December 9, 1949.

19. Johnson, syndicated column, January 1950.

20. Hopper, syndicated column, January 1950.

21. Walters, Archival Interview, *Impressions of Garland*, 1972 TV documentary.

22. Frank, *Judy*.

23. Fantle and Johnson, *C'mon, Get Happy: The Making of* Summer Stock.

24. Ibid.

25. Ibid.

26. Ibid.

27. Allyson, Archival Interview, *Judy Garland: Beyond the Rainbow*, A&E TV (1997).

28. Fordin, *The World of Entertainment! Hollywood's Greatest Musicals.*

29. Frank, *Judy.*

30. Schechter, *Judy Garland: The Day-by-Day Chronicle of a Legend.*

31. Fordin, *The World of Entertainment! Hollywood's Greatest Musicals.*

32. Frank, *Judy.*

33. Uncredited, United Press syndicated article, June 1950.

34. Muir, *Free Press-Chicago Tribune Wire*, Chicago, IL, June 21, 1950.

35. Frank, *Judy.*

36. Ibid.

37. Shipman, *Judy Garland: The Secret Life of an American Legend.*

38. Uncredited, *Los Angeles Times*, Los Angeles, CA, June 21, 1950.

39. Uncredited, United Press syndicated article, June 1950.

40. Thomas, syndicated column, June 1950.

41. Uncredited, Associated Press syndicated article, June 1950.

42. Uncredited, *Los Angeles Times*, Los Angeles, CA, June 21, 1950.

43. Ibid.

44. Uncredited, *Central New Jersey Home News*, New Brunswick, NJ, June 21, 1950.

45. Mosby, syndicated column, August 1950.

46. Heffernan, syndicated column, August 1950.

47. Rose, syndicated column, August 1950.

48. Kilgallen, syndicated column, August 1950.

49. Johnson, syndicated column, August 1950.

50. Hale, *Daily News*, New York, NY, September 1, 1950.

51. Wilson, syndicated column, September 1950.

52. Uncredited, *Lansing State Journal*, Lansing, Ohio, September 6, 1950.

53. Uncredited, syndicated column, November 18, 1950.

CHAPTER 12—POST-MGM HIGHLIGHTS

1. Schechter, *Judy Garland: The Day-by-Day Chronicle of a Legend*.

2. Ibid.

BIBLIOGRAPHY

Anslinger, Harry J., and Will Oursler. *The Murderers: The Story of the Narcotic Gangs*. New York: Avon Books, 1961.

Astor, Mary. *A Life on Film*. New York: Delacorte Press, 1967.

Bingen, Steven, Stephen X. Sylvester, and Michael Troyan. *M-G-M: Hollywood's Greatest Backlot*. Solana Beach, CA: Santa Monica Press, 2013.

Cary, Diana Serra. *Hollywood's Children: An Inside Account of the Child Star Era*. Boston: Houghton Mifflin, 1979.

Clarke, Gerald. *Get Happy: The Life of Judy Garland*. New York: Random House, 2000.

Dahl, David, and Barry Kehoe. *Young Judy*. New York: Mason/Charter, 1975.

Edwards, Anne. *Judy Garland: A Biography*. New York: Simon & Schuster, 1975.

Fantle, David, and Tom Johnson. *C'mon, Get Happy: The Making of* Summer Stock. Jackson: University Press of Mississippi, 2023.

Finch, Christopher. *Rainbow: The Stormy Life of Judy Garland*. New York: Grosset & Dunlap, 1975.

Fleming, E. J. *The Fixers: Eddie Mannix, Howard Strickling and the MGM Publicity Machine*. New York: McFarland, 2005.

Fordin, Hugh. *The World of Entertainment! Hollywood's Greatest Musicals*. New York: Doubleday, 1975.

Frank, Gerold. *Judy*. New York: Harper & Row, 1975.

Griffin, Mark. *A Hundred or More Hidden Things: The Life and Films of Vincente Minnelli*. Cambridge, MA: De Capo Press, 2010.

Hess, Earl J., and Prathibha A. Dabholkar. *The Cinematic Voyage of* The Pirate. Columbia: University of Missouri Press, 2014.

Hirschorn, Clive. *The Hollywood Musical*. New York: Crown Publishing, 1981.

Kaufman, Gerald. *Meet Me in St. Louis*. London: British Film Institute, 1994.

Mankiewicz, Tom, and Robert Crane. *My Life as a Mankiewicz*. Lexington: University Press of Kentucky, 2012.

Mann, William J. *Wisecracker: The Life and Times of William Haines, Hollywood's First Openly Gay Star*. New York: Penguin Books, 1999.

Minnelli, Vincente, with Hector Arce. *I Remember It Well*. New York: Doubleday, 1974.

Murphy, George, with Victor Lasky. *"Say . . . Didn't You Used to Be George Murphy?"* N.p.: Bartholomew House, 1970.

Pasternak, Joe, as told to David Chandler. *Easy the Hard Way*. New York: G. P. Putnam's Sons, 1956.

Pastos, Spero. *Pin-Up: The Tragedy of Betty Grable*. New York: G. P. Putnam's Sons, 1986.

Phillips, Brent. *Charles Walters: The Director Who Made Hollywood Dance*. Lexington: University Press of Kentucky, 2014.

Ponedel, Dorothy, and Meredith Ponedel with Danny Miller. *About Face: The Life and Times of Dottie Ponedel, Make-up Artist to the Stars*. Albany, GA: BearManor Media, 2018.

Russell, Michelle. *From Tennessee to Oz, Part 2*. White Haven, PA: Catsong Publishing, 2011.

Scarfone, Jay, and William Stillman. *The Road to Oz*. Guilford, CT: Lyons Press, 2019.

———. *The Wizard of Oz: The Official 75th Anniversary Companion*. New York: HarperCollins, 2013.

Schechter, Scott. *Judy Garland: The Day-by-Day Chronicle of a Legend*. New York: Cooper Square Press, 2002.

Shipman, David. *Judy Garland: The Secret Life of an American Legend*. New York: Hyperion, 1992.

INDEX

Page numbers for figures are italicized.

20th Century Fox, 48, 52, 79, 174, 295

ABC Records, 296

"Abide with Me," 119

abortions, 9, 129–30, 152

Academy Awards, 78–79, 102, 205; nominations, 106, 231, 286, 290, 291

Academy of Motion Picture Arts and Sciences, 299, 300

The Adventures of Huckleberry Finn, 83

"After You've Gone," 138–39, 141, 143

Akst, Harry, 29

Ali, Hadji, 15–16

Alice Adams, 276, 277

Allenberg, Bert, 214

"All for You," 266, 297

"All God's Chillun Got Rhythm," 57

"All I Do Is Dream of You," 102

"All's Well," 42

Allyson, June: films featuring, 174, 223, 238, 260, 280; as Freed Unit member, 86; Garland replac-

ing, 268, 270; Garland's comparisons to, 223; as MGM leading lady, 280

"Alone," 102

Alsop, Carlton: Cape Cod vacation with, 257; hospital stays and visitations, 254, 255, 257; recording royalty contracts, 273; studio mismanagement, 272, 274; studio negotiations, 234; studio warnings and suspension, 252, 271, 272; suicide attempts and support from, 271, 272; support provided by, 236, 265; weight loss harassment, 257

Alton, Robert, 200, 230, 250, 269

"Always," 53

"Americana," 46

American Film Institute, 287, 301

An American in Paris, 278

Ames, Leon, 182

Andy Hardy Meets Debutante, 102, 104, 109, 119

Annie Get Your Gun: costume, hair and makeup for, *244*, *249*, 250; demands of, 249–50; directors, 248–49, 250, 251; filming of, 246, 249, 250–51; film rights for, 244; Garland fired from, 252–54; prerecordings for, 244–45, *245*; production delays, 244, 251; rehearsals, 250; story origins, 243–44; *That's Entertainment!* outtakes from, 300

Anslinger, Harry, 246–47, 248

anti-trust lawsuits, 264

"Anything You Can Do," 243

Arden, Eve, 114

Arlen, Harold: concerts attended by, 291; *Gay Purr-ee* songwriting, 293; "Get Happy" songwriting, 266, 275; *Hooray for What!* songwriting, 185–86; *I Could Go on Singing* songwriting, 293; "Let's Fall in Love" songwriting, 53–54; radio show appearances, 88; *A Star Is Born* songwriting, 284, 286; "That Old Black Magic" music, 111; *Wizard of Oz* songwriting, 74, 78

Arvad, Inga, 56, 211

Asher, Betty, 153–54, 163, 206

"As Long as He Needs Me," 294

"As Long as I Have My Art," 191

Astaire, Fred: dance partners of, 280; films with, *Barkleys of Broadway*, 233, 234; films with, *Easter Parade*, 82, 223–24, 226–28, *228*, 229–31; films with, *Royal Wedding*, 271; films with, *Yolanda and the Thief*, 198, 199; films with, *Ziegfeld Follies of 1946*, 191; with Garland and Rogers, 236–37; on Garland's talent, 138; radio show appearances, 233, 235; USO Bond fundraising tours, 163, 164, *166*, 168

Astor, Mary, 70, 179–80, 182

Atlas, Jack, 272

Austen Riggs Center, 221, 222

"Avalon Town," 14

Ayers, Lemuel, 86, 174, 216

Ayres, Maude, 8

Babes in Arms: awards, 102; birthday celebrations on set of, 86; box office reception and profit, 94–95; director, 85–86; filming and production schedule, 71, 86, 88, 89; premieres, 94; producers, 39, 85; promotional tour, *89*, 90–94, *91*, *92*; rehearsals, 85; song outtakes, 53; still from, *84*

Babes on Broadway, 104, 120, 121–25, *132*

"Back the Attack" (USO War Bonds tour), 162–69, *166*

Baker, Kenny, 201, 203

"The Balboa," 52

Ball, Lucille, 148, 163, *166*, 191

Ballard, Francis, 271, 272

Ballard, Lucille, 183

"Ballin' the Jack," 138, 142

The Barkleys of Broadway, 84, 233, 234–37, 240

Barlow, James, 8

Barrett, Leonard, 59

Barrymore, Ethel, 257

Barrymore, Lionel, 69

Bartholomew, Freddie: dating and romance publicity, 59, 68; education, 40; films with, 70–71; at studio publicity events, 43, *43*; visits with Garland and Tucker, 55

baseball games, 84–85

"The Battle Hymn of the Republic," 294

Bauman, Roberta, 298

"Be a Clown," 219, *220*, 221

Beckett, Scotty, 45, 70

Beery, Wallace, 41

"Bei Mir Bist Du Schoen," 67

La Belle Dolly, 43–44

Belmont Theatre, 23

Ben Bernie and All the Lads, 54–55

Benson, Sally, 172

Bentz, Fred, 8

Berg, Phil, 214

Bergen, Edgar, 125

Berkeley, Busby: directing style, 85–86, 147–48; films directed by, *Annie Get Your Gun*, 248–49, 250, 251, 253; films directed by, *Babes in Arms*, 85–86, 89; films directed by, *Babes on Broadway*, 120, 122, 123; films directed by, *For Me and My Gal*, 137; films directed by, *Girl Crazy*, 147–48, 149, 150; films directed by, *Strike Up the Band*, 105, 106; films directed by, *Ziegfeld Girl*, 114, 115, 119

Berlin, Irving, 122, 213, 222, 226, 235, 243, 254

"Bidin' My Time," 149–50, 169

"Big Brother Ken Show," 18

The Big Revue (film short), 17

"Bill," 19–20, 24, 28, *36*

"Billy the Kid Street" (MGM Lot 3), 199

388   INDEX bisexuality, 186

"Black Bottom," *284*

blackface caricatures, 62, 123

Blane, Ralph, 86, 174–75, 176, 180, 191–92

"Blow, Gabriel, Blow," 164

"Blue Butterfly," 17

"Blue Moon," 21

Bob Crosby Show, 213

Bogart, Delia, 59

Bolger, Ray, 75, 88, 93, 94, 200, 203, 288

"Born in a Trunk," 39, 285

Born to Dance, 40

The Boy Next Door (film), 180

"The Boy Next Door" (song), 174, 175, *177*, 180, *184*, 186, 187

"Boys and Girls Like You and Me," 170, 171, 176, 183, 186–87

Bracken, Eddie, 262, 263

Bradley, Alva, 84

Brecher, Irving, 172–73, 183

Bremer, Lucille, 86, 173, *178*, 198, 207

Brent, Earl, 157, 158, 160

Brice, Fanny, 61–62, *63*

Broadway Melody Hour, 46

Broadway Melody of 1938, 54–55, *55*, 56, 57

"Broadway Rhythm," 39, 41, 46, 146

Brown, Joe E., 7, 43

Brown, Lew, 29

Brown, Nacio Herb, 39, 85, 102, 174

Browning, Florence, 45–46

Brynner, Yul, 245

Bubbles (film short), 17

"Buds Won't Bud," 102

Burke, Billie, 61, 77, 102, 257

Burns, Lillian, 115, 152

Burton, Harold, 84

"But Not for Me," 1, 150, 157, 169

Byington, Spring, 69, 240

Cafe Trocadero, 41, 46, 52, 54, 68

Cagney, James, 163, 164, *166*

Caine, Howard, *291*

California Melodies, 130

Cal-Nev Lodge, 29

Camp Kilmer, 160

Camp Robinson, 128

Camp Shanks, 160

Camp Shenango Personnel Replacement Depot, 162

Camp Wolters, 129

Capitol Records: concert recordings, 289, 290, 291, 295; recording contracts with, 111, 289; recordings for, 109, 110, 138, 239

Carlisle Barracks, *160*, 161

Carnegie Hall: concert recordings at, 111, 147, 290, 291–92, *292*; concerts at, 147, 291

"Carolina in the Morning," 110

Caron, Leslie, 280

Carpenter, Carleton, 262

Carroll, Joan, *178*, 182

Carson, Johnny, 297

Carver, Lynne, 61

Cary, Diana Serra, 20–21

Casa Manana, 66

Cathcart, Jack, 23, 109–10

Cathcart, Jimmy, 109

Chaplin, Saul, 266–67

Charisse, Cyd, 201, 203, 223, 238, 280

The Chase and Sanborn Hour, 66, 125, 143

The Chesterfield Supper Club, 233

A Child Is Waiting, 293

Children's Hour, 14

"Chin Up! Cheerio! Carry On!," 122

Christmas events, 62–63, 96

Clarke, Gerald, 33, 153, 252

Clary, Patricia, 257

The Clock, 83, *194*, 194–97, *195*, 210

C'mon, Get Happy: The Making of Summer Stock (Fantle and Johnson), 263

Cocoanut Grove, 18, 78, 289

Cohn, Harry, 29

Collins, Cora Sue, 44, 45

Columbia Records, 283, *283*

Combs, Carl, 26

"Comes Love," 96

Command Performance series (radio shows), 143, 162, 198, *199*, 209

Como, Perry, 233, 238

concerts: Arie Crown Theatre, 295; Australian tours, 294; Carnegie Hall, 111, 147, 290, 291–92, *292*; Cocoanut Grove, 18, 289; debuts, *157*, 157–59, 297; Forest Hills Stadium, 295; J. F. K. Stadium, 297; Las Vegas, 289; Manhattan Center, 293; musical arrangers for, 23, 109; O'Keefe Center, 295; opera house tour, 289; ovations, record-breaking, 295; Palace Theatre, 224, *281*, 282, 289; song staples at, 139

"La Conga," 105

contracts: agent, 29–30; early, 18; MGM, 32, 37–38, 113, 214–15, 277; recording, 42, *42*, 89–90, 111, 224, 289; recording royalties, 273; Universal Pictures, 27

Cook, Elisha, Jr., 52

Cooper, Jackie: charity events with, 44; dating and romance publicity, 59, *97*, 109; education, 40; films with, 114, 115; Garland's birthday celebration, 87–88; Rose introduction through, 112

Cooper, Mabel, 87

"A Cottage for Sale," 294

"Could You Use Me?," 149, 169

"A Couple of Swells," 222, 226–28, *227*, *228*, 231

Crews, Laura Hope, 102

"The Croaker," 246, 247

Cronenweth, Ed, 106

Crosby, Bing: radio shows of, 217, 237, 258, 277, 279–80, 282; radio shows with, 162, 198, *199*, 206

Crosby, Bob, 46, 145, 213

"La Cucaracha," 30

Cukor, George, 76, 197, 284

Curran Theatre, 26, 27, 282

Dahl, David, 3, 300

Daily, Dan, Jr., 109, 290

Daniels, Henry H., Jr., *178*

"Danny Boy," 9, 109

The Danny Kaye Show, *207*

Darro, Frankie, 31, 45

Darrow, George, 5

David, Mack, 261

Davis, Bette, 95, 119, 174, 212, 291

Deans, Mickey, 297

"(Dear Mr. Gable) You Made Me Love You," 28, 53–55, 58

Decca Records: compilation releases, 224, *281*; recording contracts with, 42, *42*, 89–90, 224; recordings for, 57, 58, 95, 102, 104, 109, 111, 121, 123, 143, 149, 159, 169, 186, 201–2, 206, 224; test recordings, first, 28, 42

DeHaven, Gloria, 86, 260, 262

de Havilland, Olivia, 163

Detroit Arena Gardens wrestling matches, 68

DiCaprio, Leonardo, 299

Dick Tracy in B-Flat, 198, *199*

Dietz, Howard, 117, 140, 160, 193

"Dinah," 21, 28, 29

Disney, 73–74, 106, *110*, 300

"Doin' What Comes Natur'lly," 243, 244, 249, 250, 251, 300

Donen, Stanley, 269

"Don't Bite the Hand That's Feeding You," 138

"Down on Melody Farm," 62, 67

Downs, Johnny, 52

Drake, Tom, 173, 175, 182, *184*, 215, 233, 238

Dressler, Marie, 44

drug addiction: descriptions, 246–48; early, 57, 105; film production affected by, 179, 245, 246, 250, 296; insomnia, 152; during marriages, 131, 206; MGM response to treatment, 246–47; overdoses, 295, 297; post-pregnancy, 217–18; pregnancy and, 212; public announcements of, *254*, 255; treatments for, 242, 246, *246*, 254–58, *255*; weight issues, 151–52; withdrawals from, 237, 259

"Drumhead Road" (MGM Lot 3), 229

"Drummer Boy," 106

"Drums in My Heart," 54

Duke, Patty, 296

Dunbar, Dixie, 52

Duncan Sisters, 12

Durbin, Deanna: fictional report about, 59; films with, 46, 47, *47*, 48, *49*, *50*, *51*; film test with, 45; singing style of, 44, 47; studio publicity events,

45; studio representation, 46–48
"D'Ya Love Me," 208–9

Easter Parade (film): awards, 231–32; box office reception and profit, 229–30; casting challenges, 223; director, 149, 222–23; events featured in, 82; filming of, 224, 226, 229; premiere, 229; prerecordings for, 223–24; radio shows featuring songs from, 233; reviews, 230–31; scenes from, 226–29; songs for, 223–24, 226–29, *228*; *That's Entertainment!* outtakes from, 300
"Easter Parade" (song), 222, 229, 230
"Easy to Love," 119
Ebsen, Buddy, 40, 75–76
Edens, Roger: awards, 231–32; *Babes in Arms* musical production, 85; *Babes in Arms* tour, 90; biographical information, 39; daily rehearsals with, 40; driver of Freed Unit, 248; *Everybody Sings* world premiere, 63; *For Me and My Gal* musical production, 138; Garland's identifier songs, 53–54; Garland's MGM audition, 32, 33, 34, 35; hiding Walters from Garland, 269; Kern memorial concert, 214; MGM position, 38; on *Little Nellie Kelly*, 107–8; *Oz* musical production, 73, 74, 79; songwriting, 62, 102, 106, 146, 285; tutelage of, 28; *Ziegfeld Follies of 1946* comedy skits, 192–93
Edwards, Anne, 300
"Eighth Annual *Los Angeles Evening Express* 'Better Babies' Exposition," 17
"Eili, Eili" ("Eli, Eli"), 29, 32, 33, 35
Electric Theatre, 24
Elks Movie Star Benefit, 44
"Embraceable You," 149, 157, 164, 169, 237
Erlanger Mason Theatre, 12
Erwin, Stuart, 48, 52
Ethel Meglin Studio, 14–15, 16, 17, 96
European tours, 281
Everybody Sing (film), 58, 60–62, *63*, 63–69, *65*, *67*
"Everybody Sing" (song), 55, *55*, 57
Every Sunday, 46–48, *47*, *49*, *50*, *51*, 52
"Ev'ry Little Movement Has a Meaning of Its Own," 145
"Exterior Trolley Depot" (MGM Lot 2), 177

Eyssell, Gus, 159

Falkoner Centre, 297
"Falling in Love with Love," 224
"Famous Meglin Kiddies Recital," 14–15
Fantle, David, 263
"The Far Away Part of Town," 290
"Fascinating Rhythm," 90
Fay, Frank, 41, 52
FBI (Federal Bureau of Investigation), 103, 298
"F. D. R. Jones," 82, 93, 123
"A Fella with an Umbrella," 228
Fellows, Edith, 43, *43*, 45
Fields, Dorothy, 243
Fields, Herbert, 243
Fields, W. C., 74
La Fiesta de Santa Barbara (film short), 30, 48
"Fight on for Good Old USC," 40
Finch, Christopher, 34, 193, 300
Finklehoffe, Fred, 15, 172–73, 290
Fleming, Victor, 76, 77, 78
Fordin, Hugh, 216, 219, 249, 252
The Ford Star Jubilee series, 23, 289
"Forgotten Child of Hollywood" (charity event), 44
For Me and My Gal (film), 17, 131, 135–43, *136*, *139*
"For Me and My Gal" (song), 136, 137, 139, 143, 237
Fort Custer, 126–27, *127*
Fort Dix, 160
Fort Hancock, 160
Fort Jefferson Barracks, 128
Fort Knox, 127–28
Fort Wayne, 162
Fort Worth, 128–29, 169
Foster, Frank, 103
Foster, Susanna, 59
Four Franks, 65, 68, 101
Frank, George, 18
Frank, Gerold, 3, 23, 32–33, 156, 234, 252, 269, 300
Frank, Perry, 68, 69, 101
Frank and Dunlap Talent Agency, 18
Frank Morgan Varieties, 55–56
Freed, Arthur: biographical information, 39; concert contracts, 159; films produced by, 73, 74, 77, 79,

85, 195, 217, 222, 233, 268–70; Garland's MGM audition, 32, 33, 35; Garland's mismanagement, 248–49, 251; Garland's birthday, 270, *271*; Kern memorial concerts, 213; *Meet Me in St. Louis* challenges, 172, 183; *Meet Me in St. Louis* sets, 174; MGM position, 38; Minnelli-Garland meeting, 106; personality descriptions, 248; songwriting, 102, 106

Freed Unit, 39, 86, 146, 184, 248

"Friendly Star," 261, 273, 277

"Friendship," 104, 111

Funkhouser, Clifford, 206

Gable, Clark, 44, 54, 70, 164

Gale, June, 84

Gardiner, Reginald, 61

Gardner, Ava, 276

Garland, Judy (Frances Gumm): abortions, 129–30, 152; adult roles, 140, 145; auditions, MGM, 32–35; autobiography, 290; behavioral issues and studio views of, 263, 265, 270; biographies, 3, 300–302; birth, 5, 9; childhood, 5, *5*, 9–11, 12, 14, 15–17, 20–21, 23; children's hospital visits, 96–97, 257–58; death, 2, 297; dolls, 17, 60, *61*, 140; education, 40, 63; European tours, 281; extramarital affairs, 152, 154, 245; fan adoration, 67, 103, 273, 275–76; fashion and iconic looks, 296; fashion modeling and clothing lines, 59–60, *60*, 64, *65*, *66*; father's death, 41; financial issues, 270; financial mismanagement, 233–34; flower shop, 87; funeral, 2, 297; girlfriends, 82, 98, 114, 153–54, 163, 181, 194, 206; in Hollister, *282*; kidnapping plot, 102–3; legacy, 1–2, 297–302; on live audiences, 211; movies fired from, 235–36, 252–53, 271; natural talent descriptions, 2, 138, 154, 179, 200–201, 218; as new mother, 212–13; personae and image, 1, 43, 47, 57, 58–60, *60*, 70, 87, 297; personality descriptions, 1, 223, 262, 263; residences, 45, *86*, 86–87, 126; signature/identifier songs, 1, 28, 53–55, 138; social life, 197–98, *198*, 270; solo act, 31; song standards, 285; stage names, 9, 18, 23–24, 27, 28, 29. *See also* Gumm (Garland) Sisters

Garland at the Grove (concert album), 18, 289

Garland Cult (fan base), 103, 129, 159, 193

The Garland Touch (album), 290

GarRose Railway, 130, 131

Garson, Greer, 163, 164, *166*, 192–93, 212

Gaudsmith Brothers, 82

Gay Purr-ee, 293, 294

gay rights movement, 298

Gershe, Leonard, 284, 286

Gershwin, Ira, 191, 206

"Get Happy," 1, 266–67, *268*, 270, 273, 277

Gilbert, Doris, 172

Gilmore, Laura, 99

Gilmore, Will, 15, 99, 113

Girl Crazy (film), 95, 146–50, *151*

Girl Crazy (soundtrack), 169–70

The Girl from Chicago, 238–39. *See also In the Good Old Summertime*

Gleason, James, 121, 196

Gleason, Lucille, 196

glucose injections, 234, 262

Godwin, Rack, 224

Goenne, Barbara, 23

"Go Home Joe," 283

Golden Gate Theatre, 19

Goldwyn, Sam, 74

Gone with the Wind, 77, 78–79, 102, 187, 287

"Good Morning," 39, 85, 92

Good News of 1938, 58, 62, 69

"Goodnight Irene," 277

Goodrich, Frances, 216, 222

Goodspeed, Muriel, 163

"Got a Pair of New Shoes," 58

Goulet, Robert, 294

Grable, Betty, 52, 98, 212

Grammy Awards, 291

Grammy Hall of Fame, 301

Grant, Cary, 162, 186

Grauman's Chinese Theatre, 25, 92, 94, *94*

Grayson, Kathryn, 70, 143, 147, 163, 164, 280

"A Great Lady Has an Interview" (skit), 192–94

The Great Ziegfeld, 27, 28, 117

Green, Johnny, 86, 213, 231–32

Griffith, Eadie, 224

Gross, Dean, 150

Guillaroff, Sydney, 181

Gumm, Allie, 6

Gumm, Frances. *See* Garland, Judy

Gumm, Frank: biographical information, 5–8; California relocation, 11–14; children, 8, 9; death, 41; Garland's MGM audition, 32, 33; Garland's promotion, 21–22; Garland's stage debut, 10; health, 41; homosexuality, 8, 13, 28; marriage, 15, *15*, 16; personality descriptions, 5; residences, 28; vaudeville acts, 8, 11–12, 19; wife's birthday surprise party, 41–42

Gumm, Mary, 6

Gumm, Robert, 6, 7, 11

Gumm (Garland), Dorothy Virginia "Jimmie": birth, 8; *Easter Parade* anecdotes, 226–27; employment, 125, 155; engagement, 31; film credit misinformation, 124–25; Garland's talent, 25; marriage, 112; residences, 45; USO War Bonds tour, 163; vaudeville act breakup, 29, *31*. *See also* Gumm (Garland) Sisters

Gumm (Garland), Ethel (Milne): abuse, 155, 283; biographical information, 5; birthday surprise party, 41–42; California relocation, 11–14; children, 8, 9; death of, 283; film promotion tours, 63, *65*, 67, 90; financial challenges, 23; Garland's management, 41, 233–34; Garland's MGM contract signing, 113; Garland's recording contracts, 89; Garland's relationships, 98, 112, 120, 155, 197; Garland's stage debut, 9–10; magazine articles featuring, *132*; marriages, 7, 8, 15, *15*, 16, 99; name change, 89; personality descriptions, 98; residences, 16, 45, 86–87; as stage mother, 21, 283; stipend, 113; tours, 21, 22, 23; USO tours, 159; vaudeville acts, 8, 11–12, 19

Gumm (Garland), Mary Jane "Suzanne": birth, 8; marriage, 23, 30–31, *31*, 109; sister's talent, 25; vaudeville act breakup, 29, 30, *31*. *See also* The Gumm (Garland) Sisters

Gumm (Garland) Sisters: auditions, 20–21; breakup, 29, 30–31; early years, *10*, 10–12, *12*; film contracts, 27; film shorts featuring, 17, 30; Garland's

stage debut, 9–10; kiddie performances, 14, 18; promotional photographs, *10*, *12*, *19*; radio show performances, 14; recordings, 28; reviews, 18–19, 20, 21, 24–26, 27, 28, 29; stage names, 18, 23–25, 27, 29; stage performances, 10, 14, 15, 18–19, 20, 21, 25, 27, 28; talent competitions, 17; tours, 21, 22, 23–24

Hacker, Frederick, 218

Hackett, Albert, 216, 222

Haines, William, 184–85, 186

Hale, Alan, Sr., 70

Haley, Jack, 48, 52, 92

Haley, Jack, Jr., 300

Halop, Billy, 109

Hamilton, Margaret, 74, 76–77, 81–82

Hammerstein, Oscar, II, 175–76, 243, 276

hangings, 79

"Hang onto a Rainbow," 17

"Happy Birthday," 119

Harburg, E. Y. "Yip," 74, 78, 88, 185–86, 293

Harlow, Jean, 39, 44, 126, 295

Harmetz, Aljean, 300

Hart, Lorenz, 233, 238, 260

The Harvey Girls: awards, 205; box office reception and profit, 203; director, 200; filming of, 203; Garland's behavior on, 202–3; Garland's lack of interest in, 198–99; lawsuits, 206; preview, 200; promotional campaigns, 205; recordings for, 169; reviews, 203–4; sets for, 199–200, *200*; sheet music from, *201*; songs from, 111, 199–200, *201*, 201–2; stills from, *200*, *203*, *205*

Haver, Ronald, 287, 300

"Have Yourself a Merry Little Christmas," 174, 175, 186

Hayes, Peter Lynd, 109

Hayton, Lennie, 201, 205, 231

health issues: car accidents, 70, 274; childhood, 11, 14; energy treatments, 234, 261; exhaustion, 148, 181; film production delays due to, 179–80, 181–82, 234, 235, 251; hepatitis, 289; highs and lows, extreme, 270; insecurities, 115, 152, 154–55, 202–3, 218, 238–39, 296; insomnia,

130, 152, 179–80; later years, 296–97; migraines, 181, 271; nervous breakdown, 219, 221–22; pleurisy, 295; postpartum depression, 212, 224; psychiatric, 155, 218–19, 221–22, 256; strep throat, 129; stress, 217–18; suicide attempts, 221, 271–73; tonsillectomy, 113; weight management, 47, 56–57, 64, 234, 261–62, 265–66, 267, 289. *See also* drug addiction

"Heartbroken," 283

"Heavenly Music," *260*

Heerman, Victory, 172

Heffernan, Harold, 274

Heflin, Van, 144, *144*

Hegyi, Viola, 20

Hendrickson, F. L., 37–38, 271

Hendry, Whitey, 271

Henreid, Paul, *166*

Hepburn, Katharine, 113, 257, 272, 277

Herron, Mark, 294–95, 297

Heyman, Melvin, 159

Hippodrome Theatre, 15, 282

Hodiak, John, 192, 201, *202*, 203, 210

"Hoe Down," 122, 124

Holden, Fay, 69

"Hold That Bulldog," 52

A Holiday in Storyland (film short), 17

Hollywood Bond Cavalcade, 162–69

Hollywood Bowl, 213

Hollywood School of Dance, 21

Hollywood Starlets, 17, 21

homosexuality: Freed Unit, 184; Grant, 186; Gumm, F., 8, 13, 28; Hollywood practices and, 151, 184–85; Minnelli, V., 184–85, 186, 221; Walters, 151

Hope, Bob, 95, 101, 102, 104, 198, 277

Hopper, Hedda, 47, 121, 219, 253, 260, 266

Horne, Lena, 85, 86, 171, 214, 238, 267, 276, 294

Horton, Edward Everett, 114

hospital stays, 242, 254–56, *255, 256*, 257–58, 270

"How about You?," 120, 122, 123, 149

"How Could You Believe Me When I Said I Loved You When You Know I've Been a Liar All My Life?," 271, 280

"How Deep Is the Ocean," 279

"(Howdy Neighbor) Happy Harvest," 261, 266, 273

"How You Gonna Keep 'Em Down on the Farm," 139

Hurd, Jack, 186

Hutton, Betty, 163, 164, *166*, 253–54

Hyde, Johnny, 277

"I Can't Give You Anything But Love, Baby," 16

I Could Go On Singing, 293, 294

"I Cried for You," 39, 85

"I Don't Care," 239, 241, 258

"If I Had You," 213

"If I Only Had a Brain," 75

"If I Only Had a Heart," 75

"If I Only Had the Nerve," 75

"If You Feel Like Singing, Sing," 261, *261*, 273

"I Got Rhythm," 147, 148, 149, 169

"I Got the Sun in the Morning," 213, 243

"I'll Plant My Own Tree," 296

"I Love More in Technicolor Than I Did in Black and White," 191–92

"I'm Always Chasing Rainbows," 117, 119

"I'm an Indian, Too," 250–51, 252, 300

"I'm in Love with a Uniform," 138

"(I'm in Love with) a Wonderful Guy," 279

"I'm Just Wild about Harry," 90

"I'm Nobody's Baby," 102, 109, 157

"In-Between," 70

Indiantown Gap Military Reservation, 161–62

International Photography Magazine, 104, 106

In the Good Old Summertime, 234, 237, 238, 239, 239–42, *242*

I Remember It Well (Minnelli, V.), 173

"I Remember You," 111

"Irving Strouse Vaudeville Frolics," 25–27

"It Had to Be You," 82

"It Never Rains, But What It Pours," *71*

"It Only Happens When I Dance with You," 235

"It's a Great Day for the Irish," 109

"It's All for You," 297

"It's Love I'm After," 52

"I've Been Saving for a Rainy Day," 12

"I've Got You Under My Skin," 217

"I Wish I Were in Love Again," 85, 224, 234, *235*, 237

Jack Oakie's College, 52, 53, 55

Jean, Gloria, 48

Jennings, Al, 179, 244, 249, 251, 252

Jessell, George, 23

Jewkes, Delos J. D., 55, *55*

"Jingle Bells," 10

"The Jitterbug," 77, 82, 90

"Johnny One Note," 53, 85, 234, 237

Johnson, Albert, 33

Johnson, Erksine, 265, 275

Johnson, Tom, 263

Johnson, Van, 154, 163, 173, 192, 238, 240, 241

"The Joint Is Really Jumpin' Down at Carnegie Hall," 147

Jolson, Al, 54, 126, 237, 275, 285

Jones, Allan, 61

Jones, Dickie, 45

Jones, Jack, 62

"A Journey to a Star," 180

Judge, Arline, 52

Judgment at Nuremberg, 196, 291, *291*

Judy (Gerold Frank), 3, 300

Judy: That's Entertainment! (album), 290

Judy at Carnegie Hall (concert album), 111, 147, 290, 291–93, *292*

Judy at the Palace (concert album), 224, *281*

"Judy at the Palace" (medley), 39

"Judy Barks!," 52

Judy Garland (Edwards), 300

Judy Garland: At Home at the Palace—Opening Night (concert album), 296

Judy Garland: Beyond the Rainbow (documentary), 301

Judy Garland: By Myself (documentary), 302

Judy Garland: The Concert Years (documentary), 300–301

Judy Garland and Her Guests Phil Silvers and Robert Goule (television show), 294

Judy Garland Flowers, 87

Judy Garland—From the Decca Vaults, 90

Judy Garland Live! (concert album), 293

Judy Garland Museum, 298

Judy Garland Second Souvenir Album, 90

The Judy Garland Show (television show), 62, 213, 239, 293

Judy Garland Sings (compilation album), 240

"Judy Takes Broadway" (concert), 293

Junior Troupers' benefit show, 45

Kahn, Lee, 30, 31

Kapp, Jack, 42, *42*, 57, 169

Katz, Sam, 35, 41

Keaton, Buster, 240

Keel, Howard, *245*, 249

Kehoe, Barry, 3, 300

Kelly, Gene: dance partners of, 280; films with, *An American in Paris*, 278; films with, *Easter Parade*, 222, 223; films with, *For Me and My Gal*, 135–43, *136*, *139*; films with, *The Pirate*, 215–16, 218, *220*, 220–21; films with, *Royal Wedding*, 270; films with, *Summer Stock*, 259–61, 266, 275; as Freed Unit member, 280; Garland's friendship with, 261; on Garland's talent, 138, 262; Minnelli, V., and, 220–21; support of Garland, 143, 270

Kelly, Patsy, 52

Kern, Jerome, 207, 213–14, 243

kewpie dolls, 17, 140

Kilgallen, Dorothy, 275

Knight, Robert P., 222

Koehler, Ted, 266

Koselanetz, Andre, 157–58

Koverman, Ida, 32, 33, 35, 45–46, 54, 272

Kraft Music Hall, 237

Kramer, Stanley, 293

Kupper, Herbert, 222–23

Kusell, Maurice, 18, 19, 35

Kyser, Kay, 163, *166*, 167

Ladd, Alan, 52

Lahr, Bert, 75, 88, 93, 287

Lait, Jack, 219

Lake Tahoe, 29, 30, 31, 274

Lamarr, Hedy, 60, 91, 114, 115, *116*, 119, 131, 216

Lancaster, Burt, 293

"The Land of Let's Pretend," 17
Lansbury, Angela, 196, 203
La Planche, Rosemary, *166*
Larson, Suzanne, 59
Las Campanas sanitarium, 221–22
Lastfogel, Abe, 277
"Last Night When We Were Young," 239, 240
Las Vegas, 120, *121*, 289, 295
"Laugh, Clown, Laugh," 14–15
Lawford, Peter, 223, 226, 228–29, 230, 249
Lawlor's School for Professional Children, 20–21, 40
Leo Is on the Air (holiday show), 63
LeRoy, Baby, 44
Leslie, Joan, 48
"Let's Go West Again," 245, *245*
Levant, Oscar, 83–84, 236
Lewis, Diana, 102
Life Begins for Andy Hardy, 119
Life magazine, 67, 197
"The Life of Judy Garland" (satirical sketch), 154
Life with Judy Garland: Me and My Shadows (miniseries), 148, 301–2
Listen, Darling, 70–71, *72*, 179
"Little Man, You've Had a Busy Day," 24–25
Little Nellie Kelly, 60, 104, 107–9, 113, 119, 141
Little Red Schoolhouse, 40
Loew's State Theatre (Los Angeles), 14, 16
Loew's State Theatre (New York), 64, 65–66, 82–83, 229
London Palladium, 281, 290, 293, 295
"Look for the Silver Lining," 207, 213
Los Angeles Coliseum, 40, 96
Los Angeles Philharmonic, 282
Love Finds Andy Hardy, 69–70, *71*
"Love Letter to a National Asset" (Rose), 275
"Love of My Life," 216, 220, 224, 225
Ludwig, Bill, 172
Luft, Joseph, 213, 281, 286, *290*, 291, 294, 296
Luft, Lorna, 281, *290*; biography miniseries based on memoir of, 148, 301–2; birth, 213, 283; Carnegie concert attendance, 291; concert appearances, 296; television show appearance, 294

Luft, Sid: at Carnegie concert, 291; early biographies and cooperation of, 200; management, 281; marriage, 213, 281, 283; personality descriptions, 281; production company of, 283; separation and divorce, 294, 295
Lux Radio Theatre, 113, 210, 215, 277
Lux Soap endorsements, 142
Lyons, Leonard, 24

"Ma, He's Making Eyes at Me," 258
MacDonald, Jeanette, 47
"Mack the Black," 217, 224, 225
Maestri, Robert, 64
Main, Marjorie, 182, 203
makeup: Garland's classic look, 76, 181; Garland's endorsements of, 142, *208*; *Wizard of Oz* injuries involving, 75–77
"The Man I Love," 157, 164, 169
Mankiewicz, Joseph L., 33, 153, 154–56, 171, 212, 216
Mannix, Eddie, 153, 155
"The Man That Got Away," 267, 284, 286, 295
"March of the Doagies," 201, 202
Marie, Rose, 44
marriages: Deans, 297; Herron, 294–95; Luft, S., 213, 281, 283, 286, 294, 295; Minnelli, V., 184, 197, *197*, 206–7, 220–21, 223, 236, 245, 278; Rose, D., 87, 112, 120–21, *121*, 126, 130–31, 150
Martin, Dean, 293
Martin, Hugh, 86, 174–75, 176, 191–92
Martin, Mary, 82, 250, 276
Martin, Tony, 52, 114, 115–16, 117, 118, 119
Marx, Harpo, 163, *166*
Mason, James, 264, 284, *287*
Mason, Sarah, 172
Max Factor makeup: endorsements, 142, *208*; *Wizard of Oz*, 70
Maxwell House Coffee Time—Good News, 88–89
"Maybe It's Because," 258
Mayer, Louis B.: Andy Hardy series, 69; beach house birthday party, 87–88; film release requests, 261; Garland-Minnelli wedding, 206; Garland's

396   INDEX

audition, 32–33, 35; Garland's contract, 47; Garland's drug use/treatment, 247, 248, 249, 254, 255; Garland's psychiatric care, 218; Mankiewicz affair, 155–56; *Meet Me in St. Louis* story, 172; MGM position, 264; *Pirate* scenes burned, 219; *Strike Up the Band* title selection, 106

McDonald, Ray, 70, 122

McGraw, Kathryn Francis, 7

"Mean to Me," 279

Meet Me in St. Louis (film): assistant directors, 179; box office reception and profit, 188; casting, 173; director, 171, 179, 180, 183; expectation of, 171; filming of, 170, 177–79; film rights, 172; Garland-Minnelli romance, 183–84; Garland on set of, *180, 182*; Garland's illness during, 179; Garland's lack of interest in, 171, 173–74; hit song promotional tie-ins for, *185*; makeup style for, 181; plot challenges, 171, 172; premieres, 187; production delays, 179–80, 181–83; recordings for, 169, 171; rehearsals for, 179; reviews, 187–88; scene deletions, 183; screenplay for, 172–73; sets for, 174; songs and prerecordings, 174–77, 179, 180; stills from, *177, 178, 184*; story origins, 172

Meet Me in St. Louis (sheet music), *188*

Meet Me in St. Louis (soundtrack), 186–87

"Meet Me in St. Louis, Louis," 186

Meglin, Ethel, 14, 16, 17, 96

Mercer, Johnny, 104, 111–12, 199, 203, 205

Merkel, Una, 41

"Merry Christmas," 240

Messenger, Lily, 172

Meyer, John, 297

MGM (Metro-Goldwyn-Mayer) Studios: assistants at, 55; auctions held by, 298; auditions at, 32–35; bonuses, 94; criticism of, 274; daily schedule, 40; drug treatment bills, 254; Durbin contract, 46–48; early film tests, 45; early publicity and exposure, 42–46, *43*, 53, 58; early work assignments, 40; fan support and promotion by, 276–77; first visit to, 12; Fox loan, 48, 52; Garland's celebrity replacements, 280; Garland's contracts, 32, 37–38, 113, 214–15, 277; Garland's drug

use, 247, 248; holiday shows, 62–63; in-between status at, 38; leaving, 211–12, 277–78; New York audition, 45–46; official public interviews and introduction, 40–41; party hosted by, 42; personae and image development, 1, 43, 47, 57, 58–60, *60*, 70, 87, 297; personal life control, 41; portrait sessions, first, 38, *38*; publicity fabrications, 34–35, 40, 41; salary, 37, 215; schools of, 40; script girls for, 125, 155; soundtrack recordings, 224; studio's perceptions of Garland, 263, 270, 274–75; studio spies, 153–54; suspensions and salary withholdings, 233–34, 237, 239, 271, 272; teen fashion modeling, 59–60, *60*, 64, *65, 66*; treatment of Garland, 236, 274–75; weight issues, 47, 56–57. *See also specific film titles*

MGM Club Dance, 41

MGM Records: compilation albums, 109, 299; *In the Good Old Summertime* soundtrack, 239–40, 241–42; *Pirate* soundtrack, 216, *226*; recording royalties contracts, 273; soundtrack albums, 224; *Summer Stock* soundtrack, 273, 277; *Wizard of Oz* soundtrack, 2, 288, *289*

Miller, Ann: as childhood actor, 21; drug use comment to mother of, 56; filming experiences, 203; films with, 223, 226, 230, 249; USO tours, 126

Miller, Marilyn, 207, 276

Million Dollar Theatre, 19

Minnelli, Liza: birth of, 212–13, *213*; Carnegie concert attendance, 291; Fourth of July visit, 257; godmother of, 82; marriage, 300; with mother, *212*; mother's relationship disclosures, 156; Palladium concerts with mother, 295; sanitarium/hospital visits, 222, 255; screen debut of, *239*, 240–41; Sun Valley/Lake Tahoe trip with mother, 273–74; television show appearance, 294; *Wizard of Oz* television premiere host, 287; *Words and Music* set visited by, 234, *235*

Minnelli, Vincente: artwork, 185; biographical information, 185–86; children, 185, 212–13, *213*; directing style, 195; films directed by, *An American in Paris*, 278; films directed by, *The Clock*, 194–95; films directed by, *Easter Parade*, 222–23; films directed by, *Madame Bovary*, 240; films directed

INDEX · 397

by, *Meet Me in St. Louis*, 171, 179, 180, 183; films directed by, *The Pirate*, 215, 225; films directed by, *Yolanda and the Thief*, 198–99; Garland's birthday, 270, *271*; Garland's jealousy of, 220–21, 240; Garland's suicide attempt, 271, 272; marriage to Garland, 184, 197, *197*, 206–7, 220–21, 223, 236, 245, 278; meeting Garland, 106; MGM contract negotiations, 215; musical sequences directed by, 106, 123; romance and engagement with, 183–84, 197; sexuality, 184–85, 186, 221; social life, 197–98, *198*; studio visit to, 278

"Minnie from Trinidad," 115, 119

Mirtz, Anna Lee, 9

Miss Show Business (album), 289

Modern Screen (magazine), *132*, *133*, 226–27

Monroe, Marilyn, 277, 293

Montgomery, Robert, 40

"Moonglow," 28

Moore, Dickie, 44, 45

Morgan, Dennis, 48

Morgan, Frank, 55–56

Movie Life (magazine), *83*

Movie Songs (magazine), *204*, *205*

"Movie Star Frolic" show, 22

"Mr. Monotony," 223–24, 267, 300

Munchkins, 74, 79, 80–81, 168

The Murderers: The Story of Narcotic Gangs (Anslinger), 246–47

Murphy, George, 17, 108, 136, 140, 141

"My Defenses Are Down," *245*

Myers, Carmel, 53–54

"My Intuition," 201

national anthem, 84–85

National Film Registry, 301

Neff, Wallace, 87

"New England Street" (MGM Lot 2), 69–70, 174

New Lancaster Theatre (*renamed* Valley Theatre), 13–14, 17, 28

Newman, Alfred, 163

"New York Streets" (MGM Lot 2), 119, 196, 228, 229

"Night of 100 Stars" (concert), 295

"Nobody," 106

"No Love, No Nothin'," 180

"No Other One," 42

Norman, Lucille, 17, 140

"Nothing But You," 224

Nunn, Larry, 105

"The Object of My Affection," 28

O'Brien, Margaret, 123, 173, 175, *178*, 182–83, 215

O'Brien, Virginia, 201, 203

O'Connor, Donald, 21, 48, 85

"Oh, You Beautiful Doll," 17, 138, 140, 141

"Oh, Say, Can You Swing?," 55

O'Kelly, Betty, 112

Old Mexico Night Club, 23

Oliver, W. E., 26

"Ol' Man River," 294

O'Malley, Flynn, 17, 21

"One Love," 130

"On the Atchison, Topeka, and the Santa Fe," 111, 199–200, *201*, 201–2, 205

"On the Bumpy Road to Love," 71

"On the Good Ship Lollipop," 28

"Opera vs. Jazz," 46

Oriental Theatre, 23, 68

Orpheum Theatre, 28

"Our Love Affair," 106, 123, 149, 157

Overdorff, I. C., 21

"Over the Bannister," 170, 171, 175

"Over the Rainbow": awards, 78, 301; hospital visit performance of, 96; prerecordings of, 75; radio performances of, 88, 159, 198, 237; recordings of, 90; as signature song, 1

Owen, Reginald, 61

Paar, Jack, 38, 294, 295

"Pack Up Your Troubles in Your Old Kit Bag and Smile, Smile, Smile," 138

"Paging Mr. Greenback," 146

Palace Theatre, 224, *281*, 282, 289, 296

parades, 63, 82

Paramount Circuit tours, 21

Paramount Pictures, 140, 253

Paramount Theatre (Los Angeles), 18, 27, 29

Paramount Theatre (Seattle), 150

Parker, Barnett, 55, *55*

"Parlez-Moi D'Amour," 138

Parsons, Louella, 42, 79, 173, 237

Pasternak, Joe, 46–47, 143, 146, 238–39, 259, 260

Patterson, Les, 90

The Pause That Refreshes on the Air, 156, 159

"Pennies from Heaven," 53

Pepe, 290

Pepsodent Show Starring Bob Hope, 95, 101, 102, 104, 112

Peter Bent Brigham Hospital, 242, 254, *255*, 255–56, *256*, 257, 258, 270

Peterson, Lester, 253

Philco Radio Time Bing Crosby Show, 217, 237, 258, 277, 279–80, 282

photographs, promotional: 1940, *100*; 1941, *114*, *134*; 1943, *viii*, *147*; 1944, *172*, *189*, *190*, *192*; 1948, *240*; 1950, last for MGM, *278*; for Columbia Records, 283; glamour treatment, 142; Gumm (Garland) Sisters, *10*, *12*, *19*

Photoplay (magazine), 40, 131, *170*, 241

Pickford, Mary, 17, 140

Picture Show (magazine), *202*

Pidgeon, Walter, 70

Pigskin Parade, 48, 52–53, 118

The Pirate: box office reception, 225; costume fittings for, 215; cult film status, 225; director, 215; extramarital affairs during, 245; filming of, 215–16, 218–21; Garland on set of, *217*; Garland's jealousy during, 220–21; Kelly, Astaire, and Garland on set of, *225*; nervous breakdown during, 219, 221–22; outtakes, 216, 225; plot, 216; poodle acts in, 82; prerecordings for, 216–17, 218, 219–20; previews, 224–25; retakes, 224; score for, 40; still from, *220*

"Play That Barbershop Chord," 239, 240

Pobirs, Fred, 246

Polan, Barron, 110, *110*

Ponedel, Dorothy "Dottie": finding Garland's secret admirer, 239; Garland's birthday, 270; Garland's firing, 252; as Garland's makeup artist, 181; on Garland's relationship behavior, 152–53; MGM

contract negotiations, 215; psychiatrist visits with Garland, 218; *Summer Stock* screenings and fan adoration, 275

Porter, Cole, 40, 104, 111, 119, 148, 215, 217, 220

Powell, Dick, 163

Powell, Eleanor, 39, 40, 114, 137

Powell, Jane, 280

Power, Annabella, 152, 153

Power, Tyrone, 152–53

pregnancies, 129–30, 152, 156, 207, 209–10, 212

Preisser, June, 105

Presenting Lily Mars, 46, 142, 143–46, *144*

Press Photographers' ball, 83

"A Pretty Girl Is Like a Melody," 27, 117

"A Pretty Girl Milking Her Cow," 108–9

product endorsements: fashion, 59–60, *60*, 64, *65*, *66*; Lux Soap, 142; Max Factor, 142, *208*

Pruett, Alice, 9

psychiatry, 155, 218, 221–22, 256

publicity: baseball game appearances, 84–85; early studio, 42–45, *43*, 53, 58; film premieres for, 63–69, *65*, *67*, 80, 90, *90*, *91*, 92, 93, 94; film promotional tours, *89*, 90–94, *91*, *92*; holiday events, 62–63, 82, 96; hospital charitable visits, *96*, 96–97; personae and image development, 1, 43, 47, 57, 58–60, *60*, 70, 87, 297; post-*Oz*, 82–85; USO tours, 126–29, *127*, 159–69, *160*, *166*. *See also* photographs, promotional; publicity fabrications; radio shows

publicity fabrications: age, 35, 88; American teenager personae, 58–59, 87; batons, 118; domestic lifestyle photographs, 87; film assignments, 41, 67; flower shop ownership, 87; MGM audition, 34–35; name change, 35; romance rumors, 40, 59, 101–2

"Put Your Arms Around Me, Honey," 239

Quine, Richard, 123–24, 136

Rabwin, Harry, 113

Rabwin, Marcella, 130

Rabwin, Marcus, 8–9, 11, 12, 14, 130, 148, 246, 254

Radio City Music Hall, 159, 185, 225, 241, 300

radio shows, 62, 121, 141, 159; *Ben Bernie and All the Lads*, 54–55; *Bob Crosby Show*, 213; *Broadway Melody Hour*, 46; *The Chase and Sanborn Hour*, 66, 125, 143; *The Chesterfield Supper Club*, 233; *Command Performance* series, 143, 162, 198, 209; *The Danny Kaye Show*, *207*; *Dick Tracy in B-Flat*, 198, *199*; *Frank Morgan Varieties*, 55–56; *Good News of 1938*, 58, 62, 69; *Jack Oakie's College*, 52, 53, 55; *Kraft Music Hall*, 237; *Lux Radio Theatre*, 113, 210, 277; *Maxwell House Coffee Time—Good News*, 88–89; *The Pause That Refreshes on the Air*, 156, 159; *Pepsodent Show Starring Bob Hope*, 95, 101, 102, 104, 112; *Philco Radio Time Bing Crosby Show*, 217, 237, 258, 277, 279–80, 282; *Shell Chateau Hour*, 41, 138; *The Tex and Jinx Show*, 235; *Tune-Up Time*, 82

Rainbow: The Stormy Life of Judy Garland (Finch), 300

Random House Publishing, 290

Reed, Donna, 70, 123

Remer, "Bones," 29

Reynolds, Debbie, 280, 299

"Rhythm Madness," 35

Rialto Theatre, 68

Robin Hood Dell, *157*, 157–59, 297

Robson, Mark, 296

Robson, May, 43, *43*

"Rock-a-Bye Your Baby with a Dixie Melody," 280

Rodgers, Richard, 175–76, 233, 238, 243, 276

Rodin, Gil, 46

Rogers, Ginger, 235, 236

romantic relationships: Cathcart, Jimmy, 109; dating, 109; early quotes on, 99; fabricated, 40, 59; Frank, 68, 101; Johnson, 163; Levant, 83–84; Mankiewicz, 153, 154–56, 171, 212; Mercer, 111–12; Meyer, 297; obsession and, 96, 109, 151; Polan, 110, *110*; Power, 152–53; Rooney, 101–2; Shaw, 86, 97–99, 109; Walters, 150–51. *See also* marriages

Romero, Alex, 250

Rooney, Mickey: Andy Hardy film series featuring, 69–70, 102, 119; billing complaints, 238; Christmas shows, 63; early films, 40; education, 40; fictionalized version of meeting, 40; film promotional tours with, 89, *89*, 90–94, *91*, *92*; films with, *Adventures of Huckleberry Finn*, 83; films with, *Babes in Arms*, *84*, 85–86, 94–95; films with, *Babes on Broadway*, 104, 121–25; films with, *Girl Crazy*, 95, 146–50, *151*; films with, *Strike Up the Band*, *104*, 104–7, *107*; films with, *Words and Music*, 233–34, *235*; films with, *Ziegfeld Follies of 1946*, 191–92; final on-screen appearance with Garland, 234; first film with, 58; friendship with, 40, *59*; Garland's birthday celebration, 87; at Grauman's, *94*; Oscar presentations, 78, 102; romance rumors, 59, 101–2; studio publicity and exposure, 43, *43*, 44–45; as television show guest, 294; USO War Bonds tour, 163, 164, *166*

"The Rosary," 119

Rose, Augustus, 256, 257, 259, 260–61, 262, 265

Rose, Billy, 275

Rose, David: army camp tours, 125; dating, 112; divorce, 150; engagement and marriage, 87, 120–21, *121*, 130–31; residences, 126; USO tour, 126–29

Rosen, Al, 29–30, *30*, 32–33, 35, 38

Royal Wedding, 268–71, *271*, 280

Ruby Slippers, 298–99

"Rudoph the Red-Nosed Reindeer," 279

Russell, Betty, 201

Rutherford, Ann, 69, 87, 102

Ryan, Peggy, 48

Sakall, S. Z. "Cuddles," 240

"Sam's Song," 277

Schary, Dore, 154, 247, 251–52, 263–64, 270, 274, 276

Schechter, Scott, 252

Schenck, Nicholas, 247, 254, 263–64, 270

Schroeder, Mary, 55

Schumann-Heink, Ernestine, 43

Scott, Martha, 163

Screen Guide (magazine), *118*, *232*

Sekatary Hawkins Club, 66

"Send My Baby Back to Me," 283

Shaw, Artie, 86, 97–99, 109, 111, 112

Shaw, Michael, 298

Shell Chateau Hour, 41, 138

Sheridan Theatre, 63

Sherwood, Bobby, 112

Shields, Jimmy, 185

"Shine on Your Shoes," 67

shock treatments, 246

Show Boat, 19, 276

Shrine Auditorium, 16, 43, *43*, 44–45, 198, *199*

Sidney, George, 33–34, 87, 200, 253

Sidney, Sylvia, 236, 257

Sigma Chi Fraternity, 67

"Silent Night," 62–63, 96

Silvers, Phil, 263, 291, 294

Simmel, Ernst, 155, 218

Simone, Magdalene, 244

Sinatra, Frank: "Boys and Girls Like You and Me" prerecording, 176; Christmas song lyric changes, 175; as Freed Unit member, 86, 143; Garland's hospital visit and support from, 255; radio shows with, 198, *199*, 206, *207*; television shows with, 293

Sinclair, Ronald, 58, 59

"Singin' in the Rain," 108, 109

Six Hits and a Miss, 117

"Skip to My Lou," 175, 186

Skolsky, Sidney, 40, 46

"Smiles," 53, 138, 141

Smith, Jack Martin, 86, 174

Snow White and the Seven Dwarfs, 73–74

Soanes, Wood, 27, 34–35

"Someone at Last," 284–85

Sondergaard, Gale, 74

South Pacific, 276

"The Spell of the Waltz," 138

Spielberg, Steven, 299

Stack, Robert, 109

A Star Is Born (film): award nominations, 286; celebrity attendants, 55; director, 284; filming, 285; Garland's name change at opening of, 24; Grable's favorite movie, 52; premiere, 285; production, 283; restoration of, 287, 300; reviews, 285–86; shortening of, 286–87; song recordings from, 10; songs from, 39; songwriting for, 284; stills from, *284, 285, 287*; studio finance themes in, 264; the-

atre benefits featured in, 16; vocal arrangements for, 109–10

A Star Is Born (radio production), 113, 284

Star Row (magazine), *214*

"Stars of Tomorrow" shows, 18

Stewart, James, 40, 114, 115, 124

Stewart, Marjorie, 163, *166*

"St. Louis Street" (MGM Lot 3), 173, 174

Stoll, Georgie, 90, 106, 117

"Stompin' at the Savoy," 42, 46

Stonewall Inn, 298

Stothart, Herbert, 74, 78

Strand Theatre, 15, 25

Streisand, Barbra, 62, 293, 294

Strike Up the Band (film), *104*, 104–7, *107*

Strike Up the Band (radio theatre), 113

Strohm, Walter, 251, 252–53

Studio Party, 42

Sues, Leonard, 109

Summer Stock (film): absentee warnings, 261; box office response and success, 267–68, 275; director, 149, 261; fan support and adoration, 275–76, 277; filming, 265; Garland's support during, 262–65; Garland's weight, 257, 265–66; newspaper ads for, *269*; premiere, 267; prerecordings for, 261, 266–67; press on filming challenges, 265; previews, 274; producers, 259, 260; reviews, 274, 275

Summer Stock (soundtrack), 273, 277

Sundberg, Clinton, 240

"Sunny/Who?," 207–8

"Sun Showers," 58

Sun Valley, 273–74

Susann, Jacqueline, 221, 295

"Swanee," 90, 285, *285*

"Sweet Sixteen," 82

"Swing, Mr. Charlie," 42, 46

"Swing, Mr. Mendelssohn," 57–58

"Swing Low, Sweet Chariot," 62

Talk of the Town (cabaret shows), 297

Taurog, Norman, 83, 108, 148, 149

television: biography miniseries, 148, 301–2; documentaries, 300–301, 302; film broadcasts, 298; specials, 289, 294; talk show guest appearances, 38, 294, 295, 297; weekly variety shows, 62, 213, 239, 293; *Wizard of Oz* broadcasts, 2, 78, 287–88, *288*

Temple, Shirley, 21, 56, 79, 94

"Ten Pins in the Sky," 71

The Tex and Jinx Show, 235

"The Texas Tornado," 52

Thalberg, Irving, 39, 73

"That Old Black Magic," 111, 159

That's Entertainment!, 2–3, 69, 79, 299, *299*

That's Entertainment! Part 2, 299

That's Entertainment! III, 224, 251, 299–300

"There's No Business Like Show Business," 243

"They Can't Take That Away from Me," 53

"They Say It's Wonderful," 243

"This Is the Army Mr. Jones," 159

This Time It's Love, 40

Thomas, Bob, 272

Thompson, Fred, 12

Thompson, Kay, 82, 86, 186, 192–93, 194, 201

Thorn, George W., 254, 257

Thoroughbreds Don't Cry, 58

Thorpe, Richard, 75, 76

Those Glorious MGM Musicals (compilation album), 240, 299

Thoughts and Poems, by Judy Garland, 110–11

"Three Cheers for the Yanks," 138

"Till After the Holidays," 297

Till the Clouds Roll By, 174, 207–9, 212, 213, *214*, 276

"Tom, the Piper's Son," 144, 145

The Tonight Show, 297

Topper, 70

Topsy and Eva, 12, 67

tours: concert, 290–91, 293, 294, 295, 296, 297; film promotional, 63–69, *65, 67,* 89, *89,* 90–94, *91, 92;* Gumm (Garland) Sisters, 21, 22, 23–24; MGM publicity, 2, 3, 62; USO, 126–29, *127,* 159–69, *160, 166*

Tracy, Spencer, 41, 104, 153, *260*

trading cards, *134*

Transcona Enterprises, 283

"The Trolley Song," 1, 174–75, *176,* 176–78, 186

Truesdell, John, 56, 129–30, 163

Tucker, Sophie, 55, *55*

Tully, Myrtle, 269, 271

Tune-Up Time, 82

Turner, Lana: films with, 70, 114, 115, *116,* 117, 119; marriages, 98, 109; wartime glamour girl, 129, 131

Turner Classic Movies, 287

Tuttle, Dorothy, 200–201

"Twinkle Toe Kiddie Review," 14

"Tzena, Tzena, Tzena," 277

The Ultimate Oz, 300

"Under the Bamboo Tree," 175, 176, 179

Under the Rainbow (film), 80

United States v. Paramount, 264

Universal Pictures, 27

Universal Studios, 27, 46–47, 48, 59

Uptown Theatre, 24

USO tours, 126–29, *127,* 159–69, *160, 166*

Utah Theatre, 108

Vallee, Rudy, 46, 53

Valley of the Dolls (film), 295–96, *296*

Valley of the Dolls (Susann), 221, 295

Valley Theatre, 13–14, 17, 28

Variety (newspaper), 18–19, 20, 35, 43–44, 63–64, 65–66, 67, 68

vaudeville, 8, 11–12, 15–16, 19. *See also* Gumm (Garland) Sisters

Venuti, Joe, 82

Vera-Ellen, 86, 238, 280

Vitt, Oscar, 84

"Voodoo," 218–19, 224, 225

Walker, Robert, 195, *195,* 207, 213

Walters, Charles: *Annie Get Your Gun* footage assessments, 250; biographical information, 148; films directed by, *Annie Get Your Gun*, 251; films directed by, *Barkleys of Broadway*, 236; films directed by, *Easter Parade*, 149, 222–23, 230; films directed by, *Good News*, 223; films directed by, *Summer Stock*, 149, 264, 266–68; films refused to direct, *Royal Wedding*, 268–69; as Freed Unit member, 86; Garland's friendship with, 143, 150–51, 223, 264, 268–69; as Garland's on-screen dance partner, 145, 149, 223; hiding from Garland, 269; musical direction by, *Girl Crazy*, 148, 149; musical direction by, *Ziegfeld Follies of 1946*, 192–93; sexuality, 151

Warner, Jack, 286, 287

Warner, Kent, 298–99

Warner Bros., 16, 17, 39, 40, 48, 119, 283, 286

Warner Brothers Downtown Theatre, 20

Warner Brothers Hollywood Theatre, 20

Warren, George C., 19

Warren, Harry, 111, 199, 203, 205, 261, 264

The Wedding of Jack and Jill (film short), 17

Weidler, Virginia, 44, 45, 104

"We Must Have Music," 115–16, 117, 118

West Coast Theatre, 20

Wheelwright, Ralph, 272–73

"When I Look at You," 145

"When Johnny Comes Marching Home," 138

"When My Sugar Walks Down the Street," 10

"When the Butterflies Kiss the Buttercups Goodbye," 17

"When You're Smiling," 280

"When You Wore a Tulip," 138, 143

"Where Is Love," 213

"Where or When," *84*

White, Nene, 6

Whiting, Margaret, 112

"Who?," 208, 213

The Whole Truth and Nothing But (Hopper), 47

"Why? Because!," 61–62, *63*

"Why Was I Born," 214

Widmark, Richard, *291*

William Morris Agency, 23, 24, 277

Williams, Esther, 70

Willson, Meredith, 88

Wilshire Ebell Theatre, 18, 21, 25, 26, 33, 34, 154

Wilson, Earl, 275–76

Wilson, Robert, 103

Winchell, Walter, 66, 83

Winninger, Charles, 108, 114, 119

Withers, Jane, 44, 45

"Without a Memory," 283

The Wizard of Oz (film): acting advice during, 76; ad artwork for, *90*; anniversaries of, 301; auctions of props and costumes from, 298–99; awards and accolades, 78–79, 102, 301; books on making of, 300; casting, 67, 73, 74; character development, 74; costume development and testing, 71, 74; directors, 75–76; fan artwork, *4*; filming of, 75, 76–77; finances and profit, 78; Garland portraits for, *75*; Garland's popularity on set of, 81–82; hair and makeup tests for, 70, 74, 76; misconceptions and legends about, 79–81; musical score, 74; on-set injuries, 75–77; postproduction, 77; premieres, 80, 90, *90*, *91*, 92, 93; prerecordings, 71, 75; previews, 77; producers, 39, 73; promotional contests for, 93–94; promotional photos from, 96–97; promotional tours, 90, *90*, *91*, 92; public response to, 77–78; radio shows promoting, 88; salary and bonuses, 94; soundtracks of, 2, *91*, 288, *289*; star designation, 76; Technicolor, 74; television broadcasts of, 2, 78, 287–88, *288*; trade ads for, *81*; videodisc recordings of, 300

The Wizard of Oz (soundtrack), 2, *91*, 288, *289*

Wolf and Marco Revue, 27

"Wonderful Wizard of Oz" ("We're Off to See the Wizard"), 75

Words and Music, 53, 85, 233–34, *235*, 237–38

World of Entertainment! Hollywood's Greatest Musicals (Fordin), 219

World War II: fundraising appearances, 162; military honors, 125, 131–32; patriotic film themes, 106; patriotic song themes, 122; USO tours, 126–29, *127*, 159–69, *160*, *166*

Worsley, Wallace, Jr., 179, 219

Wynn, Keenan, 154, 196

Yolanda and the Thief, 198–99

"You and I," 174

"You Can Do No Wrong," 220

"You Can't Get a Man with a Gun," 243, 244

"You Can't Have Everything," 58
"You Couldn't Be Cuter," 53
"You Made Me Love You," 54, 67, 157, 161, 234, 279
"You Never Looked So Beautiful Before," 117
The Youngest Profession, 104
Young Judy (Dahl and Kehoe), 3, 300
"You're Just in Love," 279
"You're the Cream in My Coffee," 14
Yours and Mine, 41

"You Stepped Out of a Dream," 115, 117
"You Wonderful You," 266

Ziegfeld Follies of 1946, 191–94, *192*
Ziegfeld Girl, 104, 114–19, *116*
Ziegfeld Theatre, 82
"Zing! Went the Strings of My Heart," 29, 32, 33, 35, 41, 71, 90
Zinnemann, Fred, 194–95

About the Author

Scott Brogan is the owner and webmaster of the world-famous *Judy Room* website and blog (thejudyroom.com), providing valuable information to Garland fans and fans of classic Hollywood for more than twenty-five years. He enjoys his ongoing research (which began in childhood) and the new information it brings to the clarification and deeper understanding of Judy Garland's unique legacy. Brogan's essays for the San Francisco Silent Film Festival have been cataloged by the Library of Congress and translated into different languages. He was a community columnist for the Bay Area Reporter and has written for the *ARSC Journal*. He provided liner notes for several CD projects and contributed ephemera for several books about Garland and MGM. He was also the webmaster of Liza Minnelli's (now defunct) official website.

As a military kid, Brogan grew up around the world and saw firsthand the impact that Judy Garland's legacy has had outside the United States. Brogan's hobbies include road cycling, gardening, and collecting classic movie soundtracks. He currently lives in Kansas City, Missouri, with his husband and their "furbaby" dog, Seamus.